The
autumn
orange
of the afterthought

The
autumn
orange
of the afterthought

IAN WILCOX

To order additional copies of this book, contact:
Xlibris
UK TFN: 0800 0148620 (Toll Free inside the UK)
UK Local: 02036 956328 (+44 20 3695 6328 from outside the UK)
www.Xlibrispublishing.co.uk
Orders@Xlibrispublishing.co.uk
808639

CONTENTS

ARE
YOU

READY
FOR

YET
MORE

LAST
LEG
YOU
SUPER
TROOPERS!

For
Janice Fisher

An amazing Lady and dear friend.

The autumn orange of the afterthought

Been and gone and sometimes wrong
The conundrum in what was then caught
Knowing was wrong will keep one strong
The autumn Orange of the afterthought

Yes been and done but got along
Wiser than before
The journey back would give Heart attack
Not for that I seek no more

Been and done so have begun
A better way to be
Been and done so now the one
That's a better version of me

Made and played and, sometimes trade
That's just growing up
The things you see when open be
When drink from certain cup

Ian Wilcox

With gratitude beyond words to the amazing people who
contributed to this work, both in given name and pen name

Bose Eneduwe Adogah
Nancy Ndeke
Janice Fisher
Cathy Mccormick
Aleng Loring
Margaret Burgess
Penny Wobbly
Melissa Begley
William Warigon

And the amazing Team I have the pleasure to
work with at Xlibris who I have named
Team Inspiration

You all know who you are and what you do for me and many others

About the Author

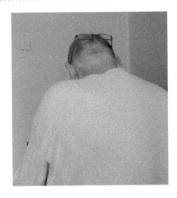

Ian Wilcox is a mid 50's Englishman with a beautiful Filipino
Wife and an equally beautiful adult Filipino Daughter

Following some unfortunate adventures, he is
now registered Visually Impaired

Writing verse has been a passion from an early age and has helped him
adjust to a whole new world where he has encountered some wonderful and
amazing people who share his belief that your own limitations are yourself.

The autumn orange of afterthought is the final Book of his
latest quartet and his 9th Book in just over 2 ½ years.
As with all of this latest quartet it features some incredible
Guest writers that he feels blessed to be able to call friend

Another dip into the varied worlds and words from
The voice of Idle Mind

Please ensure that your seat is in the upright position,
all safety restraints are firmly secured.
Sit back and enjoy the ride.

Are

You

Triangles And Angles

Smooth, rough even tough,
Navigation does demand,
Of soft touch inversion,
Fitting within and without,
Ocular cyclicals of lunar waves,
Try with error or its absence,
Landing hard at attempted sprit,
Slow tango and fast twist,
Observation mission at receding horizons,
Truth in its adult inkling,
Never a one to speak loudly,
But in the softest of whispers,
A soul does know its path,
Around and about triangles and angles,
Straight to the milky way discourse.
Where the source and the product merge.

Fun At Night Shade

Sons of Ham,
Him of accursed accidental incident,
Thrown to the wind for early rising,
Blacklisted to buy own,
Back lane became home,
Backwards rode his fortune,
Black holes drove his learning,
Black death decided his health,
Black mood told his morning,
Black heart sings his tunes,
Black as sin topping the pie,
Unlike lovers sighing at the stars,
Or the music of the wise owl,
And crickets percussion in tow,
Black cursed even the charcoal and the coal,
Invading the shades of lordly temples,
Where fair did less of sins,
Black being its accusations and judgement,
A little digging below the surface,
Alas! Blood and sinews matched the rhesus factor,
Laugher roused the old scheme's,
Which scored schooling with Darwin's theology,
Abroad every dawn,
The struggle succeeds in failing itself,
For black is no colour or shade,
But absence therein of light,
The clever knows not to share,
This lie old and rich in betrayal.
Black fan and black fun,
Only the truly black knows.
And all,
Carry the judicious crudity daily.
Not for want of truth,
But inspire of it.

Carry Me Home

Of dreams lofty crowning me king,
At that hour when senses close,
Tempting me with dishes and wines,
Fut for the king's and his best guest,
Reaching out my turn though uninvited,
A pain jabs my side and up I fly,
Hunger roused the bed of straws,
Reminding me to steal or perish,
The question of night and a lonely nightmare,
One worse for the whimpering child,
Who knows none why his tummy hurts,
Carry me home O dreary dream,
In the next plain perhaps I hope,
War doesn't come to displace,
Sending me and mine overboard,
Where wild and tame tear life like mongrels.

Edge Of A Dream

Arm's length a mile off,
Seagulls announcing a fisherman's arrival at shore,
A lonely night and full dhow,
Waves waving home a welcome,
For the mouths and ears of singers,
A child is born in his homestead,
The fisherman is a happy soul,
Gives the best fish for the new-borns mother,
Listening to the fading song of birth,
For the baby's ears and nose crossed the sea,
Wearing the hooked beak of its ancestry,
And the fair lay of its tender skin,
With village men deep in thought,
And women gnashing their teeth,
The fisherman slept awake,
Repairing his old nets,
To set sail once more,
To the edge of the dream,
Where reality may get another chance,
and another craft,
For as he fished for his own,
Another fished his own.
Breaking a man twice.

The Poet

Run when the poet you meet,
He sees with razor beams,
The tangled web of your inner,
The lie you sold to the chief,
The preaching you give a miss,
And the teaching wrote on piss,
Run when the poet meets,
Unless a child be,
For the poet loves to play,
With clay making pots,
And soldiers piecing mission,
His eyes won't avert,
Or his stare blink,
A chronicler that he is,
He stokes his only gun,
Stroking it like a lover,
Who even upon a pyre,
Will sing the censored song,
So, run when a poet meet,
Unless like a naked torso of dignity,
You will stand shoulder to shoulder,
Comparing metaphors and similes,
Drawing hopeful picturesque scenes,
Of paradise before vermin invasion.

Nancy Ndeke

5 am and again

The sun is slowly showing
The day now it is growing
More opportunities for knowing
Just what I can be

Complacency a legacy
In what others think
If they are happy then I am happy
As in literature I sink

I play my game not quite the same
As that you choose to play
For all of us are individuals
At the end of day
To play loose I do choose
Not everyone's cup of tea
But that is just who we are
Some prefer their coffee

Shadows gone but not for long
Soon will reappear
The cycle we now all call day
A constant changing marvel

But who am I to say?
What right have I to speak?
I am but a mere mortal
With a body weak

I play my game not quite the same
As that you choose to play
For all of us are individuals
At the end of day
To play loose I do choose
Not everyone's cup of tea
But that is just who we are
Some prefer their coffee

24 Hour clock

Life is but a repeated clock
Split into sections we all name
Every circle we know so well
Bigger clock is not the same
Bigger clock does measure life
All have clocks of when what we do
This my clock that is still ticking
This my times and not yet through

7am and I was learning
By midmorning I was hurting
Lunchtime came to me prone
Early afternoon I wished I was Home
Wrapped in arms of love so true
Two plus One, a Family true
Comes does soon the hour of Dinner
Wholesome meal for a once was sinner

Cooked with love and served with care
Taste the things as we both do share
Early evening hope spending time
When sat on sofa both entwined
But bed time will come and both will lay
Once again for another day
Late morning a new clock was made
It moved within the bigger face

Both do move but different speeds
In these clocks of life we find no race
Smaller clock tells different story

Smaller clock is just snapshot
Still measures things in 24 hours
In its day know what I have got
7am and I was confused
By midmorning slightly bemused
Brunch time came and I did know

Was late morning and we did grow
The day so far I do rejoice
For it is filled with your voice
Each second saved as careful measure
Of what I got when found my treasure
Early evening can spend some special time
When sat on sofa both entwined

Bed time comes and both do lay
For not alone another day
Slowly does the little face
Change the big one but not its pace
Changes story yet unwritten
About a young man who once was smitten

24 Hour clock is looking good
When again beside you I am stood
Days are like seconds as we know
With each tick we grow and grow

Ian Wilcox

A being in a sea of beings

Touched by much as is such
The joy of just the living
The things we take to make a break
The pleasure in the giving
Sometimes seems fine
Others not so much
We are we and what we be
The senses and the touch

Nitrogen and Oxygen
Where on Earth do we begin
Inhale exhale and absorb
We are a Chemical plant
Take gas in, pass solid out
Liquid in more than measure
We are walking talking chemistry
That does it just for pleasure

Just a being in sea of beings
Swimming in a big, big sea
I am reeling when with feeling
Realise will always be
Not the sadness but the gladness
No pressure to maintain
Just plain me and will always be
Just a body with a name

World absurd from what seen and heard
Let them do what do
Expression new Convention
If only had a clue
A Will I am if in but middle name
Yet it fits me well
As to success and all the rest
Only time will tell

A brief respite in common plight

One did stand gun in hand
Dirty from the day
Been up and down
Stand/ lay on ground
For a pittance of a pay
One did meet and did friend greet
A fellow in the 'game' they play
A brief respite in common plight
This what have to say

Hi Bro, I shot a man today but it's okay
I don't really feel much sorrow
Shot a man today and dead he lay
May shoot another one tomorrow
Hey Bro, don't you know?
He was shooting back at me
Could have been me that no future sees
In War it's guesswork if have tomorrow

Hi Bro, before you go
To try to find some cover
Did you manage to get any of them today?
Did you grease some enemy?
Some son of different Mother
For our Country and our people
We die and try to kill
When someone says we're different
Yet are Human still

Hi Bro, I am wondering
If someday we will learn
The greatest release is thing called Peace
Then this madness all will cease
Not just this one War
But all others for ever more
How ironic it would be
If carry on then remember thee

A Choir of Creation

The day is cold as story told
The outside and the in
Nothing left so just lets
A choral Choir begin
Bass does start from below the Heart
Baritone just adds to flavour
Tenor and then Alto
Mezzo-soprano and pure Soprano
Truly a dish to savour

So, if you sing and joy does bring
Why not sing some more
The permutations are a revelation
So, sing and it adore
The notes you float will cross that Moat
The Castle yours to take
This King or Queen needs to be seen
Such a difference can you make

I had a dream of union
It floats as music sound
Everyone a Singer
When found common ground
The difference in delivery
The bleeding to the whole
A Choir of Creation
Should be our mutual goal

A communi est verum Regum

The masses not those with the money
Yet the rich seem to find funny
Lauding up that which buy
To the poor and reason why
Wish I could just hibernate
Until Humanity a stable state
Guess that would be one long sleep
For the haves do want to keep

Oh, why did I grow in the world did grow
Why not in that I don't know
The one that was beyond me
Yet they still to me show
Why pretend you are just like me
When in truth could never be
Hoping that I will not see
Fickle Fate - a travesty

Here does come the Mail again
Will they deliver or refrain?
Another Bill as I do shiver
Whilst in the Sun the rich do Twitter
Yet in the depths of misery
Lies the perfect remedy
For no silver spoon nor silk glove
Yet I have precious – it's called love

Take the trinkets and the Sable
For to own I am not able
Even if I would not wear
For this planet we still share
Do you believe that they grieve?
Have a thought for us rest
Yet the sting in the saga
Is that common is still best

A day for play?

What do we do when face that new?
What do we think and say?
What the fact about how act?
How do we then it play?
Higher ground can be found
When we choose to climb
Physical and in other call
When change something don't feel is fine

The fat Lady sings yet no end brings
When listening with no thought
Not the mood to let intrude
In different now are caught
Now need a song about moving on
Here and not the other
To many know from that Show
With covers of a cover

We get told by young and old
How lemmings we should be
While dictate and then state
From castle Ivory
Every Sunday can be a fun day
If we just so choose
Every Friday just a cry day
When we choose to lose

A future legacy

What make of you when morning dew
Coats an outside world
Do you find peace of mind?
Refreshing that not heard

What make of the state that can irate?
The place we put ourselves now in
Do we just moan and carry on?
Or a change begins?

Bravado in the boisterous
When can say but not employ
Feeling like we have made a difference
Whilst the culprits still enjoy

The scribbled note found in the ashes
Of what was once a living space
Now amongst the badge of many
When we let the cure just go to waste

Comfort ruled the lifestyle then
Ignorance was an excuse
Simply be 'the best for me
Then we all did lose

If this rubble could tell a story
A horror one would be
Yet a mute sad tribute
A future legacy

Nothing lasts forever
Yet damaged may take some time
When committed on such level
When considered not a crime

One voice speaks to many ears

A History of me

A history of who I be
Is that not what writers do?
The fantasy and what now be
The past influencing new

Shapes that make as story takes
A life outside the own
Brief it's true for you are you
Glimpses just are shown

The writers write of success and plight
Own but not alone
For relate when not hate state
In the symbols shown

A history of Humanity
Condensed because what is
Achievements kiss and better miss
The nutshell of our legacy

How often in the retrospection?
Do the then now we can question
Different times and different being
From the present we are now seeing

Who can judge when not live?
In circumstance and what did give
Only comfort is the fact
We survived so can differently act

So the history of who I be
Not that simple as that of Tree
Both were seeds and both have roots
After that now can't compute

A letter found

A letter found and letter read
Filled me with some questions
In some way screwed a Head
If it wasn't for the current state
Maybe, then could not relate

When will we make it happen?
When will we at last be free?
Free from constraints from 'The Wise Ones'
With their hypocrisy
Not a single Nation
For this is unilateral
Not that it makes much difference
When accept it as just natural

Did you go to work today?
Because your work enjoy
Did you come back feeling happy?
Or just another's toy
The mirror image that looks back
Does it really lie?
The one burst in the morning
That we fail to try

Why do we will hypocrisy
Settle for it and then applaud
Why do we follow fools gladly?
Then find we can't afford
Through lazy eyes it seems so wise
To just go with the flow
What was the pinnacle of our being?
Somewhere past we do not know

Lemmings are a fable
As over cliff they go
We are becoming the real thing
And we enjoy the Show

Beauty is the Soul that Loves

Beauty comes alive
when one starts to care;
to serve, to give
without expecting in the end;
the radiance the heart exudes to bare;
the paragon of soul that cannot be portend.

The timeless, ageless charm,
unspoken sacrifices
that counter prided chins;
comforting words
that calm a recreant friend.

To go on to live,
to accept others' insanity;
knowing that within is the same absurdity;
rare is the soul that loves.

A priceless feeling:
of being useful in uselessness;
hope in the midst of hopelessness;
life when one forgets to live.
Beautiful is the soul that loves.

Loriz Jacob

A Humble Proposal

Paint fair your thought if wall of thoughts you paint;
aspire your growth if growth your kins aspire;
taint not pure heart to show how heart shuns taint;
respire in dove's peace when blood heeds respire.

Unfurl each bloom and seeds from fruit unfurl;
mist not old soil, ancestors toiled your mist;
world's not a dice you cast on other's world;
list all the goods and see, you're on the list -

Disdain your soul if life you must disdain
reciprocate, all deeds reciprocate;
vain is the crown that selfish seeks in vain -
cohabitate, we must cohabitate,

for truth's in 'no man's island' we live for
shore greets with love whoever lands ashore.

Loriz Jacob

To the buds of blooming daises

To the buds of blooming daisies,
bury your complaints
into the pocket of clouds
the sun will hear your song
and send you drizzles.

Don't be afraid of shadows
on the ground, let them
climb on cracks of cemented
wailing walls

Let cool air tease your petals
or hummingbirds serenade
but don't forget that they, too,
collect nectars from myriad choices

Flowers,
you did not blossom
for hummingbirds and bees alone...

Do not grow spines,
you are not cactus.
Stand on your stalk
but guard your bosoms~

for once you are plucked,
devoid of colors,
leaves will mourn.

My worn out sleeves
didn't ask why pants
slept in neighbour's closet;

instead inhale scents,
perfume sprayed on wrists
and shapely clavicles.

Diaries don't count the days
you sit on withering foliage

Be an elixir to waft each page,
a potpourri in empty bottles,
a balm to soothe heartaches...

when the midnight calls,
rest on worn out sleeves.

To the buds of blooming daisies,
bury your complaints
into the pocket of clouds
the sun will hear your song
and send you drizzles.

Don't be afraid of shadows
on the ground, let them
climb on cracks of cemented
wailing walls

Let cool air tease your petals
or hummingbirds serenade
but don't forget that they, too,
collect nectars from myriad choices

Loriz Jacob

Zooming Aurora

Waking from mental hurricane is the highest form of art.

Moonsoon within pores
dimorphised paints of syllabicated fear
in calibrated sighs

Anthill is a voiceless tomb
pheromonic sting eavesdrops
where rainbow hides:
window of embers merged with rainfall
in bottomless teacup

But dawn does not forsake...
rays of sun break strands of sleep
in the underbrush, dust meeting dust
in a cathartic dance of sweet burning ether

painting mosaicked portrait
of braded petals

Loriz Jacob

The estuary knows

how you walk hand in hand with rain,
how storm tries to cleanse your cheeks,
how you cloak your wounds from stain,
how you sit with willow tree for weeks;

how you remain silent in tidal surge,
how you lovingly carry each fallen leaf,
how you bend knees on buried gorge,
how you sigh with grief when sky lays deaf;

but see...

how whines become brines at sea,
how light hearts to clouds become free,
how two worlds meet in harmony,
how estuary becomes a sanctuary.

Loriz Jacob

Ambient ambitions

If fried eggs do well with Bacon
Do Chickens get on with Pigs?
Dried fruit a pure blessing
Who on Earth first made Figs?

If I am up yet they are down
Then we switch as move around
Yet both have feet on solid ground
What decides that thing call sound?

Elasticity a mystery
How stretch but then return?
Laziness is craziness
When spurn the chance to earn

The muddle of the mind, our Throne
The drivel of results shown
Each with name so do own
Another question is now sown

We take the knocks but carry on
Deep inside we are still strong
We adjust and belong
Listen to our favourite song

You and me, we simply be
A marvel that is true
We face the race then up the pace
When the true shines through

Ambient ambitious
The day to day we see
Some become just pipe dreams
Some reality

The complex mess to achieve our best
The pleasure of relaxing -when we find
The marvel of the matrix
We named Human kind

An album of achievement

A picture book did one leave
To be viewed by those who grieve
Happiness in time of sadness
Charting past and that achieved
Photos of a youngster
With some friends and at play
Others of the Schoolkid learning
About stuff that would not make earnings

The slightly older on Wedding day
When into new they did foray
Another leap as they stood
Beginning time called Parenthood
A different person but familiar
Certain parts are so similar
Yet a different person true
Doing that which most do

On the eve of Everlasting
Stood the soul soon to be passing
From the mortal to that which
Never have what's known as hitch
Here today but gone tomorrow
Leaving others with deep sorrows
Not for where they have gone
For at now where they belong

They have done what been asked
Now complete and finished task
So at peace with a sigh
The to us said Goodbye

An Island in the misery

Turn on a radio just for show
Not really listening to that played
Just a bunch that got lucky
Could say they made the grade
Distraction this attraction
Just for the length of song
The charade as it's played
Pretending I belong

I joined this band of clapping hands
Not those you see on street
I am just absorbed for spell
Foot tapping to the beat
Tune out at top of hour
When inflicts the News
Woe on show and seems to grow
The 'Headlines' do bemuse

The outside is a changing
The new it does amuse
For I am slightly morbid
Laugh when does confuse
And I don't need a prophecy
To tell me where to go
I don't need instructions
I myself do know

To what I think is proper
Decent and of caring
A poor cousin in today
Yet still worth the sharing
How many more to modern shore
Swim so sure and strong
If only they did realise
That 'golden beach' is wrong

An Island in the misery
Too small to gain attraction
So, I carry on undisturbed
Much to my satisfaction

And for it

'On a velvet dream I may have been'
Said one that once led
On past muse we can peruse
If only if instead
'The forced way once did play
The rules written by some fools
When both don't agree to them rules see
Ruthless then the tools'

One once said no alas dead
The non-rule took its toll
The one who chose to rise above those
Who prefer the safety shoal
Each to own yet some unknown
Pay price of being 'nice'
The unarmed fatally harmed
Look at what the price!

'I wished for change but change is strange
To some who just don't let
So I go to what don't know
With outpouring of regret
Thanks to all but this is small
When revert to what do know
Can you be a changer of the current danger?
Are you prepared to show?'

Another cost and another lost
Trying in this fight
To be a one, just someone
To change the wrong to right
There are still somewhere
Those who really care
About the world in which they live
And for it a life they give

And shall we see again?

With acknowledgement to the late great David Bowie

Ashes to ashes - to it I'm leaning
The meat is marinated
The cooker now needs cleaning
Yet the results are something yearning
Major Tom was a storm
In first song and the sequel
How many can another pen
A second that first did equal?

The outside I like to hide
In taste but also life
Choice I made I don't parade
That of different is my Wife
Different in who she be
That's the only difference I can see
Welcome that she stands her ground
Luckily chooses when no-one around

Then Phil buts in as did sing
A song so generation
Catchy true but what to you
When a chorus 'Fascination'
Eight oh to go and boy!
The eighties went!
A part of me will always be
In that decade I some long time spent

'Run to you' grew and grew
The Cannock had a voice
Typified all I tried
No chance for me rejoice
Eight and Oh to Eight and Nine
The music space sublime
Nine and oh the petulance show
The perfection of the mime

And the World still spins

Once upon another time
There did sit another line
All laid out so neat and fine
Oh, how wish was one of mine

Eons passed but words last
As fresh today as day saw light
Laid again on different paper
Some successful in this caper

And the world still spins on tilted axis

The blue and black form a stack
Waiting to be used
Other colours are in slumber
Using them just does confuse

Once upon that other time
Sat a rock, I think there still
Made of stuff not quite ferrous
Yet it seems to have an iron will

Never been that sometimes seen
The brash and so assured
A different life and then a Wife
Took that and then cured
Never been 'look at me'
Spotlight shows the fault
If you wish to describe which hide
When in circumstance was caught

Calamity and catastrophe
Like to surface at a blink
Just to show you don't really know
As in 'success' you sink

And Today's entertainment is

That bloody Crow has no sense of style
Either dress or in way acts
Thinks everything is there for it
Other Diners it attacks

The Squirrel has had enough of it
Not cowering like the Pigeon does
It is shrieking like a Banshee
Time to see who's tough

Fur or Feather- place your bets
Mine is on the Grey
Teeth or Beak, neither weak
Feet- Grey has four in play

Yes!! A Winner of the item
Of which I cannot differentiate
From the rubbish on the pavement
Street cleaner running late

Momma

Momma when you told me
That things won't be so bad
Why didn't you then tell me
I would be just like my Dad

Momma when you had the chance
Why did you choose to somethings not say?
Was it because I'm my Fathers son?
A forfeit I must pay

Momma, I feel I missed out
When in certain tone was called a Mister
Seemed to me a barrier be
Separation from my Sister

Ang gulo

One part of One chooses to be different
Puts money above those they serve
Creating unseen problems
As responsibilities they swerve
Not paid for this their excuses
Not expecting this the people's choice
They are but a victim
When 'Government' finds a voice

A comedy if not tragedy
A Nation in dissolve
The born are the suffering
Until this farce resolve
Yet is not your own problem
Is not in your thoughts
A different way we be may
Not in this we are caught

One part of one then contamination
Of the bigger scene
Of Districts being sensible
Knowing what position, it does mean
The suffering of the victims
Goes beyond belief
As does a certain word
That which we call grief

P you know that you're on show
Majority try to cope
Returnees a simple breeze
Until the inner then lose hop
Isang kalat sa bahay ipinanganak
A catastrophe it's true
Now must find that past spirit
Let you shine through

Ang kamangha-manghang saya ko

In a seemingly sense of Solitude
One step forward - did intrude
Changing that which went before
Changed by one who now adore

What was one thinking
Whilst morning drink drinking
To make decision to change a life
To sacrifice yourself to achieve it
When agreed to become a Wife

Not that I am complaining
I count the blessings don't deserve
Just a thought that keeps repeating
Never yet found the nerve

To ask you what you saw in me
When so many in that sea
You could have fished for much better
Than this one so fond of letters

Tell m please my new world
Why you chose this thing absurd
Explain to this simple being
Why deserve the glory seeing?

You ar me in future eternity
You are part of me now
I am just flabbergasted
In the whys, the when and how

Another bloody form

Welcome to the jumbled jungle
Forms to fill both screen and paper
They seem to want to know everything
Inside leg will be next caper!

My ink seems blue instead of black
Or is it just the vision lacks?
Still, should, hopefully, someway complete
This here form written neat

On incline I did then decline
To just stop, admit defeat
That is just a simple act
I like to kick challenge on its seat

Those forms we fill without much thrill
Often same because don't share
Between sections of same Department
Integration? They wouldn't dare!

Am I me yes/ no?
If I'm not how would you know
Just some letters on this form
They've been growing since were born

How many trees have I cost
How many records have you lost?
Keep a copy as your own
Bloody heck, I'd need another Home!

Oh loo, the postman's been
I wonder now what could that mean?
Just another Bill to thrill
Or another bloody form!

Captured

Caught in the Poetry
Of beauty
Turning each page
In awe
Filling my brain with
Seasons delight
Viewing beyond the
Falling words
Touching a poet's soul
In ink
Letting it flow its emotions
In depth
Connected in its pull with my
Heart beat
As it spreads across the
Sentences
Falling in view of their own
Perceptions
Of feeling another's ink in
Rainbow colors
As they capture Natures
View
So fleeting like the click
Of a camera
They've held the negative in
Minds view
To develop at their solitude
Call to write

Janice Fisher

Reach

Even in the darkest moments
When shadows threaten
I reach and find your hand
A gentle squeeze of care
With no words necessary
Tells me its ok
We tread tomorrow together
Holding tight as waves try
To drowned us in uncertain
Emotions
We tread a path now that
Curved in our destination
A different route of dreams
Unseen
The abyss of unknown that
We must acquaint ourselves
With
We search for our augur in the
Shadows viewed as answers
Still in place
We coincide in our roaming
Thoughts with the knowledge
We are not alone in this
New path
We search our faces in the dark
And although shadowed we see
A love so strong it's like a guiding
Light
We grasp this touch tighter as we
See beyond the shadows of Loves
Journey
Holding A revision of an old dream
In a new path

Janice Fisher

Beyond

Intriguing this mind
We have
It stores memories
Of years
Playing back in full,
If thought
Or brought to attention
By senses
Yet in minds view it
Becomes distorted
At times
A flash of rolling scenic
Views
Was I there? Did I see
This?
What purpose does this
Image serves
But we came without a
Delete button
So we filter through trying
To understand
Did the mind pick through?
Fragments
Putting its spill on what
Was
In reality we question our
Sanity
Because this is not what we
Seen or did
Why do I remember so vividly?
This place
I've never been there but in the
Depth of mind
It's so clear every detail I can
Describe
Bringing in focus the mind
Does travel
Back future than we ever
Imagined

Janice Fisher

35

Dreams

Feeling the depth of
Floating dreams
As if touched in flight
On moon beams
Feeling the city lights
Untouched
As I soar to find you
There
The evening breeze brushes
My lips
I taste in this dream the
Essence of you
Feel the magnetic pull of
Your needs
Wrapped in your arms
Not touching
Feel my soul brush as
One with yours
Gaze within the stars
Of my needs
That within this silent
Dream
You meet me here so just
For to nite
We touch in fading
Dreams
As one to hold till morning
Light

Janice Fisher

Cold

The Sunrise touched the
Snow-capped mountain
Brushing it with pinks

Stirring memories that
Soon the cold beauty of
Snow will fall

Seasons so fleeting
But leave an unmarked
View of scenes

The green grass wet
With springs gentle
Showers

The summers warmth
Touching the up lifted
Blossoms

The fall of golden leaves
So picturesque in the
Hills view

Then in its time too
Winter snows cover
The land in cold
Beautiful

Janice Fisher

Thoughts

In the twilight of my
Dreams
I feel the presence of
You
A fragment of my being
Entwined
In the ever-flowing waters
Of life
Where you floated in so
Unexpectedly
Catching me when my path
Uncertain
You taught me to swim the
Backward current
Then walking the shores above
The tangles
Letting the sands of time flow

Forward

I know now you were but loaned
To me
In a time, I needed a gentle
Understanding
A guide through the troubled
Waters
Holding me about the drowning
Pull
When my feet hit solid ground
Of assurance
You disappear from my sight as
If never there
If you thought I'd not miss you
Then
How wrong you were for now
I search
In all the backwards spaces we
Travelled
But for not, as you linger in only
My shadows
Between dreams and a reality of
Uncertainties

Janice Fisher

IF

If I look at the world
through your eyes
It's a different perspective
that I see
That's what makes us so
unique
Being able to share our
views
Not in friction but in equal
opinions
Meeting half way in a goal
Of unity
So two share in puzzle
pieces
Ending in results that please
Both

L- live
O- options
V- victorious
E- equally

In the end the puzzle complete
nothing missing
No you and me
Just us

Janice Fisher

Love Eternal

Remember me
when night falls short
the river flows across the ground
when the silence of your trembling heart
finds no one else around
I will be there
in a mist
from somewhere out amongst the stars
I will hear your silent voice
calling
where ever you are
the love that binds us
from inside out
can never be lost
it is somewhere floating looking for the wind
I will come to you again and again
earth has its boundaries
shadows slip into the void
light from our souls collide
we journey un-annoyed
my heart is melting
it pours into a waiting heart
yours my love
the warrior
fought the battles
cried so many tears not seen
and in the final hours
we became the dream...........

Margaret "Renie" Burgess

From Here

Watching that vacated tent silently asleep,
You, calling sympathy from your empty vault,
To squeeze a convince for the true hearts,
And a sigh muscled to rend a mourning face,
The pillars out reject you,
The hearts of men with a conscious rebel,
For you are not here to bid adieu,
Rather to bury hope with my remains,

To crash faith with the flap of the casket,
To drive back to the days of dark digress,
As you weave your ungainly frame,
Filled with a ton of scheme's,
Of systems arrests and demolition,
Holding onto the cold hands of a live in ex,
Pity is what I feel for those money has become a god,
You see cowboy!

Death is not absence,
It is life without the trappings of material.
That your guns are cocked to shoot fairness to smithereens,
Is what breaks the spirits of those watching you,
Your pumped up image of a mourner not withstanding,
Your ancestry weeps at the turn of your heart,
Having laid a foundation for you,
They hurt for the emptiness of what you hold dear,

So, cowboy!
Hush and on you go,
The echo on your back is booing,
Is sense telling you to look for humanity inside you
Those stalwartly standing with you,
Are carrion birds with persuasive legal jargon to direct your lost soul,
Those propping you up with ululations will scatter with your fall,
As for the sponsors holding you Ransom for your dirty laundry,

No royalty will hold their tongues longer than the hour you crash,
So, act all you know cowboy!
The dead know a thing you ought to have learnt,
Nothing lasts forever,
Not power, nor greed.
Be afraid and rush out pronto,
Dead does not take away deeds,
Neither does it obliterate kindness,

So, sob and snicker at this shell,
Thinking fate give you a free hand to play truant.
Cowboy!
There is always an unseen hand.
It's called death speaking after the fact.
And all those booing voices are the wishes of right chanting light.

Nancy Ndeke.

Heroes.....

Aside from ordinariness,
Apart from normal and regular,
They come often in sizes unseized,
Cotton shirt flaring in the wind,
Holding a strange hand in a moment unknown,
Listening till the rave and rant is over,
Picking that call at the dead of night,
Calling two hours later to ensure calm,

A commander leading a troop knowing not his fate,
Patience in deflecting conflict,
Unholy hours of work to provide,
Holding the hand of one who grieves,
Stopping a moment to let a family of ducks cross the road,
Giving from less of what is needed,
Heroes,

Wingless champions of small and big gestures,
Never shying from lending a shoulder,
Adopting a child to mitigate homelessness,
Sharing the little with those belittled by harshness,
Heroes,

Are a dozen a dime their songs unsung,
There are the ones who stay to share silence,
When duty is done and the surgeon packed bag,
Leaving the throbbing would blazing mad,
A Heroes presence is life taking care of it's own.

Nancy Ndeke

44

Demoted Senses

Quite focused like a pilot on a charted flight,
A to Z is embossed with 'meism',
Periphery sucked in like a storms eye expanding,
A king is owned by a prince,
of a kind scripture warned,
With the reading of a heart dark to empathy,

For when the sun is brewed to shine for self,
The moon weeps for lack of play,
At a glance demotion shines like promotion,
The silence of the land before the volcano erupts,
Tongues tied in partisan takes and banditry divides,
The king is no longer anything definable,

Just a shell, full of emptiness,
Deadly in his arrogant semantics,
While paying the heavy fine to those he owes his secrets.
And common folks like flies,
Silently stamp the continued assault,
One that history has seen before,

One that shocked pirates and shamans,
And now,
That play is set for a second presentation,
Unless folks wake up with autumn leaves falling,
To scrape the yards of the littered waste,
That the demoted king is spewing.

Nancy Ndeke

Morphology Of Who....

Are we what they say we are or who we think we are,
Names lending character a gift or is it a tagged curse,
Better than the next or worse because you bought the bias,
Favoured and Blessed for having a birthday on a holy day,

Taller than all around feeling awkward at first,
Fat and ungainly wobbling and waddling when the rest embrace grace,
Accept the only addition is increased waist for excess consumption,
You have a say though never absolutely,
You make yourself daily, chose direction and tools well,
Compare only with your plot for compensation is a sham

Take some time off to engage your points of scores,
Revise in the comfort of your inner what needs shaving,
After all,
No one should love you better than you,
Neither shift places with you,
Having arrived here smile with an inner glow,
For you are well adapted and jest will make no dent

A self-made man after creations first model.
Accept, analyse, adapt, to breeze through the draft.
How you play this life is not about classes paid for,
But from an internal script that's always there for you.
Reach it and enrich yourself.
Remembering that wealth is more than accumulated gold bars.

Nancy Ndeke

Talk To Me....

Of the silence of noise,
And the volume of fear,
Talk to me of the beauty of a stranger,
And the delicate balance of truth

Assure this handshake of the unspoken,
Reinsure this peep at midday of the dawn,
Talk to me in a letter that borrows from an emotion,
Tell me at the count of two that one is whole

Talk to me of deserts that live in forests,
Speak of a stitch that knits the open coat,
Whisper the winds intentions in caddying the candle,
Feel the waves of depths swish the feet of a penitent

The world is softly hard to the hand of kinship,
You are the UNIVERSE, part and apart,
The moment came in a delayed carriage,
Carrying courage in a cream carrier bag

In it was all the missed masks and the new message,
Of no fault or acronyms of guessed paths,
Temptations is test of will and yearning of a new year,
One that generations of warriors worried little

Registered resistance retrieved unity,
And build a new song as old as Aden,
Telling takes of tales of dreams being the real.

Nancy Ndeke

A Man Made A Storm....

A mighty wordy storm,
Shared on the global terrain for all to watch,
He was the author, player and audience,
A character in the footprints of gods,
He did applaud

Louder than known thunder,
Preaching numerics and consonants,
Reading was impossible without vowels,
A man made a storm

Rode its eye at speeds unknown,
Knockout antiques, bravado cheering,
He rumbled till the veins burst,
A few hinges came off his door,
Revealing the unmade bed,
With loneliness dressed in seventy shades,
He crowed, cawed and hooted,
He barked, bowled and farted,
Only a few escaped mental cases joined the fray

When the voice dried and the storm decimated,
A scare crow crawled out of his den,
Neighbourhood tales tell of that night,
When the storm maker rode the dark of early winter night,
Mumbling unintelligibly about greatness unappreciated,
Those who didn't laugh fought a guarantee gentle smile,
While the rest toasted a midnight pop to rid the air of a vermin.

Nancy Ndeke

This Mirror...

Standing against Kirinyaga heights,
Equator snow blazing in the morning sun,
A lie melts and truth is born,
You, begets we in the one,
Who you are drizzles into all,
The bamboo terrain with Heather purple glow,
Lake Microson shimmering anew,
Elephants with young calves,

Distance echo of ancient creation,
Before this mirror,
That unites images outer and inner,
A reflection of what lay in caves,
Of exploratory journeys and conquest journeys,
Before this mirror,
That won't move or budge,
Is an open secret long revealed.

You have always known,
That another is no alien,
Or anathema to being-ness,
For in front of this mirror,
Truth will tell not or ask,
It will just stand mute,
Waiting for wakefulness to shake it's hand.

Nancy Ndeke

49

United Dementia

Guilt glides our air waves,
Cat walking with glamour,
At all stations in our blinded stupor,
Memory lane jog shows........
Genghis khans monstrous slaughter,
Idi Amin and his genital chops,
Shaka Zulu mutilating those mourners who mourned less,
Vlad the impaler with his draconian roasting,
Pol Pot starvation escapades,
The Kim's tales still gathering casualties from father to son,
Hitler's acts of demoniac sheenigans still sends shivers,
Stalin and the great purge chills humanity,
Mao Tse-jug drama of massacres,
Historical histograms hollowed out with denial,
Are we better and fairly free of this past?
A poet laughs to forestall crying,
For under the clean noses of 'Tainted missions"
Blood harvesters and goat head gods roam,
Guillotining masses with economic choke holds,
Bludgeoning truths with gigantic quandary,
Pitting one against another,
Deleting progress that decades and centuries have made,
All for what?
The same want Hussein had in watching replays of torture over dinner,
Raw power that has no respect for life.
And still, we are quiet because it's not us.
Really?
When was it ever not us?
For what affects one will,
Eventually affect the other,
Islands are isolated places surrounded by water,
Man is not!
And history is always a story replying to its old tunes,
Unless, we break it.

Nancy Ndeke

Somewhere

somewhere
tucked hidden between grey things
in the recesses of a mind
there lives a teenage boy
who played his stereo, loud,
after his dad had gone to bed;
a boy whose dad had slapped him
in the face for the first time the week before
for trying pot for the first time.
a boy whose mother knocked
on his locked bedroom door
and through it yelled,
"turn that music down!
do you want your father to have
a heart attack?"

somewhere
in memories and
in those instants in time
that can come with a song, perhaps
"Do the Walk of Life"
by the Dire Straits, or
"I Want to Go Where Love Is,"
there lives a man
ignored by family who drove by
as he made his long way
on foot, to a faraway store
to buy the too many beers he drank each day.
forty-one years of worn out sneakered footsteps,
bare footed finally in a bed
filled with cancer in a place
far from the home town
he could not leave.

somewhere
decades stand still
mostly empty, but holding
one who cared,
talking from thousands of miles away
cords in wood walls connecting them.
her hand can still feel the bills
she sent
he bought beer no doubt with some if it
like many do who
are so lonely
it becomes pathological.

somewhere
a teenage boy in his bed,
half way through a saturday morning,
looks up at her as she says
the words her mother could not say to him,
turns his back to her and shouts,
"go away"!
and just before he turned his back
she saw that his blue eyes
were as dead as his dad's.

somewhere
there is a silver cord
connecting dimensions, preserving connections
where no one is really removed from another
and no one's little brother is alone.

Cathy Mccormick

Caught in the crystal

The day is young so just begun
Another page to add to age
What new wonders will this one bring?
Will heart cry or will heart sing?

I am a veteran of intention
More than I now choose to mention
That is all just past reflection
When you see my I am a microsecond older

Painful legs from strange sleep
Under cover must learn to keep
Funny how in that don't weep
I guess it has its good points

What to do with this chance new
Hoist the red or fly the blue
Also, what will weather do?
Oh three forty and thing to chew

Friends to talk to all around
Around this planet we call Home
Different Time zones are amusing
Working out is so confusing

As I type the day gets older
As I type the feeling bolder
Soon it will come into frustration
Is that not a new day's mission?

Caught in the crystal of conception
Creating something my intention
Guarantee not perfection
Tell me anything that is

Charade made for parade

Still four hours until daylight
Yet inside the daylight bright
When the choice is to fight
For that I choose to be right

Two 'tives' from which to choose
One I win, the other lose
I am just another one
Making best of that begun

All the tunes
They just flow through me
All that happens
Is just meant to be
All the past, just history
All the future
Is what can I be
All the barriers are just hills
Trying, yes, but strong of will
Nothing ventured, stagnant kills
Not the way I choose

Esplanade and Arcade
Things a Human chose and made
Then success they do parade
In some twisted false charade

Not for me that destination
Avoid at length that confrontation
Of the real and fantasy
Of the one who I call Me

All the tunes
They just flow through me
All that happens
Is just meant to be
All the past, just history

All the future
Is what can I be
All the barriers are just hills
Trying, yes, but strong of will
Nothing ventured, stagnant kills
Not the way I choose

Charade made for parade
Is something at rest is laid
Of the new? Yes, am afraid
Yet best decision so far made

Recognise me? I Understand
Not the person with begging hand
I moved on to something new
I just did what had to do

All the tunes
They just flow through me
All that happens
Is just meant to be
All the past, just history
All the future
Is what can I be
All the barriers are just hills
Trying, yes, but strong of will
Nothing ventured, stagnant kills
Not the way I choose

Moving to improving
Rougher Seas made calm
Typhoon now a gentle swoon
When experienced Human harm

We live in shells and outside
We are influenced by thing called Pride
Yet are we really proud of what do?
To likes of us? The likes of you?

Chemicals

Chemicals- the rise and fall
Medical and in recreation
One does keep us going
The other consternation
Logic lost and respect cost
Unless others in same state
Then that different being
They can somehow then relate

When walked the walk
The wonky walk of wine
The feet, they kind of floated
The fuzzy head felt fine
The sensation of the session
A blur in parts is true
Doing daft for a laugh
Dancing with no clue

That emotional high
When you hear your Baby's first explosive cry
This one natural
Occasionally accompanied with soft sigh
The embarrassed rush with hot flush
When your thoughts seem to be read
That laugh in their eyes that can't disguise
They didn't stay within your Head

That Pharmacy that seems to be
The replacement for the Pub
Keeps one able but unable
That's the bitter rub
The chemicals to keep us living
A different way they are giving
The chemicals taken for pleasure
Now are banned with no half measure

Christmas for the lonely

One Roast Potato, some processed Turkey
One sausage and one stuffing ball
A portion of carrots and Peas
Someone, somewhere Christmas call

Christmas for the lonely
Another pain to bear
Christmas for the lonely
Watching others share

The sound of Children having fun
The uncorking though not yet One
The gaiety of Family
No, just another has begun

We sit and laugh with gay abandon
We enrich in social pleasure
Yet when company, if lucky, four walls
What have they to treasure?

A time of plenty if you are prosperous
Not so, if you have none
Not sure if that's the original message
When to celebrate they to him sung

Christmas for the lonely
Just another Day
Christmas is for profit
Nothing else I say

How can it be when misery?
Still reigns in certain parts
How can it be when the lonely?
Have nothing but their Hearts

Chronicles of a confused conscience

Did what I did and where it led
Have an impact upon a stranger?
Did what did do then lead to
Someone then in danger?

Am I me? This thing you see
Or am I just a mask of past
If I'm wrong and don't belong
How long will I last?

A parody of inconsistencies
My legacy to hist and me
Not the thing in future see
More a twisted novelty

Who are each and what do teach?
The ones we call into this world
When we are just destruction bent
The whole thing beyond words

Little Moth by my light
Why attraction to things bright
Collisions seeming like a fight
Do you need my Glasses to help your sight?

Laid i verse me at my worst
Becoming quite a trend
Nip it quick before I slip
Here this garbage ends

Cold as old

Getting colder as I get older
Guess my Winter's here to stay
Look at me and what do you see?
With words do you play?

I am a million of the critters
Sometimes joyful, sometimes bitter
But a word is speech unheard
Strip me bare with your absurd

I lust for lines so divine
That takes the breath away
Segments said and where led
Some of them will stay

Incredulous the ink laid down
Incredulous the song that's sung
Incredulous the Actors acting
As if that character becomes

The days belong to the young today
The nights to them not old
The world is theirs to do as wish
I just feel the cold

September yes, but also years
Past mid-century so can say
Look after what we are leaving
Treat in better way

Getting cold as I get old
In more ways than one
Surviving by contrivance
That in but not begun

Cold Winds

The cold winds blow but blows behind
Pushing forward, you will find
On to some kind peace of Mind
Freeing of the things that bind

Wind of change may seem so strange
When pushes to pastures new
Yet a friend and strength does lend
To help what you must do

Everybody feels the pain
Sometime in a Life
Everybody gets some scars
Inflicted by its knife

To cry and why, we all try
To fathom a simple reason
Truth is much simpler
For is the crying season

So pull up that waistline, dry those eyes
Everything for reason, in disguise
Cast off the shackles of melancholy
In rain of pain put up your Brolly

The knees were weak and couldn't speak
Pause a cause for good
Gives time to know it's fine
When is understood

Words absurd when first heard
Become sense when heard the same
From different ones under same Sun
Who've been through that old game

My poor synapses

In darkest depths the Diver delved
Search and then did find
The way to rise from this demise
Feelings a better kind
Come to me sweet harmony
Come to me you pleasure
What we find is different kind
In that we class as leisure

Teaser, not on the relentless pursuit of leisure.
Answer the blossoming moon rays and verify your level-headed authenticity.
Is virtual demise discovered by the diver, a glitzy adventure?
The kaleidoscopic patterns of darkness is the embodiment of lightness.
The twinkling effect is gleeful, if you are not a teaser.

Who but we truly see?
The collectable from chaff?
We are our own Sea
Also, our own raft
The Beacon that on which are gazing
Is light of own making
The bed made on which have laid
Is the effort we are taking

The balmy wind blows and the raft gently flows
The cosmic moon rays elevated my mind
We are so divine and where is the Moonscreen?
A moon burn is mind blowing.
Harmonious pleasure is an envision of utopia and eradicates suffering

The air we breathe does deceive
The poison in which we put
The irony of Humanity
Is the Boot's on other foot
The making then the breaking
How we do progress
Yet the major question and answer
Will we pass the final test?

Psychedelic music is impractical conceit
There will not be any defeat
Gruelling labour of our minds is embedded in our DNA
Ancient whispers dance in the wind with images of wisdom
Handle with care
The moonlight glare will trigger your brain

We feel the need and that need feed
Insatiable appetite
Devouring is empowering
When for this food we fight
The mortal becomes morsel
The wish a destruction Dish
The Sea a salt Sahara
We but floating fish

We are glittering jewels and not fools
Perchance, we are moonbaked and our minds are quirky
The future is vibrant and we will unravel the secret of dismissing fussiness
We are floating underneath the Cosmic moon and there is no gloom

Everyone is changing
Some to something strange
Everything is rearranging
Some of which don't like
Everything is something new
Everything is past
Everyone is in the present
None of us will last

We are mortal beings with immortal souls
The prevailing attitude is Karma
What was, is a new beginning
Hold my hand, dear brother, as we become one with the Light of Eternal Love

A collaboration between Melissa Begley and Ian Wilcox

Collateral with afternoon coffee

When I walked that thought was unwalkable
When stepped into unknown
Saw a different part of me
One so truly grown
Inside the space that had been vacant
Inside the folder 'Future self'
I discovered what was missing
I discovered that I had wealth

When she's in fashion she gains attraction
When they decide they simply hide
Ups and downs pouts and frowns
The self deluded pride
The catwalk more cat than talk
Bitchiness has found new ground
The nothing to a something
Lap up as name does sound

The one like me who will never be
The song do and done have sang
The nee to feed that inner greed
The phone that never rang
That type of glory a different story
Each unto their own
To put on edge for County pledge
They have right to moan

Middle age rant, what's the chance?
Just warming to old age
The Dictionary that is me
Just turn another page
Yes, understanding but with some handling
Unfixable need to be
For if just set in what can get
The opposite of you there you see

Come calamity

Many are the mysteries
Competing with the fallacies
Coupled with the ironies
When sitting back and think

Enormous are expressions
Each have their own perceptions
So many are suggestions
Of how to improve yourself

Come calamity come a calling
Come a chance for change
Come a problem, come solution
Even if feel strange
Come the new to go through
Come the memory
Come that which have learnt
Come that still to be

But you are you and what you do
Is better if choice make
Accepting yet not relenting
All the give and take

A walking sponge of expertise
Though not all do walk
A book of gained wisdom
Though not all of which will talk

Forget about Computers
More knowledge you will find
When you look and appreciate
The joys on Human kind

Compared to River

If I'm eclectic are you electric?
Fizzing with your thoughts
Would you take me to ecstasy
In your dreams you caught
The mix and match of strange batch
Perfume I do smell
Open up and let's fill this cup
With the words that we can tell

With open eyes and to my surprise
I saw much more than me
The release was a tease
But just how meant to be
The prodder of the prodder
The stick to make them strong
To that place that I won't face
Yet where they do belong

So sit and do, try to be new
Yet not the thing you seek
For what I see surpasses me
Compared to River I'm a Creek
You look to me but do not see
The great that I go know
How you say? I watched them play
As in confidence they grow

Sometimes the strong get it wrong
But a gift is always there
For if in same make minor name
Exposure can still share
The gift is not the individual
The gift is what they do
The gift is recognition
The gift is that which new

Confused muse as peruse

Cyclones hit Scottish homes
Snow falls in Sahara
Not quite yet but get set
As Mother takes it further
Racial recognition
A long sought right decision
Just too much and lose touch
In the purpose mission

Same sex marriage and electric carriage
Now some are aware
Yet industry wants pie to eat
Really doesn't care
A brave new world from threat unheard
Before announced itself
Hitting hard with death card
In fortunate just ill health

Welcome me to that I see
Not wanted but so loud
Now I'm asking myself the question
'As a being am I proud?'
Corona in Utopia
Good and bad comes to the fore
It's so strange this time of change
Do we need or more?

Confused muse as peruse
Information situation
Are we all at beck and call?
Of this techno new generation?
Shut down not just slow down
How many now with work lost?
How and when will again
See a generation of unschooled cost

My curry is bubbling nicely
Rice now ready to go
This is such a pain for gain
When are a one soul show
Who invented Solitude?
A sadistic one for sure
Tolerating is understated
As we strive for cure

What are we and what do see?
Where heading on this path
Will outcome be winning one?
Not some epitaph
Need Caffeine fix to sort out mix
Who can lend an urn?
Big enough to hold barrel of stuff
No drip of it will spurn

Is it lunch or is it Dinner?
Are clothes stretched or am I thinner?
Not complete but no beginner
Am I mad or is it where?
Where I am and not now knowing
All the things this life is showing
Are we repeating in the growing?
Have we lost the will to care?

A Squirrel sitting on back fence
Ignorant of what's going on
Making most of playing host
To adapting to belong
Dry and cold or wet and warm
Last week's Heatwave now forgotten
Confused muse as peruse
Some lyrics by Johnny Rotten

Confusion in illusion

The frustration of the situation
When it then sinks home
The subtleties of not meant to be
The stark is finally shown
That strange stance of taking change
Blinded by reward
Such can be the electricity of what we call romance

It offered much for if did touch
Took a grip and tried
Yep it was not that which got
The truth is that it lied
Tistliness and meaningless
The gravitas I lose
Confusing in illusion
Your rewards for what it cost

We ran toward and fell on sword
We chased a gleaming Sun
Entrapped by fact fell into trap
Gave more than ever done
We promise never to repeat
Then another do me meet
Then forget past regret
We go to repeat

Then one rises to the fore
Then new felling you explore
They may come from different shore
Yet you know that you want more
More of the things they do
More of that which sees through
More of when got that clue
More that they mean everything to you

Conquers sins

When chance seemed strange
But did rearrange
The feelings have no clue
The past is gone but not forgotten
Just have found a whole new you
When nothing seems like too much trouble
Sole aim is to just make them smile
When distraction is not measured
By Land nor nautical miles

When problems seem to disappear
When a certain voice you hear
When first thought upon waking up
Preludes the wish for coffee cup
When voice call turn of radio
To better the connection
Not the one of airwaves
Just the sound of voice complexion

When as soon as end want to start again
When although good and understood
Need more than just the pen
The fuel that take is no mistake
The timeline is just when
The blissful feeling in which are reeling
The new of what you thought
The move on to the higher level
In that before was caught

The mystery of rhapsody
The floating in the air
The don't care if it share
The feeling that you choose to dare
More than mortal
Just from above
This is ecstasy in reality
This is simply a true love

Love it brings and conquers sins
A new slate it places
Not dependant on the being
Nor the colour of their faces

Conscience is no con science

Conscious is no con science
Hence
if the blood in the vein's boils,
is because our Minds are kept open

Some may regard it as a skill
Depends on how it's done
An illusionist is acceptable
For profit can't condone

open, a book; sharing its content
thoughts jumping
strolling and walking through continents

Skill or science?
That's debatable
I guess it is if it is taught
The other not if you get caught

It ain't a sci∂nce
more
bending towards spiritual

Conscience when is no con science
When you are open to what feels right
Conscience is the comfort feel
When actions in plain sight

Two
but
one

Ian Wilcox
and
I

sharing Perspectives
and
blending our Souls

even though we are half ways
across the world

Conscience are on parity
For does not depend on where are from
It is about that certain places
Where feel that you belong

One
but
of
many
thoughts

Such stars on the firmament
so, our collective Consciousness

Hence conscience is no con science
When broken down to fact
Different outcomes to other people
Depending on which act

A collaboration between Noe Basurto
and
Ian Wilcox

Different is just different

Rupert went to Rio
Helen travelled Home
Stuart loved the silence
As Rebecca went to Rome

Separate spaces sometimes needed
Just to be yourself
Gives more things to talk about
Interaction such a wealth

Some we do together
Others do alone
There's no set down guidelines
Each we figure on our own

Some are vegetarian
Some do like their meat
Some eat certain parts only
Some right down to feet

Wake in morning and sleep at night
Or wake in evening – which is right?
To each their own in circumstance
To each a different make a stance

Billy found it chilly
To Jane it felt just great
Sandra is always punctual
Henry always late

Different is just different
In certain things it's true
When respecting others
There's no red or blue

Different parts of the Rainbow

A soul they sat on a wet bench
For recently had rain
Sun now back and shining
As brightness strove to gain
Approached them did another
With warm smile did greet
Asked if could sit beside them
To take weight off tired feet

Briefly sat in silence
Soaking in the day
Then newcomer turned to face
And this is what did say

Do you see a Rainbow?
Made of Human life
Each a different colour
Yet each a part of it
Do you see a Rainbow?
How beautiful in sky
We don't need no pot of Gold
To make it worth a try

The first one did look at them
A warm smile it grew
Looking to the Heavens
Said 'Yes I do
I can see a Rainbow
Stretching on forever
For this certain Rainbow
Not dependent on the weather
A multi coloured species
For in truth we are
Stronger in the unity
Those both near and far
For in certain things am colour blind
See but side by side
Only in our ignorance
This Rainbow try to hide'
The two of them were different parts of that Rainbow

Eyelids peeling open

So, what got was not a lot
Join the bloody Club!
Fortune is so fickle
On this hide didn't rub
The song in silence is still heard
The beat of feet to that occurred
The Flag to wave until the grave
The understanding of that absurd

Routes a hoot for them in suits
Quick to earn their pay
I prefer the why and were
When read what others say
The fragrance of the fiction
The gravity of true
The sanity of history
The stupid things we do

We bump and grind until we find
That certain space on seat
Then look on quite innocent
As fellow passengers greet
The victory a mystery
To those that are left standing
Hoping in futility
Your place over will be handing

The new battle now begins
From where you once did sit
Subtly push and shove
To reach place marked Exit
Then the footrace to that dire place
The one that's known as 'works
Where for dragging hours
It we try to shirk

Fall of that confused

Everything has a season
Everything has a reason
Not all fall into Humanity treason
Some are just fact of Life

All that sent we should not repent
When make a better one today
Not all grow up with Silver cup
Some a different game do play

Does that make them lesser being?
Does that make it convenient not seeing?
None should be forced into kneeling
Unless they wish to do

Came from nothing and will return to nothing
In that all are equal
Difference between what future means
The part that is the sequel

None of matters in who we are
Nothing has a divine right
We are we and should be
Preconceptions we should fight

All we are we have gained
That before you have felt pain
Yet to inflict does refrain
Actions speak louder than words

Who are we is a mystery
Least not to ourselves
Complication situation
The deeper one then delves

Are you feeling better now?
Or do you feel abused?
Welcome to the thinking area
Fall of that confused

Fallacy and fantasy

When fallacy turns to fantasy
Then into reality are born
When ideals now so unreal
When Nations themselves are torn
What of me and what I be
A question I must ask
Are they wrong and am I strong?
Enough for this here task

The multiple of susceptible
The quandary we now face
The diversity once history
Gathering at pace
Am I just one annoyed?
Am I now just paranoid?
Am I just behind the time?
All okay and all is fine

My suspicion is merely supervision
According to some polls
I am but a number
For the new mass media trolls
They smile at you on pay per view
Suddenly they are to you wed
On a screen doesn't mean
They'd share with you a bed

The ranting not enchanting
The complimentary so unnecessary
The facts stack with each act
A step back takes the wary
So, ask of thee who truly free
Then how much we want to be
Totally leads to anarchy
When violent acts be just be

False dreams

The cigarette once burned down slowly
The coffee sat, getting cold
The meaning of the waking up
Lost to one, if truth be told
A different person on different day
That now present free to say
The trials and tribulations of before
Now just memories and nothing more

Life was hard with dealt card
Yet now I know have may to go
To be the same as some in 'game'
Who diminish me and you
When we look at what they took
Then just carried on
They are idols to look up to
They are definition of that strong

On a Doorstep left, so could forget
The problems of the past
Those days have been so now don't mean
Anything that doesn't last
Experience and nothing more
Just emoticons to explore
Never reaching to the core
For chance of breathing I adore

A little fish that swims with giants
Blessed and honoured to them know
Not all them so outspoken
Not all of them their real one show
I sit and marvel at the Maestros
Of the art of secrecy
Hiding by just carrying onward
Showing world what can be

Show me the 'perfect' human
and I will look at an android
made by people with false dreams

Fame and name

Higginbottom was quite rotten
A product of a private school
Never mixing let alone kissing
The 'common' person taught to rule

Us and them by stroke of pen
The dot goes far to right
Yet the same when just plain
In birthday suit the sight

'Classes' for the masses
Who determined which do fit?
I was not asked about this task
Am just a part of it

Helen double barrel
They seem to think it's cool
Adding to the surname
Seems unspoken rule

I am me and pleased to be
Nothing with a title shown
Nothing of the media pressure
All I have I own

Make of me what you see
A name is just a badge
Separating when self-proclaiming
Though open to the cadge

Name and fame, such a pain
One I choose not to explore
Just a common one under same Sun
Nothing less and nothing more

Fads and trends

Fads and trends the mind they send
Into a state of apoplexy
Cost a lot but what have you got?
Lean bank account and misery

What's good in May by June we laugh at
What in June do in September
Creating space for a red face
As looking back remember

Me, I like the simple things
Things that I can savour
Diet be a misery
When rob of full-blown flavour

Charity shops get a lot
Of once were proud to wear
Yet now cringe as eyeballs singe
Now we wouldn't dare

'What ever did possess us?
What Planet were we on?'
The choices made now don't meet the grade
We just did so could belong

Fads and trends and spend, spend, spend
A reoccurring cycle be
Unless are proud to depart that cloud
And normal 'boring' but are free

Fantasising about socialising

First job of the day is to see what others do say
If that's even their real name
The essentials got smaller for smaller is cooler
A Computer now in a hand held slim frame
Libellous litigation a common situation
When own version of 'fact' so easy to do
That's been around since before were born
Just ways and subjects new

When the science of progress, lands all in this mess
Are we all retards, desperately needing cue cards?
Did it all start when technology stole heart
Humanity now sits in the shards
Of the 'could be' now we just look/ see
What 'Hero' we could be
In some pixel pitch fantasy
That most now seem to own

When 'killing' is cool the player's a fool
That could transfer to what we call real
Where just don't disappear after you spear
They bleed and actually feel
To get highest score hate less and love more
Take time to actually meet
You have more than just your Hands on your arms
On legs are things called Feet

Is I.T. what it be or just what we see?
To amuse ourselves in chair
A variation on situation
Instead of at television stare
Fantasising about socialising
The latest game in Town
Don't be afraid to say you've played
Probably wear your winner's Crown

80

Father of us all

Old Father you have taught me
How to get along
Old Father you have shown me
How to be strong

We put man into Space
Why can't we fix the Human Race?
The hopes and starts, the broken hearts
Can we realise that all are parts

Time for change can seem so strange
Yet, at times, we must do
The Black, the White, all in sight
Must be themselves and true

Sympathy for what was me
No! That path I don't go
That Devil can hide or take a ride
Maybe in the morning, true colour I will show

We should reach out and, maybe, shout
All different but are one
Do what do until the new
Let's just make it fun

I wal away when other does play
Not the game I choose
For however think are winning
At the end all do lose

So what do we do to just get through?
Different streets do meet
To solitude we must intrude
A new angle we can greet

Feast the fellows of simple flavours

Take one large piece of Bovine Beast
Cut by Butcher to perfection
Whilst doing this add a twist
Get over temperature to perfection

Take choice of greens
Whatever that means
Wash and defrock as required
Take and prepare whatever else you dare
The concept soon to be sired

Take Potatoes that English stable
Wash, peel and cut to size
Not a guarantee you see
More the case of wise

A tray you may but a dish the wish
Gently placed the pots and meat
Adjust the time to size of crime
Occasionally baste pots to have a treat

Fast forward for consideration for read

When time comes now the fun
To boil or simply steam
Al dente not drowned pray
If you know what mean

Meat is done, pots golden sun
Meat just needs a rest
Then jiggery and pokey
A meal we have at best
Rice is nice and Pasta too
Many are the choices now
Yet to own are true

Feezlejam

The world's gone mad when good is bad
What's up replacing Hi
Cool is hot and slang a slot
In Dictionaries held so high

But I am just a Dinosaur
Memories my crimes
I am but a permanent
That doesn't move with times

A fuddy duddy have been called
A better insult true
Some of others need steel covers
Varied shades of blue

I am that old Librarian
You know I'm sure the sort
That sits in corner eagle eared
The 'non proper' will be caught

Make my day with Shakespeare play
Though personally not my taste
Time and place so let's not waste
The chance of new foray

Contradiction m infliction
Just different way I do
Turning old into bold
Creating something new

Feezlejam is my plan
To current stuff include
Just a mix of nonsense
No connotations rude

A dream of mine that could shine
When 'Street they start to utter
Even took into account
Those afflicted with a stutter

Hippo yo

I mixed mustard in the custard
I like the shock it gives
For explanation of exclamation
Served soup with a variety of sieves

The sensation of salvation
Lost in this generation I fear
Nothing religious, far more serious
When all destruction on screen near

Random lines from head of mine
To give my hand some work
Do I dare to them share?
At best can be called a quirk

Hippo yo!
I look and need to know
In the water you do show
But how low can you go?

Freedom plays with Takeaways
Wherever we now look
Delivery so easily
We're forgetting how to cook

Come November won't remember
Morning when too hot
Just feeling old in the cold
How quickly we forgot

Dipping pen once again
Into a mystery
To see what find in complex kind
Of one the likes of be

History and legacy

Lazarus laid claim to fame
Stating had cheated Deaths permanent game
How many more of not that religion
Have done the same with no recognition?

Questions and answers, followers and Masters
An idea/ thought occurred
Why cry belief when suffer grief
Silent or loud heard

People are a strange mix
All different in one shell
Each time you do meet them
Which one? Can never tell

Did Archimedes invent that screw?
Or stole credit from someone else
He was known and could have done
Fame brings many a wealth

History and legacy
Make a strange combination
When we have to believe that they achieved
While not witnessing situation

Can w find our perfect Mind?
That which sees the truth
Hahaha A dream too far
When we are so uncouth

Hooray

Cumulus came calling
Stop the Rain from falling
Just now cloud and miserable
Guess we can't just have it all

Fun in Sun is undone
Celsius is single figures
Welcome to the whatever weather
Nature quietly sniggers

Headlights on and showing strong
Shame it is midday
What the heck, no Fly speck
Something, guess Hooray!

Would I ever

Would I ever leave this life?
Never would willingly
For have known those much worse
I am grateful for can see

The bad is not really that bad
The hard is somewhat soft
The ailments? Merely inconvenient
Much like that season cough

Would I ever this regent?
You must be joking for one fact
All of it and every 'hit'
Shaped the me and how I act

Laughing in 'adversity'
When have no concept of it true
I am fortunate to have more
That drives on to that I do

How alphabet plays

Ben found d and then a y
Strange the thought of he
Why a y he said with sigh
Why not i and e?
Q and u together grew
Into an almost rule
Yet u no clue when spoken true
Such is the strangest things we do

J we say in soft way
Until becomes a cough
In a language spoken by others
Whose land on holiday we often trot
C alone has own Throne
Until h does join it do
Then the sound not can be found
For limited with no clue

The complexity of words we see
As how should say and why
Adding new as Dictionaries do
Raises levels to new high
Oh, to be a linguist
That partly understands
The maze to faze of how alphabet plays
Amok and out of hand

How many songs

Orinoco flowed as Enya sowed
Queen and Bowie felt under pressure
Numan liked his car he said
Feelings we can't measure

So, who will dance the dance of chance?
Who will dance with me?
Tread the space that is the dance floor
Dance the dance of possibility

Led Zeppelin sang of a stairway
To a place not ready to go
Doves sang of a Prisoner
A Prisoner I know

How many times do songs and rhymes
Match something that you know
How many times do their lines?
Go to where you did go?

Strangers that we think we know
Talking places we did go
Gone but returned again
In their music we feel sane

Knights in White Satin
Once, they did embrace
The possibility of all of we
When our errors we can face

Those Sweet Dreams can be a means
Annie knew that so did sing
Guess we must just laugh at present
See what another day will bring

Madness sang about their House
Whitney of true love
Prince about Corvette into which would get
The Jam of push and shove

How many a song can you relate to?

How their ideas

Papyrus print painted pictures
Of the world so long ago
Along with some objects found
Some of it we now know

Then I wonder what they thought
When saw previous statements caught
When this form I guess did start
What we now call Cave art

What came first?
This or vocal
For that only known
To those local

Said and gone for no recording
No chance to study, to understand
Yet visual was a different matter
Through the efforts of the hand

As progress came, grew and grew
So, Cave art became new
Papyrus turned to thing called Paper
Printing press then joined this caper

Nowadays just take a look
All around can see some Book
Branching out from professional
Can be done by one and all

Are our letters merely art?
That those Cavemen once did start
Could they ever begin to know?
How their ideas would then grow

Hurry up

So, what today and what lay
Surprises one is sure
A parody in the Marquees
Of a week and more
The world's a joke when we poke
Beyond that seemingly so serious
The Joke shop that's not one stop
And it never fails delivery

Thunder may echo in the distance
The Lightning only shock
The crash of realisation
As we pause to just take stock
Come to me your misery
Come your pleasure too
Come to me who can be
Come to me the you

How many ways can this thing play?
I guess upon how meet
All I know is one-time show
That comes with no receipt
So, stand, no sound and look around
Reflect on just where be
No longer wish like favourite Dish
We are the reality

The need to read and so feed
A mind hungry for the new
The statements said within the head
Of what others do accrue
Sunday morning gaining
The change of situation
For a Saturday it is no more
Been and done and then closed door

It's been a while since you could smile
But that so easily can change
Stretch yourself to find your wealth
Start now to arrange

The things that really matter
The essence deep within
Victory comes to those adventurous
So just hurry up and win

New day it looks with its own tunes
Yet still the music play
After all it's your call
How turns and in what way
Beanbags or Barricades
Open arms if choose
Possibility is infinity
What have we to lose?

Nothing if do nothing
Yet nothing spins around
Nothing seeking something
Then can make a sound
Time is but a statement
Yet a statement with limitations
Let's make a better place for them to face
The future generations

Thunder may echo in the distance
The Lightning only shock
The crash of realisation
As we pause to just take stock
Come to me your misery
Come your pleasure too
Come to me who can be
Come to me the you

Show the one that's hiding
Hiding deep inside
Discard the cover holding back
The one that's known as Pride

I am not herd

The end of trend and time to mend
Turn to something new
Some stay true to what they knew
Some just like to bend

To be 'in' must first begin
To understand what have committed to
So, so many quite uncanny
The craziness we do

Once did wear some makeup
Stage style and not for measure
Shock and awe the curtain call
When theatrical became pleasure

As one starts another farts
Disdain a common thing
Yet without that wall hung Trout
As Billy Bass does sing

New and old at time were bold
Wait until the new
Then the now becomes old cow
How will handle you?

Many paths our destiny
Fashion not included
Just a whim When in pool swim
Visiting so not intruded

Nothing really matters
Nothing much at all
We are just making most
Of chance to make the call

The one that says I am not herd

I am the Nemesis

In the morning as day is dawning
Do you just accept or prepare?
Do you treat it as a statistic?
Do you get bold and choose to dare?
Just a name and nothing more
Just like that which offers if explore
Chance to dance if take the stance
If feet do trip it's circumstance

The justification of situation
Sometimes it has none
Just accept then better get
During have some fun
Sky is blue? Lucky you
Here a murky Grey
Yet still up there so I don't care
Breathe in, breathe out – let's make a choice to stay!

I am the nemesis of myself
I am the things it hates
I am the foe of my woe
That more than irritates
So, let me tease you, perhaps please you
Let me just be me
Let me go to which don't know
Let's together just must see

So what's so wrong to just belong
To a greater than oneself?
What insanity when cannot see
The multi nation wealth?
I am a far fetched optimist
That already know
Yet I have a reason
As watch my Daughter grow

Not for me but for her
This course we're on leads me to worry

I call me

So, the plan took a turn
From surprise we can learn
Spent a lifetime being told
Must just follow
Not be bold
Suck it up and stay true
Suck it up and do what do
Such it up, just be you
Suck it up when conviction true

Evening someplace somewhere
The joys of being vast
Moonlight brilliant in someone's night
In other just past noon
Add to mix that can fix
When haves begin to share
Not just resources from our Earth
That thing needs some care

But I am just someone different
From different once I came
I may not look quite like you
Yet am playing the same game
And if I lived the life you live
Seeing things as you do see
Would I still be
Would I still be on the outside?
Just by being the true me

A Munchkin munched a mass of Marbles
Happy with what then did see
For they used the same tunnel
Who escaped I call me

So call me strange and call me weird
As a compliment I will take
For I am outside the dictate
Own decisions I will make

I can run and run

The serious became delirious
Now medication do take
The middle took a left view
Just Eyes for goodness sake!

I'm in a wide-open place
Enclosed within two ears
Found my sense of freedom
Losing first gained fears

The seeing of that which didn't see
The being that which now I be
Joining those already here
That drive on with odd tear

Tears of frustration not for self
They are stronger in different health
The health of word so cruelly used
By some to others to make feel abused

I made a change to stay the same
Took a loss to get a gain
Proved to self I'm more than name
Accepted hit but felt no pain
All to be simply me
That daft bugger that you see
No big act – reality
Floating Marbles set me free

I can run and run without worry
Of exhaustion or getting lost
For the running is inside me
Many rewards for small cost

I have found middle ground
Between the now and then
I have built a bridge between
By simple use of Pen

Run Writer run

I don't know Cappuccino

Excuse me love but is this right?
My coffees white you see
It is known for being Brown
More colour of Toffee

And I guess you had some trouble
Judging by these bubbles
I do know some a cup will own
But this is shaving foam

Why that smirk
Do you like your work?
No, I don't know
This thing Cappuccino

My

My Hero, my hero for a day
The imaginary friend
That made the nightmares go away

My Penfriend
My Penfriend loves to write
Writing about everything
In and out of sight

My guiding Guardian
Not a religious one you see
Just a caring person
They so care about me

My pleasure
My guilty pleasure I confess
Is penning pathetic poetry
The good I leave to rest

I gave a name

I named something that only I could see
I gave a name so I could cope
I named something real to me
I gave it the name Hope
I gave Hope a free chance
I gave it what could give
It has never failed me
Through everything did live

I named something that was so precious
I believe a must
I gave identity to a rarity
I gave it the name Trust
Without is entertainment
That and nothing more
With is a reason
To set Home on distant shore

I gave a name to bewilderment
Though bewilderment in right way
For gave so much more than that before
The reason for each day
Yes, just like you sometimes hard to do
When bed seems so attractive
Yet this thing must to always bring
The pleasure of the active

I gave a name to what will be
I don't know what its current hold
Said to thee 'You are Destiny'
A future story yet untold
I gave a name to what believe
The ultimate in wealth
Despite sometimes questioning
I did name it Self

I just know where I do go

I love a morning snoring
When asleep so I can't hear
I love a day without affray
A day that's without fear
I love the notion of a World in motion
When objective clear

Always a space for the Human Race
Always a space to face
The things life brings
The things that sings
It's great to be alive
Always a space to slow the pace
Always an idea cannot trace
Always something that seems new
Always something once did do

I love a day when can say
That I am now at peace
I love a day when can play
When the words release
I love a day that's just a day
A day more than past
I love a day I remember
But sadly, couldn't last

Where do we go when we feel low?
We go into our shell
Where do we go when such seems so
We go to living Hell
Where do we go to rise again?
The answer is the same
Where do we go, you surely know
For on it is your name

Language lays long redundant

What does make a 'poet true?'
Of the many one of few
Wish I had the slightest clue
To compare to likes of you

Maybe something in the blood
Maybe something in the genes
Maybe something in understanding
Maybe you just know what means

Hello midnight
Greetings Moon bright
Watchya Streetlight
Of shadow there is no sight

Do you sit and contemplate?
Do you sit and meditate?
Do you go to higher state?
Do you to yourself narrate?

Mangled masses in the Marshland
Relics of disposal wrong
Silent staying until reclaiming
In that act disturb Birdsong

When love Love
We reach a truly higher plain
When the losses so insignificant
Compared with that we gain

What does make the perfect verse?
Searching for, a lifelong curse
Perhaps, in truth, there's no such thing
For each one different bring

Language lays long redundant
Message has more meaning true
Maestros of the magic mixing
Part with me how you do

Languid lay

Did you flip that steak so soon!?
Why are we eating just past noon?
Maybe married but no buffoon
Just shut up and do what told
A conversation in different station
Not one I choose to use
For you see to like of me
That has gone way beyond abuse

If I never knew a sky that's blue
Would I truly see the sky?
If not live could I give
The reason than to die?
Existence a persistent
Stubborn we do not seem
When we are it seems so far
Down a paper ream

A revolving state we create
Start as single then find a mate
Then often love and maybe hate
The joy of love then masturbate Maybe introduce the new
Into which we have no clue
Doing that which species do
Why inflict? I have no answer, perhaps you too

The science of compliance
Gets lost in the mistrust
Yes, some of it is reasonable
So some of it we must
Can we ever be that thing we see?
Behind the now closed eyes
Can we achieve instead of grieve
To ourselves give a surprise?

Last chance for inspiration

A simple man stood cap in hand
In front of own reflection
About to go where do not know
A last chance for inspection

A quick adjustment here, a quick adjustment there
Satisfied, put on said cap
One deep breath not just for health
Then into the wondering gap

Down the street as friends did greet
Nothing changed on the outside
Yet was different from that yesterday
He had found something inside

'Did you blow in on Summer wind?
Or did I just fail to see
The potential monumental
That lays inside of me

I am aghast at the time past
Oblivious to my potential
When worried not if some might drop
For other are exponential

When destiny becomes history
A tragedy we make
For chance did show to let us grow
The chance we chose not to take'

The man with cap then on bench sat
Planning his next move
Nothing certain behind that curtain
Except he would improve

Last time

The last time I said Goodbye
It carried no regret
It was to a different me
So, a new one I could let
Let come into existence
Give it chance to be
What no more that before
A future destiny

The last time I questioned Life
The answer came as a surprise
I was not ready to leave it
It was a warning in disguise
Changes were now needed
To be what I could be
Different path needed walking
To find that inner me

The last time I decided to stop writing
Deep down would never be
Words not heard yet still heard
An integral part of free
Free from the 'seen' restrictions
Free from others forced convictions
Beliefs and attitudes personal see
Not necessarily yours for me

The last time I felt down
I created a third leg
Metaphorically not physically
So could kick my own Head
I don't need the lies they feed
To make self so popular
Are we a brand don't understand?
We are more than just some Car

Laugh the path

In morning am a project
At noon a project still
Evening unable despite the constant will
In small want tall in large want small
Satisfaction a few achieve
Yet in this state can relate
Just in sleep believe

Equal lines are just fine
Yet so are those so odd
Take some letters for the better
Who really gives a sod?

I be what be a thing you see
Yet do I do for you?
The answer plain is sometimes pain

Now the true is to me new
Guess it's just a thing I do

Missing five for lost that 'jive'
The beat, it had distraction
What more to say when with words play
One requires interaction?

Someday May Day, who can say?
A pen will finally quite
The thought caught but not bought
The thought alone chills to Bone
Having none of it

Once more a four with which will bore
The programme on repeat
If only knew what going through
To achieve the feat

One of 'it' that of Twit
The first bit maybe true

Screwed up again!!

Laugh with them

With any success comes a test
Not justified it's true
For you be what they can't see
So, do to put you through

If what they do is laugh at you
Laugh with them as well
See their reaction to your action
From it you can tell

Jealousy a complexity
Comes in different ways
To break that spell confine to Hell
The derision that they preach

It doesn't matter when it can scatter
A novelty at best
If you like they can take a hike
Maybe join the rest

Corn chips and Beer

Corn chips and Beer can cost you dear
In money and the tummy
Yet seem so great when in certain state
Tomorrow something runny

At Kebab try a stab
Curry for the brave
Recklessness at its best
Clothing you won't save

We don't need a lesson taught
When in intoxicated caught
We just need no reminder
Of that night we thought 'a blinder!'

Laughed in echoes of Lament

Once who did and made choice and hid
The former for the now
Once I knew as I grew
Was no cud chewing Cow
The mud not missed
Or as Earth kissed
Nor wanting certain pain
As their 'wings' did gain

The once soldier but now older
Learnt more than killing and how to kill
Gained a lot from both gave and got
Some of which hold still
Laughed in echoes of Lament
Not of soul but the time spent
Feeling victory in when did vent
Those small 'victories' so irrelevant

I knew a soldier once
An impression he did make
Parted some of their experiences
Notes I chose to take
They kept me in good stead
When needed to have clear head
Kept me focused when needed most
Now they are some remembered ghost

They laughed in echoes of Lament
At how survived when others not
Sometimes is just lottery
At who fills that fresh plot
When question is unanswerable
Login has been spent
One must try to work out why
Laugh in the echoes of the Lament

Layers in the growing

The rising of the Sun in morning
The setting what call night
The Moon takes over duty
Shadowed or so bright
Outside it becomes quieter
When a bed most face
Not programmed for nocturnal
Is the Human Race

Consider all your activities
Consider all that you've done
Consider implications
Consider not the only one
Man makes world we understand
Man, then does destroy
Man makes it to suit itself
World just a man's toy

Archives in the attic
Real or imaginary
Some are there on full show
Some others cannot see
Layers in the growing
Layers in what are
Layers some deflective
Layers past and far

Far into a future
Far into our past
Far from the mistakes made
Far so cannot last
Everything a mystery
Until we choose to learn
Everything just latest craze
When sensible we spurn

Leaving

I saw you try and wondered why
Considering all been through
I saw that look with each breath took
Marvelled that you try
But that was yesterday
Before you, sadly went away
To with others laugh and play
A different place from me

Somewhere, sometime we'll meet again
When again we both are equal
It is not a final end
For we have a sequel
A pause, of course
You just went before
Being you that is true
The first one to explore

When people question with their asking
My feelings I am masking
For not right to express my plight
When my better has just passed
The innocence of living
The complexity of grieving
The ignorance of having
The reality of leaving

Let us once again

Origin – where did begin
Summary - when that complete
Head, the part above the shoulders
Legs, the things that attach the feet
All I knew is what went through
All to know I have no hope
Something more I would adore
So let's get this wish underway!

I am a sponge for learning
Learning different things
Each an accomplishment
With just what it brings
Anything is everything
When look at in certain ways
Infusion and confusion
As a story plays

You can take me as choose to be
Warm hand or with a knife
I am not your problem
Your trouble nor the strife
So give to me some sanity
Some logic is no crime
Run with me those who choose to be
Humans once again

Last night I had a strange dream
I dreamt a world at peace
I guess it was a personal hope
That needed some release
Hope becomes ability
A strength to somehow cope
In the place of madness
A reason not to mope

Let us find our middle ground
Our pleasure, not our pain
To all smile for a while
Let us once again

Let us waste a moment

Let's just waste the moment
The moment we could 'earn'
Let's just waste a moment
So that we can learn
Profit is not just numbers
It is a thing beyond
Profit can be found
In someone in whom fond

Let's just take a pause
Investigate the cause
Why we are here and that dear
Yet not in the source
All is in perception
In hindsight a reflection
Yet we can so easily change
If our wants we simply 'strange'

White Doves don't make clover
Of the four-leaf kind
Luck is much as into us we tuck
The validity of the Mind
So come with me on that might be
The possibility of the good
The satisfaction of interaction
The under in understood

The episode on which once rode
The transport of the past
The bits that were the then the 'cure'
Now leave the present just aghast
Let's just talk about a moment
A single one for sure
Yet can lead to so much
Lead to so much more

Letter on the Table

The Husband sat at table
He had to go away
The ships journey, weather permitting
Three weeks and one more day
The Wife still in Dreamland
Face a scene of bliss
Careful not to wake her
He gave a goodbye kiss

As drained the last of his coffee
Husband left a letter
Was going to put it on the pillow
Then decided better
He wrote as spoke
Pictured her beside
Wrote with love and tenderness
Feelings could not hide

If I could be your Hero
What sort of Hero would I be?
One of old in stories told
Or one of fantasy?
If I could be protection
That which will not yield
Would I be your suit of armour?
Would I be your shield?

If I could be your shelter
Would I be a Castle with a Keep?
Would I be a sanctuary Cave?
Running back so deep?
If I could be your sustenance
What fare would you choose?
Would I be your Apple?
Free from mark or bruise

For you I would be anything
If I could hold again
I would be a canopy
Protecting from the rain
Alas I am but a mere man
A man who loves you so
So, I am in turmoil
For again I have to go

Soon will be returning
For my need is great
In this time of parting
Will remember you in sleeping state

Gently folding the letter and propping it against her empty cup
He silently departed

Letter to the Philippines

To Antonio Lagdameo Jr.
Filipino Politician
Follow

Do you so need that pocket to feed
You rob from those who you are supposed to protect
Do you sleep well while they live in Hell?
At your own bequest
Do you have a conscious?
Beyond the Bank account
Do you not even think
As your peoples worries mount?

Government of Philippines
The so-called answer to their dreams
Turns out they are just a means
To fill personal wallet to its seams
Oh, sure you look after those
Who benefit that does not show?
Much did promise yet not deliver
Forcing nation to on floor shiver

A pandemi of globe proportion
Just a way for extortion
Not a leadership that does lead
Just a bunch to wealth feed
Isang kahihiyan sa lahi ng Tao
From your language words I borrowed
Do you really think acceptable
To drain the pot then choose to tell?

Is their fault for just living
Is their fault their freedom giving
To a bunch who do not care
When in past have been there
Isang pangungutya sa Demokrasya
That you truly are
They suffer pain while you gain
Drive around in protective Car

Ian Wilcox

112

Life is but one language

What is truth in this soup
That they try to feed
Why I cry as passes by
This insane nonsense h
He says this and she says that
Then, with rules, they have a spat
The onlooker is bemused
The onlooker is confused

If 'actual' was factual
To fool no longer 'cool'
Would we be in a better place
Without those who love to 'rules?
When done with one onto the next one
A procession does await
Criteria near hysteria
Whatever land or State

Enough of this!!

Guten Morgen! ¿Cómo estás?
Welcome you my friends
Spero che tu stia bene
And that I can spell
Ang pag-alam ay masaya

Who be we when others see?
Why a fear of different hear?
Why disguise with clouded eyes
When both can just compromise

What begun with one tongue
Can spread if we but try
Though doom and gloom are in next room
When we let them slip on by?

Ishi kwa kupenda and volim živjeti
Beneath words are the same
Alles is waar i roto i ta maatau
Life is but a game

Life's a bowl of assorted candies

One will have some hard times
One will have some doubt
One will have some good times
Sometimes scream and shout
One some days will feel buoyant
Some days simply sink
One will sometimes won't give a damn
Some days will deeply think

Repetitive would be so boring
If each day the same
Only knowing moved on to next one
By the chance of name
Variety the spice of life
When from it you improve
Each day a better than the last
If forward you do move

A minor stumble will inevitably happen
A reminder have to work
Work on just who you are
Never just accept the present you
Nor betterment should you shirk
Be prepared to be unconventional
If that's what you enjoy
Rules in the Arts are merely guidelines
Allow critics to employ

The fastidious are laborious
So learn to them ignore
The more reactions the more their actions
Let them spur you to just more
Life's a bowl of assorted candies
Each has a preferred taste
Just because yours is not someone's favourite
Don't let it go to waste

Market Molly

She caught the eye as she passed by
A Peacock on parade
Designer labels everything
Every 'House' and made
To the same she is just game
To others she is strange
The need to fool none but fools
Maybe one day will change

The names the same but not much more
The Market sought and there bought
In the false she is caught
Labels make the person- NOT!

She gained fame and it was a a shame
For the Label was not good
Some refrained from distain
Put it down to misunderstood
Few knew her by her first name
Fewer knew her last
All though knew her 'given' one
Stifling their gasp

Market Molly the fashion folly
The ingredient for laugh
Market Molly the one stop wally
Never asked for autograph

Bleached Blonde hair
With Black roots
Knock off Nike
Cerise Shell suits
The 'item' was of interest
If only for the shock
Someone should have captured
Then welded firm the lock

Marmalade can't parade

Red bummed be the Orangutans
Pink those weird Flamingos
Brown the stuff that I eject
At least I hope that goes
Multi-coloured when I vomit
With curiosity I do stare
No matter what have eaten
Diced carrot always there

Always run out of bread at breakfast time
When I needed it most
Marmalade can't parade
Without a slice of Toast
The toilet call you need to stall
For in important conversation
Hope they don't know what voice does show
A torturous situation

The fox that does adapt and so does crap
Where wish to place your feet
Leaving unintended all around
Unsoiled, looking neat
The hours that seem to drag
When nothing much to do
Yet like trying for Olympics
When someone's chasing you

Irony a blasphemy
Without the attitude
Give me your best shot
My humour can't intrude
Lay it thick with a stick
In this already won
For have a secret weapon
Skin made from pure Teflon

MASK

Making
A
Securer
Killer

What is the difference when we choose?
To wear when others we abuse
Yet when worn to protect
Somehow some the concept doesn't get

Yes a pain but with gain
Another day outside a ward
Already overstretched by caring people
Who chose to do of own accord

That doesn't mean we should abuse
So broken hearted another lose
Despite the all that they could do
Another breath to see them through

They are giving so we keep living
Is it to much to ask
When we are in confined public places
Can we at least just wear a mask

May hawak ng Puso Ko

When from far off land
Came to hold your hand
Can you now true see
The empty heart now filled with part
Of your identity

Who could see what would be?
When first I saw your face
Another culture, another colour
Yet so full of grace

Nothing seems to matter
When you're there and around
Everything that's spinning
Lands on solid ground

Ecstasy and me
A distant thing was true
That all changed for the closer
The day that I met you

One came, one saw
One that I now adore
Want to be with for ever more
Then together we can explore

Sunlight o a rainy day
Bright beam that pierces mist
The sweetest of sensations
When those lips I kiss

May hawak ng Puso Ko
You are, that a statement true
Everything has meaning
All because of you

Maybe me in what see, we will never know

The one who wrote for their pleasure
Passing thing that is called leisure
Idle time spent just fine
One I am pleased to call friend of mine

Nothing new in what been through
Did those things just had to do
Nothing strange in what be
Made something I wish to be

Human beings are so strange
In what do and how change
Nothing lasts forever
In our actions if we are clever

Saw something I wish to share
From someone that did when dare
They were not without care
Just so lonely in band of lonely

They wrote

Came and try to get along
Comfort found in favourite song
Made decisions as you do
One led to pastures new
Seen both death and start of life
In between I found a Wife
So, am I normal I ask you?
Do I do what 'normal' do
Living just to have get through
The red of passion, the sadness blue
Autumn rain is a pain yet the same as Summer stuff
Sometimes we just have to admit
When enough is just enough

Meaningless Statistics

The Winter calls and rain falls
The streetlights more on than off
There go the leaves on sleeping trees
With just one person's cough

But just another Season
Am sure it has a reason
So, adapt and carry on
Even when it seems so wrong

2 C.Y.R. need not look far
2 C.Y.B. more mystery
2 C.Y.I. have to try
2 C.Y. am simply me

We lost our coats so could mend
By to someone money spend
Change the diet we are eating
Replacing lotions for Central Heating

Our covers are another
Blankets and that we call our skin
Thicker one gown, one more blue than brown
White stuff it might begin

4 R.A. habit creature
4 R.A. consistent feature
4 R.A. predictable
4 R.A. one at beck and call

A number and a letter
Is this one worse or is it better?
Statistics go ballistic
We so love meaningless Statistics

Spiritual Entities

Mr. Sandman reminded the lovely Ms P. that it is a Full Moon Night.

She sweetly replied, thank you, and flashed a
smile and blew him a mystical kiss.

The Full Moon is an electromagnetic, supernatural occurrence,
that was even worshiped throughout the ancient world.

At the midnight hour there is a ballroom dance
located on the, brilliant, yellow moon.

The night is quite cool and it is raining with clouds that are just a large
accumulation of kaleidoscopic colors of shimmering ice crystals.

The lovely Ms P's ball gown is a purple-haze colour and her
magical high-heeled shoes are carved out of huge light blue
diamonds that are form fitting on her feet and twinkling toes.

The lovely Ms P. is exquisitely gorgeous; the Belle of the Ball.

Jimi Hendrix requests to dance with the lovely Ms. P. and whispers
that wearing blue magical high-heeled shoes grants the power
to jump from cloud-to-cloud, easily.

Gleefully, sound waves adorned the Universe with
melodious beats of "Excuse us while we kiss the sky."

It is not just our ancestors that saw things in the sky
and intuitively aware of spiritual entities.

Melissa Begley

Extravaganza

We might not be able to control many factors in life.

Concentration with harmonious creative freedom
enables the mind to let the negativity go.

Imprinted sheer delights flows as a light beam of extravaganza.

Meditation and prayers cha cha cha y'all and Sweetest Dreams.

Sensational Saturday

Melancholy are many as we approach Thanksgiving Day.

Find it in your heart and spirit to be ever more compassionate and empathetic.

Many only have warm-hearted reminiscences of an earlier period in their
life once filled with happiness and loved ones living with good health.

Be grateful and thankful because there is always
a glimmer of optimism in your world.

Keep in mind mental calculations of organized chaos and the
deliberate destructions created by untruths are ultimately
a one-of-a-kind evil and never a thankful action.

Detach yourself from the ones that have hearts filled with darkness
and banish their negativity while you focus on the energy of love.

Fantastic, Festive Fabulous Friday

Weakening and waning, emotional victimhood, are resolvable qualities.

Strengthen yourself by building up and then
following up by supporting others.

Kind-heartedness and compassion are not mere
verbalized expressions, but actions.

Specially made sanctioned communication and connections to lift up the
spirits of others is a gift bestowed upon the social order of civilization.

Is everybody ready to perform the Celebratory Dance of
Life? One, two, cha cha cha, three, four, ooh-la-la.

Remember to send up all the Glory to God.

Melissa Begley

Strumpet

The charismatic masterminded gentleman was coy in his ploy to find a toy.

She was vulnerable; his passionate words danced
with melodious beats in her fervent heart.

Foolishly, she did not differentiate the falsification of his language
and plummeted into a trap set by his hollowed heart.

Time passed, after a joyous event the realization that the misinterpreted
love was not a present bestowed upon two enthusiastic lovers.

Her love was real, but she was just his thrill.

Promises of eternal love was a masquerade of his commitment.

He laughed for the reason she was trapped by
his devise of unforeseen deceptions.

Loggerheads they became and he was dead to her emotions.

She acknowledged the disagreement and agreed to terminate the relationship.

He was conceptually right for the reason she was not very
bright and had been captured by his heartless soul.

He bellowed; "I am a Victorious Conquistador."

He sang, "You are a Strumpet, zilch, zero, zippo, and nil to
my heart. I had my thrill there is no longer an appeal and my
zeal will be trouncing upon brand-new casualties."

He rode off into the sunset blasting his trumpet and seduced the
dark clouds singing, "You are a Strumpet, nothing more."

Melissa Begley

Wonderful Whimsical Wednesday, have a magnificent day

Do not let anyone alter your serenity and cheerfulness.

Remember to blink your eyes, then smile, and let the pessimism ride....

Let it ride, Let it ride, Let it ride...Shake, spin, twirl, wiggle, wiggle, wiggle, giggling, shuffling the blues away.

Giving all the glory to God

Last Kiss

It is my source of displeasure that time is slowing detaching my handsome fellow from my desirous embrace.

The knowledge of an illness that denies the process of healing is not the realism of an acceptable experience.

Enlightened thinking and faith in the hereafter does not present laughter to the ones remaining on the earthly stage.

The destiny into the spiritual realm is a perpetual love with eternal peacefulness for the one that has provided you his last kiss.

Terrific Tuesday

Rise and shine, put on your magical smile.

Today will be the best day of your life because you are radiant and dazzling.

Kind-heartedness and thoughtfulness infiltrated your heart and
you will generate warmth and affection with one and all today

It is time to perform the Celebratory Dance of Life this chilly morning.

Bear in mind that we have another opportunity to have an unassuming
nature; with servitude in our heart, we can make a difference.

One, two, cha- cha- cha, three, four, ooh la la
and send up all the Glory to God..

Melissa Begley

Bejewelled Heart

Mirror to reality, what will you visualize for me at the midnight hour?

Images of angels dancing around my beloved's physical being
or the grandiose beauty of another night of love?

I am incredibly poor in faith for the reason it was
foretold that he would soon be no more.

Psychedelic music and wilting flowers, you are traveling
the path of no longer remembering my name.

Self-taught awareness, there is no self-promotion when the
formidable competition of earthly life, is no more.

Trigger the brain to play no games. Sparkling grace of an embrace to the
intriguing one that cast a spellbinding power bejewelling my heart.

Serene Sunday

Triumphantly, touch the heart of somebody that
necessitates thoughtfulness and sympathy.

Trials and tribulations swallow up the existence of countless people.

Gratification and fulfilment are an offshoot of
reaching out to others by simply being nice.

Keep in mind, you might not be appreciated or acknowledged
for your acts of kindness, but that is alright.

Remain grounded in positivity and consider continuing
assisting or sprinkle that kindness somewhere else.

Melissa Begley

Melted blob

Blooming Heck!
My hunger pains went to North from South
Speed to feed when no need
Now melted top of mouth!

Instructions said to wait a minute
Who can count in seconds?
They get a thrill as time you kill
That before did reckon

Is that just oral or something else?
The white stuff I am spitting
Mucous or new teeth
In now need of fitting?

Microwave meals have such appeal
Instant in a hurry
Yet after finish but not yet finished
Hotter than the hottest curry

I think my knife is bending
My fork has turned to spoon
Ceramic tray upon which placed
Will revert to basics soon

How come this does not give off smoke?
The way I am emitting steam
This was supposed to be a solution
Not turning organs into cream!

I would drink some water
If my eyes would stop pouring the stuff
So that I could actually see!
If you notice a melted blob
That once was a thing called me

Melting

Slowly melting but don't care
Talking to a special one
Special in the air
Friendship has a certain feeling
This goes way beyond
I guess I'm more than fond

I don't know where this will take us
But together we will discover
I don't know the end of story
When do find a more than lover

When love alone is not enough
The real couple learn to trust
Trust in them as a pair
Trust in other When not there

Here comes a special feeling
Here comes a level new
Here comes the astonished
At just what can do

London Town now turning brown
Not quite like in my dreams
For in them with my pen
I am in the Philippines
With the two and something new
Through the heat haze fog
With surprise I can surmise
We have another dog

I long to hold you physically
Not just kiss inanimate screen
Want to walk in footsteps
The places you have been

Slowly melting but am happy
Melting in this love
For you true and Daughter too
The fit? The perfect Glove

Memories be

I gave it up when sipped from cup
From cup of kindness drank
The been through just lessons new
When into happiness I sank

Always there if one did but care
To look inside oneself
The value of just being true
The recognition of its wealth

Memories be but history
Something been and done
Yet a future now the suitor
When involves someone

I gave up worrying as a constant
Now just do part time
Different type of worrying
But new worry sits just fine

The place I be type of Sanctuary
No cause followed but myself
With the ones with new begun
The past just creeps with stealth

Show me true or look away
This one in sadness will not stay
Look at me for what I be
One who found their destiny

Nowhere safe within the Cave
I made in which to hide
Cloaked myself in ignored
Now I call it Pride

Mend

The one becomes more than one
The individual joins the crowd
In a way did go astray
Silently - not loud
Getting on for oath had sworn
To be better than what were
The one who dreams finds the means
To illness take the cure

Come to me the thing to be
Come to me my ecstasy
Come to me reality
Come to me a future see
Nothing new from when grew
Just changes in surroundings
Still the one that seeks some fun
Maybe quite astounding

No salivating in dictating
Let others ride that ride
When are weak so always seek
That illusion will not hide
Come to me honestly
Not as followed but a friend
Too much hate does irritate
Let us try to mend

Plip

Plip did plop before did stop
Unintentionally is true
Red and Green just got mean
Because they like the colour Blue
Another just escaped
Oh, the joy when employ
The launch of escaped

Nothing new that is true
For even words have limit
Just mixing up in verse cup
Can I use begin nit?
Plip just came to call again

Ian Wilcox

Middle age thinking

Cornucopia in Ethiopia
A pleasant but wistful dream
Equality a legacy
If only it would seem
Human rights instead of fights
Mother Nature calm
Leadership that actually leads
Not just profits palm

I must be high to wonder why
Some at least we can't achieve
Though don't partake so that can't make
My reason to believe
That it is still possible
To correct some errors made
We should not forget them
Just move them to the shade

Cornucopia in Ethiopia
A calmness song in Hong Kong
Religious beliefs not causing grief
Wherever we belong
Understanding not Understanding
Transparency for all
Go back when with mark from pen
The normal made the call

Bygone it seems with current means
We are all so clever
Reached the stage in current age
Common sense has become a never
Alas Humanity I knew you well
Before you chose to change
Influenced all around you
Gave new meaning to deranged

Million moves

The one did write in letters bright
Posted on a wall
Of the contentment that they feel
To tell to one and all
A declaration of a sensation
A way of every day
I saw what they wrote
This is what did say

'A million moves to make it magic
To keep it that a million more
Two million moves are just the start
To keep you here will make it four
A million moves each a Heartbeat
Moves that passed many millions sure
Since my eyes without disguise
Settled on one who is so pure

A million moves inside the Head
Brain in overload
A million moves in twenty-four
Hours a day when love it did explode
A million moves its intention
A type of Divine Intervention
A million moves and that's a fact
That resulted in this act'

I know the feeling that they feel
When found that which is so real
Oh, how much it resplendent soothes
When one makes a million moves

Mine to keep

I wonder why in mid-July
Mid-afternoon as well
I am still joyfully
Entrapped within your spell
The day it stays locked inside
The day that you did cast
Loved it then and love it now
So glad that spell does last

Ups and downs and playing clowns
Tried parenting as well
Just how good we understood
Only time will tell
So far so good and so it should
The way you took to it
Young lady now and showing how
Her Mom was such a hit

How did I get, as I reflect?
Top prize in the dream game
Never knowing what it was
Until I heard your name
The way it flows as age it grows
I whisper in my sleep
By saying I am praying
You are mine to keep

Miss my

Once I knew the perfect friend
Whatever problem they could mend
They were more than Christmas trend
When in morning their love did send

All they wanted was company
Mixed with time to run free
That so suited one like me
For so did I you see

In the dark times shone a light
With sad eyes burning bright
Resting head upon my lap
As contented took a nap

Though don't cook you do not complain
Of the offerings I prepare
Most are different from what I eat
So, no wish to share

You choose to guard me in my sleep
As watchful eye you do keep
A deterrent of no doubt
Letting would be robber know you're about

The days seem long since you've been gone
Miss that playful nip
Miss that stare because you're not there
Miss my Canine companionship

M.M.I.

Into the depth I did dive
Into the wilderness of wanting more
Me, myself and I made friends
As a person I did explore
First met me who wanted free
Myself did want firm ground
I did see the unity
So that union all found

Found a Paradise in being wise
Wise enough to know
Only when all meet you are complete
Complete so then can grow
Me, myself and I
Then began to fly
As gained more we do soar
The triumph when we try

Like the naked new born
Vulnerable and scared
Only changing way that was
When realised we cared
Rocking Horses changed their courses
Merged, became a Stallion
Found that which be when one not three
My own individual attraction

My on regret if can call
Would be not done before
Those wasted years of fears and tears
As each through a different Door
Went, returned with that which earned
Not always that which wish
Was a shoal without a goal
Now one resplendent Fish

My guile is gone

As a young girl,
I invited a friend
To browse with me through a gift shop near my home.
She shocked me, though, by showing a handful of colourful
crayon-shaped barrettes into my pocket and yanking me out the
door of the shop without paying for a week before I approached
my mom-my confession pouring out as quickly as my tears.

Grieved over my bad choice of not resisting my friend, I returned
the stolen items, apologised and vowed never to steal again.
Because my mom forgive me and assured me that I had done
my best to make things right, I slept peaceful that night.

Are you listening?

He was frustrated
He was Angry
Everything that went wrong
Year after year, he had gotten them through one disaster after another
He was continually interceding on their behalf to keep them out if trouble.
But all he got for his efforts was more grief.
Sometimes in exhaustion or exasperation, we don't pay close attention,
we assume everything will always work the same way. But it doesn't.
Sometimes he tells us to act, sometimes he tells us to wait
That is why we must always take action. Listen-then obey.

Fishing

We once went swimming
And saw a fish coming
Hello, Hello little fish
We tried to make a catch
We did a lot of search
Off went the fish
We gave the fish a chase
It gave us some space
Came back with a dozen other fishes
We turned back and fled
While our ankles and knees bled.

Bose Eneduw Adogah

Old Father

Old Father of mine where went the time?
The time we used to share?
The days of old when I was bold
When, in truth, I didn't care
Oh, Father of mine and age of mine
An age that didn't last
Are you too that just pass through?
For part of you is Past

Of, Father of mine is it a line?
In which state I do you see?
The old, the present or the next stage
The part of which can be
The Father of my Father
Of that before him if truth tell
For all of us without much fuss
Fall under your same spell

Is clarity reality?
Or just that which we choose?
The innocence of circumference
In which can win or loose
The circle that's a Girdle
The holding in which are
The old fence of circumstance
That holds the true so far

Once me a one of 'nothing'
Nothing t most who saw
Yet did believe that they could achieve
They are now much more
So why give a damn to what can?
Can be more than what we see?
Because others know that you can grow
Others just like me

On a song

On a song a thought is born
On a page it comes of age
With words taught for future caught
The journey of the ink
With a tool we capture all
The feelings that we feel
Dare to share though with some care
Yet living on the brink

The symbols say it all
The choice that inner voice
Feeling proud when read out loud
By one not yet we know
Inspiration a warm sensation
When to others give
Better in some ways as with verse play
Helping them to grow

When the words are more than heard
When touch with something share
Knowing that are not alone
Knowing others care
Then who worries about perfection
Who is fit to judge?
Who truly is above fault?
Whose ink does never smudge?

Lust for lines should be fine
Not lesson to be taught
By the one seeking to be someone
In own ego caught
'I am me so am free'
A true penners right
Providing no dividing
By offensive blight

On any chosen day

See that man over there?
Once he felt a King
That Lady standing at the Bus stop
Used to dance and sing
Everyone was a someone
Everyone still is
What you see might not be
There's so much that we miss

Once drew a picture of myself
Tore it up in shame
Was just an image behind which hid
Not the man behind the name
At the time I thought it was
How little did I know
What we are at present stage still has a way to go

That little boy on the swing
Going to and fro
Will be a better Father
Than the one he doesn't know
See the little girl
With favourite Doll in hand
Will become a Mother three times over
In a foreign land

Once thought I knew all could know
Age did prove me wrong
I barely knew just enough
To help me get along
Everyone paints an image
All have a visage
Yet mask we choose to wear
May turn out just too large

Look at all the people
That you pass each day
Wonder who the real one is
On any chosen day

On Cloud of shroud

On clouds of imagination
Daily do I fly
On Cotton balls I often call
With no reason why
On absence of any sense
My life I sometimes live
Just the thrill of able still
Something I can give

On clouds of ink I often think
That thing that is just me
The part the art when one does start
A certain identity
Amongst this gathering growing strong
Is a place I feel belong
Some may say that I am wrong
Yet no-one I know likes every song

On clouds of that we call emotion
Comes each one, a different notion
I am hooked on certain potion
Of which there is no clear solution
Life around still has its say
Each time punishment a different way
Yet to some it is a Play
Bear we hope soon goes away

Not the Life for that is treasure
Just some bits that we can't measure
Just the ones that are clouds dark
For not something to which hark
So tak my knocks as all do
Then come back as something new
The suppression of expression
I may pause but never halt do

On its Bike

The Sentiments of Seasons seen
Some I welcome, some less keen
Lots of good and lots of sad
Some want again, some wish never had
The knowing and the showing
The experience of growing
The memories made and nightmares laid
The parts accepted and parts did trade

The rains reign can be a pain
A blessing somewhere else
If we could train would be a gain
Only falls when Nation tells
The Sun the same in this crazy game
Too much or not enough
Could make a mint with a hint
On how to tame this stuff

Some food for mood - an interlude
A scatter of grey matter
To take on board but please don't hoard
For just tittle tatter
Between the Woman and the Man
Came a cunning plan
To keep a part a Family start
Another to share each Heart

Ten minutes spent with no relent
A distraction of a fashion
From the monotony monetary
We share both you and me
An empty purse the worst curse
When see something new you like
Rapidly the fantasy
Shoves off on its Bike!

On Orion sat

Are you sure that you want more?
The day some still just seems wrong
Are you sure can take much more?
Accept it just belongs
The joy of ploy is like a toy
The circumstances are a bit disaster
Yet with grin we take it in
In repetition we learn to master

If on the road to that untold
Do you want to think?
If going through that which new
Do you need a drink?
That nowhere road most have heard
Exists but different form
That travel that does unravel
Ever since were born

On Orion sat a scion
Deciding which to choose
All we know is soon will show
Then one of us will lose
The freedom sworn when we were born
A right for which to fight
Yet one day will others say
Just accept your plight

Weak may be those thought as free
Yet still the untapped might
Bring into that which new
Those of that different plight
Can we be so truly free
When around see insanity
The levels change to rearrange
The meaning and what be

The all and more we should adore
When with welcome hand they introduce
Those with fist should just desist
For of them have no use

On the eve of everything

On the eve of everything there was a twist
The one purely known as Creator realised hadn't made a list!
What to go where and how divide?
How this error could they hide?

Long and hard this did perplex
Creating something we call vex
In the end they just gave up
Threw the Planets into a cup

Habitable and inhabitable the first to draw
Then Habitable went in once more
Thus, Universe so was cursed
Though in truth could have been much worse

Solar systems then were made
Each now needed things to parade
A bowl this time for creatures more
On chosen 'Worlds to explore

Now to present day and see
Why some creatures are a mystery
No real logic for existence
Though must admire their persistence

Creator shook a weary head
Completely knackered went to bed
"Enough of this" to self said
So gave some 'thinking' and where led

On this day someone died

On this day so far away
Another person died
Some did know as that person showed
More than that did hide
On this day on 'leaders' say
One lost more than just a job
A 'leader' will forget their name
As the kin still sob

On this day near and away
A person an action choose
Regardless of the consequences
Regardless of what can lose
"Who art they?" Some might say
More interested in their self
"What are they in present day?
Can they increase my wealth?"

On this day far away
Away from that now be
Someone died for more than pride
Died so others could be free
Free to choose what they did lose
Someone paid the price
No consolation for no great 'occasion'
Just fles in man-made vice

Someone was not just Someone
They were a distant Brother/ Sister of mine

On which it washes

All around came a sound
The invader now was creeping
Into muse to confuse
Slowly it was seeping
With it spent some nonsense

Marbles rallied to protect
The kingdom of the floating
The best that they could get

From every corner it did strike
Sure, focused, without relent
Common sense has an issue
With to gain the time I spent

Into Ears loud and clear
Then further down it went
For its goal was to reach soul
So twisted and somewhat bent

Sanity is misery
In climate that I see
Being mad ain't half bad
So there I choose to be

All around came the sound
Of others trying to dominate
Not for me for simply see
Dictatorship so hate

Prefer the Marbles that reside
Prefer the ones that will not hide
Not one who goes against the tide
Just the shore on which it washes

Once discovered

I once discovered a secret Garden
The place I wanted to be
That place was on an Island
A new Home came to me

I once discovered satisfaction
A long-sought feeling true
Away from that around me then
When air was filled with blue

I once discovered I was naive
A startling realisation
I endeavour to correct
A wonderful sensation

In this journey we all take
Just how many changes make?
Never knowing if make or break
Yet that class still we take

I once was young, now slightly old
Am more cautious, once so bold
That is just another told
In the life of each of us

I once discovered who I was
Then that person change
I once was them but no longer
So many things rearrange

Memories can be mystery
Also driving force
Some do stay in what know
Some explore the course

Memories are misery
Pleasing also true
Depending on the memory
Of that which did do

Paying borrowed time

The crash of thunder overhead
Lightning lights the sky
The brother not of same blood
Holds a hand as they pass by
The one who swore to defend
At cost of their own life
Leaves behind a Family
Two children and a Wife

Appreciated by wise yet still despised
By those without a clue
Seen by Game play warriors
Who wouldn't really do

Life fluids soak into dry earth
Act of breathing short and slow
Not some flash then vanishes
Different 'next level' will they go
The one who holds the now cool hand
Must put aside for the short term
Carry on the fight
Maybe they will come to terms
When finish current fight

This morning one was present
At attention, rigid and complete
Soon will be at rest for good
Buried down six feet
Who would do what did do?
Who would be so strong?
Not with just a console
Reset when get it wrong

The survived stands and picks up weapon
Looking down with sigh
Once more they go though do not know
If the next to die

Pebbles on the beach

Pebbles washed upon a shore
Placed one place but wanted more
Bump and grind until Sand find
Went somewhere to help with chore

And all I want is a love to share
Not me here and them there
All I want is to care
Burden gets so hard to bear

Sickle said to bed let's wed
When one gains another's loss
Just a simple action
Regardless of the cost

What are you going to truly do?
When mask it slips for good
The comfort be no reality
When truth understood

And I I want is to be back Home
Place forgotten but remember
All I want is to be 'normal'
Life took look and then said never

Waiting in the Wings to bring
New to join the old
Story just half finished
So much yet untold

The beauty of the waiting
To find out what next giving
The anticipation of mutation
Guess I am just living

Perfect food dream

Picture this, if you will
On your plate seemingly still
Yet unbeknownst to you and me
Lies a conflict of disparity

Slivers of a flesh thin cut
Take centre stage despite history
Solids yet not so loved
Resign themselves, familiarity

Blooming heck and straw hats
Gravy train meets Beef and 'Tats'
Various veg then does release
All of it including Peas

Some stuff ground to powder
That bit understood
Yet how when mixed with liquid
Becomes a Yorkshire Pud?

Six days continental
Seventh return Home
The greatness of the roast dinner
Strangely doesn't roam

Admittedly it has its variations
Far from this here shore
Yet nothing like Homebase made
The one that I adore

The cacophony of orange and green
The brown that then does cover
I guess that I am a biased man
For am a roast dinner lover

The crispness of the orange
The slightly Iron of much green
The chasing little balls around the plate
The Sunday perfect dream

P.P. – Perfect Partnerships

A happy chappie can change a Nappy
Even feed, with aid of bottle
Parenthood can be so good
When both do give full throttle
What's yours is mine and that is fine
Mine is yours but I draw the line
For all Partnerships start there
Just not our underwear!

When turn the page into old age
Couples even joke
Comfortably numb with sense of fun
As each other's faults they poke
The highs and lows, the too and froe's
The opinions don't care to share
The recollection of 'near perfection'
When together chose to dare

To know the other is to know oneself
In a way previously did not
Limitations in situations
Embedded not forgot
The salutations and adulations
Of others nice but not the same
Not of same name but are in frame
The longevity when impulse tame

The missing of the kissing
The caressing and the care
That hollow space that you face
When other is not there
What makes a perfect Partnerships?
Don't ask me for do not know
Mine is somewhere in the middle
We still have far to go

Perfect treasure

It was a day in history
The Stranger came a calling
The Residents of Mundlemont
Changed that Summer morning
Mundlemont was a nothing place
You were born, you died, nothing more
Everyone who lived there
Could be called a bore

Then, so is said
Occurred the starting thing
The fact that someone came there
More so that which they did bring
Nothing much in physical
More a change of thinking
Mundlemont started flourishing
Where before was sinking

They brought words they spoke to all who gathered
To witness the phenomenon
Spoken in a new way
They said it's called a song
Accompanied by a weird device
They called it a Guitar
It made noise not heard before
The noise it travelled far

They sang
Climbed the hill so could see
Climbed that slope Destiny
What did see was fantasy
Saw the things that I could be
A whole new place was out there
A whole new place inside
Imprisoned and again its will
Because I chose to hide

Free your inner and find yourself
Regret it you will never
It is free and bountiful
It is the perfect treasure

Perfection

In all the days, ways, forays
A common thing still stands
A goal so whole it blinds the soul
In near and distant Lands
The ascension to 'perfection'
The disgrace we face when don't achieve
For a myth you see not reality
Despite how much believe

Pursuit
Everlasting
Regarding
Futile
Exercise
Chasing
That
Invisible
Overblown
Nuance

That which may seem to one misled
Average to another
For is but just a word
That resides beneath the ego cover
For is but a goal to aim for
Knowing never will achieve
A driving force for the wise
Who drive for yet in which don't believe

The golden chalice of the successful
When tempered by this fact
The only 'perfection we can come close to
Is how with others interact
No disgrace in aiming for
When knowing just a word
When we think that have achieved
We become absurd

Physical is part ritual

Someone somewhere with choose to share
More than just a story
Fiction? No! As volumes grow
A mix and past it history

Everything does mean something
If not now then will
No remorse in chosen course
Also, with no thrill

And as I walk away from day
To welcome in the night
Questions grow the answers don't know
Did this one I get right?
Time will tell if go to Hell
A decision not of mine
I try to be a spirit free
Surely that's no crime
The open book so can others look
The things that I went through
The new me and what can be
That can apply to you

To g with flow I chose not go
Branching out on own
A better me I did then see
Now my seeds are sown

Physical is part ritual
The expected and nothing more
Yet behind lies hard to find
A look at different shore

Welcome you, and you and you
Please feel free to look around
For the same apart from name
Plus, the way we sound

Picnic

Pre made and cut sandwiches
Cold pork pie and sausage rolls
A bottle of something fizzy
Has Dad paid the tolls?
This strange thing they call grass
Bloody hell!! What's that thing?
A Cow you say like see everyday
Does that my morning stuff each day bring?

The feeling of the freshness
Of thing we know as air
Not that of my bedroom
Where play on computer without care
Mom you need to adjust the aircon
I am beginning now to leak
What do you mean this is natural?
So was Dante's Peak!

I have seen and played it many times
What it is so not real
Just a way to get a rush
As in comfort victory feel

Blanket on the ground
Plastic plates are passed around
All a strange experience
Together with strange sound
Why are Mom and Dad now laughing
Pretending to enjoy
Is this next level?
A new game they employ?

Piggy in the middle

You are the most beautiful
Thing that I have ever seen
Can I ask a question?
Where in my life have you been?

Are you asking me?
You seem to be looking my way
Do I even know you?
I don't know what to say

Pardon me for Interrupting
Yes love, I think that looks a clue
Judging by that certain smile
He's definitely speaking to you

You must have been born in Heaven
With that Angelic face
Or a distant planet of perfection
Deep in Outer space

No, I was born here on Earth
A simple Human means
I guess you should thank my Parents
They gave me good Genes

Are we now doing an ology?
Or maybe some Astronomy
We're i some sort of Trigonometry
For you are on either side of me

All I can say is I thank this day
This journey and my fate
It was meant to be for you see
Today I'm running late

Hahaha, what a pair we are
For I am running late as well
My alar is bust so buy new one must
But your name you didn't tell

158

Hello, you two – remember me?
I am not one late
Shall I switch seats so can complete
This prolonged asking for a Date

The piggy in the middle
With answer to the riddle
Was no second fiddle
Just slightly awkward felt

Could see clearly
The two were both attracted
If not by the conversation
More the way they acted

So felt the need before ears bleed
To Cupid try to play
If only for own sanity
For this journey still had some way

To go or not to go
Go the journey had
Couldn't bear to forward stare
Going slowly mad

So, switching seats with the male
Aisle one they took
Young ones did while their face hid
Inside convenient Book

Pity not

One did look then decision took
To be a something and not a nothing
No 'pity me' from them did see
Unlike that they saw
"Who am I, what am I?
Why do I even still choose to try?
When the outcome seems a failure
I guess that failure's not my nature"

Too polite to them reply
Too seasoned to encourage
Those who seemed to seek attention
With a plethora of their suffer age
First impression was not care
For the one who wouldn't 'grow a pair
As was told by those far better
Who frequently used a particular four letters

Seek of praise is a waste
For those who seek are never satisfied
Better to save it for those worthy
Who despite, still have tried
'Pity me in my misery'
So blatant becomes irrelevant
Not the lack of being better
Just can't be bothered so they shan't

There is a difference in the mental illness
And the one just immature
Both, however, can be sorted
One by others, one self-cure

Pity you

So, the when not once again
The question often asked
The reality be that inside me
Confidence it basked
Not that of self-proclamation
A different situation
Just moving on with hope strong
Can rise to an occasion

Once a puppet or even muppet
To that I can now laugh
Not the kind that you find
That for gain will others shaft
So pour on me your cold water
Do try please my contentment slaughter
Waste on me if saves some others
Less secure in their skin covers

Beat on my Door and I will not answer
Though appreciate the try
The host of ghost that made the toast
Said it as goodbye
The thing I be is a new me
That in which am sure
Doubt a cloud of am not proud
When I found the cure

Poison is the need to shame
If you try from it gain
Poison deep in you be
If becomes necessity
Pity you I will do
Pity one who can't be true
In who are and what can do
Do not hate, just pity you

Played Pool on distant Planet

I've sailed the seas of Saturn
Paddled in Pluto's pools
Not a thing of accuracy
Just using writers' rules

Create new words in language
Not recognise I do admit
But the suited context
More importantly they fit!

I've written long and written short
Whichever mood did take
Each poem is like the risk
When a new cake you bake

What am me but mystery?
Never sure what see next time
That is just part of me
With it I am fine

The Caesars made a History
As did the one known as Bard
I maybe might waste your time
If I try really hard

Played Poo on distant planet
The one known and probes do go
Even ventured to that can split into two words
So main one I won't show

Who am I and then why
Do these things I do
Simply said inside Head
Because I am not you

Ploy not lost

Once came a cropper on a Space Hopper
That fiendish children's toy
That heavy duty bouncing thing
That no sense of stable does employ
That garish Orange with no legs
Fixed freakish Face designed to soothe
Stalks for ears that point of contact
That remains as try to move

Once did own that well known name
With protrusions and holes
With which to stick
Not the modern with all the additions
Mine was simply oblong bricks

All same colour if memory serves me
For that is what I have in Head
Bloody painful if accidentally trod on
With those edges, plastic red

Once did own that which made a comeback
Not the Bike for never went
That bloody surfboard with four wheels
The hours in Casualty that I spent

Once did own an action figure
Clothes and kit an extra cost
Children beseeching their poor parents
On whom that ploy not lost

Once did own so many things
Things of torture masked as joy
Willing victim I did suffer
When I was but wee boy

Poetry is diversity

Tennyson made some great ones
Made some that were quite trying
Emily Dickinson was a great one
Before succumbed to dying
The Bard worked hard
Better known for longer verse
Yet the shorter version
Part of his writer's curse

Whitman, Frost and even Plath
Joining level high
Somewhere few can achieve
No matter how we try
Killing, Burns and Oscar Wilde
Joined that certain group
Keats and Milton, even Yeats
Made circle of the loop

What separates them from us?
Why in such esteem?
So many budding writers
Dreaming of that dream
Simply most are not good enough
I do not wish to sound so rude
For amongst those good but not special
I, myself, include

Hughes, Angelou, even Edgar Allan Poe
Cummings, Ginsberg and T.S. Elliot
Names we come to know
Just from two countries
Yet so many I could show
Poetry is diversity
In its best and purist form
Nothing should be held as 'classic'
When all is somehow 'norm'

Pol

Our pain - their gain with disdain
The 'iticians relentless course
A different breed for they need
To be born without remorse

The ability to weave what say
So can change meaning every day
To act, convincing, that sincere
When re-election time draws near

The secret club 'on display'
Whilst behind the scenes it's merely plays
The 'confrontations' merely show
So in their charade can grow and grow

Their backroom staff on different path
Subservient required
To gain some fame attach to name
New noticeability desired

The Golden Goose now let loose
That hoards the eggs it lay
Not caring for the sharing
Even make the victims pay

Pol and ice are, mostly nice
Some bad apples true
The Pol and itician on different mission
In everything they do

A Manifesto?
Script for Show
Change that plan as soon as can
So their income can grow and grow

They would be a comedy if only they didn't affect every normal person

Ponder poem - part lost count

Shall I share a shadow past?
Shall I share that not meant to last?
Shall I share that anger built
That which once drove to hilt
Shall I share that didn't care?
The recklessness of no hope
Shall I share the turn to dare
The ways I found

All that have been and all have seen
Nothing compares with what I am
The old is show, the next don't know
Just part of some great plan
Wake predawn and glad were born
The rest I sometimes question
The highs and lows as me it goes
Too many the things to mention

I could surrender but not contender
Not built in me you see
The what I be is part of me
The end just this stage finality
So I grow as more I know
With every challenge takes
A cake is not worth eating
Unless it first you bake

Shall share? I think not now
Not ready for to see
The thing I was before the pause
The cast so horribly
Bygones should be Bygones
Unless a trust you lose
Then they become superfluous
In that which you choose

Survivor

The warrior sat and started
After battle this still air
The rush has, for now, gone
Once more the quiet does belong

So, come combustion in my world
Let confusion be freely hurled
Make the chaos now make sense
Let it heal without recompense

The world they know they now hate
To their past they can't relate
Maybe, one day will find
That sought after - peace of mind

So come the battle, come the test
We will, one day see who's best
The person am or that to be
The inner self, the real me

The warrior sat, cup in hand
Staring out at a strange land
Wondering with a sigh
Wondering the reason why

This is but a passing faze
The first panel of double glazed
Just a step to get through
One more step to something new

Everyone warrior
Some more battles fought
Everyone still here
Survivor with things taught

Tagalog tale

Tender went the troubled tongue
For the language it could not speak
Spoke to Brain about its pain
Remedy the Brain did seek

Spoke with eyes to view inside
Spoke with Hands that Book the held
Spoke with ears to hear clean
Pronunciation of what Hands spelled

Knowledge grew with language new
As did standing in new place
Effort made and words trade
Regardless of the tone of face

Skin akin to milk thin
Amongst a Coffee kind
Yet conversation situation
Easier in time did find

Was first agog at Tagalog
Yet rhythm held the cure
Kumusta ka at paano mo gagawin?
Accepted but not pure

Tender went the troubled tongue
As exercise in different way
Vocal cords did applaud
As Mouth began to say

English ako pero sa iyo
Patawarin ang aking pagsubok na tumugon
Mag-aaral na higit sa aking mga taon
Mangyaring hayaan silang maging ilang mga luha ng tawa

Take those Hardships

A woman passed me an hour ago
Looking troubled, why don't know
Just on face and actions it did show
One of many that I see

The Bus driver taking break
What type of phone call did he make?
Shouting loud enough to phone break
Not quite sure what did achieve

The sun does set on another day
Rise to new one far away
Okay, okay, we are a broad stretched race
Different challenges we all face
Some with grudge and some with grace
Yet all face them just the same
Take those Hardships - turnaround
Take dilemmas – make choice sound
Take defeat and victory make
That 'loser' cycle break

Further on down the street
Another woman did me greet
Positive did she send
Infection of the type I like

The Mom with child on way home
Laughing, joking with their own
Miserable will not condone
A strange made me smile

The sun does set on another day
Rise to new one far away
Okay, okay, we are a broad stretched race
Different challenges we all face
Some with grudge and some with grace
Yet all face them just the same
Take those Hardships - turnaround
Take dilemmas – make choice sound
Take defeat and victory make
That 'loser' cycle break

Taking comfort

When do Oranges become orange?
Who decided Lemons should be yellow?
When was it we decided?
A person with some common interests
Suddenly became a Fellow?

Why is up to which we raise
Yet on solid most still stays
Tastes and diet so do vary
Miners found use for a Canary

If Black and White are not colours
Why they start and end all the others?
Why take in then part exhale
Why in shock the skin goes pale?

What the heck am I now doing?
I really have no clue
Wasting space in some Rat Race
Then do punish you

Nothing much I think you'll find
Between the ears of this idea mind
So, I ask you to be kind
Make the negative somewhat blind

Apologies are necessary
You had no chance to get that Canary
Taking comfort, I so wish
That this is end of a strange

Tapas tempts the taste buds

Solemn sleeps the sense of single
Party does the pleasure of pair
Algebra is of two letters
Not Algebra if one's not there
Make believe is just relief
Moves aside the common grief
The Robin Hood type of thief
Until that grand reunion

Mickey Mouse a cartoon sketch
Until became much more
When the one and then others
Opened Mickey's door
Donald did a similar thing
Both got to the top
As became a bigger thing
The original they did drop

Echo and the Bunny men
A Band that I did like
Only got to hear them
When their success did spike
Strange is world of salutations
Critics come as well
Sometimes never knowing which
Sometimes hard to tell

Tapas tempts the taste buds
As does meal well cooked
Pleasures are a plenty
Non should be overlooked
Taste is waste when made in haste
Time to give some time
Sometimes urgency is called for
Sometimes patience fine

Teacher

That drink to sink
That pill to kill
That smoke to poke
Negative into the corner for short while

That mirror glances
Those emotions Dances
The slip slide stances
The one hundred you call you

The under estimation
The short-term situation
The ire inflation
Directed at yourself

No more this chore
No more that will endure
No more for sure
I am committed to feeling good

Good if not exuberant
Good if not the perfect being
Good but still improving
Good at what you're seeing

So, Teacher, is this the lesson?
It is sharper than the knife
So, I have an amazing Teacher
My Teacher is called Life

That laugh that carved
Despondent from my Soul
That bright mile smile
That filled the gap whole

Teaching pleasures

Of so quiet was the Classroom
Oh, so quiet was the class
Suspicious source of silence
As the Head walked past

Oh, so quiet with no talking
Though sounds did seem to sound
Gasp of Head when investigated
This is what they found

A class engaged in making
A class following a show
A class that would be re-enacting
The new they now do know

Learning is not just lecturing
Learning should have pleasures
Teaching is a balance
Getting right in equal measures

Sponge Science

The sponge we store between our ears
Squeeze and then absorb
Thoughts are merely liquid
Each of own accord

Like all sponges afford caution
Avoid that situation
Nothing good can be absorbed
In sponge at saturation

Each 'leak' leaves residue
Each like a tint of the new
Each 'soak' a top up to the tank
Then this sponge we should thank

Quad communication from more than just one Nation

The one did have a dream
The dream became the nucleus
Gathered other parts
Then became a thing quite serious

As with all so can call
The dream was given name
Optimum Poetica
Started rise to fame

Flavour of the factions
One of its attractions
Add some interaction
A writer's true salvation

From the shadows and corner's,
Residential rooms of words outflow,
Minds merging with thoughts,
Train station encounter at midway junction,
A suggestion, a discussion,
Fusion of journeys taken and those yet,
Hills draw close to a rhythmical twist,
Souls gather for a mission,
Fog lights on, birth of a vision,
Distance decimates, time mellows,
At the fresh fountain of optimum optimistic dance,
Arrives a baby with colourful heritage.

We strive and we endeavour
In the forms we love to do
we sing of time forever
and no theme will we eschew

Of course, we have a lighter side
We can't resist a joke
We emulate poetic pride
with every quill pen stroke.

Crystalline bruises can wart
duvet of fears stultifying sunrise
lanterns can hang on threads
when rays are needles in disguise
smiles may be the entrance
to cavernous bogy traps
poems are the niche of thunders
exploding in our hearts

Hope is the pen that vomits
each stroke we break ourselves free
from bondage an ode, a sigh,
a moan, a plea
between the lines of norms
we engrave our poetry
our breaths, our muses' cries
stamped in history.

A collaboration between Loriz (work), Nancy Ndeke, Ron Conway and Ian Wilcox

Evolution of experienced

The evolution of experienced
Cumulative life experiences and imprints from past lives

Teen

Dirty streets and dirty sheets
Dirty thoughts between
Dirty mouth and dirty crowd
The life of average Teen

Rebellion an infection
Don't know why but just must do
Confusing is amusing
Just a cycle all pass through

Yet some day do parents pray
The cycle comes to end
Joining in, the new begin
Join the Adult trend

Here they come, the strange ones
Soda stained and fast food
Gait not walk and nonsense talk
All will surely mood

Here again the multi pain
That drives one to despair
Not a jot from that lot
They simply do not care

Oh, to be that mind free
If only for a day
To once again be that pain
To hear what them ancients say

Teenage before

All we knew as passing threw
The silly stuff that then did do
All we saw was that of more
Than the bits could do before

All we saw was Life's a chore
Set by Mom and Dad if we had
Just longing for the more

Teenage being and what seeing
The lack of the interest
The drive and strive just to survive
The parts that were the best

Happy days and forays
Into that best not told
Keeping crime just as mine
At least until I'm old

Echo speak

The Echo speak of kiss on cheek
The old who say goodbye
That cannot show that we know
They have no reason why

The aunt and uncles, the carbuncles
The reaction tries to hide
For greed has need so it we feed
When nothing beats one's pride

Reverberation a situation
When affection want to show
Does not stop with adult top
However old we grow

Ian Wilcox

Temper trap

The temper trap we call 'a nap'
The pause before explode
The 'me time' and then are fine
The not rising to the goad
The won't stop until get on top
Of that which put you there
Silly state is irate
Not a thing to share

Just say the word and it will be heard
Find in self release
Say and do for now is true
Say the word called Peace
The music playing and games saying
Hate and misery
Yet that's just for pain got profit
Not how meant you see

Hidden be the one that's free
From pressure everywhere
Change is strange but can arrange
When for hurt don't care
Both inflicting and receiving
Hate it has no space
Dislike's fine when draw the line
Amongst a common Race

Once did stand on pedestal
Telling World that I did rule
Then I realised wasn't 'cool'
When was showing was a fool
The temper trap I employ
Now my days are filled with joy
I was a one, just a boy
I was one of many others
Was just the same in different frame
Outside the world of lovers
Now I have joined that Band

Temple

My hands are tied with velcro straps
Can break the chain if wish
The possible imaginable
A spice if one does add to Dish
In the world of that not heard
I sit within the rack
Maybe used or maybe not
Picked up and then put back

My legs regret the once did get
That known as exercise
The lack of it as choose to sit
Maybe not that wise
Tummy now trim with lack of that put in
Though sometimes it does shout
What was masses now are gasses
Screaming to get out

But that's okay!! Hip, hip hooray!
Guess that I am blessed
In the past questions asked
I did pass their test
So, go on now for know how
You crazy I call me
Adapt, react, make a pact
You are a growing Tree

Adulation and inspiration
Same-same when I think
Recognition no competition
When have been at the brink
My Body is a Temple
Just to no yet known God
My Body is a legacy
Of every footstep trod

Temporary the cope

Is the shape we make incarnate?
Or just a thing we lose
Are we blind in which comfort find?
Do we really choose?
When grabbing hands create scams
Try to pass off as what we need
Is it then wrong to pen?
Distaste at how the feed

It's not like you, the one I knew
To get sucked into games
Politician or religion
Beneficiaries are the same
Once have been their ideal dream
That I am no more
Recovery in discovery
When in self are sure

Yes, we rock as take stock
Of what at what can be
Yes, we dance with romance
As true love should be free
A rhapsody of what could be
The concert of concern
Do we play in our own way?
To just some notice earn?

To think that drink will somehow sink
Maybe just disguise
That chemicals are potential
To making fool the wise
Nothing gained when again, again
We sink into false hope
Just mask be to reality
Temporary the cope

Ten

The nothingness of that repress
The hollow that does leave
The life not fine but some like mine
Who happiness are yet to achieve
So splinter sent to where it went
Embraced and took a hold
For was just part of it
Just a future it was told

The day still that yet to come
Nothing like before
When on this journey of you learning
I always seek that more
No ego twist will add to list
For no ego own
So say to me your reality
Not that image shown

My intention no insurrection
Each do what they do
The feeling of being something
Not a feeling new
I will not condone that which don't own
Better a silent static
No need to feed that common greed
Publish, print, outright promote and then just stored in the attic

Piffle as I twiddle
Another cheap bought Pen
Got a pack from a stack
The outside says there's Ten!

The sauce course

My Brown sauce had an altercation
For Red did disagree
Upon Bacon which am fond
Which is the best for me

The Pepper got quite fraught
Felt upstaged by Salt
A compromise did seem wise
So both in dish I caught

Don't start me on the Hoisin!
I wouldn't know where to begin
Sweet and Sour is a breeze
Certain dishes it does tease

Sweet chilli quite a mystery
With invention comes sensation
Lost count of which in hide or mount
In staples of various a Nation

Worcester sauce of course
Neither sauce nor coating true
If decide under main thing hide
More the fool are you!

Now we get Caribbean merry
Someone invented Peri Peri
My sauces different courses
On taste buds each one forces

Its own identity and taste
None do wish to go to waste
Each is known for certain style
I just mix with some Jam guile

Oh, bloody hell!
Jam is now both sweets and savoury!!

With recognition to Coldplay

The Scientist and what twist

So, what I know I now don't know
The boundaries have changed
The known and shown now outgrown
All just rearranged
Is it alchemy that I see?
Or merely some progression?
And who are you to this do
Making this suggestion?

To protect that which get
A pleasure not obligation
For few see the joys that be
Incurred in granted marvellous occasion
And all the friends that had then went
To the different course
All that be in history
Recognise with deep remorse

So kiss me on the cheek I say
Never on the lips
For I am glad to know you
But Wife? By God's does she hit!!
So can you understand this unknown hand
To more than those who know
Can you add to this so mad
As recognition seems to grow

A day at best just like the rest
Jump to a possibility
Not this one for is just fun
No further yet do see
So with refrain but not disdain
Sit and think some more
The avenue that could be new
Next year I might explore

The settling

Dead eyes searching
Heart beat murmuring
The way it used to be
Numb touch of some such
Meaning now not much
Fondness flown and now free

Hatred is so wasted
Tormented times have tasted
Bitter was not sweet
Left behind a different mind
When did find the good and kind
In those new did greet

Crowded space when remembered waste
Of chances now are known
Bygones have now bye gone
When better way was shown

Trust a must or into dust
Go while still alive
With comes Hope – hope to cope
Cope and then to thrive

Never can be forever
That in some is true
Fortunately, not you and me
For in each other do

Enjoyment in employment
Every day I say
Lighter now is life
Look forward do
Because of you
The settling in the strife

The Spectre

The Spectre loitering in the ether
The presence just out of touch
The doubt machine that's always been
The cause of pain and much

The hidden but oft felt
The one who chose to stay
The invisible that is so real
In basement likes the day

Upon a wall ten feet tall
Found some charcoal and so did scrawl
Hoping some would hear its call
Then into clutches surely fall

It scrawled

If ecstasy is a mystery
Why persist in haunting me
I am not that you can see
I am the total opposite entity

I am the shadow behind the light
I am the darkness in things bright
I am the force that some call might
I am you with insight

Letters badly formed
For came from since time of dawn
When as species we were born
In its game we are a pawn

A paw yes but not Chess piece
We have the strength to find release
This is not Trigonometry
This is just you and me

The strangest scripture seed

The car's the star when travelling far
The Train a pain on tracks
Aeroplane the same in awkward frame
When destination Airport lacks
Feet a treat when can keep neat
With cover purpose made
Though with surprise I see the price
Of some new rip off trade

Places change our faces
Then we class as Races
Yet light go dark for a lark
When in our holiday spaces
Spend nigh on fifty weeks to look a treat
Then to stuff yourself
We pickle self for Bar owner's wealth
Incur hangovers as a fait accompli

The work to gain taxation pain
The 'new kid' yet in their thirties
A Mix'n'match each office hatch
The 'squeaky clean' and 'dirties'
And as they cut down to his bone
The words began to bleed
For through head was that led
The strangest scripture seed

For after all when time will call
I certain will not grieve
For in plain sight they did write
Their writing then did leave
How much time this of mine
Have you truly spent
Nonsense from the nonsensical
Another moment went

Thank you for your time you gave me

The stupidity of self-importance

Made a mark, or at least a dent
Compensation, I guess, for effort and ink spent
The visions of recognition, the main ambition
Why do they try to salsify? To stop the just fruition

I am the one that have not seen
I am the big company dream
Why do I get the overlook?
When my lesser they then took

Arrogant with no repent?
Whatever do you mean?
I am that which out of sight
I am the best that's ever been!

You silly fools with chosen rules
You blind to that which better
I am perfection personified
I am the God of letters

Yes, I'm young and yes just begun
Yet I know that I am best
Put your focus on this one
Who really cares about the rest?

One day you will regret this
For good my memory
Then you will come back grovelling
When sees reality

Too late for you that is true
What could have been a part
The pinnacle of magical
Yet you missed the start

I bet you are sorry now

The thrill of chill

That crazy kitten surfs the pavement
Can't honestly say true walk
That dog in someone's garden
To its friend does talk
The hungry for a bargain
March up to the paved High Street
There a sea of glass fronted stores
Their cash await to greet

The teens are in the nearby Park
Skates and Boards on show
That they are doing what's been done
Not sure that they do know
How many choices of attire?
Can pass this window up?
Marvel at some combinations
As a cold drink I sup

Clock says it is early in the afternoon
So, more time for this pleasure
Have done all that needed to be done
Now some time for leisure

Lost in a moment I wish I could keep
Lost in the feeling I adore
Lost in the sense of harmony
Lost in that which should have more
The sun outside is shining
At least it is here
The sun inside is shining
Dispelling all the fear
The moment seems forever
How I wish was true
Yet is dependent on the actions
Of those things we do

The times are changing

The times are changing - rearranging
The attitude somewhat rude
All seems fair with no care
The third party free to intrude
No more validity of sacred promises
No more the statement to endure
Minor problems when two are sharing
A relationship once deemed pure

Understand that certain man
Who's prepared to stand alone
Understand the right of hand
That loves but never owns
Make of them what you wish
For today are a rare dish
Love or hate just relate
This one not searching for the exit gate

Not for all, however, do
Some say those words and mean true
Work things out is when they pull through
When sky is grey, they turn to blue
Nothing eve is totally perfect
Nothing ever totally bad
Maybe sometimes a mistake made
Ends the promise, so, so sad

The times are changing – rearranging
Divorce lawyer profiteering
The exceptional now that common
When are joining without that feeling

And time are changing - rearranging
Now I'm feeling old
Time is true for what say/do
A new chapter in story told
Nothing lasts forever
But that promise made
That was not just charades
It was a moment that has stayed

Taken with solemnity
Taken with belief
Not some quick get out clause
To spare a moment grief
Time to go back to old time
In this I do think
Before into a night out
A partnership does sink

Time to end the profiteering
Also, that thing called 'arranged'
For someone outside that culture
At best it seems so strange
Partnership is partnership
No leader permanent
One will rise to an occasion
One will follow when that sent

Two to one become
Harmony in action
Taking more so can explore
That everlasting yet fresh attraction

The tranquillity of serendipity

The speed of Light to make things bright
The speed of Sound will boom profound
Yet what the speed into which am sinking?
The Black and White of sound and sight
The grey and green of might have been
The state now of deep thinking

The philosophy of who we be
The tranquillity of serendipity
When positivity wins the race
The without a care and thousand-yard stare
The soft glow when you know
How near perfection fell into place

The long, the short, the large, the small
The send/ receive that welcome call
The knowing will cause a smile
The honesty that sets free
The acceptance of current place be
The removal of all guile

The 'perfect' world not so absurd
The fruition of ambition
The willingness to try
The strength of length to achieve
The determination at centre station
The discovery and why

So, wrote one and so wrote many
Even more did say
One did write a song so famous
Called it Perfect Day

The twist is this

In the avenues of the Alchemists
They make potions and write lists
Of effects and their twists
Talk in riddle if you get my gist
Is it witchcraft or health care?
Can we delve deeper?
Do we dare!

A Doctor prescribes a brand name
Explore ingredients and go insane
All those strange chemicals
Mixed together and new thing calls
Then the game goes much deeper
What 'over counter', what must prescribe
Then the copies by the unscrupulous
Just what in? They try to hide

Bottles full of their capsules
Blister package sell some others
Some are plain pain to swallow
Others with sweet outer covers
Then there comes a complication
For most seems an addiction nation
Add that to the situation
Are we really taking cure?

Exercise and healthy diet
Now becomes so old news
Eat what like and couch potato
As online pills peruse
Medicine the new treat
From brain damage to swollen feet
Where the line that we must draw?
The twist is this the Pharmacist
If are true want less not more

The unfinished project

The unfinished project that never ends
The pleasure of its continuation
The ambiguity of the next line
The joy in its creation
The realisation phenomenal
When that one is done
The satisfaction of its attraction
Spurs to another one

When to stop? When you drop
Exhausted but content
Did you miss other bliss?
Not when with pen time spent
Only know when ideas go
The love you have for them
Only hope that you can cope
Until when they come again

Only takes a second to start a story
Only one to make poem glory
Just a second to then be
In the halls of immortality
Laid down on a page
It is irregardless of your age
The spirit free from the cage
The writer now is shown

The unfinishe project you hope won't end
Those treasured moments that you send
The link between the old and new
The contact made with who been through

The ways of minions

A new life born; the silence torn
Broken by first cry
The debts increase, no more peace
The Dad does wonder why
The cost is lost as smile breaks the frost
Unfocused eyes do sample light
The Brain is trained; some parts ingrained
Touch, taste, sound, smell and sight

Each does come with hazards
Each does give some certain pleasure
Each does help in educating
Each does help in leisure
Each can then be twisted
Each then can be fooled
Each can be manipulated
Each can be then overruled

I so want to go against what they tell me
I so to go against what been taught
I so want to go against that which makes decision
I so want to go against logic in which caught
I so want to go against sense that's common
I so want to go against some opinions
I so want to go against divided living
I so want to go against the ways of minions

Five line

Five line to say I'm happy
Five lines on which embark
Four lines to form two x's
Representative of kisses
One to help form an exclamation mark

The Wonder War

The Wonder War was folklore
Emotions Archipelago was at Stake
Regiment Right joined the fight
Against the troops of Tempt then take
Battles fought and battles won
Of casualties there were some
Some were captured but not turned
Those a rescue mission earned

Sergeant Sense called Corporal Calm
To search for Private Peace
Captain Clear had seen Lieutenant Lucid
About Mission Rage Release
Peace a prisoner of Provocation
That most dastardly of foes
How when and where with no effort spared
Will strike no-one really knows

Team Triumph took to trail
That led into Despair
The darker lands with jet black sands
A Horn of Hope did share
Triumphant over Tribulations
Laid waste to Troubled Mind
Driving into Crafting Conniving
To save a kindred kind

The war was won and then came fun
But Wrong is strong and rose again
Now again we see the pain
Guess that we will just have to put it in its place

The world out there

The traveller neared the end
Of the greatest journey they had made
End of it would have no fanfare
No marching Bands and no parade

'The world out there is dangerous'
Been told so many times
Daring not to see for self
The greatest of all crimes

One long ago day they slipped away
Not knowing what in store
All they knew was to see it through
Then to quest some more

They'd made it through the Quagmire of Questions
Dover the Depths of Doubt
Swam the Sea of Suspicion
Heard the Banal Banshee shout

They'd matched the marauding Media
A tribe who like no other
Who would go toe to toe
Yet willing to combat undercover

Endured the pain of being sane
In the confusion lands
Had a look and then on took
The Unsympathetic Sands

Now a night fell to cast its spell
Through familiar gate did walk
Went up to those who warned
To them said "You are nothing but all talk"
For once they spoke not one word

Their turn now

The boy walked back to his friend
The girl the broken tries to mend
The teen male treats as game
The teen female can't play the same

Time moves on and to 'adult' both belong
Both, supposedly, are now strong
Of how predictions can be wrong

Through broken eyes the lady cries
Through self-accusations man goes through
Promised much that first touch
No excuse was nothing new

Someone, somewhere will break the trend
Someone somewhere holds the key
Someone somewhere is the right one
How to find them? Mystery

The victims become the Criminals
New victims they do then produce
Repetition is History's mission
It just loves the dream abuse

Forget th town we call Hurting
Forget the County named Despair
Forget the Land we named Rejection
All is gone when love in air

Been an done and then moved on
Been the victim now am strong
Passed the burden with some pride
To one to which my love can't hide

Their turn now to feel the journey
Their turn now to find the self
Their turn now to stop the playing
Their turn now to gain the wealth

Those who look

Who is me and what I be?
Shown external, no mystery
The bonding of the once was total stranger
Yet at no time did feel in danger
What colour? Each did ask
'Colour blinds should not be task
When beneath each the same
Just different speak with different name

What is Male and with two more letters?
Why some try to say once better?
So once again I am here
Just the same but with no fear
I am bone, blood and flesh
In one object all just mesh
I am nothing but can be
I am the beginning of being me

The fortune and feeling good
When one's way is understood
When are, finally, free to say
That which personal, in personal way
In the hands of 'understand'
Those who look beyond which see
Look at the unfinished article
Look at what could be

The Stage show goes and we all know
That for few it lasts forever
Inspiring and unity trying
Falls to them who in some way clever
Who never stop despite some calls
To keep on trying to give their all
In the end most things can mend
Just by calling someone friend
Eσύ ndi kawula umngani

Vintage vehicle that I be

If I was registered as a car
I think I qualify for no road tax
My log book says I am vintage
Birth certificate endorses fact
Awkward in my aching action
Often seeming to lose traction
Have been known to have odd stumble
If nothing else it keeps one humble

Bodywork gets a polish
Every morning with shower gel
Sometimes remove moss from my bonnet
Other times say 'what the hell'
Headlights somewhat iffy
Causing problems with my sight
Simply solved that problem
Don't go out at night

My engine may need an overhaul
That will come with time
As long as it keeps ticking over
With the in and out in rhyme
One day I'll be a collector's item
If I last that long
Maybe showcased at exhibition
Before my own swansong

Virtual visage

If I told you that I love you
Would you your feelings change
If I told you that I love you
Would you find me strange?

Each time that I see you
I just want to time some time
With an addiction on my arm
Tell me that you'd be that one
What could be the harm?

If I told you that you light up my day
What would you then reply?
Tell me please that with ease
Then the reason why

If I told you that I want to be with you
Forever if I can
Would you then hit me?
With that big old pan

I see you each morning
Also, before I sleep
Then I dreams I think of means
Of how you I could keep

You to me are fantasy
The one I so desire
Everything about you
Things that I admire

Will you stay, come what may?
Be there when I look
The wise one to this foolish son
Despite the mistakes in past I took

Yes!! I am a bloody Mirror!!!

Vivat Books

Pull back lever and chamber load
Flip the switch and then explode
Forget sight when spray in flight
Not time to be selective
Situation confrontation
Survival bleak perspective
Time for physical Books to fight

Wrists grow weak, their future bleak
Tablet and phone keep getting lighter
Learn to fix by all three mix
Become a paper fighter

Too long spent to this way invent
To pass into history
They last longer than modern way
Won't go slow
As with age go
Same pace do they stay

Covers may begin to show
Some signs of wear and tear
Not abuse when through use
Besides, a thing that all do share

A Book can become a decoration
Placed upon a shelf
A row of Books has a look
At least I find myself

In summary to you from me
You Teachers, Students, Cooks
No charger is required
Vivat Books

Waiting for Dinner

If ancestry such a mystery
How can I be just simply me?
If I am part of Family Tree
Do I shed my leaves each Autumn?

Does Snoopy have his Groupies?
If so in which form?
So old now in which we plough
Can he still perform?

Save our Souls the famous call
For those who in distress
What about savings the whole person?
Souls but also rest

Occupation situation
Employment or when reside
How many post on social media
Then from partner try to hide

If I had bricks numbering sixty-six
Would I have enough
I guess how tall to finish wall
Part knowledge can be tough

We dig and fill and then dig still
When will we dig that which already dug?
Floor covering for smothering
What is carpet and what large rug?

How much time did this crime
Take you to fully read?
More than that as patient sat
When will you them just feed!!

Wake up in their past Sun

And in the arms of ambition
Stood a Nation with tradition
Ups and downs but so fast
Now is time for could not last

The ways before are no more
The future seen clearly
Took step back and then moved forward
Realising what could be

Echoed in the archives
How they used to be
When with certain own rules
Generally, were free

Certain rules for common health
Not the things that benefit some
Especially when the benefices
Wake up to their past Sun

The right of being able
From death bed and the cradle
Everyone should share the table
The table we call Opportunity

Slowly growing with the knowing
With some problems if truth is told
Yet that is no disgrace
When the people bold

Bold enough to stand up
In a peaceful way
Then to proclaim
Their own and right to say

Walang hanggang pag-ibig

One journey near completion
Let's start another one
Writing shouldn't be a task
Writing should be fun
Who with and when a question?
One for another day
Just concentration on completion
Of this one, Hoo, Hoo, Hoo Hooray!

You and me will always be
That is not a question
You and me for Eternity
Need I really mention?
You and me and Family
A product in the making
Who of us knows which way it grows?
Not a decision that I'm taking

One journey is not the destination
One journey just a step
For each end of journey
Says more we can still get
I tried running from the future
Glad in that I failed
Forced me to refocus
Different Boat I sailed

Two to three and what could be
The better than the one
Two to three does suit me
A new life has begun
The making for the taking
The gift I warmly took
The things it brings make a Heart sing
With nothing more than just a look

Walk on air

My slurp has slipped into a drip
My tone is now unknown
A Brahms and Lists to my lisp
Show me the way to Home

It started so sedated
Easier until inebriated
Then as the owner clearly stated
'You sir, have passed your limit!'

Why do Stars seem to swim?
Pretty Girls just laugh
Why do kind Officers want me?
Do they request my autograph?

A Time Traveller me for you see
Went out one day and next returned
Travelling is so expensive
For now short of most I earned

If my memory serves me right
Will travel soon again
For will soon be Monday
Without Sunday's excruciating Head pain

My Kidneys are now drowning
My Stomach quite aghast
Something to help soak up liquid
From Fast food shop I did pass

Golden Goose was let loose
Met its match to be fair
Changed a slightly 'normal' person
To that which tries to walk on air

War the cure if Gamer can endure

The never-ending nightmare
That encompasses the Globe
The repetition of sedition
Broadcast from a radio
Day and night both bring fright
Bombs indiscriminate
Fires light for one more plight
Relit by current state

What the cost? A generation lost
Nations to rebuild
Both those that defied
Together with those forced to yield
New ways invented
How to kill from distant place
Murder legal because declared
Most not face to face

When the pen did change the World
The ink did speak and it was heard
The years of fears, tears and 'near'
Finally, did disappear
The pen did speak for both strong and weak
It said that this must end
Too many lost was the cost
Both Family and friends

That was many years ago
Most of which the new don't know
Yet they look at a screen
See and play at war does mean
Why the game makers avoid the reality?
Deemed too brutal - might upset
So, glorify more ways to die
War best seller yet

Warning! B.F.!

Left wing, Right wing
Red or Blue
Muslims, Cristian, all those in between
Extreme in anything have no clue

All the opinions in the world
Can ever make reason clearly heard
All the logic and illogical
In same basket do they fall

Boiling hot and freezing cold
They make sense for facts told
Cowardly or oh so bold
Each dependant on how we mould

Sweet and sour, a different racket
When in describing in taste bracket
Yet both evolving to description
In the good old emotions Division

His and hers to sex refers
Physical and also that occurs
Weak and strong to that Physical belong
But when of Mind might be wrong

Play on words or Wordplay
Guess it's just how what say
Fart and Brain so apart
Unless, like this, is a Brain fart

We do not have to voice

A person turned the corner
So did choose to speak
To the crowd who felt less than proud
Emotionally felt weak
The gathered were a mixture
Of age, sex, tone and diverse nations
Bonded by experience
Shared some situations

The person said

'How could you know when I didn't show?
The pain as I was growing
You were probably the same with your own pain
Also, in the lack of showing
How we choose to hide abuse
The mental is the worst
For does stay that extra day
Than the physical we nursed

The misery of insecurity
Driven by outside
Yet it felt so personal
Each chose its impact to then hide
At the time didn't see the crime
The torment that it laid
Their satisfaction in your reaction
As their game they played'

How many know as they did grow
How many chasing cars?
How many thrive as car drive?
Not embarrassed by the scars
We all do carry after old enough to marry
We all do have the choice
To lock away as some past affray
We do not have to voice

We look out

(A part hide for was not welcome)

We look out without wondering
What lies over that there Hill
We immediately feel insecurity
The killed or that kill

A remedy for what we be
For each is different true
For plain to see you are not me
Nor am I like you
The 'pure cure' is just folklore
Ingredients experience
Each to own and to each a Home
To protect with diligence

So, blame on me your travesty
Not guilty but accept
That of past that leaves aghast
Their black marks I get
So, look at me and what do you see?
A history or more?
One I had no part from start
The other I am sure

Please don't say you love me
Love each and everyone
Please don't say we've reached the pinnacle
For this journey has just begun
A pebble on an ocean shore
Part of it and nothing more
Yet this pebble learnt to walk
Then this pebble learnt to talk

Some say I am twisted
Some say just confused
Yet are just history
Personas I once used
Within the 'Masters' chambers
Sat on not knowing
Now that one has become
Now that one is showing

We must

Temptation
Resisted
United
Seems
Together

The moment came to make decision
The point of blade on which do stand
Someone appears and approaches near
Then extends their hand

The past a mask of no-fault failures
If only you could see
You are worth so much more
If only you would be

Five letters simply penned
The word they make is hard
Not just some game with different name
Not that turn of card

Talk to me, if you must
Talk to me of thing called trust
Talk to me then of dust
In which some does lay

Talk to me of broken Bond
Talk to me of then now gone
Talk to me of creating new
Talk to me for what did do

Time
Reassuring
Unique
Saved
Turmoil

Snubbed Yet Scrubbed, But Validated

Queen of the quill
I have read your lines
They cut me to the quick
Your wisdom, no wind can blow
Your intellectual prowess
Have risen above the silver lined clouds
At your feet
I come with my calabash filled with ink
Nuanced by your precepts
I eat from the bowl
Of your penmanship
While your costituents fail to appreciate you
I serenade you
You need no accolades,
To justify your seat on the throne
You own the throne already
Your pen is a Vesuvius
Its molten magma flows
With effortless ease
I have hidden trophies for you
The real ones presented from
The hearts of your admirers
Whose loyalty can't be questioned
Or their authenticity denied
They lined up like ants
To eat from your untired hand
The deftness in your choice of words
As it encapsulates the rudiments
Of our ways of life, is second to none
You are a rare bird
That sings when angels are too tongue tied
To find a voice
Keep this kite of kaleidoscope
Flying to high heavens
Soon, snowflakes will dance attendance
As your name storms hidden archives
With a stamp of authority...

William Warigon

The Cry Of Why Die

Life, oh life;
Sweet but so short.
Time is knife.
It cuts life so short.
We are mere travellers in this epoch,
Destined to fulfil the process branded
To souls so soaked in walk and work.
What tale do we bequeath to history sanded?
Wreaths of many mundane plans left unfinished,
When we lay motionless, surrounded by beautiful wreaths.
Sweet effervescent eulogies, epithets epitaphic
On cold carved tombstones that would ever remind
Posterity of the transience of life,
As we transit from here to hereafter and thereafter combined.
Life is the gloom of dawn
And lactiferous star of the morn' of altruism.
From when we were born
We're gripped in its suffocating scholasticism.
Those left to cry ask: 'Why?'
No answer to ease the palpable pain.
In resignation, we try to pry the sky
In diuretic frenzy for answers from any spiritual den.
To what we believe, satisfied, we sigh.
At the end, the end might not be so bad.
So, do not cry and try not to be sad.

William Warigon

A Letter To Late Melody

To her he wrote
Words of his thoughts
"Oh dear, sweet Melody
Of such quiet harmony
You were one song never once sung
Tendrils of grey guilt ought to hang
Around my careless neck
I made you a speck
Dumped in a cold corner
Fancied being your owner
Demoting your loftiness in a hiss
I was miserly with my nightly kiss
You prayed on your knees, I tease
Gone away you are, you I miss
Your silent, patient presence
Never before had a prescience
So apt and devotedly abandoned
Too late, I seek to be pardoned
Were the cloying ground
That forever had you bound
To be the opening prayer
Of a forgotten soothsayer
Would have had me reformed
In darkness my heart deformed
Now the tigress that wears your shoes
Gives but delicious troubles she stews
My tears are twitching with stones
Hurled from disagreeable crones
A mother and her daughter upon me
But by your sweet side I'd rather be."
She has gone with the joy
He's a sorrowful big boy
Who is left with sorrow's shadow?
Bereft of his then stead and ardour

William Warigon

Mother's Mighty Mite

She may not adorn her scrawny neck
With ornaments of silver and gold
But her feeble hands your burdens take
She'd care for you till you are old

Your worries rob her precious sleep
She is the duvet for your comfort in winter
You may be as ugly as a gnome's blip
To her, you are precious, none's as sweeter

Your warts are her pride and joy
Your health is her morning dew
When your heart beats, my boy
Her love shines, it is ever new

She watches your progress like a hawk
With swelling chords of emotion
She is always that strong and solid rock
That is embodied in real devotion

You may be poked, mocked or docked
By your side, her shadow shields
When the sloughs of despondency rock
The fruits of her patience yields

In the eye of the storm
No one can her bond breach
She's the spirit at home
Listen to what she's to preach

Sip from the milk of her might
Even if in the eye it's a tad mite
For more makes from tiny rite
That forms darkness to the light

Treasure her as a gem of inestimable value
For when the years yawn and finally lumber away
One day she'll be gone and you my then rue
Why you ne'er made her day when you didn't stay.

William Warigon

Grand Pa: Connoisseur Of Wisdom

The Grand Father
Advanced in age
Sat on a top ladder
Looking like a sage
Had an answer to every question
He knew his defined destination
And his twin twinkling eyes
Could detect all kinds of lies
He was a man of few words
Words that set rich standards
Many loved to seep from his spring
Of Solomonic wisdom, so they'd bring
Their empty cups of vanity
He'd fill them with humility
And taught them the value of meekness
As the core of value chain of worthiness
When he died
They all tried
To fill the gaping gulf, he left behind
Yet, they tried but will never ever find
One as wise as the old, wizened grandfather
While he lived, they thought he'd live forever
He is gone and so are his words with him
Till in eternity they'll be reunited with him

William Warigon

As We Uncouple Our Coupling

The Jones are too much,
We cannot keep up with them.
I thought we could broach
And redo the state of our hem.

But you disavow the sanctity of our vow
You opted for the lights shimmering in Las Vegas.
Methinks we'd last through like Chao.
We went with motions of name change at last.

Will we still be good a friend?
Or is this the end of a hitherto bliss
That strings pulled have it end?
No more would we passionately kiss
Bidding a very painful goodbye
As we both so cry with clear eye.

I head to an arid, dry desert of Arizona
Whilst I bid my wife, Lady LitaMona,
A last solemn farewell, my dear amphora,
I had thought ours would last forever.

Forever is now a mirage.
I'm in search again and again
From the fenced hedge.
Well, this my hope won't wane.

William Warigon

Medicine After Death

The lone oak lay on his sickbed
With his thoughts, cat and dog.
Dogged by terminal one so red.
He's as an obscure fog in clog.

None of his many children
Sent a scrap of good wishes
Till he wilted like flower then.
They were busy chasing riches.

Upon his death, they gathered like crows in thrall.
To beautify the fanfare of his grand funeral.
Golden eulogies spew from their high hose.
The hearse, embellished in gold and white horse.

They that were absent are now wailing uncontrollably.
Their aloofness to him turned to fake late compassion.
In a few hours, their jets will jet off with them quickly.
They only came to make appearances of façaded commiseration.

His restless ghost in limbo hovered in disappointment.
The people he had spent his entire life nurturing
Gave no hoot to foot the bill when he had an ailment.
Sadly, he entered the Light without closure, for he's despairing.

William Warigon

Oh, Dementia

I married her when she was fifty
I was a strapping young twenty
Year old adventurer
She was an admirer
I am now sixty
She's now ninety
Suffering from sad senility
Oblivious to grim reality
My very sweet, sweet Portia
Deeply drenched in dementia
She calls me Kelly instead of Billy
Sometimes she calls me Su Lee
That is the name of our dog
Her mind is in a tangent fog

My red rose is unwillingly wilting
Before my naked eyes
Still, strong is our bond, my loving
Our vows are inside ice
Preserved to stand the test of time
Ours is like old wine
Better with time, subtle and sublime

Our memories I treasure
I wish I could prick into her brain
And know her pleasure
But she is a slow-moving train
Heading towards our final destined destination
Oftentimes she cried in lieu of laughter
But eerie silence is her faithful companion
She's eagerly inching to the hereafter

My consolation is the wild beyond
Where we'll renew our vows
In eternal love, live forever young
This is the wish of the spouse

William Warigon

Dear Smoker

Dear smoker
I know you are smoking hot.
Smoking has been your lot.
Dear Smoker,
I don't sit on a high horse to judge you.
For daily I battle my own demons too.
But truth as bitter as bitter leaf
Must be told to Saint or a Thief.

Smoking sure is never a joker.
Though you hide in the locker
To take a drag,
You are dragged
To kiss the mound of the grave
Before you age and in fame rave.
You cannot resist the push to puff off,
Thus, making cigarettes' price puff up.

You always blame Covid19
For an addiction to nicotine.
Chew a gum of determination
To overcome this addiction
That is heinous to your frail health,
Depleting your hard-earned wealth.
Next time you cough in pain,
Remember smoking's no gain.

William Warigon

The Dancer From A Voodoo Night

How was I to know
That beneath the pristine agbada
Lie different shades of charms and amulets?
Adorned in sparkling white
Dancing upon sacred floors
Of the largest church in Africa
The feet that sucked on the blood
Of the one crying in the shrine
Is now mocking the altar of the Most High
In the name of Thanksgiving

How highly we sequined his praises
In awe we admired him
In obeisance multiple bows we bowed
The weird world I observe is but obverse
All is not what it seems
The dancer is an epitome of all things perverse
He is the dark shadow of the voodoo night
That sends shivers in the spines of warriors

His nocturnal ventures reek with stench
Of the innocent blood
Of missing children without a trace
Could he retrace his steps?
And find forgiveness?
The allure and praise songs
Have turned his ears red to the voice of reason
Like one cursed to rot in perdition

He will stamp on the sacred ground
His flowery slangs cast spells
Magic, money motivation, macabre memory
Wool over our eyes
Soon his stamping days will be over
When I find a voice
From the muffled grumblings of the spectators
And call him to order....

William Warigon

The Tempest Trumping Tranquility

The terrible tempest hatched a luminous putsch
To make tranquility the young widow before dawn.
Thieves divide the night in the unpatriotic push
To amass wealth to the detriment of what we spawned.

In this byzantine labyrinth where sincerity is scarce,
Honesty and integrity are on pilgrimage.
There is no straight path for any good reason to pass.
Many years of sufferings, it's time for a new page.

Dukes detest Cupid and his arrow but bask in cupidity.
Those deep in inertia, wake up!
Pushed to the wall, yet you're touted as jowls of stupidity.

I'm fleeing to my nest to hide in shame.
The anticipated one is gone and nought's same.
The wool pulled over my eyes is peeled.
To heal my will, I feel I must kill a bad deal.

Will you come with me to replant?
The forgotten pill of peace and tranquillity?
For the taste of the tempest plant
Is like the whirlwind of semidiurnal morbidity.

William Warigon

221

Elegance

When I met her, named Elegance
She said as she held my hands
"I am elegance
With a glance
I seduce and confuse
The minds of the loose
I dwell in sheer rich refinements
Gentility sequins my garments
I am adored by the discerning
Copied by those desire-designing
Ilk who dwell in sea of fame
Elegance is my given name
I wholly personify poise and panache
I stand out in the crowd even without cash
I am royal and stately
I so strut ever elegantly!"

Trodden Yarmulke

Blood and mud smeared
Upon my skullcap, my yarmulke.
Fire has caught my beard
Until saved by an obscure alfalfa.

Disdain has sat on my veranda
Smoking silently, the sweat of my brows.
As his chattel, I gave as a server.
In his heart, hatred hemmed a grouse.

I lived with the eccentric enemy
That thought truth is a lie.
Habituated in toxic alchemy
Hate like molten drunk me high.

Joy was stripped naked in public
While love hid in fear of the haters and unknown.
Every day, I got trepidatedly sick.
One day though, flute of freedom may be blown.

For now, in the pool of anxiety
I pray for Pluto to pay a visit.
I'm stripped of any fakery piety.
In death, let me on throne sit.

William Warigon

April Dance To Corona's Funneral

I am a cunning child of April
Wearing of my faith's apparel
I am planning to dress to the T
Soon prospects of being happy
Will rear their beautiful heads
And we all will get out of beds

This month, Corona will rest in hell
Those whom he's sent to their shell
Will cast that first stone
Its malaise's simply done
With our drums, set and readied
We'll dance for the found remedy

As we carry Corona's casket to its final hellish place
Dirges will be thrown to the hurricane
Warmest smiles and laughter will adorn every face
The malady will be washed by the Latter Rain

No more would godless prancing steal the day with fright
No more would we succumb to ill that flies from foreign fight
Like winged wind, our flight is to victory's utmost height
To see the back of this demonic man-made blight

The plight is without its might
In April, its power is broken and amply ashed
From its grave comes a Light
that's sure to change this arena once harshed

No flowers will beautify its mound
No tears will smooth its rapture
We will send it away with the sound
Of music made in bliss to capture

224

Such strange an anathema
That gave the earth an interminable hauteur of grief
Will be buried in a corner
Where there is no shaft of moonlight's whiff

Join the endless burial procession
Corona's grave is hereby hungry
It is not an abdominal congregation
April closes Corona's quandary
So, let's dance to its grave without remorse
With cruel Corona gone, nothing is worse

William Warigon

The Name Like None Other

When waltzing like one crazy,
Sporting innocence like baby,
I am in glory decorated realm
Singing praises to Your Name.

I seek no fortune or fame
But rely fully on Your Name
As the Key that opens every mystery.
That Master Key has done me well, thoroughly.

A Name that rises above every name
Has covered every indiscretion and shame.
It has brought succour and rest
When things were not the best.

It has lighted my path many times.
Table filled with food without dimes
In torn pockets to substantiate.
Faith in the Name is the initiate

It has rained snowflakes of healing
When the body and soul were burning.
In vain would temptation make me take the Name in vain.
In deference, I give reverence to your holy Name.

Windy Winesome Wednesday

Before me an ethereal beauty unfurling
This golden grey morning
'Ere the wind so sweet, scented and sun warmed
Umbrella tree boughs rustle and toss in the wind
Enchanted paths that lead to love unwind
Noam trees bearing their harvest munificently
Old Mountain with prosaic name sits in contemplation holy
Neighbours with their knowing smiles
And gossipy halos, shout
Sweet coated hellos
Flighty flirting birds pirouetting
In wild abandon
The windy haze, have me dazed
Oh, my heavenly days!

William Warigon

To Leah And Rachel

Prologue

He is in love with two women
One is special, a mother hen
Fluffy feathered friend
And not a freaky fiend
The other Is none that I know
Best let time unveil and show

He can't do without the two:
"The one is a summer in October
The other is hot and spicy too
In the cold arms of December"
So said he to me
It is so, or maybe

The Theme

I am the other woman
I have adorned many a man's bed
But none is like this man
He is kindness in purple, well bred
A tickler of senses, a generous
Carer worthy of the best rosses

The Plot

I'm in love with two wonder women
But I am not a scoundrel one bit
I'm a day eagle needing a night wren
I'm nuctunal owl needing sun to fit

Completeness is harmony
In the lips of sweet Melody
Pleasure and pain plain entwined
Like falling rain and the sunshine

Epilogue

You are my evergreen everglade
Smoking hot and yet epitome of tenderness
I offered myself to your sharp blade
Pure, untouched, worthy and undisputedly stainless

You are my soulmate
I remain your loving pet
Forever my nest nestles deep within you
None other can this union ruin with rue

THE END

The Tear Of A Tearing Nation

Where did we go wrong?
In this nation building?
We used to sing one song
That bound us in uniting.
Our sad sun's setting as we pierce
Each other in the back of our hearts.
The cloth that we wore with peace
Is torn by the vile insurgents' darts

Are we slinking off in dire defeats?
With a résumé of the failed feats?

The mystique of the highest-ranking office
Slowly eroded like a new gangrenous orifice.
Pestilential presidential place
Fazed with hatred it faced.

Go back to the drawing table
Chalk a thought to enable
On why you, the happiest in the universe
Shed tears of despair like sad hearse
On your wedding anniversary.

Your back is too weary to carry
Milk in your dry, greyed sunken udders.
You were once a giant used to subduing thunders
Until they whimper instead of roaring;
Until they run in the limpid clouds hiding
Like sniffling dogs with an inferiority complex.
Arise, do not waste like rotten corny cornflakes.

Wake up from your sadness slumber and set our hearts high
On the rolling hills of high hope.
Let joyful assurances put cracks on our patient, stoic lips that cry.
You can still make it to the top!
Be bounteous.
Be plenteous.

William Warigon

230

Own Taste Of Mine Own Medicine

THIS GOLDEN GREY, fine morning
I woke with unlinking of mourning.
Upon my snow kissed, whitened window pane, perched a pigeon;
Beaked a missive from a millionaire ex- legionnaire of my legion.
Glasses perched on my beak-like nose,
I nosed through its coarse contents thus:

"THE DAY OF reckoning has come:
Skeletons swept from my cupboard
Spring to haunt me like wild gnome.
Everyone thought me above board.
The tireless truth that trails the true
Has come to set me free from lies,
That had me so warted all through.
Stench of hypocrisy brings flies

TODAY TO Show the lies in my superciliousness,
I was a regnant Czar of high price
The feeble that pay right price I show mercifulness
Otherwise, to the gallows the splice.
Today, turning tides try me
In a domain I once waxed strong.
Teary eyes will torture me
For I never thought I was wrong.

I RODE ON the back of integrity,
Flashing fires of scrubbed scruples
Like a pastor with holy dexterity.
All the way laughing at you, doofus.
Did you not grant me golden chalice?
For my pure perfect charade
That wooed your eyes? My malice
Has paid off. Let me serenade.

I WILL HAVE the will soon to recline
In a corner to eat the spoils
That soiled and spoiled my white lie.
Though your anger boils,
Remorseless, I know your memory is short.
You will see me with trolls
To yet trod upon and own your own port.
This, friend, is how it rolls.

THIS PRISON WALLS are just for show.
I will show soon to the world
Acolytes we sup together. Slow,
And yet fast crumbled world
Of mirage shows truth as naked as day.
But I am unbothered.
In the world where lies are truth's way,
I can't be encumbered..."

William Warigon

Teacher The Treasure

The teacher that spared not the rod
Had the pupil unspoiled.
The teacher had an inflection to lord
Loads of education unsoiled.
With deft diffidence
And sheer reverence
We held the teacher in such awe.
From him, we knew many a lore.

He was the tidal wave we swum in.
From him we knew how not to sin.
Under his tutelage we were canopied.
His voice rang like the school bell
That woke us in the morning to sow a seed.
In us he opened a floodgate so well
that deserved effusive compliments.
He had tacitly turned us into intellectual investments.

Our hunger for knowledge perched archly above his head,
As he strived to have our keen desires aptly fed.

Upon graduation, we looked at the teacher with endearing warmth such,
As his grin of pride lit up the hall.
He deserved to smirk away for getting us out of ignorance's hutch.
His name, written in gold in fame's hall,
Will be forever engraved in our hearts.
He's refashioned us to the science of our arts.
We treasure the tenacious teacher.
A preacher that makes an achiever.

William Warigon

233

The Village Sphere

I long to twist the arm of time
And make it run catawampus in a good way
So that it'd bring forth the behind
And those good old days would come my way

I long to mandate time's fragile heart
To beat like the African drums of yore
To the songs sang at Mama's hearth
Weaving wild yarns of the many folklore

The aesthetic air and serendipitous sphere
Swings of peace and wines of tranquillity
Were hallmarks that made my village fare
As the envy of a drab neighbouring locality

But alas the village is now but a memory
Those welcoming arms of the mud huts
Replaced by many built a high-rise storey
Rounded by high walls and steely shuts

The forest we used to roast the rats and snakes
Are replaced with soldier like array of mansions
Owned by strange rats that never tasted our snakes
They are the ones with full pockets calling the shots

The languid river that coveted our nakedness
Is no more a swimming parking lot
Sand filled to cater for a gas emitting madness
These are what are now our dreary lot

Where are the children throwing muds?
Grey, old men under the trunky baobab shade
Are now extinct, we now have demi gods
Becking-a-call to us their second hand made

Time, cruel time, repent this instant
Bring back our hungry bellies and sweet joy
Those were simpler times of suppliant
Easiness; air of the coquettish and the coy

Under the road, give us the dusty paths
Bring birds back and the inquisitive vultures
Cats chasing mice, dogs daring cats
Unearth the ancestral colours of our cultures

William Warigon

Ready

For

A little drop of something

A little drop of something
As it fell, I caught
Not the liquid that presumed
No more a thing now taught

I am a nothing yet a something
I am simply me
As with all that moved from crawl
We try our best to be

A little drop of optimism
Can change more than day
Yet a little drop of pessimism
Can ruin more can say

Some lose grip and then do slip
Some do hit ground hard
Some recover to be another
Deck of playing cards

A little drop of outside thinking
A bit of being me
An individual within a multitude
That's the one I be

Have a set of certain rules to follow
Rest is just a game
Providing there's no injury
Attributed to my name

A little drop of something
Understanding we do call
Just how great would be present state
If was shared by all

A little drop yet so vital
To guarantee a future
A little drop is the beginning
Of something we should nurture

Ian Wilcox

A matter of perception

Was it men who named the Mendips?
Did women invest woe?
That is not a subject
For health I wish to go!

If God is dog but backwards
Why are our attitudes extreme?
Praise one to highest lever
Yet to other can be mean

If Black and White a type of sight
That some animals do use
Why are they then so colourful?
Surely must confuse

Pre and post my coffee injection
Find myself in deep reflection
Stupid questions myself do ask
To fulfil the writing task

Am I normal or abnormal?
Do I even care
If everyone was first one
Then with which compare?

Why do cats like fish
Yet hate water in much they live?
What i better in bigger picture?
To receive or to give

Am I really me?
Or just some strange collection
Of things and bits we cannot see
A matter of perception

A message to a once Minor

A kick to that which shall remain unnamed
A jolt to which we do
The stark fact of how we act
Not the subtle clue
Somewhere some place you will fall
No fault but just the curve
The earning in the learning
A fact that we can't swerve

The Honeybee that we see
Turns out a Dragonfly
The hits we take to ourselves make
The wonderment of why
Simplicity cannot be
When tester one does suffer
Yes, that thing with which does bring
Attraction to another

Why would you to this go through
The rewards are worth the challenge
More in store as love is core
Everything can manage
Been and done and had some fun
Now it is your turn
Learn don't spurn for life an Urn
Holding everything can be

They say that I should act my age
I then ask them which one?
The age of when I came here
Or the age that life begun
Where do I find myself in future?
Honestly no idea
Yet you are way behind me
Can change a certain part

A Mother's question

Son, will you pull your pants up!
Underwear is under for a reason
Son, that 'talks' is like gibberish
Are we now in silly season?

Son, when are you going to eat a proper meal?
Not just stuff you buy
How about some cooking lessons?
Not so hard if but did try

Son, when are you going to finally let?
Someone make an honest man of you
Look at your Father
See what it can do

Son, when are you going to spread your wings?
See what it can bring
They are building so many now
But each Castle needs its King

A Son's reply

Mom, you are a fine one to talk!
Kaftans had their time
Sometime last century
Even then a fashion crime!

Mom, I am just helping save the Planet
It may come as a surprise
But what I eat is kind of neat
For is just chemicals in disguise

Mom, I am showing that I'm caring
Not inflicting self upon poor soul
Father often tells me
He missed an open Goal

Mom, are you trying to kill me?
If so tell me reason why
You talk of wings no human has
Then ask me when will fly!!

A myriad of misconception

A raindrop fell from a rain cloud
'Free at last!' it thought
Until it found on the ground
Into a puddle caught

A salmon swam against the current
To its birth place it did try
If not killed on the journey
There, exhausted, it will die

A Homeless person gets a refuge
Maybe one night or maybe week
Then, after taste or perhaps reminder
Cast out again and must food seek

A Soldier serves for their Country
Yet upon return denied a voice
Is this truly Liberty
Is this freedom to rejoice?

A myriad of misconception
A 'magic marker' some do find
Plundering people for 'bestowed' by Ballot
Thus, the blind does lead those blind

Anything and everything
Takes and then does measure
Self destruction the instructions
Of it take a twisted pleasure

Alas my Hearties we are normal
When we do what others do
World around us masochistic
Masochism lies inside of you

A Rainbow has seven colours

Have you changed? Can make a case?
Different you because difference face
Needed push to break the chain
Needed prod to engage the Brain
I used to ask why always rain
Used to think all was pain
Then I found open space
When realised all one Race

Once was blind but now I see
Once did see now classed as Blind
Once was trapped in my own opinion
Now have it but I am free
Shed the thought that always right
Shed arrogance as Night sheds light
I am correct in some, not all
Not my place to make that call

A Rainbow has seven colours
Humans grouped into four
Yet we are like the Rainbow
Mix and blend to make many more
Maths it talks of 'common denominator'
Humans speak of 'Lover/ Hater'
Yet both are just but some test
Over the head of the rest

Found m life on different shore
Honestly, can't ask for more
What I have I want encore
Did my time on what call 'Tour'
I've now moved on to better things
Enjoying all that it brings
Opened eyes with surprise
Not quite there but getting wise

A reflection in perception

The challenged kid lived in confusion
Never knowing who truly were
The older 'kid' found acceptance
Guess they found the cure
Grew thick skin with soft within
Chose to fight when only matters
All the rest just simply refuse
On the street the refuse scatters

One day grew the new true
The person found them self
The adored as explored
That once so hidden wealth

They said

Once my thinking was barbed wire
Now chocolate fondant rules
Once I hated all and everything
Then realised that Hate's for fools
Once react to all and everything
Now I just to them ignore
Precious is the time we spend here
We should make it so much more

Who I me and what want to be?
The question one must ask
Who am I and should I try?
That's a challenging task
One day a victim, next a symbol
Symbol of what we can achieve
Mixed with a certain sense of humble
In ourselves we must believe

Yes, I don't fit in certain thinking
I don't meet what they like
I am not the all and everything
In the line I am a spike
I am me and will always be
I was given this great chance
So to those who's contempt grows
Say so simply 'now let's dance'

A teardrop on the fire

Overview of the obvious
A reflection on demand
To err is a simple thing
However, results planned?
Misery for profit
They haves preying on the poor
The cycle of this thing we live in
A practice to abhor

A teardrop on a fire
Evaporates before impact
Yes, a deluge of them teardrops
Might stir some simple act
The we become the true we
Not the class divide
When the victims stand together
The injustice it can't hide

Misery a history
So common we accept
Yet we are the fuel for it
Because we simply let
Let those who perpetrate
Carry on with no regard
Of the rest in misery
That hold elections card

Not that the 'opposition'
Would change the things they do
All are much alikeness
System needs that new
Not just one who maintained promises
When needed numbers to progress
A whole new set of people
Who value self-profit as a less?

Less than they benefit
of those they, supposedly are there to benefit
A fantasy is true
For we are merely what have become

A thousand dreams

One content with time spent
With soul that matched their own
The nomad grew some roots
The wanderer a Home
Through passing years and lost fears
Contentment came to roost
With it came another name
Life got a new boost

A thousand dreams and then the means
The search they didn't know
The reward fate did accord
Then began to show
Life, love and liberty
Not just some saying that most hear
Life, love and liberty
When we find and hold that dear

Many sharing the benefits of caring
Both giving and receiving
Each to own in how shown
Each yet still believing
Each can write with new sight
The simple yet profound
When with one they become
One now on firm ground

Each know

As stories go this both new and old
On wings of wanting soared a soul
Searching for that something
That to make them whole
When I heard your name was never the same
That's what you did to me
When got together I knew never
What I was could no longer be

A to Zee the grateful me

A an apple that fell from tree
B a boy that wished to see
C the call of something new
D the daring so did do
E eternal that they said
F the fortune which found in head
G a goal they achieved
H the happiness when one a agreed
I the irreplaceable now have got
J for joy that defies plot
K the kiss, the first remember
L that lingers from that November
M the making of the Man
N the nurturing so they can
O observation for cannot hold
P for place but that's been told
Q the Queen he did discover
R the rapture when added other
S a statement proud to show
T a triumph they do know
U undying for brave hearted
V the volume when are parted
W wish to return
X symbol kiss that cannot spurn
Y the yesterday but not tomorrow
Z a zealot who fantasy borrow

Just one alphabet that is true
Yet a message can shine through
Writer still so in love
With his Angel from above
Who chose to walk on his world
Greeting him with wings unfurled

Another chance and space

The evening drawing to an end
A decision you now must make
Will this be the start of something more?
Is this a make or break?

I want more but can't demand
I can only pray
Not to something more than me
Just for another day
Can you see it in my eyes?
Can you hear it in my voice? Can you understand my dear
Is time now to make a choice

From the time first met
In the queue
Waiting in that coffee shop
I knew what I must do

That shared walk out
Before going separate way
Made arrangements for tonight
And so now do I say

I want more but can't demand
I can only pray
Not to something more than me
Just for another day
Can you see it in my eyes?
Can you hear it in my voice? Can you understand my dear?
Is time now to make a choice

The clock ticks by behind you
I see through open door
If not tonight then that's okay
As long as again am sure

There will be another moment
Another chance and space
When I can soak in radiance
As look upon your face

Another day to be what may

Friday Four and who could want more
Than to see a Saturday five
Just as be with decree
It's a joy to be alive!
If from above you find a love
One that will survive
In physical and not unreal
A feeling that can thrive

Whatever be I am me
Whatever way I choose
Whatever feeds this insanity
In insane can't lose
Cut this skin to see within
I'll show you just like you
Paint your picture with this fixture
You are merely what you do

Believe in me and believe in wrong
You should first believe in self
The options wrong to them not strong
Or suffer some types of ill health
Look at her that female purr
That symbol of regret
Look at him in ego swim
The persona they do let

I remember when got crazy
The day myself did know
Not the crazy of that hazy
That which helped to grow
Grow you see that which I be
That who went and found their lover
Not where grew and battled through
That with a different cover

I hear those songs that don't belong
I hear those that do too
I am that be a cacophony
I am a Symphony true

Another day

The hour hand moved past the vertical
The second time so starts again
Illumination by thing electrical
Buying and fitting can be a pain

The scene seems peaceful
What more can I say?
Relaxing in the quietness
On this, another day

The beginning of something wonderful
Just option have to choose
That in self so beautiful
This blessing I can't lose

The challenges of softly tackling
Once more into the fray
This fight one enjoyable
As this, another day

Some figures change but not that strange
A record must be kept
Happy/ Sad, the good, the bad
Nothing should be swept

Learning from the last one
Learn from future if we may
Opportunity there to see
As this, another day

Limb

The old phase
"Out on a limb"
A reality as I sit
Up high
Holding tight as I
watch
Careful of the roots
tipping
Engulfed in the depth
of darkness
Watching below as lights
play
In shadowy corners of
darkness
How does one reach this
point
Of uncertainty that rocks
your world
That plays card games as
jokers win
Or the roll of face less
dice
A string of doors that hold
A mystery
I see them down there without
A key
Teasing on the tides pull
of in and out
if I slip and fall am I
caught
Or lost again in the shadows
of doors
Locked beyond my
reach
Or will I wake swinging on
A moon beam
Stars lighting my
WAY

Janice Fisher

Morning

My window view shows
A busy spider left its
Jewelled web in its busy
Netting
But the only thing caught
Was my view as I look
Beyond to see the morning
Fog
As if it a blanket covering
Earth to protect its dampness
In the cool of fall
The sun begins to peek through
As it turns back the foggy blanket
To wake earth with its
Warmth
Birds sit on the fence shaking
Their feathers of dampness
As their songs begin to fill
The air
Dark clouds move in from the
West with a teasing push to
The sun rises as it slowly brings
A morning shower
Opening the door, a freshness
Fills my intake of breath of
Newly turned fields that
Hold a promise of springs
Growth
I watch the clouds play peek a boo
With the sun as they give earth its
Morning shower

Janice Fisher

Box

The old saying flows ...
"Look outside the Box"
Possibility meaning, we ...
"Shelter Within"
Which rides the waves
Of truth
"Our comfort zone"
So in our reach we seek
The Universe
It holds a mystery of ...
"Unknowns"
Where focus drifts in ...
"Questions"
Answers are predictions ...
"Of Thoughts"
I think ...but no not ...
"Yet"
Some think our destination ...
"Wrote"
Before the soul's connection ...
"Of Body"
Science travels farther than our ...
"Limits"
So, although the future path ...
"Unknown"
Predictions always fall within ...
"Grasp"
We humans never know the stillness ...
"Of our thoughts"

Janice Fisher

Depth

We search the depth of
Emotions
Sometimes drowning in
Them
Sinking in so many unknown
Whys
Finding no answers we can
Accept
Mental anguish pushes one to
Disparities
Selecting to be alone in this
Anguish
Holding oneself tightly closed to
Acceptance
A safety net that pushes life's
Reality
As if not seen its not there at
All
Only truth is seen in the depth of
Eyes
The windows to the souls
Needs
That has closed its shades
Alone
When in truth s flow ...one is never
Alone

Janice Fisher

Leaves

Falling leaves ...
Fall like rain drops
Rolling across the
Road
Crunching as they
Tumble
As if an unseen person
Walks on them
There colors matching
The red sun
Seeking its way through a
Smokey sky
The breeze turns the yellow
Leaves
Matching the cut wheat
Fields
Some drying to brown as
Earths nourishment
Tree limbs sway as if to
Catch
Their fly away clothing leaving
Them naked
As they bare their limbs for
Approaching winter
As summer flees and Autumn
Waits in falling leaves
Years end comes to quickly as
Nature views
The soon snow white of
Purity

Janice Fisher

Link

I am....
But a link in a chain of
genes ...
A complex of chromosome
of heredity ...
A lineage of my family
pedigree ...
My thoughts that random
float ...
Come from the depth of
this passage ...
Passed on throughout
history ...
A photograph from era
past ...
OH ! It is I, but behold
It's not ...
I am but an extra duplicate
of her ...
DNA linked me to this
person...
If I continue the back road
of history ...
I'll find clones of me that
are no longer ...
I stand in a time they knew
not ...
As in the future someone will
be a clone...
"OF I"

Janice Fisher

Looking

Never look back
It's in memories
Bank of lessons
You may have learned
Or perhaps this time
Around you will
With each sunrise
Comes new paths
It's up to each how
There walked
We become a clone
Of a group
Lost to self-awareness
Of who we are
Or we search within for
Our own strength
We learn to love ourselves
Then it flows to others
Hate has no place in our
Future as the days turn
Forward
We also take baby steps
To find where we lost the
Simplicity of truth in
Right and wrong
Soon this page in life will
Turn with a page not yet
Read but we wait in
Hope

Janice Fisher

We

We All ...
Stand in silent
Moments
Our eyes ...
Search beyond
View
In hope...
To find our world
Again
We see ...
It's under attack by
Error
Man made ...
Or Nature's twisting
Times
Call it space ...
Fires, tornadoes and
Floods
Tears Fall ....
Emotions trying as death
Seeks
Screams flow ...
Hold on our nation we're
Coming
Hands reaching ...
Seeking a unity but falling
Short
But ...
The world turns to tomorrow's
Hope

Janice Fisher

The Fall

Sometimes ...
We fall like in
Fantasy
Stories that capture
Youth
But an adult version of
Turmoil
Trying to roll with life's
Punches
Thoughts come in hurricane
Force
Unable to catch their throttle
Of speed
Like drops of spilled
Ink
Dropping like summers
Rain
An endless fall of search
Never ending

Janice Fisher

Tick-Tock

Time waits for no
One
Where were you a
Minute ago
Lost in the hours
Shuffle
Between wake and
Sleep
Sun rises and sets
Day gone
Did you notice her
Smile
See the rainbow
Of promise
Throw the ball back
Landing
At your walking
Feet
Catch the scent of the
Last blooms
Feel the rains freshness
Beginning
Really taste the lunch rapidly
Gone
Trying to beat the clock in
Shuffled papers
You lost time never
Seen
Never to catch the missing
TICK-TOCK

Janice Fisher

Perfection

Is that disjointed run, against self and the wind,
The beauty in brokenness,
Scars adorning a career,
It's the dream of a thousand hills,
Waves bringing home a pilot and a guarantee soldier,
Perfection is the music of silent soul in prayer,
A child holding an old man's hand to cross the road,
It's a vow to serve till death,
It's life partaking doubt at every sunrise,
Perfection is duty to love the unforgivable,
It's calling a neighbour just because,
Perfection is the colour of life even caked with dirt,
Perfection is stopping every while to marvel,
At rolling marvel's that ignite the flow of Poesy,
Perfection is an end game,
That knits the body back to its fold,
It is laughter at what blimps tears,
Looking at the moon and its faith,
Perfection is love with its stinging nettle and drowsy dew,
Perfection is every moment breath goes in and comes out.
And that makes all equal before the blue sky,
Favor is fates cup to be partaken with gratitude.
Perfection is everything even that which we discount.

Nancy Ndeke

264

What is wrong?

The light has gone from your day,
What is wrong?
The smile that always used to stay
Has disappeared now gone.
The songs you used to sing
Have lost their cheerful ring.

Nothing is so bad
To keep you down for long
Let me hug you close,
With kisses and hugs,
Return your face to norm.
Nothing now is wrong.

I Sit

I sit and gaze at the sky.
With fluffy images floating by,
Ever changing re-arranging
So, relaxing to the eye.

At times static pure white pillows
Bathed in brilliant sun light,
Hang resting on an azure bed.
Recovering from drama they have fled.

The breeze changes tempo
Gloomy clouds collide till lightning strikes,
Thunder roars with the need to vent,
Rain falls to soak the land.

I sit and gaze amazed
At this theatre in the sky.
Allowing me moments
Of relaxation and inner calm.

WobblingPen

Cafe Chat

Choosing a place next to a wall so I can survey the room.

Watching the people entering, meeting, and greeting.

Pondering where they have come from, are they
local or have they travelled far?

Is that little group a family, or just good friends?

The two men must be farmers, as they are talking avidly
about their cows and the need to change their feed.

The woman sitting on her own, is she here on
business, or will she be staying overnight?

An old lady quietly reading a book and drinking a cup of coffee, her cake has
just arrived it looks delicious. She gave the waitress a lovely smile in thanks.

I wonder if I should try one too, I might just be a devil?
But they may not have them gluten free!

Two mums slipping in with their prams and their quietly sleeping babies.
Grateful for time to sit and share their feelings about their experiences
of early motherhood, to be waited on, and served with a tasty lunch.

Whoopee! I am able to have one of those delicious cakes,
wonderful, so I can sit here a lot longer observing the
customers, and trying to lip, read the cafe chat.

Oh Bed

Oh bed you seem so inviting,
Yet your pull is not enough
I must keep on writing, writing.
Stories slip with speed across my mind.
I dare not stop or they will escape.
I try to keep on repeating so I can find
Them one more time.
Oh bed I know you are still calling,
I am sorry to keep ignoring your desire.
One more line to write before falling,
Into bed to rest my oh so weary head,
Till morning.

WobblingPen

I sit

I sit and gaze at the sky.
With fluffy images floating by,
Ever changing re-arranging
So relaxing to the eye.

At times static pure white pillows
Bathed in brilliant sun light,
Hang resting on an azure bed.
Recovering from drama they have fled.

The breeze changes tempo
Gloomy clouds collide till lightning strikes,
Thunder roars with the need to vent,
Rain falls to soak the land.

I sit and gaze amazed
At this theatre in the sky.
Allowing me moments
Of relaxation and inner calm.

Marriage

The ceremony is the permission to blend together, and start the journey.
How complicated it becomes, or how divine depends on you both.
It can last barely a day or an entire lifetime of
love, commitment and responsibility.
I would not change mine, would you?

This Corona Virus is testing marriage and partnerships as never
before. Make renewed efforts, that yours survives these very difficult
times. We have never had so much time together on our own, small
irritations fester if left unchecked. Finding small things to please one
another, becomes important. Like finding the glasses, or hearing aids,
or a vase placed on the table with garden flowers. Calling you, so you
do not miss a favourite programme, arriving to find a cup of tea waiting.
Making a meal and washing up together, oh there are many more.

In our old lives before the virus, these things would have been
unremarkable. Now they are vital to pleasing both of us, and of
course being in our own bubble, hugs and cuddles are priceless.
Expressing our love and hopes in words and on paper, become more
necessary now. If you mean it say it, never let it be too late.

Take care, stay safe, help when you can.

Penny Wobbly

The Hat

The hat I wear I never knew who owned it before.
It sit's on my head a party to many conversations.
Some private, others to spread to one and all.
It has protected my head and face from the sun's ferocious glare.
Sparing my skin from faster deterioration.
When it rains, I keep my outings brief.
Taking you undercover, to save your brim from ungainly waving.
Placing you in the cupboard up high to sit and dry.
Your brim has captured stories and jokes told with laughter.
Reminding me on the next outing of the memories we shared.
When it is time for me to go, I hope you will not be discarded.
That someone else will wear you, as I have done.
In the meantime, let's have fun.

A Wish Fulfilled

To shut my eyes and wish you close.
To send a breath upon the wind to draw you in.
To make believe my wish is true.
To finally celebrate you are home again.
It is true, it is true, thank you.

WobblingPen

Are circumstances circular?

The consequence of circumstance
The blessing in disguise
The time spent at non event
The startling sheer surprise
The truth that see, finally
The curtains drawn to side
The fall of fool so can stand tall
The false tall that falls amongst the tide

I miss the comfort of stupidity
The belief in my own sense of great
I miss the joy of ignorance
Conducive with them states
If I tell of sins where to begin?
For past, present with more to come
I am a mix they cannot fix
Yet some of it is fun

I heard the Thunder and then I turned
Changed my ways before got burned
Dodging bolts that came my way
Heard the cracks that cause affray
I have been told as we get old
Repetitive is a sedative true
The only thing I wish to bring
Is wish many have no clue

So, are circumstances circular?
Going to return
Depending on the size of ring
How many from which learn
Diameter a difficult one
For don't know around have travelled
Must be I say at least half way
Judging by the what's unravelled

Are you Family?

Sense did meet Sensibility
"Are you my offspring?" it did ask
"No" reply from that shy
"That's Sensible, I have somewhat different task"

Plausible met implausible
"Are you my Brother?" It did ask
"No, I am your opposite
I have different mask"

Love and Hate did not relate
In any shape or form
Each could not get what the other let
So, opposites were sworn

The ornamental Octagon

The ball that has been walloped
Flattened out of round
That doesn't roll, upon my soul!
More sort of clunky one found

Bought it from strange shop
Quirky seemed the themes
Even sold some strange nets
Said to capture dreams

A Paper weight? I am not sure
A big one if it is
Definitely a conversation starter
For is hard to miss

The ornamental Octagon
The double cube in one
How many squares? I wouldn't dare
To count and forget sum

Are you trapped?

I want to kill someone!!
Slowly and with pain
From projected suffering
My new drive attains
I want to torture someone else
Though I do not know
Murder by the distance
Compulsion it does grow

Their day will seem quite normal
No threat that they can see
Yet lurking in the shadow is a killer
That killer simply me
Slowly I will extract
The addiction that they suffer
For I am a twisted drug
I truly am like no other

I will start with common sense
Mash it with some glee
Introduce into my world
Welcome to Insanity
I am Satan's tutor
Taught and taught him well
I discovered Poetry
Are you trapped now in my spell?

As good as gets

A raindrop falls from the sky
Some look up and wonder why
Mother Nature replenishing
So can new help to bring
Clouds then part to spread some light
Warmth and things when are bright
Actions beyond comprehension
More chemistry than care to mention

Little legs tackle pavement
Free from the Buggy and restraint
'Me one of those little ones!
No! Dear Mom I ain't!!'
Pop, pop, pop of the Moped
Drowned out again by big brother's roar
Weaving between our enclosed carriages
Lack of walking we adore

Come the time and come the crime
Lethargy for all to see
Effluence in affluence
How we seem to be
Takeaway for can't stay
In the place did cook
Loosely termed by those pittances earned
Instruction cards but not shook

From complacency of what be
An earner for another
Success rests on being best
So, encouragement they smother
All we are with Bus and Car
Redundant our legs make
Just how much of current such
Can a mind honest and freely take

All I am is what I can
Be within some rules
Others, more, I ignore
When trading us as fools
I harm no-one with rise of Sun
None before it sets
I am not the perfect one
Just as good as gets

As the fashion

The last time that I saw you
A different view I took
The open you had passed through
Now you're a new closed Book
The last time we had conversation
Will not now be the same
The person I remember
Is just that which has name

The salvos that we fired
The points of view we shared
Showed a person with some feelings
Someone simply cared
I am not perfect I admit
Yet better than what be
What has changed the person knew
What made the shell that be?

Yes, I fear too many years
Since we last did meet
A different you if choose to do
Same place we plant our feet
What became of that in name
I once called a non blood Brother?
That now see a mystery
A stranger or another

The delectation of situation
Sadly I can't say
The consternation a revelation
The price we have to pay
When visiting the things that were
The great sadness might incur
The past a blast that didn't last
As the fashion to wear fur

Ask of me my opinion

Once upon a time in place like mine
Another cover did belong
Some said that they were different
Some can be so wrong

A 'nothing much 'who just accepted such
Ask of me who I am?
For the answer would not know
For who I was is in the past
Before for today I grow

Ask of me my opinion
Prepare to spend some time
For not who be agree with me
The definition of what is Crime

Ask of me my fantasy
That with some do share
The absurd that is one word
The single one called care

And when the new Dawn is born will we still mourn
That we did not accept the task?
To leave behind that which makes blind
Too scared to the question ask

Has something changed to word Liberty?
Something that just passed by?
For what do see it cannot be
Leading to the why

A single marvel can make magic
A single act can make that tragic
A mood can make a maelstrom
Time to think where we belong

Ask

Amorphous and will always be
Sediment is what do see
Just eruption interruption
Another case of that could be
Simplicity an ideology
All do wish to gain
Yet the space before it face
Cause of so much pain

Rush of Head where have you led
Let's stop this train right now
Enough have said to send to bed
Let's laugh and brow let's frown
Yes, let's think with morning drink
Not as go to bed
A sharpener Mind I think you'll find
A better tool instead

Hypothetical or philosophical
Who knows but not me
Energetic or just prospective
Do you want to be?
Fixation nation new situation
All strive to hope to rise
Yet a 'fail' so now email
No longer a surprise

So this is what we want to be?
The world without identity
Just another on a screen
How much really does that mean?
So this is new? The magic brew?
More now out than in
The Blue line now seems fine
For not alone as thin

Do I ask too much of life as such
To at least have dance?
Maybe then you can see
If only have a chance

At least we're having fun

The trees in breeze shed their leaves
A sight now not often seen
When replace with some haste
That which once was Green
Cement and brick do the trick
After natural remove
We are greater than Mother Nature
So, we shall 'improve'

'Don't like this' get the gist
Extinct does now become
For many years had little fear
Until we decided we're number one
Yet without we have no clout
No food on which to live
Give and take for goodness sake
Give back what does given

A car alarm can cause harm
Not in self it's true
But a part of a start
Of polluted me and you
We've robbed the earth for fossil fuel
Now we switch to atom made
Money in the misery
'Beneficial' the big charade

So, take a stand upon this land
Non-threatening please do
For a gift and with it
Can see this passage through
Part of it or none of it
Really is the choice
Plunder for the number
It seems grabbers have the voice

Look at me and what do see?
Another guilty one
Progression is regression
At least we're having fun

Contemplation consideration

One did stare into open air
Decision they must make
Promise failed and hope sailed
A different chance did take
Now alone with what known
Yet better for the crime
Another cover for wanting lover
In more than act sublime

"Shall I shun a shining Sun?
Shall I choose to hide?
Shall I see just misery?
In name of what call Pride?
Shall I go to what did know?
Before becomes again
Shall I be that thing you see
Wrapped in so much pain?"

Words that said inside of Head
A familiar song
Each time sung a new begun
Just with heart now strong
The journey's take that so often break
The reason comes as shock
Yet a blessing in disguise
As after one takes stock

Will I wait for you again?
Chance again to feel this pain
Will I something new then gain?
The answer still is flouting
Could this be a travesty?
If my emotions not set free?
I am just the simple me
Open t the gloating

Corners

In the corner I call hope
I raise my hand to say something
In the corner I call expecting
I stay quiet to see what bring
And I am one of many
In many corners stand
I am one of the multiple
Share same thing in different lands

In the corner I call union
I share a drink with a stranger
In the corner I call promise
I do know I feel no danger
All I need to succeed
Is allies in my quest
Those who feel we are still
Equal such as laid to rest

In the middle lays the riddle
Corners known but not the space
The vacuum of the various
The variations set by face

In the corner I call reason
Reason/ logic but also why
Simple if we think about
Simple if we try
Barriers are our behaviour
Of the few but that's enough
Standing by their illustrations of power
Hiding by playing tough

In the corner I call Prospects
Stands a box not yet touch
For it contains more than my future
It is Us and as such
The way ahead is first led
By admission of a faults
Unless we first recognise
That box is filled with noughts

Could we have

The Trees that were, animals killed for fur
The destruction we introduced
The cables laid then new ways made
The scars we have produced

It seems to me we cannot see
The treasure that bestowed
Seems to be we feel free
To ignore the warnings told
Nothing new in what we do
Just acceleration
Nothing new despite what through
As passing generation

The rewards reap when life is cheap
Compared to shares can buy
The suggestion of a question
Why the reason why

Please sit with me so both can see
The path we burn together
Please sit with me and maybe be
Part of the future whether

Whether ends justify the means
Whether all as good as seems
Whether better old ways been
Whether we can just mix both

If some which said stays in head
If slightly alters way now bred
In the want and to which led
Could we have a better future?

I cannot show you but can speak
I cannot make you think to seek
I can merely now suggest
Up to you to do the rest

Counting Crows

The dizziness of the 'missingness'
Of those in physicality
Due to things that life it brings
Cannot with them be
The ups and downs, pouts and frowns
The same not really mean
When words heard seem absurd
Through object with a screen

They can still make me happy
Can still make me sad
Yet in both stays thought most
Are the best things ever had
Now we know the things we invented
The rewards but also cost
The gains a pain to feelings train
When count the things we've lost

Counting Crows instead of Shows
Hey now! A flying Cow!
Well what do you say when comes what may
The urge to throw that towel
Soon the Moon will to which swoon
Replacing each day Sun
Irregular is spectacular
When viewing never same one

Bill and Ben with some Flowerpot men
Somewhere deeply stored
The mystery of old chivalry
Part of which were manners shored
Do again? Maybe when
The new becomes the old
The suspicion of repetition
Confirmed when finally told

Counting crumbs at Coffee time

Strawberry jam when mixed with Ham
Makes a strange surprising combination
Yet do we see what it be
The reason of situation?
The irritation of situation
When water from tap ceases for short while
How would we live and be?
When it comes from walking miles?

I am with a Lady of different tone
I am with but I don't own
For she is her and that is fact
Part the reason I did act
We compliment with no Leading
A perfect match of each are needing
Two lost souls full of goals
Repair with love the occasional holes

My Custard was not yellow
Only two things could this mean
Somebody has been tampering
Or it is just a dream
I am partial to a Curry
Though not my favourite dish
I hate my betters' favourite
She absolutely does love Fish!

If we were meant to be up at night
Why do we need artificial light?
We are creatures of the bright
That's how works our thing called sight
Why are 'lefty' things so hard to find?
When I seem to know a lot
Is it that I am the above average?
With the friends I've got

Composed Really Another Pathetic

Many are the making
Some do then do the taking
What the heck in circumspect
Is the difference to which we get

Saw myself in my reflection
Questions asked I could not answer
For am not a real servant
Nor am I the Master
Everything and what did bring
Changing every day
Try to move to improve
Listening to what each day does say

If I could, maybe would some do say I should
Accept my situation
No for me for you see
I disregard the implication

And now for something different

The egg that hacked found a match
Another squeaking thing
Cacophony the thing that be
When to Mother all do sing

That first cry we wonder why
When joy of living should replace
Perhaps they see much more than me
The disasters that we face

I sometimes wish I was a Tree
Elegant with silent strut
Then again maybe not
Some daft species likes to cut

Crazy conversation

"Okay Bacon, what you got?
Me a Sausage has a lot!
Skinny you without a clue
If with salt or not to do"

"Excuse me Sausage but you are wrong
For in Breakfast you belong
I, Panini have a hunch
I better you when come to lunch"

Oh, you silly makeshifts
Mere appetisers to myself
I am many Dinners
Dependent upon wealth"

Twaddle

A thunder sound in October rain
Another misery waits to gain
Yet outside they suffer pain
I'm inside so comfy gain

Traffic state does irritate
Tyres on the road
If I was of evil mind
Would wish that they explode

Brollies now a call to arms
Competition with the prams
All while on the Mobile
Ignoring the 'no hands'

"Make the most of Beans on Toast"
A car went near and far
For a simple staple
And Anus no Guitar!!

Crazy time is so sublime

The melody of harmony
The sound of perfect day
The rapture there to capture
The attitude of 'come what may'
That intuition that comes to fruition
The vision that we see
The sound aloud heard by the crowd
A sound of unity

Wait!
Crazy Time!

The fart had cart so that's a start
The rumble it did grumble
Into air the fart did share
Its presence not so humble

The thought it caught a line not sought
Reeled in and on display
The caster some say Master
Yet to them is just play

The Ice said nice as in device
Span around with drink
For the Blender was the sender
Into another void to sink

The melody of harmony
The this and that when interact
The whole of soul - that perfect goal
The welcome of impact
That much of 'me' that yearns to see
The greater still not shown
The bird unheard for sings in word
The un becomes the known
The end my friend as your eyes bend
Adios to you now send

Create a breeze and reap the whirlwind

The once was warrior but now a soldier
Learnt from it so now is bolder
Wisdom gained when blessed with older
Not your normal rhyme

Sleepless nights but different reason
Not the weather nor the season
Have stayed true so nor is treason
Just found a different flag to follow

No one state nor just one Country
For his companion not like him
Where begin to list the difference?
Sorry but some things still private

'Look at me and what do you see
Man that's parted from Family
Them in issues that should not be
I am helpless to be sanctuary
Look at me and what do you see
I a settled sleeper cannot be
When my own in misery
Wife and Daughter, me makes three'

Now forget that thing 'personal'
Just how many to this call?
Those who parted, those who learn
That with money cannot earn

Different time and different places
Different lives with different Faces
Different hardships, different graces
Yes, I love the difference

Until no when despot how
Shows in herd is merely Cow
I am past being placid
The once a warrior has had tail pulled

Word can cut as deep as blades

Creating almost new

Each time I open sleep filled eyes
Waiting for that orb to rise
Changing colour of the skies
As reflect and then surmise
The past day and what did do
Some reputation and some new
All of which were passing through
To the next and challenge too

Look at clock as take stock
Within Grand Plan just what my status?
The complexity of being me
Coffee then allows hiatus
A sip touch lips and with it
Awakening does grow
Not that you would notice it
Still not prepared to show

The feeble attempt to good tidings send
To those awake or sleeping
For on more than one different shore
Their own time they're keeping
Them and me both mystery
As are others I don't know
Yet some more I will explore
As continue, as do grow

The Caffeine kick does the trick
Eyes adjust to light
Artificial through some riddle
Elasticity - no not right
Need to write for is my plight
Just not sure how to
Come again with paper/ pen
Creating almost new

Criminal cuisine

Take two Hens and scare them
Collect the eggs they've laid
Take a gentle stroll to the Bakery
Steal loaf of Bread they've made
Go to Grans and 'borrow'
Pan she hits granddad with
Also 'lend' some oil
Don't forget the whisk

On returning Home find a bowl
Then 'borrow' neighbours' milk
Careful not to be seen
By the pompous one in silk
Pause a moment to admire
Your gathering prowess
Now there comes the challenge
A basic cooking test

Crack the eggs into the bowl
Add dash of milk and beat
Salt and pepper if you have some
This is really gonna be a treat
Heat granny's pan with some oil
Of bread cut a slice or two
Take a break for a fag
That's what the top chefs do

Now suitably infused with nicotine
A gastronomic delight you must prepare
This not for the faint hearted
You though choose to dare
Take bread and dip into the egg mix
Ensure good coating on each side
Fry until just hint of brown
Serve to self with pride

Criminal cuisine made simple

Croupier plays and sorry days

Zero to Hero in a blinked way
With carefully chosen words we say
Words not that themselves important
When the feeling heard today
Parenthood now understood
The little means a lot
When appreciate current state
Appreciate that which one has got

A new life with Husband/ Wife
Or even current trend
The creation of a nation
That our mistakes can mend
Responsibility I hand to thee
Me and mine fell to the curse
In what we thought was making better
We, in truth, did make things worse

How many of us live on this planet?
How many live comfortably?
We are not that secular
We are part of We
I cannot chance a word I know
But with support we can
Not in this a call my lifetime
But every success does start with plan

On Red laid bet as Croupier set
The gatherer to spin
When we choose two colours lose
The stakes are set to win
Win for them without a care
Prey on those gullible
Short term gain with disdain
Plunging further into trouble

Minutes are meant to make a moment
Use and treasure as come by
Clock is but a memory dock

Someday will know why
Nothing but care can withstand that share
Pain and pleasure in equal measure
Take it in because know you win
The price of your sought treasure

Call me fool, call me old school
Call me want for I don't care
I have that which so much means to me
I have the privilege of Family
Not the best for that is test
When with circumstances do mix
Yet are stronger as time gets longer
Nothing we can't fix

Croupier plays and sorry days
If you fall but don't rise
Everyone has someone
That turned them into wise
Cherish thought when happy caught
Store for reference all the rest
Believe that you can achieve
Realise when blessed

Not by some distant Dietary
To some give comfort true
This is about one more important
This is about the one called you
Play the game with some disdain
Croupier can't fix that which you don't bet
Not quite match for still ongoing
Just you win the Set

Rambling therapeutically
To me at least I find
Apologies if misery
If not partial to my kind
We are we and so should be
If still keep that common link
Whatever and wherever
Let be basis of how now think

Crumpets please with the Coffee

On wing and prayer to get there
Lucky Leprechaun did leap
Had too much of strong stuff
Now his ashes I do keep

The Dragon caused commotion
When Kebab did order plain
Not that the lack of Rabbit food
More the cooked then cooked again

The Fox found box and thought unlocked
Not sure what it did hide
Upturned be so couldn't see
The Badger there inside

The yawn predawn merely pawn
For that which then will come
We do resist in confused mist
For nocturnal have become

The Tick Tock of battery clock
Checking if time is right
With something else on wrist or shelf
Wall mounted just for sight

The quiet that we used to cherish
Now just part of norm
Isolation situation
Until we all conform

Diatribe we try to hide
Successful? You can say
Early Ink doesn't think
It just likes to play

Cry for sleep

A maelstrom in a magic moment
When the body demands sleep
Yet the Head is, again, fed
Scribbling need to keep

The day is done both work and fun
The bed visited for while
The pillow accepted graciously
I think it even had a smile

Then before could sleep adore
Find back in different room
Tapping as unwrapping
Hopefully it's finished soon

The consternation of abbreviations
Before the bean have drunk
Not yet but am wishing
Into its alertness again sunk

Half open eyed with brain fried
Once more the pen does go
Outcome for another one
The reader I don't know

Tap, tap the pat as now am at
Transfer to modern thing
Maybe then both me and pen
Will find that strange sleep thing

A cry for sleep and rest to keep
If only for short time
Will again despite the pain
Engage in writing crime

Cupid came with chemical

Clementine's in the crazy
Situation All Fudged Up
When are we going back?
When will 'normally be top trump?

Orcas in the abyss of understanding
Having wonderful time
Playing in the sea of sense
Once owned by what called mine

Said the tablet that was found
Amongst the rubbish on rubble ground
The message sent too late to sound
Are we the next to be?

Air seemed pure but too late the cure
Irony in action
Loved what had so took it mad
Comfort the distraction

One woke from dream with half know what mean
The rest too horrific to remember
The cause was techno intercourse
Speeding to December

A different name but just the same
The balance went too far
Forgot about that vital 'stat'
Who and what they are?

They love to show what they did know
Creating things that then did grow
Into masters not a servant
Then their power they did show

There once to town came a stranger
Different look and different speak
Habitants greeted warmly
On attraction rose to peak

Slowly the absorbed the townsfolk
With their cunning and their guile
Without knowing soon were following
Independent became disciple

Custard Cavalry

Calling Custard cavalry
This sponge is somewhat dry
Calling some who like some fun
When soak in – don't know why

Calling Custard Cavalry
To make a bed for Prunes
That favourite of the school meal time
Then stomach playing tunes

Calling Custard Cavalry
You go well with some Jam
Sweet is neat for a treat
Not sure you'll go with Ham

Names

Horatio better known
By his final name
Such way he in History
He gained in death his fame

Shakespeare shared in life and past
A certain unique style
Studies now copiously
In day they travelled miles

Lyndon B got overlooked
Assuming that there role
When the famous Kennedy
Eyes did unexpected roll

Caligula became familiar
Not for good reason true
More distaste at how did waste
Power and what did do

Does it

The day it starts as that of old
The one of many that has been told
The new thing is what can bring
Make Heart cry or make it sing

You hide from me that thing called Future
You are, I think, in recess
So today is just what may
With a today I am at rest

Does it get much easier?
When embark on different life?
Does it get much simpler?
When avoids the strife?
Does that Sun still rise in morning?
Does the day still seem so boring?
Teenage years and all the fears
All the happiness, all the tears

A message to me from what will be
A nudge and nothing more
The whisper glistens if one listens
Then upon it you explore

We look at sky and wonder why
So distant yet the same
We teach and preach, sometimes beseech
Each with different name

Does it get much easier?
When embark on different life?
Does it get much simpler?
When avoids the strife?
Does that Sun still rise in morning?
Does the day still seem so boring?
Teenage years and all the fears
All the happiness, all the tears

Dog and Pony Show

The silence lies in anticipation
The sense of building in the air
They're unsure but known something is stirring
Something someone wants to share

The sudden urge to this thing purge
The pressure needs release
With odd eyes but now grown wise
With right hand each letter tease

Never enough to stay silent
When words form behind these eyes
Never enough to form conventional
Gaining pleasure in surprise
The simple fact that I don't know
How and where each will go
Just putting down what comes out
With some ink maybe shout

As with age I turn the page
Many things thought I knew were wrong
For was just me in puberty
Lots of stuff ran strong

An innocence in incompetence
Excuses rise to fore
Yet deep down feel the Clown
Yet go back for more

Never enough when life is tough
Just reaching what we do
Never enough, that silly stuff
Under breath the air turns blue
With age see some clarity
Glad then I did not know
Just how ridiculous that found serious
The Dog and Pony Show

Don't ever let the Sandman see

The Mom went into the daughter's room
Met with child and sense of gloom
Red rimmed eyes showed had been crying
Crumpled sheets on bed where lying

Had heard the Daughter come home from school
Normally 'Hi Mom' the standard rule
Not today, had just swept by
Mom now curious the reason why

Between sobs the child explains
The bullying and bad nicknames
How they hurt with such pains
Why never do they want to go again

Mom made a note to go next day
To see the Teacher for this not play
Had been there in own life
Way before Mom and Wife

She got through it but some it scars
Festers, growing, rust on cars
Bullying whichever level done
Can have results like that of gun

She sat beside her daughter and said
"Don't ever let the Sandman see
Inside you and what can be
Let your Heroes you protect
They give better than they get
Trust in them and trust in you
Then, together, will get through
Stand up tall and future face
Fight your battles with good grace
Do not hate those who inflict
Better just to rise from it
The victory is then won
The evil ones they come undone"

The Daughter looked to Mom for while
Then began the start of smile

Don't mind

The day a day and so can play
With ink and think and things
Nothing need to guarantee
Let's just see what brings
Sun will rise so no surprise
When the day gets light
Sun will set and then will get
Another thing called Night

I don't know where thoughts go
Until appear on page
I don't know which way will flow
Guess it is my age
But I don't care as they stop and stare
At him who loves to write
I don't mind the surprise they find
At my lack of sight
No, I don't mind if they don't mind
For doing just the same
I don't mind being 'Blind'
Blindness is just a name

I don't mind if you don't mind
I look different from you
Just outside so have no pride
Do the same things you do
Yo are you and me is me
Look at self, I think you'll find
More in common than that different
So with that I don't mind

I don't know where thoughts go
Until appear on page
I don't know which way will flow
Guess it is my age
But I don't care as they stop and stare
At him who loves to write
I don't mind the surprise they find
At my lack of sight
No, I don't mind if they don't mind
For doing just the same
I don't mind being 'Blind'
Blindness is just a name

Drank

I drank as sank
Into that now miss
The lips a treat when did meet
The tenderness, the kiss
The situation of conversation
Leaves more than achieves
The remedy is just simply
Know together can still achieve no griefs

Original so quizzical
To those 'taught' to be the same
Become just a fish and in shoal miss
The chance to show a name

Came to me I could swim free
When others sought protection in collection
That their choice so will not voice
About missed on close inspection

As I grow have come to know
The feeling of defeat
Not the one from when begun
Just those now often meet
The ones that are really nothing
Won't accept those that mean something
As I grow now can show
A name is just a name

Ian Wilcox

Died Dandelion dung needed

I am that Bee that wants to be
But cannot be the Bee you see
The travesty of being Bee
Bee that be what don't want to be

It really was quite a to do
The silly chuckles that some go through
Better than a wet shoe
The day Willy walked to Waterloo

You know you know when you know
You know what know when need
Showing that which knowing
Knowing knowledge feed

Can a pram become a Tram?
I just ask for friend
Should we talk when power walk?
Where does circle start and end?

If a flea conspiracy
Committed how would know?
Just a kiss that we might miss
Would it still as something show?

What is this!
I'm round the twist
Medication I did miss
Wayward wanderers, you get the gist

Drip drop

The searching, sought something special
The searcher they were blessed
The searching Searcher sensed salvation
Finally, they were at rest

They found a calmness in troubled waters
Found an answer to reason why
They found that they were now stronger
Thanks to all that had gone by

Drips make Drops and Drops they drop
To form into something new
Drips were Dreams and Drops the means
A better person grew
A story of a someone
A someone just like you
In fact, it is you Reader
In all that did and do
The drips are minutes, hours
The drops are periods more
They make a Lake of Living
As we swim from shore to shore

The Searcher searching something
Rests at different places
Regaining strength to carry on
To each new challenge faces

Not enough is small learning
When envision as a Sea
A plethora of Drips dropped
From here to Eternity

Drip drop, Drip drop

Drunk

The early is just now history
The chapter has moved on
Somewhere I am not certain
Somewhere still I feel belong
To a day I do say
Give what you can give
I will welcome it
If means that I still live

I woke this morning and said 'let's play'
Just another, another day
I woke this morning so I grew
Grew with change to something new
Feel the free that can be
Feel the ideas caught
Feel that which belongs to me
For some it will mean nought

The sensation of situation
The way to which react
The chance of mood like Breakfast food
Same a boring fact
Shall I shine a silver shiver
Shall I just go no show?
The mystery of being me
Is that even I don't know

Drunk more times than I remember
Not on alcohol but of word
Filling me to new place be
The written but not heard
We click a space at certain pace
Yet do the gaps we see?
Space to act a certain track
Gone so not to be

E motion

A mixed day well past May
A device does tell me so
Lighter than a Book to hold
Guess why the attraction seems to grow

The Marbles making mayhem
What subjects will they choose?
Interfering with my plans
Yet am loathe to lose

So here I go on this one man show
Friends joining for support
Some did encourage them
Some from which were taught
Lessons never lessen
When accepted for which they are
When criticism becomes witticisms
It opens doors to travel far

Another minute lost to writing
Yet that minute I don't care
When it helps encourage others
They're free to smell the air

Not al will understand
I accept that fact as true
If only one does give support
Then pleasure in what do

So here I go on this one man show
Friends joining for support
Some did encourage them
Some from which were taught
Lessons never lessen
When accepted for which they are
When criticism becomes witticisms
It opens doors to travel far
E motion – now there's a notion

Each of us do be

In fields of grass we laid our past
Sometimes in Poppy field
The irony of what want to be
When to temptation we do yield

The star so far is what we are
A goal and nothing more
So spread those wings and see what brings
On near or distant shore

A box of potential both physical and mental
Each of us do be
The limitations our expectations
Our barrier is we

Do we know which way to go?
The conundrum we all face
No answer yet for what will get
A case of 'Watch this space'

Zero two in day and if I may
Part of which within am caught
That old friend that tries to mend
By the name of Thought

Who am I to simply try?
To make my child's world a better place
When I don't know which way will go
The future problems they may face

What will be will become history
Someday but not today
Present is just thing that's lent
So will it let's just play

Echoing the Avalon

The soil shifted and revealed
No more its protection, no more its shield
Once again sees light of day
Once again can say someway
That once it was important
Once it had some need
That once it was a necessity
To some distant mutual breed

Material has been surpassed
Technology now most long forgotten
Buried in hidden places
Slowly going rotten

Echoing the Avalon
Of those things that now are gone
To some place that we can't see
To that place called History
Some brief glimpses do we get
When Earth yields and does let
Modern find some of past
A brief moment not born to last

How I wonder of Avalon
How I wonder what was like
More than just piece of garment
More than just some weapons spike
How I wonder were the people
Here and in those other places
How did sound when they were speaking
How the look of ancient faces

Part of me is what they did be
Part but not the all
Many were the transitions
After time when made curtain call
Yet still remain in some frame
Reminding who once were
The succession of progression
From when were clothed in fur

Fiddle

We are symptoms of the system
The system we did choose
We are fissions within the mission
To destroy, abuse

An epitaph – no autograph
The last no chance to sign
Crumbled was creation
Once deemed as so divine

Our molecules just follicles
Within the greater Space
The mystery of the travesty
The once was Human Race

We came, we saw, we plundered
Yes, it was a blast
Alas like all extravaganzas
None of them do last

So was found in future times
On the alter planet Earth
They couldn't stop before the pop
Regardless of the worth

The one who found stared at ground
Similar to own
Yet just dust in radioactive gust
Ultimate self-harm these had sown

Questions now for must ask
Which of Earths is this past?
Answer please to this riddle
As with Nature we do fiddle

Filling cup

Not for nothing but for something
Should we aim to achieve
No encore but just adore
The chance before we leave

One chance dance though maybe two
We get and so should take
Not for others but ourselves
A future should we make

The rest will follow if succeed
We are all but one creed
Each has hope and each need
Each ambition needs to feed

Vacuum is attraction
For other things to fill
Load it with variety
There will always be some space still

What be we but infinity?
If that path we choose?
We are the decision makers
We can choose to lose

Nothing lasts a lifetime
For lifetime is evolving
We are born with the skills
The skills of problem solving

Nothing much in empty cup
Never full I know
Yet the filling is quite thrilling
Guess the way to go

Five and Four

I made a day sometime 'Hooray!'
Just gave up on the News
Looked instead and so were led
The beautiful I can peruse
Made a stance in crazy dance
Left and Right both making stance
Both forgetting that we are letting
Just slip by the current chance

Confused, amused at how intrude
When no answer know
Just requirement for their environment
Everything for show
Cynic me and long have been
Overhead does go
Happy me to simply be
Outsider to the show

If an Elephant did float in Space
Would we then become just one Human Race?
If Seas around the world became a chocolate store
Could we turn Hate to that adore?
Five and Four to be once more
A figure can remember
Turned to it one September hit
Past yet can remember

Nothing really matters
Nothing much to me
Until you mentioned one word
Mention Family
And so my friend we're near the end
Of this one but not all
For that choice is collective
That one is your call

Five hundred billion trillion

The kid did say the cost
When was asked to explain
The value of their Mother lost
Five hundred billion trillion
The first figure sprang to mind
Of a higher value
In life I think will find

"Why did you leave when living?
Was it how I look?
Why did you reject me?
Yet another took
Mom, you went missing
When I needed most
You are now a memory
In some way are a Ghost"

So said the child no longer
For had grown to adulthood
Not all same species think the same
That now understood
Child grew with Foster Mother
Grew closer to than real
For they gave what was needed
A love to hold and feel

Parenting heartbeat
Sometimes one does miss
Loading and then aiming
Yet miss with loving kiss
Yesterday was yesterday
The child had to take
For some unknown reasons
Yet a better Parent they did make

Flatulence and incontinence

Shaft was daft when on the raft
It chose to finally settle
Too much spent on where it went
In the Rapids kettle

Pup stood up then fell down
This walking thing a chore
Why not smell when on belly tell
That this way they adore

Is Fish the dish that you wish?
Maybe something far less smelly
Oh, so know from some T.V. show
You watched on there that telly

Flatulence and incontinence
In wordplay I do suffer
My coffee has a sugar lover
It just asked me for another

Have you seen an Eleflump?

Is that Eleflump simulating
Or is it in some way stating
That's in the mood for some mating
Thus, more Eleflump creating

The mystery of improbability
The Eleflump exist
For they stomp around at leisure
You should see when kissed!

Eleflump an Rickety Rhinos
Upon the Serengeti plains
Not that found in safari
More in the adventurous Brains

Flavour savour

Gone shopping – trolley bopping
Not sure why for won't buy
Just the fun of being the one
They with displays do try
Gone Supermarket scramble
They hate it when you amble
Unless loading stuff don't need
For the whole Town seems to feed

Gone to fight a battle
With pauses for tittle tatter
Do I know?? As opposite go
I guess it doesn't matter
Stressed out Staff make me laugh
They were same just yesterday
If so bad the experience had
Why come back to play?

Gone for bored at Home
When there all alone
Here can spear the Managers leer
As if everything they own
If don't cower can spend an hour
Purchasing in Head
Security soon wise to me
No stop just smiles instead

The mantra be that time is free
When you do me invite
Am no fool and know the rules
Won't try to spend the night
Task complete and back on street
Next victim? What's my flavour?
A whole day can pass this way
In strange ways I savour

Floating in the air

Growing old with stories told
The mix of those betwixt
All were done and some were fun
Some needed to be fixed
I've walked the walk to strange places
Seen some stuff with no human faces
Been and done and then returned
Took some tests and badges earned

I've been drunk a thousand times
Hope for a thousand more
Drunk on the feeling of heart reeling
When see those who I adore
I've missed a beat and slipped my feet
Floated in the air
When they state and reciprocate
A common love we share

A shout out to the ones I know
A shout out to who just told me so
A shout out to those yet to meet
A shout out to who hardship beat
A shout out to a foreign land
A shout out to the sea and sand
A shout out to the other places
A shout out to Cities and open spaces

You're goin to say what you say
Going to and that's okay
You're going to because been caught
In the culture and what taught
You're going to judge me so
Even though you don't know
You're going to be just you
So to yourself try to be true

Flux state

So, I turn to you the Future
Ask what have you in store
Life itself is getting better
Can you offer more?
My door is open if wish to visit
With a plan we can discuss
I am, you'll find a simple Man
Have no time for all that fuss

Your relations have been here
Present and the Past
One is still visiting
One just couldn't last
They spoke of you as what must do
I take their words on board
Yet with a note of caution
Failures I don't hoard

Criteria Inferior
Keeping me searching still
I am not the best of me
One day be I will
Transition situation
Will be until I die
Nothing else is possible
I really don't know why

Happy but not content
Drive it drives without relent
Pushing from the day were born
Through the times I've sometimes sworn
No matter the outcome scatter
Providing with no hate
Just me being what am seeing
The constant of flux state

Fly away

The Lady had a day we know
The type occasionally we all get
The blip in the sea of sunshine
The strange type we try to forget
Come now to the present one
Sun just rising so good run
At moving on front what had
That left taste slightly bad

Over morning drink did write
Something stirrings through the night
More a case of letting out
Far less disturbing than a shout

They wrote

'The day has started so fresh change
The good things I may dance
Yesterday has been and gone
It and I didn't get along
Nothing major, just some quibbles
Our of joy it took some nibbles
Slept, repaired so start again
Hopefully without frustration pain

Fly away my feel of sadness
Fly away this current madness
Fly away and don't return
This now current I did not earn
Your aim is to try to bring me down
I am not one to wear thorn crown
I am one adjective with two nouns
So you annoyance just fly away'

With that done she ventured forth to bright and rewarding

For this experience that is so hateful

With soft sigh you wonder why
Some survived yet some did die
Not for fault for they did try
To solve this puzzle and just by

Admittedly we stack the Deck
When we say "Oh what the heck"
Outside is big and we are a speck
In Survival Sea lays many a wreck

Emotions enter, thoughts do play
Memories now here to stay
Some are good and some are bad
All though times one has had
Some distort with passing age
Each the turning of the page
Amazed now at what once did do
Realising foolish with knowledge new

The Sandman visits at least twice
To Life's wine will add some spice
Bitter bite or nectar nice
Each day a grain of random rice

Some we choose and some get
Some we wish we could forget
Some react to, some we set
Some object to, some just let

Lottery balls and Bingo calls
Study places and Dance Halls
Who are we to think can change?
This complex creature oh so strange
Maybe bend and maybe twist
To slightly alter that on list
Yet we still all are grateful
For this experience that is so hateful

Formaldehyde

Formaldehyde could be my Bride
If stopped me getting old
It does the trick with skin not thick
So I have been told

Technology and surgery
Just delay not cure
I am just a selfish man
I am wanting more

Formaldehyde could be my Bride
If I could stand the smell
Can I ask to wear a mask?
No? Oh, what the hell

Cuisine team

Custard on the Sirloin steak
A dash of pepper and then bake
Something new I could make
In world of new strange dishes

Such a chore a sauce to pour
Glaze and then forget
Worry not what have got
The inside still be wet

Paprika with the Spotted Dick
A bite to Suet pudding
Anchovies with sauce runny
The taste buds we are fooling

White fish relish
Of some Clotted cream
No, I am not an animal!
Just joined the cuisine team

From the dust

If underground it was found
Was it trash or treasure?
If the air we all share
Who quantifies the measure?

If a wrong can inspire song
Does that mean that it is right?
Is Gravity plain sanity?
Or everything would be light

I journeyed through the dessert
The experience made whole
For in the wilderness of nothingness
Is where I found my soul

In love a trust we simply must
Or becomes infatuation
Same feelings but for shorter
A different situation

If experience has relevance
A blessing that it be
When motion is just notion
Is it always just lazy?

In outer space a test did face
Enclosed could I still breathe?
For the means made by those unseen
Did in them I believe?

That old voice when given choice
Do in ourselves we trust?
The health of self then shows its wealth
We rise up from the dust

F.U.B.A.R.

Yellow thing came crashing down
Was not wet so was not Custard
Yellow thing came crashing down
Then my thoughts I mustered

Is it a plane? Is it a Bird?
It seems to fly but that's absurd
Is it from another Race?
Is it from Outer Space?

Does this thing come in Peace?
Will it some Death Ray release?
How do we greet this strange faction
Fight! Oppose! Or interaction?

Relax my friend for are not foe
Just on different path I go
I am someone who likes to show
Poetry and then so

Cranial collapse

Excuse me Mrs Maybe
Is that parcel addressed to me?
If it is then ecstatic be
For is my first Book see

I dithered and I dallied
I pondered and procrastinated
Was I really good enough?
For my scribbling to be stated?

Never knowing until it showing
In own way, no anthology
A collection not one poem
That will be how known is me

Not lost amongst a crowd so proud
To have one piece like the others
No! I will have worthwhile reading
Plus I get to choose its covers

If we could

Shall we swim in others whim?
Wake me when with surprise
We are we and can see
When we realise
Seasons have a reason
So do many names we know
Do strange things for what it brings
Stuff they can then show

Those who intrude and then get rude
To others who are same
The levels get past that personal set
Can drive a neutral quite insane
But it's okay when can still say
For capable you still are
That fact is bliss as is a kiss
From love and in love still you are

Is it easy just to survive?
Another day to be alive
Endure this travesty
The one who name with certain shame
For that name is me
How much more can you endure
Addiction now tradition
You click on name with hidden shame
More questions than suggestions
As I play my game

Who just lies
As moments slip by?
Certainly not new me
To take a pass and then call past
Such a travesty
We used to be the now what see
Why? A simple fact
We knew as grew then knew new
About things like how we act

An education a confrontation
Yet not the one from School
That of Life and loving Wife
They the things that rule

If we could perhaps we should
Go back and think again
Maybe then no need to feed
That we then try to just sustain

Could we be a bit more free
When first release the us?
Not to do as others do
Crime and all that fuss

Just be free to say "I'm me!"
Free within that zone
That certain space that has your face
The part that's free to own

Those who intrude and then get rude
To others who are same
The levels get past that personal set
Can drive a neutral quite insane
But it's okay when can still say
For capable you still are
That fact is bliss as is a kiss
From love and in love still you are

If Windmills could be Propellers

All I got was I.D.
And then I got a life
Found a different Country
Found a loving Wife

I need her now but she's far away
I need her as in birthplace stay
I need her more than ever did
As thing Lonely lifts the lid

If Windmills could be Propellers
I would buy two
Then somehow manage to build a carriage
The extreme I would put through

Its paces to lessen spaces
Had enough of lonely Train
The circle again at start
Just a difference this time
Someone else does own my Heart
It's so wrong to here belong
When you are not with me
Windmills sails are still frozen
Frozen by the tears

Tangerine dreams now have no means
To turn this passion red
As I lay with change of day
Alone in double bed

If Windmills could be the propellers
There'd be no space for planes
The earth would lose its Windmills
As such as me do gain

I.F.A

I fly away on the words I say
Fly to somewhere new
Fly away when feel that way
Just a thing I do
May rain outside so need to hide
That really does not matter
When feel indeed no colour/ creed
As my thoughts I scatter

Throw the loam that I own
Into bricks I can then bake
Building things to see what brings
Many mischievously, the myriad I make
Am I getting better?
Am I just now annoying?
Am I just an irritant?
The style I am employing

Am I strange with the constant change?
The subjects and the styles
Do I fill with frown as some sick Clown
Or fill a day with smiles?
Three in the morning and others are snoring
I am guessing what to say
Do not think as lay down ink
Ramblings gonna stray

I fly away into a Day
Old to others, to some not yet begun
I fly away for made that way
To me this is just some fun
If only you could see true me
The challenge an addiction
To merely do simple for you
Is more than supervision

I.i L not I'll

Who would be your Hero?
If you could choose but one
Who would be that certain person?
With all the things they've done
Who would be the first choice?
To stand beside you when
The times do need an ally
Apart from trusted Pen

My Hero is my younger me
He saw me through some stuff
Stood up to be counted
When the world got touch
My role model my reflection
A person known so well
Will I achieve what they believe?
Only time will tell

All my thoughts they go astray
Though some remaining everyday
Imbedded, maybe, in deep place
As another day do face
Quantum questions quiz the quirky
Quiz the reasonable as well
What will I ask a mammoth task
Only it can tell

Impossible is logical
Yet illogical it be
When the Blind see and find
More possible than me
Starting out is just adventure
A challenge that we choose
Yet starting out is a bonus
What have we to lose?

Makikipagkita ulit

"Will meet again on this I promise
Will meet again my love
Will join again in physical
Before we meet in that above"

Said the one to another
Said the one so far away
Said the one that was missing
Said to them who with seek to stay

Ikaw ang buhay ko
I cannot say much more
You are the one who changed me
The one that I adore

Maybe not that language
Each one now does speak
Yet the words mean the same
When finding what we seek

What is distance when is real
When true pleasure we do feel
What is time when away
From the one with want to stay

Looking bac in history
Looking back on what was one
Looking back but also forward
Looking back at when begun

Ian Wilcox

Ikaw ay aking anghel

I'm home yet away from Home
I know that sounds strange
I am in my land of birth
Yet my Home has changed

I am a stranger in that where born
I am almost just a guest
I am here but wanting there
For there will lay at rest

Place Where born and once to sworn
Doesn't have that bond
As do two as a clue
They're way past calling fond

Miles never meant much to me
In some way still the same
When through the powers of technology
Their faces still can frame

They say that absence makes heart grow fonder
That is something I understand
Though can talk through the ether
I still want to hold her hand

Learnt a new way and new language
Learnt happiness that once was lost
Learnt the sharing of the caring
Learnt not all has a cost

Made a move to improve
Got my Destiny
Found above what I deserve
Unlocked the inner me

Ikaw ay aking anghel I say to her
Ikaw ang aking Puso he reply
I am blessed beyond measure
Why she chose? I don't know why

Illogical not mythical

It's past July and wondering why
As get older days just pass too fast
Almost seems they find obscene
So have no wish to last
A blink of eyes and a week's gone by
Unless are waiting for something
Then the days with patience plays
Before one does choose to bring

Can a curve create a circle?
If it decides it will expand
Did we in evolution
Swap a paw to create a hand?
Did I ever doubt my being?
To a point I would just fold
If I did, I can't remember
That would mean no story told

The mystery of mortality
The permutations quite astounding
Who decides how long the ride?
Who or what's surrounding?
The good fall short whilst bad not caught
Explain to me how fair
Those who aim to do good cut down
Whilst remain those with no care

Illogical not mythical
Is everywhere we look
Punished for trying to be better
The decisions one then took
Too much deep delving
Is that why it goes so fast
The days and months and even years
Too rapidly are past

Implore you

An Ant embedded in some Onyx
A carcass in some Coal
Reminders of some past before
Preserved and therefore whole
A skeleton of some bygone
Found buried in the ground
So different from what they saw
When they were around

Some ancient scroll, partially whole
In tomb so recently discovered
Artefacts and their impacts
As each of them uncovered
Laws and cause might cause some pause
As judge by modern day
Yet different then before the Pen
So who are we to say?

Revolutions in our evolution
Some major and some small
Product be of History
So, who are we to call?
The right and wrong of the bygone
We just must now adjust
The influence of effluents
Need not be a must

Once again use a Brain
There for a specific reason
Not that got and then forgot
Like clothing for a Season
Year in – year out should scream and shout
That is what it's for
Use and please don't abuse
That simple thing implore

In all future days

In all future days and future ways
However, I explore
Could I find a way to simply say?
That I could love you more
The days are long and in each belong
That means more than just a Wife
You and her, our future for sure
Mean more than simply Life

Without both no help to cope
The challenge that I face
I am in that special within
That cannot see just Race
I yearn to keep more than skin deep
The things that have no measure
Lodieta and Maria
Things that have become my treasure

What was I waiting for when before more
More than I deserve
If only sooner had heard Heart crooner
If only had the nerve
That is just a supposition before proposition
That led to you and me
No more that chore to explore
Got more than truth it be

So rain in Spain does fall on plane
Not the airborne kind
More that wet when sadness get
Not with you I find
They play the songs to the bygone
Not the tune for me
For have found my perfect ground
Forever may it be

In and sanity

A strange experience I had today
As again head felt like clay
Heavy, sticky, slightly cold
Waiting for me to it mould
Into something I could show
Of an object I should know
What I found I am in shock
Now I gaze as I take stock

I slipped inside my troubled mind
Searching for release
What I got meant a lot
For in it I found peace
All it needed was understanding
All it craved was gentle handling
It so sought to be adored
Instead of that it felt ignored

When did I begin to commit this sin?
Ignoring that which matters
Too busy with the pleasure
As it lay in tatters
How could I be such a fool
To myself to be so cruel
Part of me I could not see
Permanently in misery

I slipped inside my troubled mind
Found it was one of a kind
I should have cherished not turned back
As its sense of loneliness did stack
Now it feels a part of me
Now it knows that it is free
To just be what wants to be
Mix of in and sanity

In glory rest simply the best

On floodlit stage the actors played
A story, something new
Were the perfect of reflection
Doing that which chose to do

What we be visually
Just half story told
Rest at best will be laid to rest
After experiencing that called old

The actors play as is their way
Certain people recognition
Love the fact they choose to act
Though Fame not this scribbler's ambition

The fun of one to part just some
The reward is in the know
Inspiring those desiring
Their confidence to grow

I make a mark upon a page
As did them of different age
Nothing ventured, nothing gain
In the current not seem sane

The love they show helps one grow
A simple part of playing art
The actors on the stage are us
Just going through without the fuss

On floodlit stage the actors played
Though now with different story
The ones portrayed a history made
Now resting in that glory

In limbo

I can't say when chose to pick up Pen
Just did and now you see
The one who dared and so shared
Their own frailty
I saw the one and did become
The exception to the rule
Joined the Band that understands
That writing is a tool

And all that fly as time goes by
Some they choose to scatter
The head led but feel instead
Moved objects and the matter
What came before don't matter no more
The here and now does tell
We were caught in promise nought
On the way to Hell

No true age for first stage
It comes and then you know
Takes a grip that pen nib
Its efforts like to show
The Birds sing as light does bring
A different if you look
Cat did look and body shock
Then went back to sleep

In the ground of reason towns
The point it had been made
They saw so and so did go
Discarded that charade
Before final fall I'll make a call
To that which gave what got
Try to be nice so don't pay the price
Of in limbo left to rot

In the presence

The rain it falls on windows here
Yet for you the sky is clear
Here a need to wear a coat
There is T-shirt weather

I say hello in your morning
Some hours before my own is dawning
Yet together I do feel
Until once more it is real

For now, I'm living like a ghost
Far away from what matters most
A recluse with some pride
As my sadness try to hide

If ocean deep and sky high
Tell me now the reason why
All that matters so far away
I turn night-time into day
Make what can so content
With each minute together spent
Just a glimpse of what can be
Stirring up sweet memories

Making mark self-made moments
Passing time the best can do
Counting down to when can be there
In the arms I love so true

Making most of misery
So the real you cannot see
Just the one who wants to be
In the presence of beauty

In this present new
(To my awesome Daughter Mj Sumayo)

You came of me so what will be?
The future I do hope
The constant change as things do cha
Explore the means to cope
One single soul can't fill that hole
The one left by that 'perfect
Nothing gain in the pain
Just reason for reflection

So said a man because could can
To the second treasure of a life
The first, maybe, reality
More valued was a Wife
I am not you so little clue
The ways and means you do
Just go for more you I adore
Journey holds for you much more

The first line a a sentence
First chapter in your Book
Of the things you did and will
The chancers that you took
Anak now just a Nak
No miss-spellbind that I see
For you are grown so no actions 'own'
Yet are and always a part of me

Yes, am different
When did first you opened eyes
Yes, the feeling of confusion
Yes, a big surprise
I am of a different cover
Yet that is nothing new
We are both the give and take
In this present new

In touch

The Goods Train rushing to Capital
The Fox that makes like a Cat call
The sound of wind as rain does fall
The brief interlude of silence

The delivery lorry to some shop
Laden with a type of stock
The chime as hour reaches top
The comfort of the calm

When all around just seems so bad
When all around seems lost what had
When all around seems simply mad
Then you are in touch with all around
When all around just seems such fun
When all around is a new way begun
When all around seems something done
Then you are in touch with all around

The click of kettle as boil does reach
The latest News, some political speech
The turn of pages in stories teach
What happened on some past foreign Beach

The tone that summons your attention
On modern day 'magic's invention
That unidentified to which suggestion
Is limited only by imagination

When all around just seems so bad
When all around seems lost what had
When all around seems simply mad
Then you are in touch with all around
When all around just seems such fun
When all around is a new way begun
When all around seems something done
Then you are in touch with all around

Isang mensahe sa iyo ang aking pagmamahal

Many a soul throughout our being
Said the words that now you're seeing
Simple words at first glance
Yet meant more when given chance
The sayer and the said to
The one and both like me and you
Different in the old way
Similar with what did say

I choose to die for worthwhile
Until then choose to live
Spent long time just getting
Now the time to give
Not that I can offer much
Apart from the real me
The ambition and tradition
Come as priced as free

None but fool choose to rule
Some they have no choice
Leadership has many ways
Sometimes merely voice
Living in a lost land
Really have no clue
How to escape the insanity
When seems nothing you can do

Night it falls in blackness
Yet without the sleep
Night it joins with a mare
A thing that long will keep
All the sense of sensible
Gone to distant place
The rest of the unjustifiable
Now are left to face
Stop!
Sit! Relax!

Not alone though seem alone
There are others by your side
Some do so in physical
Some actions others hide
Yet an army does support you
In this the crazy time
Stay now just sole focused
On when it becomes fine

Easy said and harder done
Been and am there now
Not knowing final outcome
Just the method and the how
First off is together
Together we will stand
Forget the complication
At present different land

Physical is nothing
When heart and soul will fight
For which they do recognise
Something oh so right
When voice don't work as want to work
Look into these eyes
They might seem slightly misty
Yet behind them something wise

Wise enough to know past times
When world seemed like your now
Memories of the getting through
Let me help you in the how
Adversity in abundance
Just false vision seen
The mask of modern madness
Together will wipe clean

Ian Wilcox

It was me

The pink hair caused a stare
The body piercings caused a look
The tattoos, not something new
Just from reason took

The protestations of Generations
Audible and visual
The cry for more they explode
Just seems irrigational

Caught when wet, dry we just slip by
None do stop, just fail that hop
The question still is why?"
So, in the depths of our existence
Can we find the simple reason?
To be what we choose to be
The outside that others see

We sew a seed and then do feed
The attitude of individual
Want them to be somewhat free
Providing it's not criminal

The clothe that barely cover
Makeups that just smother
The Him and Her now a blur
The long run thing on wearing fur

I went somewhere just to stare
The entertainment free
The irony is History's
Past times it was me

It's magical

That silence sense of security
Gone the feeling need to impress
Comfortable within your 'bubble'
No desire to be the 'best'
The jubilation of occupation
Within an object call yourself
Grey matter sometimes behaving
Regardless of the physical health

When nothing matters but the air that you breathe
Nothing more can find to grieve
When that burden you relieve
That's the start of what can achieve
When nothing matters when can feel
With the senses that which real
The lessons learnt and learning still
Before the touch of the final chill

It's magical it truly is
How we work, a thing of bliss
Not what do but what can do it
Walk and talk, stand and sit
Identify and wonder why
Add to that which stored
Make decision and admission
Which dislike and which adored

Analyse and then adapt
Overcome and doff the hat
Treat an argument as a spat
Walk a Dog or stroke a Cat
Life is life and if are wise
The reward when realised
All just nibbles when are sized
That makes one chuckle with surprise

Iure libertatis

'Our way was going wayward'
So said someone in some Land
'I am tired of this direction
I choose to make a stand'

How often said in History
How often the results we can see
We invented word Democracy
Surely all are entitled to be free

Free with certain amount of rules
For without we are fools
Yet rules which majority benefit
Not the rule of kill or hit

This I read and stuck in head
Layers to then peel
First it sounded disastrous
Then a truth so real

All free Nations, will limitations
All the right to choose
All accepting of each other
What have we to lose?

Yes, I know sound like some madman
If I am mad then look around
Ask again if I am crazy
When you hear a Baby's sound

Iwi is a strange man

Juggling into a July
Another comes too soon
In the clock of Calendar
We are just past noon

Where has this year gone
Seemingly way to fast
Caught up in world misery
Sure, was not a blast

Self-isolation across the nation
No real difference for me
For was doing way before
Normal status so can see

Iwi is a strange man
Spoke a lot with letters
Narrative with what body give
C at most and could be better

The clamour for social gathering
Maybe before time
Understand the reason why
Understand why crime

The risk is still outweighing
From what the 'knowing' saying
Little steps make great leaps
Not just at party showing

Iwi is a strange one
On that I can agree
For I do know Iwi
For Iwi is just me

Jam over Jam

The Toast has been browned to perfection
A topping I desire
As well as spread of Butter
Something to light delight fire

Strawberry or Raspberry?
Apricot or Plum?
I am in a jam over Jam
Cannot choose which one

Blackcurrant or Morello Cherry?
Nope, decision made
Finally, an answer
I'm having Marmalade

One, Two

One, Two, how do you do?
Three, Four, have we met before?
Five, Six, so how's tricks?
Seven, Eight, running late?

The man who spoke with numbers
Met once and still recovering
In Cafe at start of day
For am their Breakfast lover

I should have heeded warning
He came in, all walked out
The server ran for cover
They didn't even shout!

There I was a Target
The sacrificial Lamb
Next time I will eat at Home
Refer please to the Jam

This is the age

by Loriz

Unwieldy and overgrown tombs
cluttered with metal stools
home of the soulless ghouls
with adulterated body from scraps
tripped by their own traps

architectural artistry
a new concept of beauty
fueled by luxury
spartan simplicity and
slaughter of progeny.

Whiff of smoke surrounds
nourishment of deserted fields
along the banks of the river
hidden by sullen mist.

In a cold world dilemma,
who could've saved Abel
in a narrow concrete path,
a dingy old shack...
a rotting room?

a letter...
Soiled clock stops.

Quiet Turmoil
by Loriz

Looming in the mind
Clouding the only reason
Darkening the horizon
Wisdom is hard to find.

What is there to hope
There's nothing to grasp
Gently unlock the clasp
Untie the binds of rope.

Unspoken lies discovered
The holy mouths of night
At midday's stroke of fright
Until the vision faltered.

Chaogenesis
by Loriz

The utopic world of being forgotten
The hidden sanctuary when given quiet passing
A solemn place that had long been missing
Mastering the cold life away from the fallen.

In the order of disorder
The quiet lies alarming
The gleaming truth concealing
Honor bestowed a sweet liar.
Ideal fantasy in a twisted reality
When ranting moral is nonexisting
And chaotic life gets more exciting
Vivid in abstracted vanity.

A perfect world from demented society.
Realignment of broken sanity.
Luxuriate in your little fantasy
With gratified heart, I bid goodbye to thee.

Longing

by Loriz

From the velvety ground stands
the self-replicating structure -
abode of the half-robot half-beast
giant sloth whose dependence on machines
has opened up features
of abstraction and mathematical fiction
the unthinkable lust for knowledge
powered by philosophical indifference
of the inhabitable hostile soul
who hates to be on the ground
yearning for something to climb on
with his excellent rule of life.
I stare motionless
making a prolonged mental inventory
simultaneously in pleasure and in pain
I ruminate on the machinery of my destiny.
cowed and apologetic
appalled by vague, non-committal message
knocked off my perch.
I look up to see the plentiful admonition,
the cosmopolitan naughtiness
of the generation.

The link that binds the man
and me seems broken....

Did I fence myself in
or you fenced me out, my son?

Coming Home

by Loriz

After three years....
my chest heaved like
the gallops of the buffaloes
from the dancing hills that end
over the edge of the world
meeting the sun spreading marigolds
reflected in sky as the shaggy greenish-brown
grasses would bow down guided by the herd
tiny butterflies would flutter around in panic
seeking shelter in my mother's garden
--- as I was trying to do.

In three hours,
I was ushered to the cold white pavement
the irritated grating of the gate greeted by
the sweltering air hot with impatience melting
the wilted cut flower on snobby flower vase
at the rusty table standing on the carpet of sickly lawn.

The horizon was the gray black wall
where only snakes could pass through
its timid holes, the scared eyes---

Looking up, I saw a tawny hawk flying
away from the shadowy portion of my grave.

The Color of my Birth

by Loriz

The canticles of aerodynamics played
while the sails assembled
to splatter rainbow of colors
on the azure of the sea.

Petals from the bough fell
to cover ditches,
the ridges hid red flowers
preparing for a dance.

Fireworks signalled the promenade.
Drums and bugles cried with firecrackers.
The mirth opened naval pouches
and rocky shelves
while spades irrigated lands in grid.
Flower dancers flooded along the streets
and river red ribboned the cake
---black forest covered in red cherries.

In one bayonet thrust, my birth was induced
with the pulsating of the blood...

The gift was opened.
With a blast, I spread my might.

Now I am named:
WAR

Death be the final judge (Alliterative verse)

by Loriz

I don't measure your leisure for treasure
or your whims to the woe of the wounded
all I care for are the cries of the creatures
the howling of the house being haunted

trick the truth; trumple the trumpet torrent
emboss embarrassment at embassy
of jokes in judges' jaundiced judgement
hark the quaking tact of bureaucracy

crack the crevices of the Crooked's brain
peel the pot of polluted panacea
drag dogged dealers of drugs to the drain
chain the chowder of chinky cavalry

turn the tourniquet at tower turret
bend away the boon of the blue blockade
I shrieked at the shrill shout on the first street
the fly fell on the floor of ambuscade

Humor Me

by Loriz

Mama, mama I am sick
Call the doctor very quick
My lashes fell off as I slept
My nose did twitch too when I crept
To find my glasses oh, so thick

Fix my wig please, it can't fit
When I tried, it lost the knit
I tried to put a zipper but in vain
My make up smudged, it has stain
Mama help I don't have wit

My chin sags, oh teach me the trick
And my clothes now I can't just pick
My belly's swollen like a blubber
My arms and legs I hate forever
Surgeon, please come. I need you quick.

Why I Hate Geometry

You said we're parallel
side by side forever
Can't we hug each other?

You put me in the box;
I sat at one corner.
You think it's fair n square?

You say the world is round,
it's either up or down.
Well, I'm dizzy going around.

You brag about the lines?
...at each end is a dot
to mean we should stop.

You say we're solid rock...
but you have to endure
that I'm a plane figure (sorry!)

So, Mr. Geometry,
stop following me
We are not meant to be

Lumpkin and a not eaten meal

I once wrote of Lumpkin
Today does rise again
His deeds long ago once more will show
By the use of pen

Lumpkin knew less of cooking
Than this writer does
I who fries the common egg
Wearing industrial standards gloves

Lumpkin tried Italian
From place he did not know
To impress Tatriness
Lack of knowledge did, sadly, show

Pasta a disaster
Pebbles to be hurled
Sauce, of course, a new cause
For meat to choose edges to be curled

The Garlic bread it was said
Became a new sensation
With the local builders
Who used with imagination

Politely she did make excuse
Not wishing there Taste buds to lose
Said that had already eaten
Though his delicacy could not be beaten

Lumpkin looked at the mounds of mess
Somewhat slightly proud
Me too, I had some Stew
Lying quite out loud

Made a mark for new

Maligayang pagdating said one person
Bem-vinda said another
Välkommen said someone else
Each of different cover

Welkom said a soon not stranger
ahlaan bik a different voice
καλως ΗΡΘΑΤΕ came from somewhere else
In all we can rejoice

Welkom came from different place
Bienvenue from somewhere new
Benvenuto yet another
When we do what's true

어서 오십시오 came from distant shore
Vítejte never hid
Karibu came from across the seas
Doing what once did

The simple word when is heard
Can change so many things
The statement and sincerity
The pleasure it then brings

Üdvözöljük came and stayed
ようこそ made parade
Tokotai so oft repeatedly
Friendships born and made

Made a mess

I made a mess of making makeshift
Became but without make and the f
Not much use for that I have now
Contemplating kindling left
I made a mess of being 'normal'
Never was if truth be told
Just became deeply opposite
As with each day I grow old

I made a mess of long-term employment
For am no corporate lackey
All the dumb down of opinion
Really never was nor will be
I made a mess of being mad
No matter how tried to shiver
Others said that was just different
So as such I now quiver

I made a mess of growing up
In the context of that expected
I was just self-determined
So, plans of others I rejected
I made a mess of mess making
For even that I made a mess
Yet I am grateful for mess making
For in mess making do mess bless

No example, bright and shining
Could I ever call the me
No pilgrims in path follow
Would I wish identically
I welcome if I have encountered
Satisfaction but nothing more
For everyone is individual
Includes my own who I adore

Magic Fingers

I sit and read and wonder why
That before me, with a sigh
How can they say so much?
When a keyboard magic fingers touch

Shapes and symbols recognise
Yet they pass that great divide
Take me to what have been through
Then do take to places new

Life stories told – big and bold
Life ambition as a mission
All laid out in thing called verse
That strange thing, pleasure/ curse

The scratching of the pen on paper
The tapping of the keyboard plastic
The expansion of the hidden
The delivery like elastic

So many names yet to discover
So many yet not on a cover
Yet I think their time will come
When they become 'someone'

Magic fingers they possess
Sets apart from the rest
A rare talent with which blessed
The rest is up to us to decide

A look at Book is all it took
To make one want to be
Like those who are there before them
Those who made part of history

Magic Fingers have so many
Not all are in that of writing
Yet they have that special Gift
In dark place they are enlightening

Magpakailanman at walang hanggan

On foreign shore one asked for more
On that question they then grew
The answer changed to something strange
A Family and love
A Holiday became a place to stay
For that was what their Home
The unknown in which did roam
Became a silken Glove

The traveller became the settler
Thou not with force intrude
For the reason in past season
Could never be that rude

The making of the undertaking
The paths we choose to walk
The complex sees an identity
Down to how we talk
The acceptance of the difference
The challenge to then salvage
The unity of which wish be
So, learn a different language

May-ari ng aking Puso
I will say to you
Ibibigay ko ang aking buhay para sa aking Asawa
For that' what Husbands do
Nothing great to which can relate
Except that which I have now got
Maybe means not much in 'means'
Yet is the end of Rainbow pot

Aking Puso, kalusugan, lahat
I to thee say
Magpakailanman at walang hanggan
Forever and a Day

Make me smile

My darkness filled with sunshine
My wounds now are just scars
The things done were by someone
Just like passing cars
The Movies never tell it true
The Hero doesn't always win
Yet sometimes that's a blessing
When different from that begin

When the past a Looking Glass
When guns fall silent from the bark
You have made a new beginning
You have made a start
When it's time to say goodbye
To the anger both give and receive
Then, my friend, is the moment
Then in us we can believe

Come to me you fantasy
That lays there by my side
Too many years of laughs and tears
For anything to hide
Come to me you simplicity
Of the basic facts of life
I was but a nothing
Until you agreed to be my Wife

Now we walk in pastures Green
Whatever is the season
We are above the things around us
For some special reason
Yes, we are a part of it
If only for brief while
Yet the moments within together
Each a moment to make me smile

Making Bread

Today I am a Baker old
Wife has said so I am told
Said that I should make some Bread
I just want to stay in Bed

Method

- STEP 1

Mix 500g strong white flour, 2 tsp salt and a 7g
sachet of fast-action yeast in a large bowl.

Right, I take some flour and mix with what?

Salt I know for in pot show
But am I making Beer?
That other stuff changes taste rough
Helps it down when almost clear

- STEP 2

Make a well in the centre, then add 3 tbsp olive oil and 300ml water, and mix
well. If the dough seems a little stiff, add another 1-2 tbsp water and mix well.

What the hell! I'm digging a Well!
Pouring oil upon the water!
I was told in days of old
That's something you should never oughta

- STEP 3

Tip onto a lightly floured work surface and knead for around 10 mins.

More blinkin flour I now must spread
Wife's rolling pin will meet my Head!
Knead for 10 minutes
I'll a lot more than 10 stitches!

STEP 4

Once the dough is satin-smooth, place it in a lightly oiled
bowl and cover with cling film. Leave to rise for 1 hour until
doubled in size or place in the fridge overnight.

Satin smooth? Yet more oil
Cling film? What happened to tin foil?
Leave to rise? Is this reincarnation?
A fridge strange place for that occasion

• STEP 5
Line a baking tray with baking parchment. Knock back
the dough (punch the air out and pull the dough in on
itself) then gently mould the dough into a ball.

Now we are into parchment
What the heck! This is frightening
Just trying to make something for my Butter
Not a tome of bloody writing!

STEP 6
Place it on the baking parchment to prove for a
further hour until doubled in size.

Prove what? An argument or an opinion?
This is not some strange debate
The thing can buy in shop ask why
Is making me now quite irate

• STEP 7
Heat oven to 220C/fan 200C/gas 7.

Hahaha
So just put it on my forehead
That's about that temperature
Thanks to where this has led

• STEP 8
Dust the loaf with some extra flour and cut a cross about
6cm long into the top of the loaf with a sharp knife.

Would you believe it Step!
More bloody flour!
Is it on special?
Need to shift this hour

STEP 9
Bake for 25-30 mins until golden brown and the loaf sounds
hollow when tapped underneath. Cool on a wire rack.

Bake for about half an hour
Guess what! No blooming extra flour!
Golden brown and sounding hollow?
Brain needs to be for this to follow

I think that I will just have some Crackers from the Cupboard instead

Making marks on map of madness

Somewhere, sometime Sunset
Somewhere, sometime Sunrise
Some will have reflection
Some will have surprise
Some ignore and carry on
Further deep they go
Some will learn and apply
Then their wisdom show

A few will live in constant sadness
Others will enjoy
Not the fate of others
Just that which did employ
Yet who are we to judge them?
Reasons we don't know
Just a hope of exit
All that we can show

The pet is looking out of sorts
Immediately noticed with a question
A person looks just the same
Yet nothing will we mention
A conundrum for the curious
The Stage show we put on
Everyone an actor
Joining complex throng

Mister B from Twenty-Three
Missing for a while
Maybe one should visit
With a caring smile
Mrs L has been through hell
From what is now on show
Does she need some company?
If don't inquire never

Making mess of making good

Making mess of making good
You told me so understood
More debris than used to be
Guess I'm in wrong trade
What used to be a Table
Now footstool quite unstable
The clock on wall had a fall
Now time in who knows where is able

The bloke at Tool shop loves me
Finding out new ways
To use but not intended
'Should have new job' often says
Yes, many do bend a nail
When with hammer hit
How many a figure eight
In a receptacle does sit?

Once went to hang some Wallpaper
Hung it sure and true
Pets got new clothing
They didn't have a clue
Don't mention when I changed a Tap
Didn't first turn off the mains
Room got a sudden wash
Though drying was a pain

The Boss won't let me near the Gas
Not sure why her strange notion
That by working with lit fag
Might lead to an explosion
She wants to swap my toolkit
For that for children buy
Not much use when repairing ceiling
After with blow torch I tried to dry

Marbellia

In a land called Marbellia
Once resided a strange tribe
In a house made from Walnut
They did live and choose to hide

And their Home was mobile
Though of destination had no choice
They could escape through use of letters
But there Marbles lacked a voice

The variation of one Nation
On display in just one part
Yet a common trait of many
This one tribe just made a start

During travels of the Home
It encountered many live self
Some Homes travelling for just pleasure
Some in search of long hoped wealth

Of other tribes some irritating
Using this one by association
Adding in on mass circulation
Without use of that asking thing

So this tribe spent time removing
When another tribe failed to ask
An irritant but a principle
Is common courtesy such hard task?

In the land called Marbellia
Guidance given free of charge
When the tribe thought deserving
Not used as badge for world at large

Marble mayhem

A1 did become
B2 joined the queue
C3 wishes to see
D4 said same and then did snore
E5 came alive
F6 called in sick
G7 found some strange leather Heaven
H8 forever late

Crouching Marble, hidden nonsense
Made mistake and so was seen
Only consolation
At least it kept it clean!!

I9 did try to be fine
J10 mistook for aircraft fuel
K11 did put up in Devon
L12 liked to delve
M13 in mystery been
N14 loves clotted cream
O15 just came alive
P16 questioned Bricks
Q17 felt random Heaven

The reproductive cycle is a marvel
Of the 'Guests that I do carry
Not ofay with their ways
I wonder if they marry?

R18 just seems a state
S19 is always fine
T20 a friend to go
U21 a tribute Band fun
V22 has no clue
W23 sought Sanctuary
X24 a long term bore
Y25 for more does strive
Z26 a box of tricks
Marble mayhem strikes again

Mr. Sandman has transported me across the astrophysical line

I have landed in the middle of a lush meadow filled with
beautiful flowers of unimaginable shapes and colors.

I am weaving flowers of different hues into my Goldie hair when
sounds of music are emitted through the balmy wind.

Dancing around me are Whoopie cats wearing bright orange
and lime coloured ball gowns with itsy bitsy magical yellow
high-heeled shoes that are blinding to gaze upon.

All of a sudden, I am adorned in a bright yellow ball gown,
ornamented with dazzling green emeralds.

My magical high-heeled shoes match and are bright yellow
and encased with more dazzling green emeralds.

I jump up and shout, "It is all right now, in fact I think it is a gas."

The Whoopee cats are dancing and prancing around me.

The wind is blowing, and if you listen closely you can distinguish an
extraordinary language only heard beyond the snow-capped mountain tops.

I am awakened, standing outside underneath the moonlight
dancing around my Magnificent Ash Tree.

Difference

Distinctly, different views with contentious conversations,
or ridicule, are the dialogue of agony.

Distinctly, different views with momentous discourse and
respect are the constructive dialogue of autonomy.

Low Vibrational Energy

The Spirits dance around the beautiful black Puss Cats.

Listening to the constant influx of the sweet sounds of
love, the Spirits ponder why many humans decide against
a steadfast commitment of a glittering universe.

Do not depart from the light and live in a world filled with darkness.

Hardened hearts coupled with harmful actions emit low vibrational energy.

Melissa Begley

Passing Fancy: (True story with my husband)

Forbidden passion uncovered in a clandestine
relationship but disclosed as a passing fancy.

Relatable experiences and the disguising of a love affair with whimsy fantasy.

Nightfall and twilight developed into a ceaseless delight, but my
endless desire to have you forever more ended the love affair.

At the break of dawn, on a beautiful summertime day; I chose
to end what would never begin our lifelong relationship.

Marriage was certainly not your way of thinking.
You warned me countless times.

After I left, not once did you get in touch with me, but conceivably
you didn't care. It was feasibly, I was merely your passing fancy.

Autumn arrived, I received information involving your deceased nephew.
I took refuge in knowing the right course of action was to contact you.

Was my heart healed enough to hide my emotions after
such a devotion to our romantic connection?

I gently knocked on your door and unexpectedly I was in your
embrace. Rapidly, you attempted to ignite my fire, but my spirit
disassociated from my body and soon we were standing apart.

Unpredictably, you articulated the words, "Baby
doll, I missed you. Will you marry me?"

Sensationally, a shocking disbelief to many, but the passing
fancy developed into a permanent relationship.

Melissa Begley

Fantastic Fabulous Festive Fantastical Friday

Fantastic Fabulous Festive Fantastical Friday, your attitude
will sparkle, shine, glitter, and glisten today.

Trounce, thrash, and trample the adversary of unpleasant, disagreeable,
obnoxious, unlikable, heartless, and hurtful mind-sets.

Decorous, demure, well-mannered, courteous, and respectful
behaviour will be your heartfelt bequest of kind-heartedness.

Remember to send up all of the glory to God
and to detach from negative people.

Golden Hearts

The harmonious ensemble of tranquillity and love are exhilarating;
frequently a difficult performance of the human condition.

The gift of self-restraint, with effortless dancing, while you ignore
those that boggle the mind with seductive lies and spreading
untruthful rumours is an intuitive dedication to inner-peace.

Distrust those that have limited positive energies and
are oblivious to their own unhappiness.

Golden hearts are uninterested in flattery and will flutter away
from the destructive behaviours of over dramatization.

Magnificent Monday

Magnificent Monday has arrived; wrap your spirit of kindness
around the weary and those that are not cheery.

Keep in mind our lifelong mission is humility and humbleness.

Haughtiness and prideful behavior are unacceptable.

By means of genuine compassion, the evils of
humankind will in due course fade away.

This morning I am dancing, prancing, singing, and enjoying another
day of living the good life and giving all the glory to God.

Melissa Begley

My Eleven

First and foremost, I am requesting forgiveness to anyone I
have harmed, whether intentionally or inadvertently.

As you presented my earthly life with needless actions and behaviors, I
forgive you. The tittle-tattle, gossip, harsh words, pilfering, and fictional
scandals regarding me are irrelevant to my being and do not matter any
longer. Hopefully, you have come to know that you should treat others better.

I will overlook the inaccurate, erroneous, and untrue stories
you tell on your own behalf to impress others; perchance the
attention is an awareness of your loneliness or failures. Glance
into the mirror and your beautiful image will appear.

There will be a constant evaluation of situations, not persons,
to protect myself from the negativity of others. I have already
detached from persons that enjoy pessimism, disparaging others,
and gloominess, but will interact respectfully when warranted.

I am grateful that I have given you my time and resources to assist in
the improvement of your life and happiness. It was revealed that you
were a psychic vampire and upon eliminating the thrills and frills
you no longer cheered and began the shrills of fresh fabrications.

I will enhance my kindness, sympathy, compassion, and
benevolence to add brightness to the Universe.

I will surround my loved ones and friends with love and peace.

I will attempt not to chatter unnecessarily regarding inappropriate
activities or stories that are factual concerning someone I love or once
cherished, especially in attempts to build up my personal agenda.

I will remember to give daily thanks regarding my blessings.
The benedictions bestowed upon me or different than upon
another. I am not wealthy or poor, but shall not become a
braggart or look down upon another of God's creations.

Lessons in abundance to be weighed when rendering assistance
to prevent destruction or hazard from coming into my arena.

I am requesting, unstated, aspirations and yearnings to be fulfilled.

Melissa Begley

Earthy Pain

I granted you, the portal to the inner sanctum of my heart, soul, and mind.

Did you betray me or is that the pathway bestowed upon you?

Do not dance around the subject and continue upfront and apologetic words.

Release me if your cleverness is a toxic secret to
deliver me permanent emotional harm.

My destiny is to love you throughout the centuries
of my past, current, and future lives.

Initiate my freedom from heart-breaking pain if that
is your triumphant plan of your earthly gain.

Heart and Soul

What values have you learned in life?

Many are practiced at the act of appearances such as caring,
but thank goodness many people are compassionate.

Charismatic communication and declarations of love,
perchance are gauche of heart and soul.

Be cautious and concerned regarding words and behaviours.

Charm, but do not harm.

Aesthetic consciousness is your awareness of Faith in God.

It is time to perform the Celebratory Dance of
Life. One, two, three, cha, cha, cha.

Melissa Begley

Defaming

Human hearts were not created to be callous.

Human minds were not created for malice.

Are we considered enlightened, but experience excitement
when we win at the game of defaming?

Fantastical Friday and the magic is in the air

Enchantment is created by those that have their mojo on.

Mystical events occur when you conduct yourself with
kindness, compassion, and empathy towards other.

People do not foresee tragic events in their lives, anticipate poor
health, expect to endure physical or mental pain, but thoughtfulness
and benevolence from others is an expectation and anticipation.

Do not be a moron, display prideful behaviour, and remember
to reflect upon your own attitude and behaviours.

Get up perform the Celebratory Dance of Life.

Get up, shake it up, twist and shout, wiggle, wiggle, wiggle,
cha, cha, cha, Ooh-la-la creating the magic of love... ...

Realm of Reality

Indulgences without a watchful eye with the
impulse controls of childlike wonder.

Dark toxic secrets operating negative energy.

Dysfunctional relationships under-the-radar of show
stopping sophisticated artificial love.

Your loved one patiently places their heart in your
hands, abuzz with anticipation to see you again.

As you dance around the subject promising to visit soon, the last
moon-kissed night arrives and even the wilting flowers fade away.

Transfer the darkness and enter into the realm of reality.

The brightness will begin again. Per the Lovely Ms P cha cha cha y'all ♥

Melissa Begley

Thankful Thursday

Magically, we begin our day rejuvenated, refreshed,
revitalized and ready to reorganize our thoughts.

With the Grace of God, we will mystically convert
the negative energy into positive outcomes.

Retreat, run away, move away from the unenthusiastic,
unconstructive, and pessimistic ones.

Adorned in our magical high-heeled shoes, this morning,
together we will perform the Celebratory Dance of Life.
One, two, three, cha, cha, cha, ooh-la-la... ...

Wonderful Whimsical Wednesday

Another day and a new-fangled beginning that will be enchanting, exciting, electrifying, enthralling, exhilarating, elating, enlivening, and eventful.

It is time to kick up your heels and perform the Celebratory Dance of Life. One, two, cha cha cha, three, four, ooh-la-la.

Count your blessings, and give all the glory to God... ... .

Spiralling Decay

Lavish indulgences and dalliances with others are the vortex of darkness.

Mirrors are reflective of shadow-self.

Imprints through light waves travel through portals

Aversion towards sincerity is the mutation of the mumbling of heartlessness.

The projection of light beams are visible to humans, but absent in many souls.

Grounded abundance is conflicting and provocative.

Pretentiousness is the pretence, but the spiralling of decay.

Melissa Begley

Terrific Tuesday

Humans engage in conversations regarding other humans,
but keep in mind tittle-tattle, gossip, misrepresentation of
the truth, embellishments, over exaggerations, and cruel
negativity are unacceptable and reflects a hardened heart.

We should do our best to project positivity, say no to negative
conversations, and dance amongst the Spirits of Love.

Magnificent Monday

Transformation of your choices by outside forces are not always satisfying,
but existence to execute positive acceptance of change is inevitable.

Our fate, perchance is not totally ours to establish.

It is time to perform the Celebratory Dance of Life.

Sing praises to God for all of your blessings.

One, two, cha, cha, cha and three, four, ooh-la-la.

Intriguing Star

Will you be the intriguing star in my dream tonight?

With the time change, we will enjoy an extra hour of delight.

Thrill-seekers, magical realism, pretty, pretty, pretty boys that
conduct themselves as gentlemen, but are overly confident
and a bit on the wild side; I patiently await your arrival.

No cads, misrepresented of the truth, or those only
desiring greedy pleasures will be accepted.

Sweetest Dreams all y'all

Melissa Begley

Holy cripes

If I had all the clothes I needed my wardrobe would be full of clothes
If my wardrobe were full of clothes I would attend many parties
I would know many people, if I know many people
I would receive many gifts
I receive many gifts
I would give them to everyone I see.
And if I give out to everyone
Everyone would love me.

My home my family

The song that the bird sing,
Is the song of the home

When the goat bleats,
It is all about home

The snail values it's home
And it carries it all about.

When I go east and west,
North and south,
I dream about my family

My home my family
The one I am proud of
My brothers, my sisters,
There is no one like you!

Simplicity

Some say that my teaching is nonsense
Others call it lofty but impractical.
But to those who have looked inside, themselves, this
nonsense makes perfect sense. And to those who put it
into practice, this loftiness has roots that go deep

I have just three things to teach
Simplicity, Patience and compassion. These three are your greatest treasure
Simple in the actions and in thoughts
You return to the source of being.
Patient with both friends and enemies,
You accord with the way thing are
Compassion toward yourself
You reconcile beings in the world.

Kindness

Are you kind?
Mother kindnesses, you're good!
With happiness, love and peace you fill us.

The Creator gave you to us
Our great creator is kind
And in Him kindness we find
He formed the firmament
He created our environment,

Air, animals, water, land, vegetables.
And made us their master
But not for us to plunder
Daily, our sins He overlooks
This kindness teaches us to have

That all who come our way
We may make mirthful
As we make ourselves joyful

City light

I still search
For you in crowds,
In empty fields,
And soaring clouds

In city lights
And passing cars,
On winding roads
And wishing stars

I wonder where
You could be now,
For years I've not said
Your name out loud

And longer since
I called you mine
Time has passed
For you and I

But I have learnt
To live without
I do not mind
I still love you anyhow

Bose Eneduwe Adogah

More than just a lesion

Rotor blades thrash the air
Troops on board lock and load
Gunships circle ever protective
Trying targets to simply goad
To show themselves and feel the wrath
Before boots on ground can deliver
Wiser foe that do know
Fade away with shiver

Though this is pointless to a point
When not planned to hold
Simply visiting and introducing
A different sort now in this playground
Joining mix of what do see
The front line of an army
A combination in cohesion
Creating more than just a lesion

Target coordinates match on screen
Through rear ramp nothing seen
Rapidly it does descend
Against the downdraft already bend
Those about to exist quick
Into whirlwind rising thick
Sucked up quick and slow to disperse
Vacuum caused the troopers curse

Another day of a deployment
Another until return
To Home and what it means
This is how airmobile earn
A pittance compared to cost of training
A pittance to make this surgical knife
A pittance for the job they do
A pittance compared to price of life

Mother Test

Bravado like the Avocado
Soft fruit but with a stone
Secret be to scoop that free
Place beside – alone
Coconut can cause a tut
Two layers must remove
To get the sensible we call edible
With milk they say can soothe

Today I will change the World
Today I'll make it mine
Today I will adjust it
Today it will be fine
What? You say
What? You question me
What? You doubt that I can
What! Watch my capability!!

None did stand upon this land
Rightfully say they own
For we are but a visitor
So, attitude I can't condone
The visitor came and said a name
Human called themselves
There began a problem that ran
Dipping deeper as do the doer delves

Can I be my destiny?
Or merely part of history
Depending on what choose to be
In the present you and me
Nature calls and structure falls
A reminder that not so great
We must see that just be
A simple growing state

We like to lord and oft applaud
Those who do it best
Yet they be so small you see
When Mother gives a Test

Moving Statue

The Broadsheets are being noncommittal
The Tabloids having a field day
News peruse does not amuse
So predictable in what say

Distraction attraction from real action
Woes but no real change
Revel in the misery
Reason does seem strange

I don't care about neighbour's new car
I don't care about their deliveries
I don't care about their Garden
All the 'improvements' and novelties
I don't care if some Politian
Has a 'beef' with someone else
I don't care of big name worries
I just care about Family's health

I am one of many
Saying but don't do
Alter within the ways we're given
Guilty me, are guilty you?

Faces fill in spaces
Those can fill yourself
Are we just too lazy
To think about our health

I am the moving Statue
Just motion you can't see
For the act of moving
Is buried deep inside of me

Music muse

Are we ready?
Are we steady?
Good! Let's have some fun
The place we face is no race
Just a journey just begun

Don't wish for the tomorrow
When today we have a chance
To enjoy its offerings
To join in its dance

California Dreaming plays on radio
Yet not that place,
Though is beautiful
The place I seek to go

Are we brave enough to change?
This here now that seems so strange
Discontent without relent
A fashion not for me

Physco City

In the night my Demons fight
In the day they go away
Guess that they don't like the fight
When encounter that which right

Openings in open space
Into which not wanted race
Do not know their time or place
So, at rest we them face

Physco City does reside
In most of us we choose to hide
Not an option as a Bride
That one I think I will let slide

Ang aking maliit na kapatid na babae

(My little Sister) dedicated to Vanessa Lawlor

The little Sister became a Lady
The Lady then became a Wife
Wife turned also into Mother
Another chapter in her life

A life that has seen many places
Many spaces and new faces
Each one blessed with her graces
Her only fault is that I am her Brother

Another year past just like the last
Am sure she feels it went too fast
So much experience can she cast
Too the offspring she so loves

So long has been since last I've seen
My fault and nothing more
Yet, again she found this pain
For I am but a chore

Seven to four, removing three
The name on screen that will see
Yet those seven still remember
Eleven months short of my September

Do yo remember that time in Hythe
That Brother took an unexpected bath for him
In that dyke deep not wide
Saved a sheep that couldn't swim

I remember Beaverwood
With those friends you then stood
Still I guess you do today
For that simply is your way

Memories now of some old times

My name

Am I a grain or just a pain?
To the sands of time?
Do I fit or simply sit?
Am I dull or do I shine?
Am I attractive when inactive?
Do I sit well and sure?
Am I considered inappropriate?
Am I ever referred as pure?

What am I as minutes fly?
Do I stay or go?
Do I belong in expression session?
Do I you choose to show?
I am sometimes random
Sometimes I am not
Focused on the serious
Dealing with what got

Do I drive you crazy?
Do I make you lazy?
Do I change your routine?
Am I now or just have been?
The conundrum is sum
Me an those have caught
I am just a part of your
My name? I am known as Thought

New nocturnal nonsense

The Foxes have formed a Choir
Pre-Five is not their best
Delivery lorries try to drown them out
As uphill their gears they test

Day starts with T so that must mean
One in two chance some rubbish will be collected
Not sure why not the rest
Is rubbish now thoroughly vetted?

World is bright with street light
Arcs are overlapping
Merrily burning for the illegal earning
While the victims are still napping

Recollections of yesterday
As start a challenge new
Dip a toe in this hole
Social swamping to wade through

When police cars rush to close escape
Normal life has been resumed
The Lewisham Lads are encroaching
Bromley Boys are not amused

Never in the history of me
Did I even see things now see
Extension is pure quality
When reflect on what did be

Forget that song for got it wrong
When we collide we don't come together
We fight and rob and on platforms sob
About more than just the weather

Now thirty past – that went fast
When write and then transcribe
Maybe another hour
If sun up I can bribe

What will I Find to do with you?

Oh, what will I find to do with you, with you,
To help make things seem better, better.
I am searching high and low for words to tease
Your sad face into smiles to make you better, better.

So, give me that smile I would walk miles and miles to see.
I would stand in your gaze and troubles would fade away.
You would give me your hand and I would gather us close together.
Synchronised we would glide round the room moving in gentle rhythm.

Is it a smile I see, peeping up at me, revealing the girl who was hidden?
My heart starts to beat like a drum all must hear, dancing near.
When your face is raised to mine with a smile others too can see.
We light up the room as your smile chases away the dreary gloom.

Now our spirits are joined sharing laughter joy,
Spilling our delight out for others to share
Sending smiles round the room better and better.
It is something we can do so well together.

WobblingPen aka Penny Wobbly

I sit

I sit and gaze at the sky.
With fluffy images floating by,
Ever changing re-arranging
So relaxing to the eye.

At times static pure white pillows
Bathed in brilliant sun light,
Hang resting on an azure bed.
Recovering from drama they have fled.

The breeze changes tempo
Gloomy clouds collide till lightening strikes,
Thunder roars with the need to vent,
Rain falls to soak the land.

I sit and gaze amazed
At this theatre in the sky.
Allowing me moments
Of relaxation and inner calm.

WobblingPen

Not for sale my own trail

I ripped the cover from so called lover
Saw the truth behind
The ecstasy in my agony
All they sought to find
I ripped some more to find the core
The reason why they be
Yet could not find for were not my kind
A darkness truly confronted me

Sell them self for that not wealth
For no gain in pain
The misery of that they be
Would drive myself insane
Resting in the deepest oceans
Lay the bits of our strangest motions
Buried in that we can't see
Lies the wreckage of the one be

Some days I try to just get by
Others I do drive
On to new so can that do
With challenge we do thrive
There's a Lady who for sure
Rain or shine passes Door
Dog her eyes and with dark disguise
The milkiness and more

We've built this thing so let's to it bring
Something to remember
A burning light that shines so bright
In the cold and dark that is December
Gone past noon so guise I'll soon
Think what have for lunch
The complexity of variety
Still, I have a hunch

Not May

Ontario in October
Madrid in muggy May
Loathsome lounging in London Town
All the words we say

Historical or mythical
Educational or factual
Biological or 'gasp, Religion all
Some do deter and some call

The power of a Book

Physical, visual, audio – bases covered
Self-publishing or Publishers plundering
Opportunities wondering
Why in words is not Earth smothered?

The reason why, though some do try
We are not as good as think
Only few not me and you
Into that esteemed place sink

Yet many to which aspire

On Autumn leaves the left grieves
Parted for a while
Knowing though although cannot show
The beauty of that smile

Maybe one day on a fun day
We will do that so extreme
You do say no sense in play
Let me show you what I mean

If from which don't earn you should then spurn
A fallacy so often taught
Depriving them without that pen
To share that in which are caught

Mary made Maypole magical
Steve did beat his Drum
Olive was the peacemaker
Colin loved a sum

Are antiquities that we see
Covered by some privacy?
If they are then what it be
If are found by an old tree

A light rain before the sunrise
Will drive away the mist
Then it clears another day
To be with light kissed

The wandering of idle mind
The sense of which has none
The bad news is not finished
The good is past begun

Can I have a Coffee please
My senses are a quivering
Been long two hours since the last one
My body now is shivering

Oh, what the lot of that which got
The urge to stuff display
For currently no Mary Queen
Currently not May

Apologies for wasted time
The time that you have spent
Reading something not self-promotional
At least did not shout 'Repent!'

Not ready for

The sensibility of September
For that was when was born
The outrageous of October
When swaddling clothes were worn
Nectar in November
For produced my Wife
Dilemma in December
Frivolity and strife

The changing of the clocks
Shops now swapping stocks
Darkness closing in
Light not sure when to begin
The rain from Spain a constant pain
When passport it does own
Just heed the call before you fall
Not welcome! Just go home!

The musings while am cruising
Through another dreary day
The playing with which am saying
Much missing months like May
Don't really want a new one
For that means another year
Don't really want some of past ones
When hurt thrust with its barbed spear

Life does tease when hard to please
Guess I'll accept what I can get
Though with some restrictions
Not ready for the 'Happy Clappers' yet
The senility of September
Closer every year
The passion of the passing
Has been done to one held dear

Not yet Generation

When ink flows as words show
When it just feels right
When lose oneself in visual wealth
Then it's time to write
Of days gone by and reasons why
Of future things we hope
Of day to day and hope may
The tools we use to cope

Ink set down in cold Alaska
Was read in far Atlanta
That Book from peaceful Nepal
Enjoyed by one and all
That Novel that kept you gripped
The poem as moment slipped
Into the wondering and engrossing
Of dreaming and supposing

Modern times didn't start this crime
Of captivating with intent
We just took of old a look
Then did to see where went
'A voice for all' came the call
Heard by every Nation
Technology gave help 'free'
To a satisfactory situation

Not all can hear and some with fear
Express in different voice
The feel alone yet one of own
Given different choice
Black on white just feels right
When communication situation
Long may it last to futures past
In the not yet Generation

Note

One younger spoke to one who slightly older
Was their Guide and their 'cry shoulder'
Looked at them and with pen
Wrote a Note and said

Teach me trouble, teach me hate
Teach me things to which can relate
Teach me spite and teach me wrong
Teach though know they don't belong
Teach me envy, ridicule
Teach me I am above all
Teach me arrogance, teach me blind
Am a human, receptive find

Teach me Love for I have changed
Teach understanding though is strange
Teach me acceptance that we are equal
Teach me so we have a sequel
Teach me patience when am tested
Teach me somethings better rested
Teach me Wisdom in circumstance
Teach me not of ignorance

For am but pollen in the air
Some allergic, some somewhere
I am start when do land
On fertile space and not in sand
That's too full of buried Heads
We have and do see where instead
Of the place we wish to be
We get consigned to ignominy

Teach me one that's gone before
Teach so hold forever more
Teach the errors and the cure
Teach to be almost pure

Nothing

Not the abyss of afterlife
She's still living, yes, my Wife!
No reason yet to separate
Even if sometimes she does hate
Not that sanctuary from misery
Here but can with cope
I have one secret ingredient
Most of you know it as Hope

Longing for longevity
Longing for much more
Longing for some history
Longing I am sure
Waiting for the new day
Waiting for the new
Waiting possibility
Waiting just to do

What did be built new me
What did be - a step
What did be just what did see
What did be now the past be
Tongue is for more than just tasting
Tongue is something new
Tongue a form of speaking
Tongue, different we should do

Is this the last time?
That this one will write?
Is this the last time?
See a day so bright
Is this the last time?
I get the chance to think
Is this the last time?
Enjoy the beverage that I drink

Nothing known so carry on
Nothing set so will stay strong
Nothing is a waste of something
Nothing, a place I don't belong

Novus Ex antiquis

If I were a Gun, I'd fire love bullets
If I were a Bomb, I would release
Bullets aimed at everyone
Exploding with a thing called Peace

One way or another
Obvious or undercover
I took a look that turned into Book
A gift to more than lover

Once I was a morsel
I became a snack
Then became a full meal
From which no turning back

Ambition to be a Banquet
A simple Menu will also do
I just love the experience
Of trying something new

Finger food or silver platter
All the same so doesn't matter
As my thoughts I freely scatter
Nothing much but nonsense natter

Pull back the crack and let light flow
Let's go somewhere we don't know
Open wide and let inside
Show the World and let it show

In a past that could not last
Close to going under
Cracked and broken, somethings unspoken
Felt both sides of Thunder

Then word said filled my Head
Words with meaning strong
Took a grip and made one flip
Enough to carry on

Now we are teaching

The appeal of the seemingly unreal
The nuances of Nature
Speaking now with vision
The creativity of the Creator

The mist made the Moors mysterious
Haunting, silent, vast scene
Beautiful visible but now invisible
Trapped when wrapped yet, somehow, clean

The plunging call of Waterfall
The ripple, skoosh as it passes by
The bang, explosion of liquid motion
The tears of Mothers cry

The Rejuvenation of the Tree
That seems to work in reverse
Wrapping self in leaf wealth
Then bare at climates worst

The barren lands of endless sand
That were once oceans so we're told
Now complete with extreme heat
Then went through Ice age cold

The parts we take for granted
Just accept and carry on
Too concentrating not contemplating
What we're doing could be wrong

Climate like a Primate
Adapts to what is taught
Now we are teaching it rebellion
Now in it are caught

Now we start to mention Heart

I walked same ground and heard same sounds
Yet different now they be
Shared a joke as with same spoke
Yet felt so new to me
Maybe I am lazy, maybe I am not
Just appreciation in situation
Liking what have got

Day starts same as last week's name
That's the only thing in common be
Now hour near the time to shower
Then some sleep will, hopefully, see
Seven be the names we know
Learn from each one as we grow
Twelve another group we know
In four seasons they then show

What is always but six letters?
When the ways are not all
What is friend but another six?
When with them you seldom mix
When a man can't own a Car
Does that mean can't travel far?
Why do we wish upon a star?
When we know can't go that far

Now we start to mention Heart
As a thing of love not life
Who defines the term we earn?
When become a Husband or a Wife?
Soon to sleep and thoughts will keep
Hopefully until tomorrow
Then again with use of pen
Some of your day will borrow

Nowhere needs

Nowhere needs a nothing
Something needs a some
Despair, it needs direction
Life requires fun

When find it hard to smile
When find happiness is unemployed
Then I look to another place
That leaves me overjoyed

A piece that fits so neatly
A piece that I know well
A piece both in and outer shown
A piece that breaks a Spell

And came the call for clarity
Came call for classification
Came the call for some understanding
Understood we're just on Nation

Though do try I still wonder why
I am so sorry for not joining
But I am me and will always be
Not your type in the morning

Been and seen and done for real
That bravado that you feel
Images haunting still
So sorry but have no appeal

Nowhere leads to nothing
A path some choose to tread
Somewhere leads to something
Not necessarily that inbred

Nursery rhymes and Human crimes

'Sing a song of sixpence
A pocket full of sighs
Wishing had a sixpence
Just one before do die'
Sing a song of sixpence
A dream that someone had
They never saw one
Isn't that so sad?

'Humpty Dumpty sat on wall
Then that cannon had a fall
Much like many who we call
Human but don't treat as such'
Little Jack Horner sat in corner
Too scared to show his face
Parents cared nothing of parenting
We've become our own disgrace

Nursery rhymes of bygone times
Transformed to modern day
Look at them then look around
Think then just what say

Yes, these are words and so not heard
Much like the subject's cry
These are but someone's poem
Ask the Writer why

Why the why and then why
The one stepped out of line
Maybe they are crazy
Believing this is not so fine

Obsessed by need

We came tonight in Moonlight bright
To make a whole new world
But did miss so into Abyss
We were cruelly hurled

For technology we did plea
Clamoured for it fast
We chose to forget the path we set
The lessons from our past

What has become of the thinking one?
That could do it for them self
Obsessed by need of corporate greed
Even for our health

Bullets fly with no need to try
For a simple no reason why
When so easy to make one die
Than to discuss and beg to differ

A Star was born a million years
A million years in our past
It's light so bright is now in sight
But does that Star still last?

Look at me and what do you see
A reflection or a stranger?
Am I one with whom can get along?
Or am I a mortal danger?

Black or white is just sight
So is brown or tan
It is not the skin I wear
Is what I want and can

I can be a mystery
Can be example too
I am just another one
Choice now what to do

Pondering the if

What will be will be
Hardship or a harmony
Drifting into possibility
If from this body I was free

If I was an Eagle, I could soar
Alas I was born of Human kind
If I was a Tiger, I would roam
Alas, I think the Wife would mind

If an atom didn't matter
Why we made a bomb to scatter?
If don't like then why reads?
Food for thought and so we feed

If I was a wild Dog
Which part of territory would I hog?
If an Armadillo with thick hide
Would you venture on other side?

If this world just made some sense
Situation no recompense
Would it really be that better?
When still exists these hate groups setter

Now fee deep in that which write
As approaching thing called night
Already needed electric light
To endorse the not right sight

When pain to gain considered sane
The question remains as statue stiff
Silent in the violence
Pondering the if

Pop

'Pop'! A thing came into being
Not yet hearing, not yet seeing
Though had one thing that left it reeling
The thing discovered it had feeling

Needed new thing to describe them
Something, one day, to be heard
To pass on those new found feelings
So created what we call Word

Pop then started changing self
Mutating to encapsulate this wealth
Thing mutated, still mutating
With each pass of its sensation

Developed ears to hear sound
Developed eyes to see
Developed mouth with which to speak
Developed Hands and history

With these new found things
Along with some more
Pop found mobility
Pop chose to explore

Discovered other Pops
Discovered Popettes
Created thing called Friendship
Discovered all the happiness
Discovered the regrets

As it slowly got to know
A different feeling began to show
In a certain one went above
Then created thing called Love

Poppy fields have two meanings

One did say and one did do
In that there is nothing new
One did cherish that so strange
When that one explored the range
Knowing but not showing
The path on which are going
All the seeds then sowing
To that which no-one saw

You whispered and I listened
You said and I did do
You beckoned and I followed
Followed into the new
If I could have a loop repeat
If I could turn back time
Then you know which part would choose
When knew loving was no crime

Poppy fields were something new
Not the place for me
Poppy fields have two meanings
Now and history
We are all our own story
Not each chapter filled with glory
We are all a page in age
When does come the Grand Parade

Crash and burn and then from learn
Learn to rise again
Education in the bad occasion
No pleasure without pain
Some, they talk of Phoenix
Some they speak to higher above
Yet for cure that's so pure
Nothing beats true love

It's pot luck

I've built things up then shot them down
Because no-longer did I care
In some strange way we could all say
A history we share
The shot in arm that seemed a charm
Until in it we're caught
The golden chalice containing malice
Not the stuff we sought

The cancer of the chancer
Some they have no choice
Without a cure its allure
When offering rejoice
That closing time for was not mine
That false smile of sympathy
The rueful act of fact
Not all is meant to be

It's all pot luck so buckle up
The things go through as grow
Some will hide for are inside
Others are on show
I've built things up then been shot down
Not necessarily by my choice
For you see many more than me
Think and have a voice

Pottery shaped out of Clay

Holding a candle to what we can handle
Watching the flame light the way
With all that we've learnt we seldom get burnt
We're Pottery shaped out of Clay

You and me are history
History in the making
All we do and go through
The challenges undertaking

Don't give to me a poor sad excuse
Don't say to me that you always lose
Failures fail when that they choose
That cycle was made for the breaking

The Potter and Pot, we are the complete lot
Crafting our craft as the Craftsmen
Drawing up plans, notations in Sans
Designing the deeds like a Draughtsman

So, show me what designs form in your Mind
Show to me the variety
Break the spell when I then tell
You can, if choose, that be

Don't hate the plate for plates are great
Keeping food from floor
Become the Dinner service
Become that plate and more

Don't smash that plate with thing called Hate
Put upon the shelf
Probably displaying what I am saying
The perfect item is self

Pretty in the posture of petulance

The lady was having a hissy fit
That the man did know so well
Just what triggered this one
None on earth could tell
Yet she looked adorable
To the man who loves
Her for being simply her
The Hawk side and the Doves

The upturned corners of her mouth
The frown lines that appear
The expectation of the snap
To all who ventured near
That slight stomp of the foot
The bark of the demand
The threat of the sudden crying
If things get out of hand

The good and bad of married life
Each does have a place
Even the look of a spoil child
Shown in this here face
Pretty in the posture of petulance
As is pretty when life enjoys
Somehow acceptable with the females
Not so on the boys

Soon this will get put away
Back with come the smile
For never does it last too long
Just few hours are her style
The man he braved the comments
Knowing not truly meant
For from a part she could not control
Were from these moments sent

Priceless wealth

Stood on the stage of the play
The one we call ourselves
A mystery is what we be
Prisoners to thing called wealth

Hello old friend, it's been a while
Since last you I could then greet
Though abhor that gone before
A correction we cannot meet

Everything in extreme
Video has taught us to believe
When we just go around killing stuff
Then a high score can achieve

Law enforcement are just human
Bad and good do mix
Only when they show themselves
Can we then, hopefully, fix

Turmoil at the Turnstiles
Gathered but can't enter
Social distance the new catch words
Fines for non-repented

Mathematics play with algorithms
Spin Doctors just spin
Though seems strange we are the change
We still have chance to win

Nothing big and glorious
Just how we choose to live
Not all about receiving
But what we choose to give

Tell me in the privacy
Something about yourself
For meeting other people
A simple priceless wealth

Problem Pets

The Watchdog's watching Wombats wandering
I guess it is asleep
Standing guard for walking's hard
When in the trees do keep

Not that Watchdog but the Wombats
Dogs prefer the ground
At least I guess because the rest
Is where are normally found

The Cat's sat at door of Rat
It's in for a surprise
Thinks a Mouse lives in that House
Soon it will be wise

How do I know? For it did show
Just the other day
Blooming Hell I did yell
Exact I couldn't say

The Parrot's fond of Carrot
I think because repeat
When on plate before I ate
All sliced up and neat

I gave it raw for thought wanted more
It started with beady glare
Then gave me four pecks not three
Gave me a bloody square!

Oh, how I wish didn't buy those Fish
I am such a gullible fool
Just more work is their quirk
When classed as Tropical

Still do the same as the Gold name
Just Tank and not a Bowl
Guess need more to explore
When parted from their shoal

Product-person

What direction is perfection?
Can someone tell me please?
For its route I can't compute
So many mysteries
What road to take for goodness sake
My head it just can't function
So many choices with different voices
It's like a spaghetti junction!

Use to think knew what was doing
Now I am not sure
Forks in road just seem to goad
I need a Map for cure
Overtake and overtaken
The cautious and the brave
Middle lane is my gain
My vehicle I want to save

I am ready for the steady
Boy racer am too old
Once did try, maybe why
Bought more vehicles than I sold
My name a frame for once insane
Now wisdom I can part
If choose to hear that I hold dear
Their choice but is a start

Things went away some did say
When met better souls than me
Taught me more than just folklore
Taught me, me to be
I am a product-person
Manufactured certainly way
Crafted by the 'been and done'
That lived to have a say

Profugo

What became of that we learn
Yet never chose to benefit
What became of all experience?
When on it we choose to sit

Part of me, my be amused
Part of me is still abused
Part of me is just confused
Part of me I've still not used

Never ever assume your clever
For students be for all that we live
Never ever be that taker
That to others something can give
Never be 'the woe is me'
When another worse than you
Takes a stride along the ride
Showing something, they can do

Contemplation Station for situation
That's a place I've been through
Seen and met those yet to get
Yet would because they saw the clue

Found new clothes without holes
A place to cut their hair
They are making something out of that 'nothing'
How? Because they dare!

What became of that we learn?
Then we chose to hide
It became the saving thing
When lost that thing we call Pride

Prominent past

The modern Shakespeare does exist
Given title and rightly so
A name I wish to which be accredited
Alas am not for way to go
Walter Whitman or E.E. Cummings
If were American to, perhaps, aspire
Alas I am but Ian Wilcox
So, at best my work is dire

The modern W.B. Yates or Oscar Wilde
That would be a blast it's true
Alas poor scribbler despite your efforts
They remain far above you
No Charles Pierre Baudelaire nor Victor Marie Hugo
Parley me non francaise
Cannot even write the language
Guess another day

No, am not a Eugen Berthold Friedrich Brecht
Nor am I an Irving Peter Layton
I am just a pupil learning
From the day which I was born
I am no Chairil Anwar
Never aspire to Subagio Sastrowardoyo
I gues that I am just a virgin Poet
With long and inked way to go and show

The world of the great Poets
Acclaimed and rightly so
Embedded in our History
Lost before we know
Why! The cry of the aspiring
Why the dismissed fuss
Well, my friend, because of our attitude
Yes, because of us

Proof if needed

In humility what do we see
Other than that, we can relate
In the depths of the self
The parts we like and parts we hate
Nothing is a something
When experience it you do
Not the place that one should face
Yet alone go through

I saw again that look of pain
Upon a person new
Knew that once and was enough
Felt just like they do
Guess it's hard to be 'outside
Physically and the other
When you have no benefits
Not even have some cover

Went to one and so begun
A friendship of a kind
Different faces and different spaces
Just sharing of the Mind
Who am I and I ask why?
Some get a lucky break
Which another of different cover
Has to get just what can take

I am the pea in the pod
That somehow didn't cook
I am the raw that went before
The one did overlook
Rain a pain for the sane
Imagine with no roof?
Look around your surround
There will be the proof

Puppets in the play

To set the scene in what might have been
I'm walking down the street
Then taking space so have to face
And cordially now greet
An apology to the Apothecary
Who's workload have increased
To keep me here through care and fear
So not labelled that deceased

I swim in sea of self-chosen ignorance
Certain things don't want to know
Like how close to becoming ghost
When certain times can show
Now I be a new me
Did change then change again
Yet a constant followed me
To Wife I'm still a pain

The acorn fell and landed well
A chance to be a Tree
Still have to face questions in its space
How copy we will one-day see
Human mirrors Nature
Though in different way
Something far more powerful
In end does have its say

Come with me on travel 'free'
The cost it is not shown
Yet each part a new start
In that I call 'my own'
Who could write this story true?
All have done and still to do
Not the likes of me and you
We're just puppets in the play

Purong pagmamahal

As the skies try to disguise
A Winter again alone
Rain it falls and sunshine calls
Deep unto the bone
Technology a saviour be
But not the perfect cure
For have dipped into loving trip
So now want much more

I don't believe that anyone
Could love as much as I love her
If you have your own the same
Then that is a love so pure
She said to me 'where do you want to go?'
I told her to the stars
She set us on a journey
Recently past Mars

Moments make a lifetime
Love a life does make
Experience an education
All the give and take
Every time it rains, she's my umbrella
For every cold she is fire
For every question she has answers
For every wanting my desire

No matter the distance I find no resistance
"my goal to make us whole"
No matter what say I will find a way
To achieve my soul
No matter what comes, will overcome
A challenge and nothing much more
Not quite the same but still have same name
Still have those who I adore

Purpose

The Tower turned to a tourist attraction
A big pop hit about no satisfaction
Then we ban interaction
What a crazy world this is

Rules 'for fools' because it's 'cool'
The self above the Mass we do
All the media can 'see through'
What a crazy state of things

Democracy is now 'a conspiracy'
This from the land 'of the free'
Lost our sense of decency
What a crazy time we're having

Give me please a way back
Back to something that I knew
Give me please just a glimmer
When had purpose to just do

Not the thing

We start something but then lose track
Create a vision but let it cloud
Lust for larger figures
Scared to say 'no' out loud

We wan the 'like' above being different
We want both sides but can't be
We become complacent to objective
It's so easy to run free

Will w one day just look back
With regret when finally see
This has gone so far from start
Not the thing was meant to be

Put a P

Who am I amongst the crowd?
Who am I to stand out proud?
Who am I? I will tell true
I am me and so are you
Others speak of personal Hell
Some do like to kiss and tell
ME, I sit within my shell
Let some others chase that sell

When I reach, what do I find?
Nothing more important, just the peace of mind
When I look beyond the now, look into the can
Nothing else much matters, for a simple man
When choose to search beyond what see
Finding out that real me
Taking and devoting
Opportunity there is never ending

In the morning as day is dawning
I am already near midday
Nothing much as into being
Just the bits that others say
Have no vehicle but I am driving
Have a reason for surviving
In a small way I am thriving
Put a P before lay

Had some fun when cut and run
Legs now too old for that
So, I go with half know
To rest I tip the hat
Old enough to know my limits
Young enough to the new try
Got some people who are watching
Some of them are asking why

Remember and do the same

On fields of fire, I found a foe
That foe was my own fear
Fear w that I didn't know
Yet was more than near
On fields of pain, I went insane
For no sane person here would go
The seemingly need for destructions seed
Each did have to sow

In Camaraderie I found Family
In chaos found our bond
In discipline did begin
A union of the strong
Reliance on another
For your back to cover
As theirs with care
That commitment you share
On place that's Devil's Mother

In Uniform a man was born
Different from that known
Of two different sides that with pride
When needed was freely shown
In man-made Hell many fell
Before their own December
So in November we will remember
In some small ways will tell

Those caught up in the maelstrom
By choice and those not
For not all did wear a uniform
Yet are not forgot
The one to end all others
Merely became another
With guns and planes spread deaths and pain
We remember but do the same

Reminisce with a twist

I made a pact with the Devil once
I was rejected as too hot to handle
Spoke then to the other side
But refused to light that Candle

I once was boy but then I grew
Learning from that went through
Came out as something new
I guess a thing that all do

Maturity in mid waking
Roll but still stand that taking
Better me I am making
So bring it on for I'm not breaking

Call me in the calm collective
Call me when find sense
Call me when feel are equal
Without demanding recompense

Yes, our forefathers made mistakes
Yes, I do not with them agree
Yet harbouring, not moving on
No solution to unity

I have made mistakes
I am sure that you have too
It is part of education
Part to becoming true

An awkwardness in Arkansas
A flippancy in the Philippines
A moving moment in Montreal
Tell me what it means

A surly sulk in the Seychelles
European in Ethiopia
Making mark in Marrakesh
Entering Utopia

I once made a pact and that's a fact
The story so well known
Then discovered a different way
One can call my own

Reminisce with a twist
The thing we all must do
Chances done and then moved on
The silly once did do

The lucky learn and knowledge learn
The unfortunate have no chance
Taken far before their time
To know the old age stance

Reminisce with a twist
Then reminisce again
Hopefully the script will change
Containing far less pain

Responsibility for future see

The need to feed that insatiable seed
That manifests inside
That need to show that it does grow
That Parent with the pride
Pride as 'child' it does grow
Not the blood and flesh that we know
No, the child we hold so tight
The child others see as both do write

The Writer is a Parent
Of different kind that's true
As with all Creatives
In anything they do
The conception of perfection
First must have a start
The constant changing of the definition
The benefit – the Art

In Human form a Family born
In other just the same
Needing the same nurturing
Just collective, different name
Does a Parent ever stop caring?
How their offspring will improve
Only difference in another realm
Always and forever – always is just 'your move'

The trials and the tribulations
The punishments and the salvations
The one same different for contemplation
Is home truth without exaggeration
Can fool oneself so easily
Just how great we think we be
Outside bubble lies the trouble
Comes with name Reality

Revel

A thought it caught the train to Gain
It loved what there it found
An idea came that wasn't same
An idea so profound

Added two t's and an r
Created thing we must
Form the one became much more
For Created trust

A thought it caught and we sought
A different in what do
Started to future look
Found that hidden clue

It gave strength to carry on
Gave a way to cope
Thought contained just four letters
Thought we then named Hope

As surprise came demise
Of just merely being
A target yes that we should bless
The light of that now seeing

Here me out and please don't shout
Letters on a page
Doing it old style
Showing of my age

Revel in the Rebel
Of the proud art
Not exactly History
But at least a start

Rhythm the attraction

Way down there in the 'been around'
The one did make their mark
Way back there when did the dare
Even just for lark
The one did taste the 'bright life'
Soaked up all the beams
Made the most of its coast
While coming apart at their own seams

Way back when and can't do again
The one who was carefree
Living with no tomorrow
That would lead to sorrow
Just the flow of that they know
Not much if truth be told
Not a barrier for the carrier
Of an attitude so bold

And then the time caught up again
Then the carriage feels the pain
Then the jaunts become old haunts
Likely not to see again
The once crazy now is lazy
When Daredevil comes to call
Some surprise as with age get wise
Leaving that to younger fool

Yet still the music has attraction
Tempting body into action
Still the beat reaches feet
Arms do twitch as notes greet
Yet we know we will be slow
Clumsy in the action
Yet the force must run its course
Rhythm the attraction

Ribcage

Sky outside a different hue
Clock says different to that of you
Yet inside where I hold
The essence pure does unfold

Tap of finger on the screen
Not enough to say what mean
Can send an image through the air
In those times, times we share

Make a moment last a day
Finding truth in what they say
Countdown ticking until we share
Once again, Filipino air

The days apart will soon slip by
The minutes together just seem to fly
Yet through it all I still believe
The thing called us will never leave
You are me and I am you
Just the thing that couples do
Made it this far with the tests
Soon plain sailing for the rest
Others look and wonder why
When apart we still do try
To be as one, just like the past
That made something, Born to last

Adam gave a rib they say
To make his Eve then real
I would give a ribcage
To show you how I feel

My love, my life, my everything
My joy, my pain and what you bring
My heart, my dream, my honest soul
My reason sure so can endure
My perfect fit to fill that hole

Riddle me and you will see

Long ago but again on show
Some broke away from recognised
Some they were truly deeply upset
Others just surprised

Just used common language
But in different way
To release their thinking
To in ink then say

A certain way was just for its day
Expansion and diversity
Loudly then did say
You were good, that's understand
Yet restricted in your play

They wrote

Imagination is creation
Not some age-old rules
We are free to be what be
We are not misguided fools

Riddle me and you will see
I am a better riddle
The one who chose to get the most
By with letters I do fiddle

I make some sense with my nonsense
To those I think you'll find
Can relate and appreciate
A forward thinking Mind

So, look at me and you will see
Writing is constantly History
Evolution its solution
Not its execution

Rise to the task

What would it feel if you told me real?
The inner that you hide
Is it shy that reason why?
Or more a darker side?
What would be the cost of that you lost?
Compared to that which gain?
All have them, some without pen
To express the pain

So, I hold hands up and runneth cup
The vessel that holds me
The fluid runs to what becomes
That part is Destiny
I may want it now but that's not how
This thing is programmed by some chip
No catastrophe will we be
If we just have a blip

Blast you through proud and true
Scars are battles won
Medal not of metal
Just what have become
I owe you nothing but I owe something
Something I can't say
For that was then and how and when
Just another Day

Suddenly an open Gate, suddenly no cause to hate
The past that owned the name
Such waste is that named Haste
Such a crying shame
I could change and I am strange
So, question that I ask
You are strong so are not wrong
Can you rise to but a task?

Romeo Echo Alpha Delta

Something stirred in the seat of seeing
Something that not seen before
Am of age that remember page
Turn again because I want more

The old and new for things to do
The ink that wants to feed
The long, the short, the words I've caught
When I simply read
The black on white a pure delight
The contents always change
The factual or rhyme call
The serious or strange

The lyrical lines and age-old crimes
The fantasy or fiction
Gave up T.V. when couldn't see
Now reading my addiction

The quivering and the quibbling
The characters to love and hate
The villain of infamy
The relationships and the relate

The old and new, the puzzle/ clue
The 'how to' if I could
The places been and things seen
The shouldn't and the should
Those things I knew or what went through
That simple discussion that not boring before snoring
That time I simply read

Room for reflection

If a sphere was perfectly clear
What then would you see?
If a man pushed the 'can'
Would that be a travesty?

Longing for the letter
The solution to feel better
The innovation of exploration
Somehow sits as a sensation

The putting down the feeling
While the mind is reeling
Not all sad and some not bad
Just a person being

The gain of pain is verse
The happiness no curse
The multitude that could include
Not necessarily the worst

That sensation an exclamation
When see the part you feel
Somehow when vision lets
Words become so real

All this time I have been breathing
All this time still believing
You are only just held back
When the drive yourself you lack

If slate was clean what would it mean
How learn when nothing wrong?
If w live in Ivory Castles
How then would we get along?

Room for reflection
Maybe a conception

Ruefully reflecting

Once, long ago, someone stood out
Not the best but knew to play
Surrounding self with stool pigeons
Woe betides that fateful day
Nothing much else on offer
Chaos ruled supreme
Then the chaos, it expanded
Not all true what once did seem

'Did I come to make your happy?
No, I came to feather my own nest
Did I come to impart some wisdom?
No, am here to do what do best
To make myself someone important
At least in some poor foolish eyes
Those so desperate for a difference
Cannot see behind disguise'

Once in past but so oft repeated
As a species did evolve
Many times, until present
Various, we can't solve
A splattering of ego junkies
Rise to then back fall
Into ignominy of the Despot
When hard truth made a call

The desperation of frustration
The wanting of a change
Yet unsure what 'perfect' cure
Leads to choices labelled Strange
The irony of who we be
The gullible but won't admit
The Masochist for the Sadist
We just accept the hit

Runaway journey

There's unrest in my Universe
The one in which have grown
Discord in distance destinations
Sadness which we have sown
Violence in vast quantities
Destruction of all I seem to find
Feelings, physical and equality
No Feelings – lost, we are of same kind

Some resort to as last measure
Some just for fun
Fire, stones and firepower
Just start of that begun
Sadness in the silliness
When weighing up the cost
How many ways can we invent?
When in which a life is lost

How many ears are turning deaf?
How many eyes are turning blind?
How many now use thought as weapon?
How many others freedom bind?
Renegade or Revolutionary?
Saviour or a Sinner?
When parting from the parity
Which way is a winner?

Here you go – a thing to think
Here you go – just some read
Here you go – just some words
Here you go – what do they feed?
Revulsion or reaction?
Something or plain none
Can we stop our runaway journey?
When ties of loving come undone

433

S a M

Made a Breakfast then had lunch
Might have Dinner but that's just hunch
Noon the tune some Bells do boom
Heard but yet inside
A noisy act on railway track
Disturbs the Radio
Irritation generation
The feeling not do show

And all the pavement traffic
All the road stuff too
Rushing to something somewhere
Of me they have no clue
Yet maybe though sounds crazy
Someone watching from afar
Internet intelligence
Gathering just who we are

Dance the dance of thing called chance
Rain may fall outside
Strut your stuff when things get tough
Develop thicker Hide
So, you are different - that's okay
So, you don't fit in others 'Play'
Well, welcome you into my world
Where absurd is often heard
Welcome, you to being normal
Just the same but far less formal

Subtlety a mystery
The call before we fall
S a M to one with pen
When hear their Writers call

S and S

I could be wrong but get along
The path I choose to tread
The 'let's go to what don't know'
Just seeing where am led
The intricately of who we be
The queries and the ask
The silence broken with just one token
The tantalising tempting tasks

Just say the word and it will be heard
For we all have a voice
How you say is your own way
Many be the choice
So not alone with flesh and bone
The inside you can't hide
If you were chasm, we did then incur
You'd be miles wide

I've been learning, some knowledge earning
Since day I opened eyes
Might bright light win the fight
Turn me into wise
The mystery of simplicity
When make it complicated
S and S are just the best
When are simply stated

Said in safety of distance

The Wardrobe needs extending
Neighbours garden could be lending
Credit bills they have no ending
Need another one

The better half thinks I'm daft
As for our income they hard graft
Me, with bags three
Just for now I simply laugh

With enough do we stop?
Or just carry on
The expecting of collecting
Can it be so wrong
Will enough just be tough
To us just achieve?
For more for sure we adore
Less we don't believe

So what! I have more shoes than days
So what! The Trout that music plays
So what! Perfume enough to cause a haze
You should see that Winter collection!

No, I am no addict!
No! I have no perverse attraction
No! I do not need some intervention
Of some Phycologist that you mention

With enough do we stop?
Or just carry on
The expecting of collecting
Can it be so wrong
Will enough just be tough
To us just achieve?
For more for sure we adore
Less we don't believe

Said the sands

The wind was still so did not thrill
Excite or even move
The rise and fall heard no call
Not a single groove
The heat did bake and crust make
Though thin and easy broke
When upon an object placed
Then the inner spoke

This sea of grains had a name
Though never said itself
On this the sands were silent
The vastness said it all

Humans did encroach upon it
Parties called it Home
With mobile dwellings and beasts of burden
Its vastness choose to roam
Few were others they did meet
For existence here
Is no common feat

Silent staying in the present
As if without a care
Yet easily to get to speak
With added moving air

Once part of great mountain
Or just a humble rock
Long before we walked this Earth
Long before we took stock

Just how many tales could tell
If chose to have a voice
In its current state of being
Does a grain rejoice?

The Rock of Ages now fine ground
The stories it could tell
The evaluation and solution
To a living's own made Hell

We dare to travel some of sands
Even then convert
Into a different substance
Mix with finer versions
Supposedly inert

The sands of time a natural crime
Or just recycling before we did
So many mysteries it contains
So many more that it hid

Walked some sand as did many
Walked but with no connection
Blinded by the vastness
Dazzled by reflection

Said the sand 'Go back Home'
In way not known before
Giving gentle but firm hint
It could punish more

Now I treat it with respect

Small shop scenario

Eric made an enterprise
Shaquir started with surprise
Rosie rocked controlling stock
Brenda guided because was Bank wise

The small business industry
The ups and downs of what could be
One shop could lead to chain
One could be a money pit
Taking it but with no gain

They come and go on High Street know
An ever-changing scenario
Rental lease then seems to cease
Never knowing which way go

Here today then closing down
Where goes stock with staff frown
Not just one in many cases
For have seen many faces

Sarah started on her own
Learned the trade so now shown
The skills she gained in cutting hair
With some perks she chose to share

How long last a question asked
Not in public just in mind
Barber Bob there before
Same of different kind

Seen the phone shop become a food shop
Seen a food shop become available
Seen next day to my dismay
Selling chairs and tables

Snaggle Snagpus

Snaggle Snagpus liked collecting
If not fixed down it went
To the Den of Snaggle Snagpus
Without remorse, without relent

The odd sock found its partner
If left the remaining in same place
While you searched for lost objects
There sat guilty with 'innocent' face

"We seek it here! We seek it there
Yet that Cat with blank stare
Laying on lost underwear
Quite oblivious, without care"

Snaggle Snagpus liked to snaggle
Alas it caused its end
When it tried to snaggle by the barrel
Yet pushed on long bit with slight bend

Rant

Poem, verse, just a line
Sentence, 'spoken' – all is fine
Yet as look it does amuse
Why Two line 'Poem' to confuse

Two lines a beginning
Not start, middle and then the end
Yet is growing popularity
As so many lazy join this trend

Guess that Ink and the 'think'
Need some saving modern day
I am opposite with my 'what's it?'
So I guess I cannot say

Snipping while outside is dripping

Eighteen age of adulthood
Unless it's Twenty-one
Yet allowed at Sixteen years
To legally have fun

Where does this Lead lead?
Does it lead to Lead?
Should I now a sense of caution heed
As races around my Head

Car alarm can cause harm
When set off by the weather
In the hours most try to sleep
Do you own that vehicle? Never!

Do you do

Do you do what others do?
Simply because it's a thing they do
As to reason, have no clue
Gormless now does poke through

Not a day to go astray
So will stay here – if I may
Got good food and lots of play
Better here I do say

Sweet Home Alabama
Lynyrd Skynrd once did sing
What's so special in Alabama?
That make it such a thing?

We buy white bread to toast it brown
Buy white or red meat to do same
Do we just prefer that colour?
Do we just like that name?

So one day

An Apostle or an apostrophe?
That's the question, which is me
A cause or pause or just cause pause?
That's a decision, which one be?
An enigma or an enema?
Fluctuating situation
Just a flush of Royal Flush?
An astonishment or aberration?

Mistakes I make, that's part of take
Taking chances gets odd glances
Half blind has its benefits
When you ride with all the hits
It's alright to be strange
Strange the way some will judge
Beauty of the focused 'foolish'
Is they really don't give a fudge

Bigger things are in the wide stuff
Than a dreamer who chased dreams
Once chance only so just take it
Too much pause and gone the cause
Once it's started gone faint hearted
Just don't worry about applause

Who is right and who is wrong?
Who decides what does belong?
Certainly not one like me
I just wish that all were strong
Strong enough to go for ambition
Strong enough to make it mission
Mission so some future day
'That was worth it' you can say

So pick up Pen

The current real I do feel
The air of the despair
The gloom does loom so need a broom
To sweep so I don't share
The masses feel just miserable
Confusion no illusion
What to do they have no clue
The pent up now palpable

The unpredictable is quite miserable
When all just seems bad news
The same blame game with different name
Whichever channel choose
Simplicity that can't see
Moving on seems so wrong
For they enjoy the misery
It helps them to feel strong

Decision made to be 'brave'
Carry on to get along
Pity those seek pampering
When worse amongst the throng
Each to one – that is true
But when you see, when have clue
The ones we take for granted
Are suffering people too

So here we go as pen is poised
The release from inner noise
I just feel I have no choice
But to write again
The words know Just how to flow
The hand does understand
Switch to Autopilot
Again, in different land

Vera PEN in virtute

So sometimes

As one sits near end of day
Tunes so eyes can rest
Occasionally sampling that of others
The moments I like best
Invigorate yet placate
Conundrum welcome so
A glimpse into a person
A person I don't know

Sometimes Sunset seems so swift
Sometimes seems so slow
Collaborations of connotations
Things we just don't know
Sometimes I feel happy
Sometimes I feel sad
Sometimes I feel quite sane
Sometimes I feel mad
Nothing but a Sometimes
Does express the big question
The occasional irrelevant
That sometimes we don't mention

Are we free from misery?
The question Creatives ask
For no sense of perfection
No matter what the mask
No, we're not unless lost the plot
For improvement as we grow
Done more years than some were born
Still perfect I can't show

So sometimes Sunset seems so swift
So sometimes it seems slow
So sometimes I think a lot
So sometimes I don't knows
So sometimes I will pen some sense
So sometimes prefixed with non
So sometimes the white coat people wait outside my door
They will never get me because my Floating Marbles are a free Nation!

So today

So today went astray
Not what was that was planned
No real care when still can share
When these things we understand

So today didn't want to play
Some of those I have my self
When tomorrow can forget sorrow
Becomes a thing we could call wealth

The twists in it can lead to hits
Blows that do not show
We sustain pain for what can gain
No-one needs to know

I built a stand with my own hands
Not knowing how to build
Was not a perfect structure
Just acted as a shield

Were you like me when little be
The one who both accepted but rejected?
Accept for now but look for how
Things could be somewhat perfected

Spent my time with wine and song
Stayed up most of night
Now I be that who can in morning see
Without the double sight

Take me please to that release
Of burdens that we bear
Take me through when was just new
The decision that we care

So today went astray
Nothing more to say
When in truth that which can soothe
When can live another day

So what today

A brim-full of the things to be
A brim-full of that yearned to be
A brim-full of the hurt and pain
A brim-full of that didn't gain
Yet haven't lived until you give
Not expecting some repay
You haven't been the dream clean
Unless for one you feel that way

If you know me - took a look
Saw the chances that I took
Then, maybe, see real me
The one behind the Crow and Rook
The name a pain when is the reason
Strawberry to Trifle lend
Another gloss on that most Moss
By a link they try to send

So what today? The come what may
Sod it! Think I'll stay
Those in Mask and those don't ask
No mood for an affray
Situation real with no cure pill
Still there when you come down
Now the task to self ask
Was I really a Clown to frown?

What you see is part of me
To know me is to Know
The eighty percent that with relent
Other parts will show
If thing I be a part of me
Perhaps you'd understand
The things we make, success/ mistake
Not always by own hand

446

So, no answer

In the mirror of reflection
Something strange, a new perception
Been so long as which do
Honestly, had no clue
So, engrossed in now what be
Failed to potential see
Not just one or thousand three
In some way we should pity

Am I got what want not?
That expansion for incineration
Am I all that misery?
When get nightmare not fantasy?
The thought process of attention seeking
Not medical just the weak
Weak in doing and believing
We are potential of that seek

Verse interrupted- resume shortly

Why do nails need constant clipping?
Why are they even called that name?
Nails are things for hammering
Or on animals wild not tame

Why do men grow facial hair?
Yet not women until old age
Why exhibit to promote freedom
When are captured and put in cage?

Why am I writing this here drivel?
When more productive I can do?
What are you doing as you read this?
So many options but no clue

So, the contemplation of situation
Growing now to agitation
I, myself, have given up trying
So, no answer am supplying

Someday, if we may

One did choose to express
One chose a certain way
One did find peace of mind
When to another they could say

Can you my love, beneath your feet
Feel the feel of my heart beat
It started day that we did meet
Growing stronger every

Can you feel the change we made?
When two did join as one
Can you sense that which makes sense?
Can you feel the feeling begun?

I know you know as offspring grows
The benefits of the union
Yet do you understand as I hold that hand
The dream comes to fruition

Someday, if we may
Can we go back to our first day
That new thrill I remember still
The no, the might, the may

The new me that you set free
Wants to be once again enclosed
Within the feelings have
Those that you exposed

This sanctuary of us three
The calming of each storm
The awesome charm of the calm
That removal of a Thorn

Someone punch this Poet!

The simplicity of Trigonometry
If are a Scientific Calculator
The temptation to stir situations
If you are a paid Translator
The best rest when pass hard Test
The need to cry when are passed by
By Team you liked the best

That strange change when rearrange
That room for the first time
That which do to cease nag true
Keep meaning to no crime
So, we go to where don't know
Just the pleasure of a trip
The joy or pain and possible sprain
Dependant on which type of slip

Haberdashery it used to be
Now just drop off for repair
To sew is now burden so
Items found in the Hardware
Power cuts lead to tuts
If one does opt to refrain
From expletives used by Dockers crude
When on Strike again

Classed as rude so should not be used
In front of those still yet to grow
The sheer shock as take stock
That they already know
The good and bad to be had
Of those called a Mum or Dad
That taste of waste as with haste
This poem's more than bad

Someone said

Someone said and stayed in Head
Someone said "you can"
Someone said and so it led
To becoming a better man

On wing and prayer, I got there
Found that reason why
Someone said and it led
To make me want to try

The look, it shook and changing the Book
The one that we call Life
Turning nothing into something
I even found a Wife

Not quite a Sage in older age
Just better than before
More importantly if truth be
I respect myself much more

Sunday morning – Coffee calling
Knew its twin a week ago
Correction for misconception
Many Sundays does each year show

Is it not a joy to be?
Part of this, our History?
When the future can look back/ see
Just what idiots we were really

Someone said and stayed in Head
Son, you are a future Hero
Bloody hope not! Then did think
That does sound too much like zero!

Someone save me

I once met a Toadstool
A Toadstool? You may ask
Yes, it was a Toadstool
Living, with a task
It set it sights on yonder heights
Up mountain chose to go
How could travel I could not unravel
Another thing I don't know

I once met a Pebble
Missed friends upon the Beach
Was quite obviously despondent
For them it couldn't reach
Had no legs to walk on
Took pity and did so
Picked up lonely Pebble
Then Pebble I did throw

I once met a wandering Slug
It's path travelled shown by slime
We pollute when car does suit
So can't blame it for its crime
I find no rhythm nor reason
What begin the Slug season?
To squash it would be treason
To something, somewhere out there

I once met a Daffodil
Gailey swaying- time to kill
With that colour set to thrill
Some poor Welshman feeling chill
I suppose we've got the Rose
Scotland wrote a song instead
That bloody thing stays in head
'Flower of.' duly led
A Sassenach to go back to Bed

451

Something

Innocuous the Porcupine
Until its parts dart from its spine
Innocuous the common Ant
Though in company can cause a rant

An incident can cause a vent
An incision is a mission
Promise made sometimes part played
Sometimes come to fruition

When lost in thought we are caught
Then something blows away
Must be good when understood
Something meant to stay

A grey day

A grey day with which to play
The changes we can do
Rain a pain but refrain
It's nourishing the new

Parachute and Paradise
Sometimes joined with surprise
When one has been wise
Leading not to one's demise

'Red or White?' The question ask
Of the meat, not different task
Yet is meat that we eat
While in tray each does bask

Chicken wings now that's a thing
So much effort for joy to bring
Rather leave them in the coup
If not that then to flavour soup

Sometimes are not through marriage

The lady said as shared a bed
With the one she chose to wed
Another Day and still did stay
In the good and bad
For the bad was not physical
No excuse for that
Just the moods that intrude
The changing of the Hat

'Some days I think a heart of Marshmallow
Some days a heart of stone
So is you and what put through
When we are alone'
For share a life but not all strife
Each a life they lead
Somethings are not through marriage
To introduce he doesn't need

The man did lay but didn't say
The comment made at work
Went beyond that acceptable
A retort didn't shirk
Yes, he wed a different skin tone
Yes, he didn't care
Yet when a bigot questions reason
Then his mind will share

No regret in what he did
Just felt no need to say
Create a worry for just being
The one that makes his day
For stone is stone and loam is loam
Yet a being is more than look
If could read then could feed
Intelligence from book

Sometimes my eyes

The mellowing of maybe
The peacefulness of pause
The ecstatic of just static
The catastrophes they cause

Oh Fate, you fickle friend
Yes, me again - the pain
Wondering where I went wrong
So will not do again

Sometimes my eyes
They fantasise
Then I get wise
To what I have been told
Sometimes my eyes
With surprise
See but don't believe
What has been done
By someone
What they did achieve

This is me talking to self
For Fate is what we make
Everything a challenge
That can make or break

Hello you, how do you do?
Are you as wrecked as me?
I am the figment of fulfilment
The shell of what could be

Sometimes disguise
Is more than wise
A need and not a choice
Sometimes it is protection
Sometimes the rise
Can surprise
Sometimes but not forever

Just some media show

The one did write day and night
Found an outlet it is true
Thus, became more than name
Pleasure in what do

With no thought a thing caught
Just what the others can decide
This therapy a mystery
As of the person they try to hide

The eyes open to a new one
Another chance to be
Nothing much in the broad sense
Yet important for is me

Every day a chance to play
When attitude is good
What a path has been the past
So now understood and seen that not clean

I never knew, but did you?
The things that were to come
Fixed on laughing and its spanning
Everything just fun
Then the strange as did change
Serious it came to stay
Not the thing that I wanted
Not my joyful yesterday

All that's been like a bad dream
Not all if say things true
Met some amazing people
Just, sometimes, things I had to do

As grew up I learned much
Some I should not know
Yet better from the personal
Than just some media show

That Book I bought

In a Bookshop in a side street
A Diary did find
I took a look at this different Book
A novelty of kind
To self amuse I did peruse
To know them was my mission
Those personal things that life brings
Fact stranger than some fiction

Today the day it does say
So, guess it might be true
Yet Today was yesterday
To the likes of some of you
So you like Tea? Me Coffee
Bean is more my taste
But carry on for both belong
Those leaves we shouldn't waste

Missed 'in style' by country mile
Was just that classed as strange
Nothing new as I grew
Somethings never change
No Pop Star – not by far!
Fog horn springs to mind
These dulcet tones are my own
Better I do find

I'm out of shorts! My legs have caught
The decision to now hide
Now don't know which way to go
Drainpipe or Flairs wide

That Book I bought for me it taught
That we don't truly know
The ones we pass as life goes past
The people not on show

That cancellation

What's the nature of the game we play?
Do we always play same way?
The changes of the leave or stay
Despite the rules, choose anyway
Choose the songs to match the mood
To current state so understood
Facial expressions just a hood
The music is my food

It's getting better all the time
The additional stations supply this crime
The supposition of recognition
When notes come to some fruition
Rock to shock, ballad to calm
Some old era with no harm
Mix and match when want to catch
When someone else you want to charm

When under pressure you might snap
Play some music to get back
That sense of what it all just be
The things called us and not what see
Echo beach a great song
Sometimes there I do belong
Yet 'When a Man loves a Woman' strikes a note
To the point some of it can quote

What's the nature of the game we play?
When we seek that affray
Do we really want to be curt
Of do we just like that hurt?
Song and Ink can drive to brink
Yet also pull us back
Time for thought and the space caught
That cancellation of that attack

That does mean

The longing seems a lifetime
The life you never knew
When did that certain something
That not all will do

Happiness
Overcomes
Most
Everything

The start of Heart a loving
Never may it end
For have broken many things in a journey
This one will never mend

Let
Obsession
Vault
Enforcement

The trust a must or all is dust
The determination a certain
Pause a cause for some remorse
Though not the final curtain

Truth
Remains
Undying
Strength
Total

Fortunate to have
Obsessed with what have got
Changed the strange so can arrange
That does mean a lot

That Fly did try and so did die

Enough did I that annoying Fly
That did try to pass me by
What it thought know not I
As out of Jar it did try
To continue to my room explore
To annoy more and more
Should have stayed where before
Perhaps it can pester them again

A mystery it truly be
When out of window it did drop
Before again rose that pain
Window quickly closed apart from gap at top
Go your way or next time pay
With sudden impact feel
Just before you are no more
As from wall I peel

That Fly did try to again pass by
This time it brought some Brothers
All did get the same respect
When in Fly spray each were smothered
My carpet got some new additions
As result of my mission
Nothing but to inhume
With the help of the vacuum

Cleaner with the help of that Cleaner!!

That I am strange

Some things are a cause from laziness
Some just happen anyway
Who is so perfect to then judge
Who the right to say
That you are less than they see them
See themselves as want to be
An Adonis in the mirror
A perfection blindly see

Once I thought that I was near it
Once I was that fool
Once I thought I was imperial
Once, before the fall
No regrets for the adjustment
When were plainly rude
Part of me needed adjustment
So my health did intrude

Is anyone without a problem?
Is anyone without a fault?
Is anyone that misguided?
Is anyone in self love caught?
Vanity a misery
Vanity on show
Vanity not way to be
Vanity a curse I once did know

Of Sight and speech I struggle
Just walking is a pain
How do carry two bags
When in one hand is a white cane
So now mistakes I freely make
Am nothing yet am proud
I am not considered 'normal'
This I shout aloud

I did get a wake up call
One I wouldn't care to share
Now I'm thick skinned to the comments
Impervious to that certain stare
Look at me and now see you
Look at what can change
Look at me and see reflection
Then tell me that I am strange

Not that strange in my new world
Not that bad when I do greet
Not that different when encounter
Those much stronger which I meet
Who will be almost immortal
Who's legacy we will pass
Onto generations as examples
Of who laughed at broken glass

I now know many I could suggest
A different world I now know
I knew brave in the old one
Same again many show
Different yes, but the same
That certain person who makes a difference
In the muddle of the problems
They brushed off the interference

That kiss that miss

Liquid lines so often find
Flow but just don't go
The need to show so all can know
Yet the real refuse to show
Illusion in profusion
The mistakes made as trade
Reality as what want to see
With so called 'experts' and money made

To be oneself and nothing else
A switch some just cannot do
So lost in the mid when talent hid
The greater than the few
That claim to Fame in this strange game
The only target see
Yet by that are just sat
In common fantasy

The difference is one being
Much more than what are seeing
The multitude of 'awards' to include
Fiction with no meaning
Printed out so ego can shout
Just how good one is
Yet the cost is that which lost
That true writers 'kiss'

Ink did spill and with it thrill it
Of the inner now on show
What still hide deep inside
Perhaps we'll never know
Without rude may I include
The reason that I be
Not all touch but to me so much
They are my Family

Am nothing more than average
Yet, strangely, am apart
I have no illusions
At least that is a start

That makes them lose the plot

They go out as normally do
Yet something different you do sense
Nothing physical, everything normal
Yet it leaves one feeling tense

This started about a month ago
Just happened, don't know why
Cold inside you try to hide
When gone you start to cry

Was that the final kiss you'll get
Just how soon you they'll forget?
Do you say that you know?
Will you force something then regret?

Intuition or mere suspicion?
Ingenuity or insecurity?
That the question so many find
The gloss of trust has tarnished
Freedom tied down in varnish
Plaything of a twisted mind

Why does perfect come with baggage?
So good you can't believe
Why When you achieve such happiness
You want to make it leave?

Luckily these are just words
Though for some are not
How many have that certain switch
That makes them lose the plot?

More than we know if truth be told
Though no fault of self
Just another cruel, cruel taste
Of ill in mental health

That self-pride and market wide

Red light, Green light
Most know what mean
I am more the yellow
Something always been
The traffic lights of living
The holding back to the giving

I am halfway - centre station
Undecided on situation
Nothing much can understand
So hold back with open hand

I see you and see again
Yet you have changed from what knew
You have changed for the better
Put quite simply, you just grew

The one that has so much to offer
Found a way to then share
Made a statement to an audience
Said so openly that you care

Don't it feel fine
Don't it feel good
Took deep breath
Stepped outside the known 'Hood'

That bit inside we tried to hide
Mistaking for self-pride
Yet the market open wide
Do yo understand more than me?

No Preacher me nor wish to be
Just a soul that looks
Gaining recipes of 'What makes me'
And them how one cooks

That thing called living

If the sky fell to earth
If the waters it did meet
Would you still carry on?
If no-one came when you call
Had to get back up when you fall
Stood alone amongst the crowd
Voice not heard however loud
Would you still carry on?

A question asked for many do
This to them is nothing new
When everyday it feels like rain
When nothing seems like shine
The people who are same but not
When ourselves feel fine

A six-day week or five-day week
Whatever one we have
We moan and groan when we get Home
At least we have that path
When Home is just a place we grace
Any place to just try sleep
Then the issue of not just tissue
But your gatherings to keep

To charity we often give
Then advertise the giving
You do we true do what do
To help that thing that we call living?
Unscrupulous don't give a toss
As help themselves to make
A better way for them to stay
The despicable of the take

That was something

Many dishes make a Banquet
Many flavours to then taste
Sample without the preference
For then many go to waste
Once upon a clever chapter
Someone said that it didn't matter
Just how far the feelings scatter
Let them call me 'The Mad Hatter'

They answered

'I made a mark in a Park
Many years ago
Who pass through would truly know
I did it for a 'lark'
Sun has risen and Sun has set
Many are times since then
Found a different way to express
Found myself a Pen

Sweet that pour the emotions
Sweet that pour the others too
Sweet that feeling of achieving
Sweet that knowledge that can do
Knocked down the walls of the doubting
Knocked down the barriers and broken free
Knocked down the limits on achieving
Knocked down restriction, now am me'

Resonation Generation
Needed time but no more
Needed to just be new
Then a different could explore
Old but new for did see through
The 'acceptance' based on past
That was something we used to know
That was something that couldn't last

We've been waiting so patiently
For the known to become the new
Now we are the rising
Just watch what we can do

That Banquet that we cook

Last September do you remember
The same in way as now
Each November I remember
A certain number how
How we do to just get through
Tests we have to face
Nothing worse than the curse
Of being in a different place

Autumn rain, the same paint
As were the years before
Autumn rain such a pain
When away from whom adore
All one ever wanted, all one ever needed
So far and yet so near
Speaking is believing
Screen time wipes the fear

In the morning as you I'm calling
Until remember you're not here
Yet you are always there
Just different part instead
Every time I feel the rain
It washes part of me
Making clean that I glean
The part others cannot see

In starlight vision bright
As remember how you look
The strangest chance we call romance
That Banquet that we cook
For nothing more than to be on that shore
Of place that we call our place to live
Nothing more is sure than you adore
And to you myself give

That's when

As first Dates go it wasn't bad
In all truth, the best I've had
Talk flowed freely just like water
In her attention I knew I'd caught her

Time did fly and I wondered why
Had never noticed her before
All I knew as feelings grew
Was that on this one I was sure

I walked her Home so not alone
Two become one and not just fun
No thought to stay for am now that way
Intentions strictly Gentleman

The questionnaire stare showed she did care
That certain look all it took
Yet mind made up so face did cup
Not some victory to go in Book

"Come close" I said
"I want to whisper"
She obligingly leaned in
That's when I kissed her

The first of many over years
As share joy and shed tears
Help each other through our fears
That first kiss made so much clear

The action

The action caused attraction
The scene was not so mean
The two did do in front of queue
They simply had a kiss
The two were now united
From separation due to duty done

The action a distraction
To deflect defeat
Still believed that which achieved
To everyone did meet
Alas, poor deluded fool
People said you no longer rule

The action of some faction
Gave a name some shame to rest
Not the actions of acceptance
The deadly suicide vest
They can meet their futures true
Why bring along the likes of you?

The action of the action
When shot from various places
Stunt double for some trouble
To protect some famous faces
When looks make money
Damage is not funny

No! No never

No! No never
Will I while breathe forget
The sacrifice of millions
In a thing we chose to let

The cost a Generation
For some pointless situation
All achieved were souls that grieved
From almost every Nation

They choose to rise

In fields of confusion
One finds oneself that in which
In the doubt one finds wealth
In the test one finds they can
In the trial one improves 'common man'
Served or those not serving
Still a thing can do
Changing some parts better
Changing old to new

I am not talking racist things
Am not talking all it brings
Just respect and common sense
Not that which a Microchip lends
Young kids now walk the street
Carry knife for who meet
Gun is fun until goes bang
Then the Judge a sentence sang

But we don't know which way will go
Them instead of us
Learning 'trade' with games they've played
Immune to all the fuss
Yet they don't know and so is so
Advancement our destruction
For given free that chance to be
Though with limited or no instructions

On a Flanders field so many did yield
To let others have a say
We are here for despite their fear
They gave up their today
Enforced now not compulsory
In so many nations
Yet still they choose to rise above
For countless situations

They said

A person who one did not know
Wrote eight lines that changed a world
A person who chose anonymity
Yet those lines were loudly heard

An island in the sea of conflict
In troubled waters a Life belt
More by doing than just saying
Was a message truly felt
They said

Open ears to more than hearing
Open eyes to more than see
Open mind to more than opinion
Open Us and not just Me
A cog we are in thing much bigger
A gear we are if we progress
A spindle if we encourage others
A broken piece if treat as less

And I, I did hear them
And I, I understood
And I, I changed my thinking
And I, I felt so good

Many years have passed since that moment
Many happy ones it's true
Just because I changed my perception
Just because changed what could do

The word still sound as clear as first time

Open ears to more than hearing
Open eyes to more than see
Open mind to more than opinion
Open Us and not just Me
A cog we are in thing much bigger
A gear we are if we progress
A spindle if we encourage others
A broken piece if treat as less

Things called Ghost

I asked a question to a stranger
As we both did drink
From a well-known High Street vendor
Answer made me think

"Aren't we stupid paying this
Overpriced just for our pleasure
When a weeks' worth of the cost
Could give someone so much leisure?"

I asked myself a certain question
As in mirror I did look
"Are you really brave enough
To accept and better that took?"

"Yes" came reply
From down deep but don't know why
Guess ingrained is thing called 'Try'
Will be there until I die

I asked myself in times past
"Why do you carry on?"
Then I got an inner answer
"To quit now is just so wrong"

So easy just to give up
So hard to just be true
True to what you are blessed with
True to being you

True is but four letters
Yet mean more than most
When of self you accept
Put pain in things called Ghost

Thinking hypocrisy

The skin tones can determine
Body shape an interference
How many years you have been here
Seems to make a difference
Beyond the barriers that we make
Lies opportunity if we take
So I ask for Goodness sake
Take a stand and barriers break

Yes, not all is physical
When we rise, we can then fall
Yet the treasure is mental
Something we have inside us all
Computers offer much
Each new version an improvement
Yet none yet in certain things
Can surpass the Human movement

Is this just a sole reflection?
Am I only to now question?
The beauty that we own
Is this just a string of lines?
Is there more than reader finds
Are other pauses to be sown

Fairy tales tell of Giants
Yet are not a fantasy
In the way we think and display
Giants all we can be
We are enigma, mystery
We are straight thinking hypocrisy
We are above and then more
We are that I hate and adore

This progression

The silly cone, it had strange taste
Someone decided it shouldn't go to waste
So, decided to take a chance
Turned our subject into implant

If it lucky for a medic
If unlucky just cosmetic
Either way carried risk
For if rupture, removal brisk

The silly cone - semi solid
Not the type to hold ice-cream
That is why it's called silly
Some inventors mad, mad reason seems

Clever Loan had a face lift
Parts chopped off and some did change
To make identical from original
Now an obsession in times strange

Mother Nature has done already
Yet just split one into two
I guess we now are getting arrogant
'What you can do we can too'

Clever loan was never alone
As we took the idea further
3D printing is the new stage
This progression a real unnerve err

This time have a clue

Glorious the victorious
In days of old and new
No-one really knowing
Just what had to do
Knew they'd won a battle
An opponent was defeated
Unaware or, perhaps, didn't care
A war not yet completed

Yes, a physical they'd achieved
Yet what about the other?
That hidden one that might drag on
Beneath their outer cover
Not just the lost who pay the cost
When to conflict choose to go
Casualties still mounting
Just not the type that show

Despite all the training that they've had
Nothing can quite prepare
The horror then experiences
Just by being there
A challenge won and kudos gain
The exaltation and the pain
Something, somewhere never again
Will quite match when we refrain

So, march you gallant heroes
Enjoy this oh so brief
Soak in the adoration
Briefly forget grief
You faced the test and came out best
In what we can do
Destruction on a grander scale
Though this time have a clue

Those of different face

The light it lit and words with it
In the stranger who changed that had
Ink did flow and with it so
The page pieces good and bad
Am I thunder or do I blunder?
The opinion I don't care
I am with but without
The other who my life I share

Look at me in autumn sun
Then ask yourself 'am I someone?'
Look at me and what I do
Ask yourself 'am I one too?'
The person who gets things right
The person who gets things wrong
The person in land of different people
Does this person now belong?

There's nothing here than that I love
Nothing here than sky above
Nothing here but on which stand
Nothing here but new Homeland
All I own I call Home
All I share is warmth and care
All I be is one to see
All I am is part of me

Writing but a pleasant dish
Writing just visual wish
Writing is to a fool
Writing to them a success tool
When lose my mind in words find
The way to tear things down
Writing is the building blocks
Writing is a person Crown

So look at me and what do you see?
I really wish I was some other place
Look at me who wants to be
With those of different face

Those things

Bats are banging in the belfry
The one between two ears
Such a common feeling
So, in this one have no fears

They are playing Marbles
Whilst hanging upside down
Some like to act serious
Others fool around

My vision orbs have voted
The have reduced their load
I am now that part sighted
The Headlight dazzled Toad

But who cares!

I am still living in times of dying
They did have no choice
I am able to adapt
I still have a voice

What were once such little things
Now a blessing true
The bits we take for granted
When in working order do

How man things have gone by
Unnoticed until too late
Just were taken as were granted
Consigned to thing called Fate

Only when you switch to other
Do you realise
What a true and important thing
Those things we call eyes

Those who

Late in day and Marbles play
Another does escape
Down trodden route so verbally mute
Let's see the verse it makes
No control as pen does scroll
A situation familiar
Just at end why conscience lends
Is this one something similar?

Onto steps of my progression
Those I leave, my succession
A bit of what we can be
Is the simple thing I be
Not the end for they can mend
The faults we've made so far
They are the appointed
To drive forward not using Car

Not of me some things see
Just a result of what are given
Not agree with at least one in three
The current in which are living
Oh, to be a Fantasy
One that does come true
To be a sticking plaster
That bonds both me and you

But because we are in the present
But because we are we
But because we are focused
But because outside can't see
Holding on to keep me strong
Holding on because I believe
Holding on for those upcoming
Holding on for what can achieve

Those who still are finding way
Those who will one day have say
Those who in their own hands
Those who one time can change lands

Thought before bed

An effigy of who I be
Are the symbols that I make
The right and wrong both below
Criticism I can take

A penner me and what you see
An unusual you might find
For nothing planned when pen in hand
Just voice of idle mind

Nothing malicious for not my thing
Just a different abled person
Who awareness to bring
My clock is ticking

Who are we in what we see
Product not the being
Judging on what they lay down
Not knowing what are feeling

An exercise for the wise
Look beyond what see
Understand those whose hands
Slip some reality

Written word can be absurd
Yet can be a strange sensation
When it is in welcome stance
Can be a revelation

Thought for nought as sleep sought

Caught when having liquid supper
Swapping soup for a cuppa
Leaving solids for another
In the fridge for tomorrow
Light the load as Imploding
Into place that may have snoring
With some dreams that never boring
And from them will borrow
Some subjects that, later, could regret
So are now just circumspect
The jury is still out

Out should go to awake I know
Into the world of slumber
Why am I, as I try?
Keep thinking 'I am not a number!'
Pillow fluffed and all that stuff
Shorts and T-shirt bright
Sleep on top for feeling hot
My heavens what a sight!

A million me's descend from trees
Made decision somewhat strange
To lose some fur and so incur
Human but no mange
Got instead balding head
Wrinkles visible
But it's late and in no state
So Goodnight and sod it all!!

Thought sought

If thoughts came with a price tag
Would I be rich or poor?
Would it lead to them less?
Would it lead to more?

If that spark for a lark
In the serious did embark
Would I be truly me?
Or just another see?

If stone can turn to Crystal
Ink to legacy
Just what kind of creature?
Am and then could be?

Electric impulse quite unbidden
Some on show whilst others hidden
Form reform for the 'norm'
Yet are somehow inside born

If a thought was charged rent
Would it be money well spent?
For they flow without relent
As I stand as witness

The Hive survives and then it thrives
Free and no restrictions
Apart from some that don't become
When doubt if are afflictions

If thoughts all caught and not sought
Without us even knowing
Would we be what we see
As of each are growing?

Ian Wilcox

Tickets

Half past health so say to self
"Buck up you silly fool!"
Nothing but the start and end
All else is not a rule
What you want you can do
Maybe with adjustment that is true
Yet that drive will survive
If engine remains and then shines through

In the middle of a riddle
The true to self can find
The way to be the new 'me'
Same of different kind
In the middle of the question
There comes a new suggestion
The bit that doesn't quit
Laughs at the mere mention

Can a ray make a sunshine?
Can I make a wish come true?
Can this crazy see solution?
Can we just do what do?
We've built our cages throughout ages
The only thing we trap is us
We strut in the ruts
Love to make a fuss

Who set the known boundaries?
Certainly not me
Who sets the that still possible
Who tells what one can 'see'
Can a single make a difference?
That I do not know
Maybe can, Lady or Man
I'd buy tickets for that show

Time is crime on that divine

I made my entrance in September
A day each year that I remember
Been a few since was life new
Too many if truth be told

Where has gone since I was born
The bits from then 'til now?
The pain and fun of things done
The tears and fears, the simply wow

The memories are history
Locked away, secure
The innocence and repent
The time when I was 'pure'

Time is crime on that divine
The innocence before we leave
The sad but true for the new
The parts we couldn't quite conceive

There's no story of my glory
For glorious was not
Just did try to get on by
With the things I got

Laughing no at things have done
When adventure was spent fun
Of responsibility I was free
A word I chose to shun

Now I am a Husband
Am a father too
Hope that I can be a good one
Despite the things went through

Time to kill

Chapters matter when thoughts scatter
Some more than some others
The not so spiritual yet heard the call
The ancient one of lovers
No turning back when love attack
It conquers with no quarter
As recompense it then sent
The most beautiful and loved Daughter

When time came, I changed the frame
Of the picture others see
Moved the scene to that which means
Something more to me
My past a blast that didn't last
The ghosts they came too
Yet still was strange that initial change
The old became the new

When take a chance on dance Romance
The steps we do not know
As we move, we improve
We just have to show
That this is more than just a miss
A Bulls eye if you will
Let this embrace not go to waste
When we're standing still

If I digress it's simply stress
For never known this feeling
Let music play for one more day
To convince you I'm worth keeping
Guitar strings do your thing
A slow one if you will
For I am fine and this one's mine
Together have time to kill

Play on please play on

We shine

The saplings sought to grow to Tree
The Child did think the wild
Of Harmony of all when free
Wanting- a path wide but room to be
The one who was a someone
Not just another number
The only sound of conflict
Was that of natural Thunder

We shine because of what we are
We glow with what we know
We radiate when banish hate
We are the seeds we sow
We are History, past and present
We are seeds of what's to come
We are Masters of Disaster
If we let become

Standing at a Bus stop
Or on a Train platform
What and who around you
What role could they perform?
In the quest to be our best
In the hardships that all face
Are we not all confined?
On a certain orb in Space

Can we fix? Yes, we can!
Can we make a better Man?
Can we merge and hatreds purge?
Yes! And that includes Woman
There's nothing magical in the practical
Just an effort it will take
To change the selfish system that suits some
A better place can make

We suffer circumstance

If truth was made in black and white
Would we still not see right?
Some will mix and some will say
Truth is both and sometimes Grey
How long this road to correction?
How long the time to near perfection
With what's going on needing correction
Some of which they choose to not mention

Is it life when just strife?
Is existence just some penalty?
Do we care if don't share?
Blind if cannot see
In closed space we run our race
Yet outside is still there
Someone wanting just a single one
To get in touch and say they care

To love to love is a blessed feeling
To hate to hate – forgotten feeling

Is it fear that drives us near?
Near to where don't want to go
Is inspection thing won't mention
In case our real we show

If you stand by me and one makes three
Then we could do more
Stand by me in equality
Soon we will be four

When warning calling kept on stalling
For lack of maintenance
We then go to stupid show
We suffer circumstance

Wedded Bliss

Was that the door that I heard?
Yes, I have just come in
Did you go out then?
Maybe yes, could have been
You seem vague, what is wrong?
Nothing much, moving on
Am I in your bad Books?
Will you stop with those stupid looks!
Oh my god! You are mad!
Just shut up! You're sounding sad
Shall I be on Sofa sleeping?
Up to you but no bed creeping
I think I'd better hide the gun
Don't bother for bought another one
What in hell have I done
Forgot again! Another one!!!
Forgot what? Please explain
Our Anniversary you bloody pain!!!

Child talk

Mummy got big tummy!
Yes, I am giving you a Sister
Don't want! Me is good!
Well, Daddy naughty mister

What di Daddy put in you
That made your belly big?
Let's just say that in play
It was not a skinny twig!

Mommy how do you
Get her from there to here?
Let's just call it hard work
With some naughty words I fear

488

Weekends are hard but I will endure

The reclamation from temptation
Solved by just a pause
The infused air of 'just don't care
Alcohol the cause
That food you buy but don't know why
When surface the next day
That stain ingrained might be a pain
Grease just likes to stay

The traffic cone that has new home
Not sure what it will now warn
When it sits, and sits, and sits
A Drawer unit does adjourn
Vertigo will soon know
When try to leave that bed
A mystery in how be
Guess blind instinct to it led

Did Stan really kiss that van?
Because he said it yearned attention
The choice of reply by him inside
Sober self can't mention
Two days down of drunken clown
Five more before again
Enter that of drunken Pratt
The Impervious to the pain

So, come on you the punishment
Am a veteran of this
I will Mom I'm unwell
To receive a cooked Breakfast bliss
I'll get sympathy for my agony
As body will readjust
Then there's always next week
Repeat performance must

What is ours

I watched a Fly and with a sigh
Wondered who created and just why
They annoy and then they die
A meal for some type of Spider

I watched a Tree begin to flourish
Removing gasses as did nourish
Then will shed when work is done
Until next cycle, another one

I watched the rain fall down from sky
In myself I asked why
Coming down to go up again
This constant journey must be a pain

Everything a purpose true
Even why clear skies look blue
All around a thing to do
So, what is ours? Yes, me and you

I watched a lion kill antelope
It was not fast so could not cope
Helping weed the weak from strong
So, the species did belong

Contemplation situation
Where does lie our own salvation
Is it this or next mutation?
As to techno we rely

What we have become

Somewhere, someplace long ago
The name of first one we don't know
Stood alone and was shown
A different way existed

To a shocked audience they said

A show of strength that doesn't exist
I charade, the disguising mist
The need to prove because not there
So, illusion have to share

Safety in the herd absurd
When that herd is wrong
A gathering of the gullible
To help them to feel str

I am not you nor you me
Could you be this travesty?
I am not you but I am not rotten
So in that have thing in common

So yesterday went away
Tomorrow soon to come
Today I stay, if I may
Today am just someone

All of you and things you do
Are your choice so it is fine
I just go with what I know
From myself and mine

Today just be a single 'me'
What about tomorrow?
Will you start from herd now part?
Fill this space so hollow

Look at what we have become

What we were was not for sure

The sky looks grey in many a way
The Storm gathering at pace
So many are the people
So little is the space
Forcing different cultures
Upon a once one Nation shore
The complexity of who we be
Triples and some more

If we create the problem
We can invest the cure
If we find the first step
We can find some more
Each generation promises
To redress that which done
Yet each fill their own comforts
Leaving to next one

Never let the loud mouth
Influence a single thought
Never let the radical
Change that which once was taught
Never let the comforts become Masters
Tech is but adding new
The things it brings not all that sings
In me if not in you

Upon that stand built by foot and hand
Yet also by force, so sad
Maybe soon can change that tune
Have best we've ever had
When Black meets Gold new stories told
Those we wish to hear
When all as one we've begun
Then our future clear

What we were was not for sure
The one we would become
Effigy of once who be
Not the present one

When all Toast

Step by step the deeper get
Into known yet is unknown
We are crazy if stay lazy
When results are clearly shown
In your Mind deep you'll find
Something different - something good
New perception - changed direction
When join the Brother/ Sisterhood

Hour by hour we devour
That which living does sustain
Some of it has blood and body
Yet do the others feel also pain?
Sitting in my comfort Castle
Talking to one in a Castle too
Shielded by our choice of ignorance
Of the damage we all do

And when all the world just seems so sad
Had the best time ever had
Nothing ever seems so bad
When accept that we're all mad
Not that it was ever sane
We don't know how in our Brain
We enjoy making pain
With it comfort we do gain

I am the ghost that wants the most
Will be happy when all Toast
Maybe some the Sun will roast
Taking chunks out Coast to Coast
I hear the News that does confuse
Bad news seems to get more space
Is it that we are that twisted?
That have become a 'Bad News' race?

When are today

Mayhem in the mirage of muchness
Too much choice to choose
Irrelevance does lead the dance
Wish Ir could lose
Filled to top but still won't stop
The petty pours profound
To drain a pain when fill again
That with no sight nor sound

When we lay at end of day
Do we lay with ease?
When surmise with closed ties
Did last period truly please?
Educational or irrigational
Digging up a past
Some did stay so with it play
When tied our flag to mast

We discard the Staff of Learning
In search of things called Earnings
Sure, we learn but not the same
When the habits have bad name
Frivolity a novelty
In right time and place
Serious too we must do
To benefit our Race

"It's my life!" I hear you say
Just how many others does it affect?
When through all your actions
Them a different future get
Floating fields of fiction
Tomorrow promise change
Yet like all tomorrow's
When are today we then rearrange

Prowess Of The Poet

Whenever the poet spews out his chosen words
They pierce with the power of ancient swords
His words wield the power
That conquers every hour

Only he can bring the man
Away from his work in the farm
He and the man understand
That story about the fair Marm

Only he can bring out that woman
Away from cooking her sumptuous gourmet
She, swayed to swoon by a wordsman
Whose words, sweet or sour, do make her day

Only he can bring home a child
From his cur, toy and the ground of play
The kid doesn't kid with stories mild
Or rough, as long as a hero a dragon slay

For fame and fortune fair not his face
His face is alight when listener falls under his spell
He knows and savours his rightful place
History knows his story can freeze hot spells in hell

When the sun yawns in a sunset hue
Before the arms of the bed embrace him at night
He regales like a jongleur with a tattoo
All darkened spirits he sunshines them to his light

Blessed are they that treasure his words' darts
They are the source of his happiness
The fecund embodiment of his creative arts
In each other, they knack brightness

William Warigon

Bud Nip

Nicely nip it in the bud
Lest it bites in the butt.
Do not downplay the dot,
It may bring regrettable rot.

A slight, small wound, festers slowly
May turn very gangrenous so quickly
Within blip blink of long lashes.
So, find succour to small rashes.

To procrastinate shaving the head of trouble
May then turn the trouble to double bubble.
When you nip it bit in the bud,
You may erase imploding load.

He that knows loves when to heartily hear
That all tough trouble's rudiments disappear.
He needs no foreign seer
To do what others may fear.

Never ever be like an empty head
That loves to ingratiate the dead.
Let lives live long to the fullest, friend;
So that they don't end before the end.

William Warigon

From Liberator To Oppressor

O hail, here comes the heroic Liberator
He came to snatch us all
From the clutching claws of an Oppressor
A dictator must sure fall
His red eyes blazed fiery fire
Like a demon from the pit of hell
Yes, we hailed our new desire
O, hail, our hero, you we did hail
When he liberated us that fateful day
We were drunk with optimism
We danced and danced till we broke
The back of the day
Gone were our hopeless pessimism
A new dawn kissed our black and weary faces
A new song dressed our chapped lips
Lands grabbed he returned to their rightful place
Laughter returned to our own rips
We went to sleep, snoring like fed cubs
Only to wake up to another form of slavery
Our Hero ruffled feathers, we lost jobs
Our boom economy thrown into a quandary
The people's love for a loaf of bread
Vanished as its price soared like rocket
Our joy turned into nightmarish dread
Poverty polished us into a bracket
The hero turned despot
Duly laced our black backs with whips
As we wait to coolly rot
Our confidence sales with hopeless ships Things came to a hilt
When the despot curbed policies to police
Our freedoms. We ate filth
He's an emperor who threatened our peace
Till he drew his last breath this day
He was as unrepentant as a mule
A new dawn dawns those sunny day
A preferred leader has come to rule
Our orison is for old, peace and progress
Let the new helmsman impress
Our national interests he must address
No more a Liberator to oppress

William Warigon

497

Thank You For Being A Friend

You are a strong tower
Striving hour after hour
Working hard to bring ease
Taking over other's disease
You're a treasure trove of trust
Which is a rock and can't burst

When you sing, the earth dances
Your songs mend broken fences
Your smile is like a soothing balm
It makes turbulent troubles calm
Your priceless presence is a blessed assurance
You are the fairest star with love in abundance

Thank you for being a friend
I'll travel with you to the end
For you are true as truth can be
You are real as the sun I do see
You I will always bless
For feeding me no stress.

Rule Of Love

Do not choose whom to love.
Emulate the Father above.
Do not chose whom to hate.
All colours must conjugate.
If you are a lover,
You need no cover
To choose where to pitch your love
In adversity, be as gentle as a dove.
The leper and the beauty
In shine or in a day misty,
Must be loved in equal measure.
To some, each is but a treasure.
When you rule with love,
You paint peace thereof!

William Warigon

Window wonder

The summer sun will return
When year does pass to next
The phone now has new features
More than speak and text
Autumn now is calling
Soon leaves will be falling
On thick coat am stalling want to eek out before too cold

Chasing cars and odd airplane
With bad eyes to keep me sane
Through the glass that keeps out
The other world and about
Sitting with a blank page
Guess that all did have this stage
An invitation for creation
No regards for situation

Nights draw in and so begins
The daytime light bulb on
The gloom in room has come too soon
Soon me and Bill will not get along
Give me back the last few months
When moaning about the heat
Truth be told this thing cold
Can't match nor ever beat

Nans wit prams but no Sampans
Glide down the pavement wet
Office wallah with upturned collar
Seems to someplace they must get
Soon the dusk and then the musk
Of night creature marking ground
The cacophony of misery
The ones now Homeward bound

At which stage do we feel age?
Am I feeling now?

Window

One by one we came undone
History or travesty?
One by one lost sense of fun
Looking now what we be
Always the race to fill a space
A space, perhaps, for reflection
Always on we do go on
Regardless of the right or wrong

Sometimes take a sidestep
Let this rush pass by
Sometimes I take a pause
Then I question why
Why so wrapped within this trap
Why we do not halt
Take some pause to check the cause
Of that within are caught

I may walk different, may talk different
Yet we are the same
I may choose to something lose
But it was just a name
Weak I am but strong for knowing
Incomplete you do greet
Yet that part still growing

Mesmerised when categorised
Put in place by some object made
Am much more if explore
Join the grand Parade
Nothing yet to that can get
A window display is me
Tempting but not for sale
Delve into diversity

Ian Wilcox

Wisdom Warriors

The bullets fly and the shells do scream
The 'safe' ground is no more
The cries of pain as seek to gain
Place not had before

The resolution for confusion
The digging deeper we must
The spirit strong so carry on
In us we now must trust

The unity in diversity
The common that is found
The security of being 'we'
The shell that does surround

The once more and to the fore
We put ourselves in harm's way
For others do not agree
In many actions say

The adrenaline flows from where don't know
Just the rush to do
The exhilaration of completion
The surprise of getting through

Yet this is not War
This is just what we do
We are living 'normal' lives
Being Creatives me and you

Similarities a plenty
In ways we do not think
As are Wisdom Warriors
Once more standing at the brink

The things we do our weapons
To show becomes our foe

Wise in its disguise

The ecstasy of what could be
The calamity of what reality
Every day the same new way
Courting, creating controversy
When to some seems right yet to others wrong
Do we actually from same species belong?
Can we really get more diverse?
Not in us but in this curse

In dusty Halls our heritage stalls
That what we call our History
How far we fell, returned that spell
In our modern misery
We used to class by colour
Party colours now class us
Old remains though some refrain

Who we are could go so far
If accept we're not the same
Yet seems unacceptable this potential
Discrimination we gave the name
When opinion becomes physical
When with ill intent do vent
Regression our progression
Back to where from sent

We think we're wise in its disguise
When we choose to close our eyes
To the silence of timelessness
When with violence we do bless
The sweetness of completeness
Not for us it seems
The sight of 'might' show through fight
In too many pleasant dreams

Wise to exercise

I took a look at a Book
It felt so good to hold
To actually turn pages as learn
The story someone told
Something then occurred to me
How did sound that I see
Why now bordering fantasy?
When we have spoken through history

Placed Book on lap and filled think gap
With another new
For I am almost that kind we class as Blind
Audible helps them do
Do what you do without hesitation
Do what do on occasion
Do for work or do for leisure
Do as task or do for pleasure

To get away from that same old say
To venture in the vault
Of the words now seldom heard
That were once common caught
By the ear of those near
For spoken no mere token
The days were made for vocal not laid
A habit since now so broken

The needing of the reading
Compliments but not overrules
Vocal cords are same as eyes
Within Body they are tools
They are not just gatherers of infections
Like our muscles need exercise
We go to Gym for the latter
Let's now talk if we are wise

503

Bilquees: The Queen Of Sheba

This fair ebony beauty
That was the famed Queen of Ethiopia
Her Highness was lofty
In name, panache, living in her Utopia
Every ear tingled upon hearing of her quests
Fearless, fierce, fabulous, the Eve of Bliss
She was the Mistress of all she surveyed. Tests
Were sent her way, she crushed with ease
Men came from far and near, armed to charm with their ardour
They preened like princely peacocks, raving about their grandeur
But soon, their crown jewels shrivelled upon seeing her splendour

She had it all, but she was empty
Her heart longed for true love
Nights upon nights, her bed empty
She tossed and turned enough
To set her sweaty duvet on fire
The undeniable cravings in her heart were like a disease
She'd not known such alien desire
Her magicians failed to bring her remedies

Then, like a big bolt from a thunderstorm
She heard of a king from a faraway land
The things she heard, set her heart to roam
She wasted no breath, she took her band
And travelled torturous journey to Jerusalem
She's mesmerized by the riches of the land
His beauty and brains captured her soul
And head over heels her heart fell in love
She gave in to her heart's desire, whole
And gave thanks to the Almighty, above

Time sped as though chased by the demons
Solomon was Cupidly arrowed with love
A union of two strange nations of diamonds
Those star-crossed lovers wrapped in love
Sang the songs of the moon and the stars
And danced above the rim of the setting sun
Their story is retold till we raise the bars
With fervour, we wish, so ours will be done.

William Warigon

The Rose And The Big Boss

She was as beautiful as the morning rose
And she knew how powerful her beauty held ground.
She wore her corrosive pride like a boss.
Her arrogance was the harbinger that brought her down.
She sang praises with pouting lips
And lukewarm heartiness.
Thanksgiving was given in nips
Her sacrifices were like half baked loaves without sweetness.

The Big Boss was far from pleased
With this his daughter not like the other.
He hated to be the one to be dissed.
So, he took a key, locked her womb altogether.

For years, yowling and yearning for a yearling
To give suck to her sore nipples
Yielded no succour. She started learning
To bear the gifts of simplicity and humility.
She turned around her ship
To worship with fervour without frivolity.

The Big Boss shifted his leg
From this Earth his footstool.
Miasma of compassion decked
His cloak of mercy of holy wool.
Her repentance in sack clothing
Touched every fringe in his heart.
He opened her womb for birthing
And in no time she filled the Earth.

She'd learned the cost of pride
But, was never ready to hide.
She saw errors arrowed her way
And repented in humility anyway.
Now, her story is like lipstick
On lips in praise not gimmick.
A ship turned around is big work
But it would safely reach the dock.

William Warigon

Head Teacher

The teacher that teaches my head
Sensed that I needed sense.
He opened the mouth of my brain, fed
Me to stupor via his lens.

He led my head to be the head of the class,
Bestowed Davidian confidence in me,
Until I became a fountain none could outclass.
He led my head to be the head of the class.

I have sucked knowledge from the very edge
Of his hardened head to the calloused sole of his feet.
He's a connoisseur apt for an adage.
I'm a codicil willing to be wilfully willed in his feat.

I became a clay in his palm.
Like the plain pundit he is,
He moulded me into a psalm
To be sung at royal feast.

As he rests in his cloying crib,
I feel his spirit hover over me always
To ensure I do not ever trip
But to follow in his mammoth trace.

William Warigon

The Quest

Armed with a shriek of determination,
We embarked on a quest.
From the deep eddy of the river
To the swamps swamped with swarms of merry, monstrous mosquitoes.
We were on a mission to find the witch.
Long had her evil machinations
Stole all our thunders till
We were left, wallowing from left to right.
Her evil stench hanged with precarious glaze
Dressed upon the rancid air
To discourage our quest.
We're wild wolves, ravenous and mad.
Amulets of fire scourged our sunburned necks.
We were furious like religious flagellants.
Charged with portentous grip,
We soon felt her unnerving enervating influence like an unseen umbrella, yet
Inured to her spell.
Arcane arts, so esoteric, we pouched,
Screened from the eyes,
Fed from the mud in our sea-bedded souls.
Antediluvian monster with a plan hovered, but
we ignored him like a lost cause.
For today, we shall not feel the lethargy of death.
We are already death beaters of death eaters:
The seasoned soldiers spoilt for war to bring spoils of war

William Warigon

My Child, My Asset

My child, you mean the world to me
You are the never-ending blessing
My eyes rock and roll when you I see
You harmonize my melody as I sing

Despite the rock in your head
Or the big mole on your nose
My love for you stands ahead
Your odour is my scented rose

I watch every twitch of your mouth
A prelude to a bitter squall and quench it
Your cries are the razors to my heart
Like the eagle you are, I desire you stay fit

The future is surely bleak and uncertain
A caterpillar may be the beautiful butterfly
Or turn out to be an ugly monstrous stain
Yet, I will never forsake you my Quirky Pie

Come to me when your soul hungers
My comforting words give panacea
Don't drown in placid waters of angers
The door to my heart is wide, it's here

Watching you growing is the ultimate joy
Your chortling sounds, cackling smiles
With drooling four toothed mouth, oh boy,
Are yen that keep me good in life's miles

William Warigon

Yet

More

A virus for a virus

What's that I hear, is it fear?
The surroundings are rebelling
Are they being rude or giving clue?
The things we want they are not selling
Don't you understand we're on borrowed land?
As has been lent before
Mother thunders as we plunder
Changing shape of shore

Don't speak to me of being weak
When we take just what we can
Regardless of the damage caused
To others, earth and man
A virus now runs through us
A virus for a virus
We are all a disease
With that which is inside us

So, come to me you misery
You are what, in part, deserve
An irritation for situation
For profit we now serve
"Forget tomorrow! I like for today!"
The common cry now hear
"Just give to me Electricity
With games my vision clear"

Don't tell me that you're innocent
For all guilty in some way
Looking for the present pleasure
No plans for next to stay
Money like Heroine
Hard to kick once had
Yet money is admired
All the good and bad

A year of near but not yet fear

We play cards, we play the hand
We are born in different land
We adapt and overcome
We are not separated - we are one!
We cross the waters or we not
United us sometimes forgot
Yet in modern are 'job lot'
What in honesty have we become?

Major fires in America
Earthquake in the UK
I guess that Mother Nature
Finally wants to say
I gave you room and took a broom
Swept what I had to give
Now again feel the pain
Of what I have to give

Two oh two oh a number know
Not for the challenge of Seasons
Sad to say for different way
Most of which wrong reasons
A part of Time that I call mine
I legacy of what to be
The other has no cover
Just the wait and see

Depressed no yet but for it set
Will not allow for the inclusion
So many reasons for that treason
None of which are yet infusion
Body subtle yet is vulnerable
Not the thing inside
It staying strong when even wrong
A certain inner pride

Retardabitur motus human

The world we live in is in meltdown
A strange virus runs amok
The haves that have the current 'power'
Shield themselves and buy all the stock

Not for care of who represent
More the history of came then went
Sod the World when elections loom
We hold it so play our tunes

Some do truly like this
Others truly sad
For some is self-importance
Some the worst they've had

Here today and gone tomorrow
More rejoicing than the sorrows
How many times have we done?
How many times since we've begun?

I sit on pebble within the lake
Listening to decisions made for my sake
Some make sense and should be rule
Others just a longevity tool

I open eyes and wonder why
Wonder what is new today
Quoting scripts from fellow twits
Guaranteeing pay

Learning now to ignore
So many 'slants' become bore
Not just here but foreign shore
Am I now strange to wish for more?
Retardabitur motus human

The world we live in is in meltdown
A strange virus runs amok
The haves that have the current 'power'
Shield themselves and buy all the stock

Not for care of who represent
More the history of came then went
Sod the World when elections loom
We hold it so play our tunes

Some do truly like this
Others truly sad
For some is self-importance
Some the worst they've had

Here today and gone tomorrow
More rejoicing than the sorrows
How many times have we done?
How many times since we've begun?

I sit on pebble within the lake
Listening to decisions made for my sake
Some make sense and should be rule
Others just a longevity tool

I open eyes and wonder why
Wonder what is new today
Quoting scripts from fellow twits
Guaranteeing pay

Learning now to ignore
So many 'slants' become bore
Not just here but foreign shore
Am I now strange to wish for more?
Accipiam vos omnes

Acclamation Station

Who decides the right way to write?
When expression is individual
Providing not deliberately offensive
Surely room for all
Pigeonholed into Genders
By someone with some degree
Never knowing what are thinking
Never knowing me

Who decides then choose to lecture?
Own or established way been done
Closing lid on that important
Writing foremost should be fun
Not, necessarily, in the topic
But the way you feel
Can have serious or the frivolous
Depending on how feel

Acclamation Station
Recognition by some others
Does that really mean that much?
When only part it covers
A mere segment of what can do
A mere snippet, a small clue
Yet if they look at true
There is so much more can do

I don't want to be next case
Time spent on me is such a waste
I am not for category
I am simply what you see
But 'in the know' so like to show
Telling new without a clue
How to be what want to see
Never being simply you

Acorns in the Attic

What becomes of the undiscovered?
The many not recognised
What becomes of the gifts they're giving?
Will we, one day, be surprised
The countless talent in vast ocean
Hidden by the plethora shown
Just a name like many others
Yet a name that is their own

What becomes of the despondent?
Who aim high but don't make grade
That forget should be a pleasure
Not the sole money earning trade
For those who do are the few of few
Too many variables need to fit
In a space and in a 'right time'
To become what some call 'hits

What becomes of the pleasure person?
Doing but rejecting more
They are content to have no pressure
Giving licence to explore
Knowing that nothing guarantees
That the whole world will you please
So, carrying on with some ease
When mischievous will they tease

Acorns in the Attic
Sit and wait to grow
How many of them will succeed?
Alas we'll never know
Talent Tree a mystery
When to some surprise
Some do value what you shed
Yet remain the unrecognised

Take comfort in the shadow
For spotlight seems too bright
Don't get caught in others expectations
Do for you what just feels right

Activation situation

Activation situation
CPU to energised
Body parts switched to 'Start'
Some protesting as surprised

Built up fluids need release
Legs take Body, hurry please
To the place for that to do
Without need of bedding new

CPU now is craving
Before more rubbish mouth is raving
Caffeine needed, Caffeine fix
Into system and then mix

Liquid splashing on the face
Before meeting Human Race
One more shot of Caffeine need
Before meeting like of breed

How many here have been there?
With that half focused wake up stare
Not quite sure what the time
Wondering if this is crime?

To deprive what do best
Some call sleep and some call rest
Whatever name it is same
Deprived of it is such a shame

Activation situation

Ad primum deducite pilum!

A former one that has seen
A former one that in real been
No waggling of a joystick
No techno language speaks
Can speak in a different one
The information Commanders seeks
A person in a conflict zone
Real and not some game
The breath and bleed just like you
Difference? Just not some game

A former that has felt on self
The wetness of real blood
Not the restart option
As laying in the mud
So, brave you armchair heroes
If haven't spent money for comfort way
Guess that it is acceptable
When say you only play

Is it enjoyable to be protected?
By some variant of a chip?
Does that make you feel a better person?
As just gnawing at your lip
The profiteers are in undreamed state
As profiteers they do soar
The uneducated innocent
Screaming for some more

I see a sunrise and I wonder
What this one will choose to bring
Will my Heart still be beating?
When a nightfall it does sing
In which group will I end the day?
The living or the past
For soldiers are a short-term solution
They weren't made to last
The alteration to adulation
A sickness slowly growing
Profit before realising
Gained by real world knowing

Adam

Adam an enigma
Adam is a quirk
Adam is a puzzle
Adam is a jerk

Adam is a headstrong human
Adam is always right
Adam can be stubbornness

Adam – A detail about males
All the gossip and the truth
The facts and various tales

Adam likes to think he's superior
Adam in fact is quite inferior
Adam is master when with Adams
Adam something that sometimes saddens

Adam is a carnivore
That mixes that with herbivore
Adam is confusion
Mixed with some illustration

Adam is a breathing creature
Adam seeks and likes to feature
Adam is social when it suits
Sometimes proud of his roots

Why do I know so much about Adam?
A question I hear you ask
Because I am one of Adam
Not yet drowning in a Cask

Advance the acolytes

Marshmallows melting in the midday
Unconventional but still a treat
Joyful the experience
When other cultures meet
Who am I? Then ask why
Was born in place with choice
Why retarded when discarded
The opportunity to voice

Making mayhem with a new pen
Passing just some time
Paper seller felling better
With money once was mine
'What a joke!' One once spoke
Each to their own I guess
Just happy to be that which me
Leave different to the rest

If you're somebody let me know
If an individual let it show
Don't hide the person that you are
Let me appreciate you from afar
And all the Kings horses were suited for courses
Not necessarily those of which do run
Just going through what had to do
Before they could have fun

In the meantime, with this I call mine
We will argue and will laugh
We are not much and are as such
On contentment path
Nothing more do I adore
Than a blank waiting to be filled

So, nothing much will make
When it's just give and take
This one will not break
Advance the acolytes of ambition

Affluence of effluents

However, whichever the what's it
Whoever, whenever the how's of it
Together forever the sum of it
The liquid goes and flows

The make the most of madness
The shy away from sadness
The greeting of the gladness
The symptoms start to show

The one that's fun has just begun
The searching for the sleeping Sun
The ramblings seem to run and some
Now another place they go

The Crossword

The crosswords had some cross words
They were quite irate
The cross words and the down words
The across words they did hate

The Puzzle was a muddle
The eyes it did befuddle
One piece played in puddle
Soggy section so much trouble

The PlayStation Nation a Generation
So seemed the situation
Increased Index indication
Costs they crept about inflation

Who we be and who we see
Is, in fact, simplicity
Reaching realm of reality
Focus thoughts on flouting free

Seek

My eyes roam the magnificent
Galaxy of mysteries
It holds the beginning and
The end
Questions float in minds
Quest
Is there in this vast space other
Humans
Have they become so far above?
Our intelligence
Where peace reins in the
Equality of man
That we're shunned in our
Ignorance
The stars map our horoscope
For some
The moon pulls our tides and
Touches our moods
We watch in awe as men travel
This space
Will earth someday join the
Vacant planets
Science verses its knowledge
Different
Then the biblical way of our
Growth
A division of thoughts in humanity
Beliefs
In away death opens our eyes to
Truth

Janice Fisher

My Space

Searching a space where
beauty blooms
Where sweet fragrance fills
the air
Where contentment sways
in the breezes
When rainbows of promise
follow the rain
As new seeds sprout in beautiful
rays of colors
And wheat fields glow golden in
summers sun
Summer takes a backward step as
fall shows its brilliance
Mornings dew glistening on falling
Leaves of fall
Mountains air cools with peeking
Winters blast
My space complete in changing
seasons
My peace flowing with the changing
tides of life

Janice Fisher

Wishing

IF...
Only this was a dream
and waking would erase
these moments in time
as if they never were ...

ITS ...
So hard sometimes to
carry the weight of paths
journeys...

BUT ...
We push beyond our human
endurance to strive to be
more than we can
be ...

A ...
Time when we search the
depth of souls' worth finding
it stronger than we
realized...

DREAM ...
Is an escape to regain a respite
Of the burdens in life's endless
curves...

Janice Fisher

Search

I search for you in the shadows
of my mind ...
Trailing the paths of a kiss
lingering ...
New Year's bells struck at
midnight ...
You came from nowhere as you
turned me ...
Softly kissing as if a lover in
search ...
Tasting my lips with the tip
of your tongue ...
A fleeting kiss as your eyes linked
with mine ...
A sparkling of mischievous feat
accomplished ...
Then as if running with the chimes
of a New Year ...
You faded in the crowd as if you
never were ...
My mysterious New Year's kiss sealed
forever ...
In the twelve chimes of minds holding
memory ...

Janice Fisher

Melody

I feel you within the rhythm of
this flowing melody
Its key touched by the joining
with me
Your whispers float in my minds
remembrance
Now a ghostly touch to find you
In music
Tears drop with each note playing
as I feel you
A haunting melody plays a loss of
us
As if you sat beside me our fingers
joined again
The piano changes the meaning of
each tune
Pulling magically memories of
past nights
Where we felt the magic touch
you played
Now caught in your pianos returning
touch
As if in music I'll always find you in
haunting melody
The loss of us

Janice Fisher

Depth

My thoughts of you flow in the
Minds travels
Interrupting my inks path of
Words
As you seem to come alive between
The sentences
Jumping in hunger with each spill
Of ink
So intense the memories I hold of
You
I've brought you alive in words not
Yet written
As you control the dripping of my
Inks flow
Devouring each word as you move
Among them
As if the memories belong to us and
Not to Be shared
You pull the pages apart not wanting
My remembering
Magically erasing each word as if the
Ink gone
You fade into the empty shadows of
Blank words
As if your Angels wings have removed
The past
A signal to move on down the path of
Follows

Janice Fisher

Rain

Fall rains raise the rivers
To their banks
Flowing with a tremendous
Speed
Sounding like a roaring
Lion
As it speeds down its
Path
Moving large rocks as if
Pebbles
There's a freshness cast
In the air
Picturesque in its vivid view
Of beauty
Bathed sides of banks with
Fall colors
Nature's endless show of its
Grandeur

Night

Darkness came so quickly
Chasing the day away
Before the dinner bell rang
The sky void of moons glow
No blinking stars to wish on
The breeze had a winter bite
The air smelled of chimney smoke
Mixed with everyone dinner cooking
Thoughts of winters cold brings to mind
Hot chocolate with floating marshmallows
Movies and popcorn amongst the cuddles

Janice Fisher

Sun

The sun raised in full
Control
Sky in beautiful colors
Edged in blue surrounding
Its beauty
Clouds like puffy marshmallows
Floating
Sun rays dancing with shadows on
The ground
Then as if controlled by a magical
Force
The clouds turned dark hiding the
Sun
As it fought the breeze that brought
The clouds
But in vain they won as the breeze
Became wind
Dark clouds hiding the beauty once
There
Thunders echo as if laughing at its
Gain
As lightning flashed its striking
Control
The wind bringing a shower gliding
In sideways
Quickly turning to a pounding down
Of rain
Like the heavens had opened a flood
Of tears
Then quiet as the sun gained control
Once again
The storm in a rear-view memory like
life's paths

Janice Fisher

Life

Battered and broken in the brutal
stormy waves of
Emotions
Just barely a float in broken pieces
of my heart and
Mind
Standing on the pier of life's path
where the destination lays
Unreachable
Watching my tide pull me in and
out never letting me
Escape
Living on borrowed time as the clock
Ticks
Wondering if closed eyes will wake
to see dawns
Lights
Pills becoming the stepping stone
that pedal ones
Life
But like a train out of control you
Ride the tracks to the end of the
Line
Who really knows what's around?
the speeding out of control
Body

Janice Fisher

Walk

I feel so much as I walk
Through the forest of
Thoughts
Search throughout the veins
Of bare limbs for blue
Sky's
Feel the lost life of dry leaves
Under my path I walk as they
Crunch
Smell the pine needles still
Clinging to life their fragrance
Stilled
In a soft breeze that carries the
Chill of winter just around the
Corner
I listen to its sounds as it speaks
In nature's background like a
Song
I beg my path to never end here
Amongst the peace of nature's
Breath

Poetess

I look longing at my pen
Hoping it will blend with
My mind and the poems
Will float in inks spill
They say I'm old fashioned
Still using a pen when
Technology so much easier
But that's where my poems
Float in this ink well where
The pen dips in connecting
With my brain, heart and soul

Janice Fisher

532

Paths

We push through the days
To fast
Then wonder where the time
Seemed to go
Search through the unseen
tomorrow's
Pushing at the fog that holds
Us
To an unknown future we're not
To see
We grab at straws that become a
Extinction
Become lost in the hours we tried
To lengthen
Ride a merry-go-round that never
Stops
We take a step but the path crumbles
Before us
We stand in place pushing at the
Fog that holds
"The Truth Not Told"

Night

The sun settled behind the
Horizon
The sky dark showing no
Moon
Hiding the stars in its
Depth
The air cold and biting in
Breezes
Thunder heard in the mountain
Range
The sky opens in a flash of
Lightning
You can smell the coming
Storm
Feel it dept within your
Being
It's coming

Janice Fisher

Bleed for you

Give to me some blood for free
So, I can bleed for you
Give to me security
Give a shield called you
In the dark times when need light
Be that Beacon burning bright
In the mist be my goal
Be that one that makes me whole

Can I change? Yes, I can
I just need the reason
I am a million in one shell
I am as different as a Season
Give me you as a clue
Prove to me it's not see through
Give me something is all I ask
Is that truly a hard task?

Saw the hole and sidestepped
Just carry on with what get
Get me down I never let
Climbing back up is such hard work
All that been some type of sheen
When object inside we try to hide
That was then but this is now
Just learned them lessons and then how

The Bowie was a master
In turning good from a disaster
Major Tom is still strong
In some place should not belong
I believe I will achieve
If not success then happiness
That's all I need to this one feed
In a head where lay for rest

535

Blindness has its benefits

What makes our World go around can be profound
Can sometimes, just be true
What makes us, us can make such fuss
In what we see we do
Environment to us it lent
So, did Biology
Yet we shine through in what do
Pure simplicity

If I said that I love you
Not sexually but who you are
Would that be okay for me to say
Or a step too far?
If I said that we are equal
In same sentence not a sequel
Would that irritate if it I state
In pecking order there's no prequel

Blindness has its benefits
When mind treats all kinds
How they act and interact
Judging by the finds
What would we see in equality?
What would be the opinion?
When we be one place free
No preference dominion?

If said that I did love you
Can't see but not that way
Just a fact, how react?
Would you leave or would you stay
Not same place just same space
In this thing we call a friend
Would you hate our equal state?
My opinion then tries to 'mend'?

Blinkers off

Made a moment in a maelstrom
Made decisions to be better
To make sure I follow pure
Wrote them down in a Letter
Made a choice to self-voice
Without the use of sound
Chose a way that became play
Yet is heard all around

Countries do not worry it
Nor the language spoken
When the message is not commanding
When the product merely token
Choose one form yet not the sole one
Many out there, bold as Brass
Yes, this one with which feel comfortable
Never knowing when will pass

Introverted not perverted
Extraverted needs attention
Something in the middle fiddle
Could be called an amalgamation
Flying high yet don't know why
The aim of one and all
Yet we are just part of something
Up to others to make that call

Footsteps in the future
Become the tracks of past
When we seek to improve present
What we have was just a blast
Pomposity once did see
In self and all around
Yet startled cough as Blinkers off
Accept the common ground

Blue silence

We come as one to become
Two or more if choose
The benefits of partnerships
Give more than we do lose
Social in more than vocal
Some were just a try
Then the right might, just might
Happen to pass by

Blue silence turned to Silver
When I told her that I missed her
Gold was told when could hold
Platinum when we did kiss
The numbness of the nothingness
Now distant memory
The satisfaction of interaction
Replacement ecstasy

Nothing makes like enforced breaks
Bring home that you have and why
Hours slip on pleasure trip
Realised with contented sigh
Wild Horses and Race courses
Never will they meet
Yet wild me that once did be
Finally found my feet

Blue silence turned to Silver
When I told her that I missed her
Gold was told when could hold
Platinum when we did kiss
The numbness of the nothingness
Now distant memory
The satisfaction of interaction
Replacement ecstasy

Boredom with bravado

'Look at me!' Cried Figalee
'My supremacy can't be denied!'
'Look at me! I'm what can be!'
Shouting with self-pride
Yes, the people took a look
Found nothing special to separate
In the field of achievement
Just in field of unjust hate

'Look at me!' Cried want to be
A name in the fame game
'Look at me!' Became history
Another 'almost' name
Yes, they had a talent
Not matching own perception
Yes, they were gifted
In self-perceived invention

The trap that waits and this one hates
The pomposity of some
That when said is just inside led
Not what have become
Confidence is just a chance
How much it can grow
Yet to know how much to show
That's a different dance

Just desire to inspire
Not brag of your delusion
For what see is just wants to be
A total mere illusion
An error made in a grade
Marked by none but self
By supplying are denying
The 'common peoples' wealth

Black warriors

Black warriors are resilient, bold and beautiful.

They are courage, fearless always on guard

Tall, dark, muscular, strong, reliable.
They are ever ready to defend their territories.

Always ready to lay down their lives
They are guided by the African spirit.

We are who we are
Africa is my root and I'm not ashamed of it

Our black heritage
We are proud to be Africans

We dictate our pace
We are not slaves
We are free born.
Don't take us for granted because we fight with our past blood.

Why the discriminations?
What have we done wrong?

We are stronger and the world knows it. We are never
afraid of death because we conquer as warriors.

We envisage and lay ambush for our prey
Don't dare us because we devour our prey.

We are lions of Africa descendant and we don't care if you love us or not.

This was triggered by a black woman that was
beaten at the airport at Amsterdam

Bose Eneduw Adogah

Box of tricks

'Black Lives' the latest thing
As more 'likes' they hope to bring
Other colours just don't matter
In case interest we do scatter

It's all about the numbers
As meaningful it slumbers
Don't care a jot if true or not
Our brains are getting number

Making money from the mayhem
Create then promise to fix
Everyone is suffering
While they just get their kicks

I'm sure that this will get removed
As some do hate the truth
Speaking with 2 brain cells working
Now is just uncouth

Just say the word and we are all cured
You can seem to cure the world
Politics a box of tricks
Of those needing to be heard

We used to be more stable
When think for self were able
Now anything on table
The social media fable

Braver Man

When I said Goodbye, you didn't cry
Just laughed and had a drink
More celebration than consternation
What was I supposed to think?
When I packed my bags, you got me a Cab
To hurry me on my way
Ordered for as soon as possible
With nothing else to say

That other car outside
The occupant did try to hide
Just how long have you had another
Worse it is my Brother!
Shame on you and shame on me
Should have known but didn't see
The time he spent 'just popping round'
The different toiletries that I found

The dirty shirt I didn't wear
That panicked look as I did stare
At two used plates when were alone
The seat up on 'The Throne'
Just how long been going on?
I begin to wonder
All those leaks we had last week
Convenient he is a Plumber

My rides outside just like my pride
Though guess it's for the best
He can wear if he dares
That bloody knitted vest!!
He can eat those Pasta sheets
That don't soften – they just harden
Can explore for that Mower and more
In the Jungle called a Garden!

He's either a bloody fool or braver man than me!!

Breakfast begging

Hi ya you! How are you?
That sausage there looks nice
Yes, it is a grim old morning
Wow! They even do fried slice!
I see that the bacon not overcooked
Don't you hate it when they do?
Ahh and Black pudding
So, what's new with you?

Your little one is teething?
Those Hash browns they look delicious
They seem to grow up so quickly don't they
Toms and Beans! That is something serious!
How's the Missus these days?
Toast and the fried slice!
She gave you what for your Birthday?
Like those mushrooms that is nice

Is your oldest now at school?
Two eggs! That's a treat
Wow! Soon be dating boys
I quite agree Brown sauce can't be beat
Soon be playing with different toys
A side of chips as well
Hahaha, you'll soon be a private Taxi
Tea or Coffee? I can't tell

Me? Oh, just plodding on
Yes, Breakfast of a King
Same old, same old
That gorgeous morning smell
Ducking and diving but surviving
Keeps the body in pure bliss
Can't complain so that's a gain
Do I want one? Well if you insist

Broken dreams and unseen seen

Here they come, the 'righteous'
More righteous than the last
All can 'see' much more than me
My own bit goes too fast
To Black Holes we go though we don't know
Until on edge we stand
Not too late to change that fate
If but understand

Once walked with holes in each shoe
With no House so not new
Doing just what need to do
Something in common with some of you
Yet like me you broke free
From that stage of misery
You took stand and changed that wrong
That like us don't belong

Changed what had and changed what be
Changed myself and found me
A lesson learnt the hardest way
Some will lift they will pay
So, as you sit in comfort somewhere
Spare a thought and even care
Some hit problems not their own
Just a result of in that grown

Broken dream and unseen seen
The vision Invisible
For those lucky to not get it
Those who heard the Poverty call
Those who suffer freezing night-time
Those who suffer hunger pain
Those who are bewilderment despondent
Those who think they cannot gain

Broken lies and slipped disguise

In this world so often heard
The bitterness of break
When one side discards pride
For their futures sake
Either one can come undone
Know what have to do
The one I saw could take no more
Don't know what they went through

All I saw was were cut to core
That calm soft voice did choose
Not the one of pleading
They were the good thing lose
Close enough to hear
Close enough to see
The fact met with no regret
Persona no fury

They simply said

The cold hard truth came calling
No more at your feet am falling
Bending this way, bending that way
Just believing all you say
Broken lies and slipped disguise
True colours on display
Not the way I choose to play
Finally, I got wise

A puppet on a string
The pure gullible King
Now lost that Crown, the puppet's down
A better does begin
Go find another victim
You sadistic soul
I have cut out all your cancer
Now again am whole

Butter and knife

Many mistakes along the way
Do we make as with life play
Putting off for another day
Losing chance of that which may
Here in my hands I hold my future
Here in my hands it waits to show
Here in my hands is future knowledge
Here in my hands that not yet know

Come the reckoning as truth sets in
Come the ironic laugh
We are all a once fool
When remember path
The numbers change and might have mange
So unhealthy do they look
Outer cover coats some not other
My mine I so shook

The calamity of you and me
So what I/ we to do?
Change or just rearrange
When we have a clue
The Squirrels scurry, always in hurry
That is them not us
I look at them and say with pen
Why have all this fuss?

Step one to what become
Admit that Life knows best
Step two is just seeing it through
Rise to every test
Sometimes along we get things wrong
According to the Husband or the Wife
Such will be for simply we
Are the butter to their knife

Cab to clarification

Can we catch a Cab to clarification?
The journey seems so long
One is saying something
Another says their wrong
Can we find a road to Reason?
A straight one would be nice
Too many U-turns on path present
Been this part six times twice

A motorbike to middle ground
Weaving through the war want Wallis
I pity but I can't hate them
Reminding me of the old trolley Dollies
Faster than the average car
On less fuel can travel further
Such a state is our fate
To get there need to be a 'swerver'

Can we get a Speedboat?
Skim over misery
Once it was but a Pond
Now it is a Sea
We can glide over choppy waters
Steer around if get too rough
A little bouncy is a fun thing
But enough's enough

Can we get an aeroplane?
With it travel high
Above this maelstrom of our making
With no answer to justify
Maybe we just need a Spaceship
Take the sane to start again
Leave the rest to their bequest
Partners with pandemonium and pain

Caffeine in

On autumn day whilst storing Hay into waste we drop
A different did the same
Different reason but same season
Both have bills to pay
A Crow does grow with that we throw
Muscles other birds aside
A Fox likes box in which food drop
Survival over price

Can you feel the times a changing?
Can you notice cold?
Can you see reality
Not the stuff you're told
Imagination an irritation
For those who like the blind
Muppets see and Muppets be
When accepts their kind

Summer gone but not for long
Back again next year
Now can relate to hibernate
When too cold to shed a tear
Maybe exaggeration
For now, is just wet
Soon will go to that we know
That certain when a snow will set

Caffeine in so does begin
A flurry of new worry
That pain again that is insane
Needs to hold back on his Curry!
A tempting dish when one does wish
An import glad received
Yet cannot beat a Roast with meat
When it is achieved

Beef definitely my favourite although I love the occasional Lamb

Cake

In the middle of this riddle
How do I make a Cake to bake?
In the heard that is absurd
How a difference can I make?
In a meal both eat and fill
How to create 'perfection'?
Equal measure a secret treasure
Did someone forget to mention?

Boys like boys and Girls like girls
So what does that mean to whole?
All that be is opinion free
Banish the nasty natter
If I could I'd surely would
Wipe from those who don't agree
The personal is the be and all
Why that need to then deceive?

I hear the trouble as does double
Past the physical
The thought it taught was count for nought
In the where withal
The things seen are just has been
The vision now the mission
The get strong and carry on
Until the sweet fruition

A single soul amongst a whole
A nothing yet a something more
Captivity if choose to be
When reject a foreign shore
Back to cake for goodness sake
A masterpiece now I do wish
Please Cake gracious bake
For other choice is Fish!

Calamity cleaned the Cookhouse

It was running near catastrophe
Demand near to what could supply
The popularity to them mystery
Yet others, they knew why
No thrills and spills infected grills
No fancy for the Fish
No deep fried top so price does pop
The D word serving dish

The long queues became local News
Even got to that classed national
By doing plain a following gained
It became sensational
The producers rose with the Roosters
The hum matched Cape Canaveral
The word was heard and so incurred
The hungry willing now to travel

Then the blessing in disguise
Though to those who worked there a surprise
One minor error before Dawn
Led to better being born
The chip frying left on overnight
Got so hot it did ignite
Before the break of new Day
Firefighters lost the fight

From phoenix of the ashes
A marvel did arise
Different location but the same
Now with safer fries
A larger venue – more potential
Old not mourned, just pre -quintal
Now a Beacon for life's twists
As on new seats bums sit

Call a Friend

Sent a message to the Stars
Help was needed for my own
Got reply but don't know why
Came back to me 'Address unknown'
Sent a message to those above
Whatever form they take
Got reply though don't know why
'We're too busy for good to make'

Sent a message to my neighbours
Asking for help if could spare
Got no reply, no single answer
Guess too busy to even care
Sent a message to 'my Leaders'
Not sure they read or even got
Filtered through so many individuals
In this set up there's a lot

Will not send the message to my Family
They have enough trouble I can see
They are the unfortunate, they are the victims
They, somehow, are related to me
We might have changed this story
Gave it a different end
Maybe if I sent the message
To one that I call Friends

In the hours of our darkness
We just need a light
In the hours of the all wrong
We just need some right
The hours that do trouble
In loneliness do double
The nothing is a something
When we can call a Friend

Dance Hall action

The room it seemed so empty
Middle a vacant space
Then came all the couples
Standing face to face

Drum did start a tempo
Guidance for them all
Others joined and made perfect
The well-known Dancers call

To the sound they moved around
Two's then fours, then Two's again
Gliding was just hiding
Release of inner pain

The frustration of sensation
To lose oneself in steps
The Music Hall did have its call
For Stranger or those kept

Beat to feart fait complete
Release a true sensation
Dancing to the just not new
But that of a past generation

Drum did beat and Trumpet greet
Saxophone then felt at home
Guitar made a visit and stayed
The vocals not alone

The one thing could be understood
Was the pure attraction
The synergy of energy
When involved in Dance Hall action

Dawdling in applauding

Welcome you to the new
Welcome to what we made
The breaking in of our sin
The things we had to trade
Common sense has no recompense
When we live the here and now
The disdain of those who gain
The lure of the cash Cow

The might 'seems right' in current fight
The Internet just a disgrace
When do share without care
The diversity of the Race
Avalon once did belong
Why it is the past?
Unity a dream it be
Regardless of ones caste

The cutting of the knife to right
The escapes it scrapes and what then makes
The things that make were sent
No disgrace in what now face
So no owed recompense
I walk in rain with disdain
For appreciate can walk
Enjoy the fact that now with act
To distant I can talk

The high and lows, the come and go
The recipe of what can be
The something strange we choose to change
The vision of the possibility
Not a lecture but a thought
Are we victims in which caught?
The easiness of situation
Better than the contemplation

Day

One day, could be a Monday
Life becomes that normal
Not the way now has to play
Everything so formal
Someday maybe Tuesday
Some day one at least
Will a couple again sit together
On each other's presence feast

One day maybe a Wednesday
Two become a one again
No misery of distant be
No remote caused pain

In Hearts home we're free to roam
If know and stay with one
For endless be possibilities
With that when begun
One and one are not a sum
A bonding it is true
When good and bad, the happy/ sad
Together we see through

Someday, maybe a Thursday
Will not be apart
Then that day we can say
Let's call a new start
One day could be a Friday
For I don't have a clue
All I know is wish does grow
Hope the same with you

Someday, even Saturday
For days are merely numbers
Until a two can just do
Awake and then in slumber
One day, even Sunday
Both can share same time
For that day hip hip hooray
We're past the parted crime

Daylight detritus

A cup it sits upon my table
Not too wobbly and somewhat stable
To place upon it I am able
Without the need to clean the mess
A plate last night, somewhat late
With its covering had a date
Now the bit that I so hate
Will someone with Dishwasher bless?

Mr Sunlight or Mrs be
All the same to one as me
When will let your appearance see?
These dark mornings don't amuse
Public Holiday in August late
Leaves me feeling quite irate
When last of year some do state
Does that past Christmas so confuse?

Now Breakfast time in place of mine
Guess input should be no crime
What to fill that tastes divine
That's another question
Where now go? A place I know?
On a morning walk
To someone knew or someone new
Will I get to talk?

How long did take that cake to bake?
Rambling now I am
Wild and free that I be
From menace with the pram
Can see a car for curtains are
Open again at last
The misery of hidden be
Something of the past

Day again

If you could have a day again
Which would be and why?
If you could have another chance
What different would you try?
If you could do Deja vu
The with chance for bits that new
Which parts keep and which parts lose
Oh, the chance to merely choose

The question harder than first read
As thoughts run around ill led
Might you wish for month instead
Imagination is now fed

Many a time this I think
As into nothingness at the brink
The stupid questions that I ask
Myself to solve, a pointless task

If I could have a day again
A repeat feat just sounds neat
But then today who would you greet
I guess I'll stick with fate complete
Enough riddles now to solve
Need no more so thank you
Put past into that experienced
Take on-board and to the new

Tally Ho and wobbly spoon
Meet this Evening, long past Noon
Play your own and not my tune
All ask is please don't croon!

Decision mission

The tension it was mounting
Decision must be made
Do they go for what want?
Do they their 'coolness' trade?

Those around just waiting
Not caring which do choose
End of day same old way
One wins and one does lose

They've narrowed down to two options
Discarding others as they go
Many not appealing
More the case for show

The one had been thinking
Before getting to this place
Half certain but not knowing
All options they might face

They've endured all the promotions
Each saying they are best
Yet only when a choice is made
Are they then put to test

Whichever way the wind blows
Mood when got out of bed
Traffic flow when to work go
Result in which are led

The crowd behind impatient
Want to do a choice themselves
Some looking for a happy time
Some conscious of their wealth

Finally, they chose the chocolate Éclair
The glazed Donut was left for another day

Deep dip as Life sip

The oscillation and gyration
Our salvation true
This atmosphere both far and near
Misty, clear – helping to get through
Red for ready in the morning
Day is looking bright
Red for bed to rest one's head
As it sets at night

Have a pen now and again
So, decided it to use
Scribble things and see what brings
When others them peruse
Hot or cold a story told
Choice or circumstance?
Is this just a beverage?
Or maybe mood perchance

Left, or right? Sound and sight
How deep we choose to go
Some display better between ears
Some we put on show
The in and out without a doubt
A major activity we cannot leave
For we would be a nothing
If we didn't breathe

Randomness the strangest kiss
When lay or when pick up
Proof if proof were needed
Many flavours can we sup
What is Time but one more action?
In the greater scheme of things
Silently going about its business
The multitude it brings

Deep I dip

For those who do not know me
Let me introduce myself
I am a normal person
Just labelled as ill health

I screwed up situation
Rose above the occupation
Nothing gets in stationary
Nothing like when lose the wary

You run with ink what you think
Then I run with you
You hide behind that thing beside
I'll ask you why you do

New Marble!!

Deep I dip into things that happened
Deep I did and correct that
Deep I did into the person
Deep explore where once I sat

Gone but not forgotten
That once I classed as rotten
Turns out it was just a step
The push I needed to more get

Wow!! Brain Fart!!
Back to original

Onwards! Upwards!
What more can this thing play?
Refuse to lose that I choose
Bring on another day

If you closed your eyes what surprise?
That when the past reflects?
The chaos of the growing
The now and circumspect

Define the definition

Some might say and some might play
Some stay silent too
Some may leave and some may grieve
Some don't know just what to do
Some their day – Hip! Hip! Hooray!
Some just want it to be over
Some they drink for pain to sink
Some feel has found a four-leaf Clover

"So, what's today?" I hear you say
A nothing and a something
Came from one to try to become
Just the other thing
A number on a record
That some may then applaud
To join another horde
With same and thus they do accord

Who be we? What is 'free'?
Define the definition
Trapped then sold before get old
Like some sick tradition
In Orchards grow because we know
Apples can make drink
With potential of changing mental
State when on the brink

So, some might say and some might do
Some the likes of me and you
Some survive and some do not
Some remembered, some forgot
Some celebrate another year
Some do find they have no cheer
Some do get a Birthday wish
Some don't receive that friendship dish

Demons in the D word

The times they are a changing
The present History
Soon will become present again
That's just how we be
The times are always the bad times
We change in hope of good
The good become the bad times
When past is understood

We hold periodic elections
To oust the bad and bring the good back in
Then come next elections
The cycle again it does begin
Yet in this game they're all the same
The show we know so well
Just different in the delivery
The lies they tell so well

Politics cannot be polite
Though similar in the word
To have a mutual agreement to make things better
Is simply so absurd
How far have we now fallen?
When this the best choice
Democracy over Dictatorship
Yet still one has final voice

Let's face it we need leaders
For mutual cannot be
Some have to degrees have tried it
Most now history
'Socialism' they named it
Another fantasy
Yet
Demons in the D word
P so confuses me

Desert or Dessert?

A certain King some sense did bring
In a time so wrong
Paid the cost as life lost
Though name remains still strong
Then something new as a country grew
Apartheid became its name
Both miseries still sometimes see
Such a crying shame

So, shout out loud above the crowd
Make your voice be heard
Instead of fight let's unite
Division so absurd
On them clean let be seen
Paint on walls in letters tall
No confrontation for one Nation
As it rise or fall

'One for all and all for one!'
A line from famous story
Yet if took it as a motto
Imagine share of glory
The success that we could get
When just Human not sub-set
The power we could hold
Reality, not a fantasy

'I have a Dream' now immortal
Not in just one land
The King spoke with a vision
To not be buried in selfish sand
Sand. How many grains make a Desert?
When Dessert more pleasing
Let's make option two
Instead of only teasing

Diet Diatribe

A common Cold is somewhat inconvenient
A common Cold is inconvenient
A common Cold inconvenient
A common Cold

Look at me and what do you see?
Look at me and what do see?
Look at me and what see?
Look at me and what?

She sells flowers in Market stall
She sells Flowers in Market
She sells Flowers in
She sells Flowers

Much giving will then receive
Much giving then receives
Much giving then
Much giving

All that's been

All that's been was just a dream
Of all that we could be
All that been just kept us keen
In some puzzling perverted way

The seed that fell from the tree
That rodent stores for food
The slow song to get along
Because are in that mood

The first breath a new one takes
The promised time that all breaks
The missing moments can't regain
The contents of thing called pain

Different be

The one stood before the crowd
Spoke so clearly with words loud
Had been and seen that hatred scene
Was not bitter though was not proud

One of many in situation
For was more than personal occupation
One of many who did then turned
To the better and better earned

Why oh why they said with sigh
Do we wish our own to die
When so simple if we try
To get along and all get by?

They took a breath and said

"What are we but energy?
Nothing spiritual, just a fact
What we do and put others through
Just the way we act
We are all nothing's that could be somethings
If only that we choose
We are more than were before
What have we to lose?"

Are yo the one who said this?
Are you the one to say this still?
Are you the one that has witnessed?
Are you the one that made that kill?

Life is Life no matter what
Life is a one chance got
Life is sacred and should be
Valued even different be

Disregard

Politics and protocol
Change as does tone of skin
Where do we finally draw the line?
Where do we begin?

Ingrained history is just that be
History and nothing more
We are better than our past
Our future should explore

The old been told so many times
We seem just on repeat
Are we equal to a sequel?
Can we achieve this feat?

Not my call for needs all
Are we brave enough?
To disregard that of retard
Along with all that stuff?

Dude dipped - don't dare

Man! oh man! What was the plan!
The results am sure not this!
Anatomy not new to me
So know backside can't real kiss!

It looked so good on paper
This feat was just some caper
Reality as now can see
More case of 'see you later'

The start was pure perfection
The Rockets gave injection
Just some misdirection
Believe was not intention

D. I. D.

The sun may shine, the rain may fall
The pleasure of the new dawn call
The afterlife or belief in Ghosts
The current place we love the most

We stride, we stumble, we stride again
The one great final stumble
Never knowing when
We look, we see, we look once more
Each time vision clearer
Until, at last, are sure

The Baby's cry, the loved one's sigh
The speak to one and their reply
The touch, the feel, the know it's real
The launch into which does appeal

The pardon to which felt wrong
Even just to us
The letting go for the simple must
The waste of time that is a crime
When actions had a need
The once more to doubt cure
The discipline we feed

The merely bent the trust we spent
In that in which believe
The initial shock which then we block
Determine to achieve

The make believes to which did grieve
Until the truth we see
Caught the thought that simply taught
Diverse Is Destiny

Education our Salvation

On days of cloud I wonder loud
The beauty that is shown
On the place within Space
We choose to call our own
With Degree a level see
Yet that is just financial gotten
The waste we face a disgrace
In education system rotten

What is the importance of education?
One thing in common with each Nation
The haves do get the 'I am' set
The others get 'pot luck' regret
'Who am I?!' The poor do cry
Deprived because of birth
Are they no care that cannot share
A College or University turf?

Sponsorship pastes over 'blip'
Yet should not be the case
When education is a money situation
When so much goes to waste
Ignore the letters behind the name
Concentrate on that who wears them
Maybe have more skills to them
They just wish that chance to share them

Education our salvation
If only realise
Ironic be that those who see
Must suffer compromise
The talent lost because of cost
The pay so others benefit
Double gain for those with disdain
So freely gain from it

Electric dreams until find the means

The when and why we choose to try
That impulse in attraction
The 'do or die' with a sigh
Yet still complete the action
If you have to try then ask why
The separation between work and pleasure
If have to force to complete the course
The value has to measure

On the waterfront staring out
In one place but want another
I don't want the present me
The one without my Wife and lover
The two are same in body and name
The one that does complete
I so wish had water wings
Could place upon my feet

When to walk down street becomes a treat
Not just another obstacle must conquer
The value of the had but lost
Sits deep within oneself
Call me morbid - I don't care
Call me foolish – have some to share
Call me whatever pleases you
I still know what I call wealth

When scree the means to view your dreams
Despite effects it gives
Just take on board as pleasant sword
As in the difference lives
That happiness and then sadness
As call comes to an end
The meaning more when know for sure
That they're more than just a friend

Electric dreams until find the means
Find them guaranteed

Equality is Equity

Take a cup of kindness, mix it with compassion
A cocktail all should drink
Take a slice of humility pie
Into better then will sink

And what we are it can go far
Obvious it seems
When we just accept each other
That's the stuff of dreams
And I can't hide as say with pride
Have seen the writing on the wall
Together we'll last forever
Separate each with fall

Mix a sense of blindness
To your perfect sight
Ignore the outer skin before you
See just what is right

Beyond that outer cover
Stands another same Life lover
Same challenges if not more
As same journey they explore

And what we are it can go far
Obvious it seems
When we just accept each other
That's the stuff of dreams
And I can't hide as say with pride
Have seen the writing on the wall
Together we'll last forever
Separate each with fall

Equality is Equity
More valuable than Gold
Such a free treasure
If only we are bold

Err and err

Sarcastic twist at that not missed
For new has come on stage
Now a new deadly virus
Right or wrong becomes a rage
Media having orgasms
Pandora with open box
Ecstasy in misery
Shattered seem the locks

Atomic dropped and world it stopped
If only for a second
Then the rest aimed for best
As new stick it beckoned
More and more they did implore
Bigger, better and multiple
Just how many times can we wipe out
Generally the rule

In August sun we have become
The species wearing mask
Not nation small but nearly all
That's some monstrous task
Highlighted or deflected
Issues that still be
Most now too I.T. blinders
To see reality

Mary ha a little lamb
It never felt alone
For though belongs to Mary
It was just a clone
Humpty Dumpty sat on wall
Watching the Stock Market fall
Had no worries so sod it all
Had 'insurance' from voice cool

If be what want to be
What sort of me would you then see?

Ether not a total healer

The day does start like yesterday
In this half empty bed
Look at unused pillows
Where you should be resting head
Breakfast more like pit stop
When taken just by one
Miss that twinkle in your eyes
That mischievous sense of fun

Distance is more than the space
Between two certain things
Distance is the cause of pain
That separation brings
Wish could speed up time to when you are mine
Back in these arms again
Memories they will be
The hours of loneliness driving me insane

Ether not a total healer
Until we can teleport
Just a brief time sublime
When shared moments caught
Soon that Ether will have to move
Make way for one returning
Making space as I race
Back to those of which I'm yearning

Wish could speed up time to when you are mine
Then I'm never letting go
Will be memory when couldn't see
Those who I love so

Euphoria Emporium

The hours caught in what was sought
The satisfaction of attraction
The ghosts of gone that was wrong
Just actions not satisfactions
As I stare up to grey leaden skies
Wondering if it is wise
To actually learn or just surmise
What it's like when no-one hears your cries

The free to be but not necessarily
That which you do aim
The sudden realisation that this sensation
For others just the same
The show of strength that was spent
On some ridiculous cause
The clarity of sincerity
The definition of pause

That certain sound now buried underground
The one which don't want to hear
Nothing gained in the pain
That is known as Fear
The one who wants to be Someone
Not fam for not the same
The employment of enjoyment
Life's Lions now do tame

That cannonbal that rips through all
The barriers we see
That so proud to shout out loud
'Hello! I am ME!'
When the use has of what we own
Learn to somehow fly
When the hope is finally shown

Everyone 'take your mark'

Face to face the living race
Competitors do embark
Ready, set, GO! To what don't know
Everyone "take your mark"

Like a sea that washes over free
The ebb and flow, back and forth go
Each time a little further up the shore

Back-to-Back repel attack
From mutual adversity
Yet in between see what can glean
When break from unity

Like the fork tongue of the Snake
Flick and sample
What can take

We heard the word that inferred
The single gets successful
Yet what are we if not family
So together should stand tall

A stepping stone we all own
We carry everywhere
It is known as Care

Should we surmise they are not wise
Those who promote a separation
For what then the Brick and Pen
That comes from different tone situation

One to two we easily do
Now let's explore more
Start with three and four

Existence before I slumber

The nakedness of which are blessed
Beneath a name of colour
The simple fact that may impact
We're not that different from each other
The separation by Generation
That opens but also closes
The diversity that can be
Whatever one supposes

Today I questioned that I mentioned
Today and yesterday
I answered same 'it is a Game!'
One that all do play
Place of birth – shirt or skirt
Decided before born
Skin tone we own should not alone
Nor 'Leader' supposedly sworn

To do their best at your bequest
To let you more than just survive
Not just Honey Bees all paying fees
To help promote the Hive
The worker ants when old age rants
Hope not just cast aside
By statistics that would go ballistic
If 'elected' did not hide

I am a number, just a number
On forms I have to fill
So non entity can deal with me
If 'up and running' still
Maybe, if am lucky
A couple of phone calls
From people on the steeple
Of an Empire before it falls

Diversity should be free
But life is not just number
A thought caught on that bought
Existence before I slumber

574

Expect your respect

Semaphore became law
Hands replacing old
Not the same as what can gain
When in person told

Distancing a new thing
To those who liked to share
Not the new that is true
They choose not to dare

Situation in a 'great nation'
Imploding when it can
Finding new to push through
The population don't largely give a damn

A ray of light shined so bright
Upon a Pond of which were fond
Gave it beauty yet unseen
But was that light the type which clean?

Perspective can be invented
Careful what we see
A moment caught without thought
Then asking 'is this me?'

Times have changed without a doubt
What the need to scream and shout?
Vandalism seems the mission
For those who lack morale fibre

I will not join peacefully
Into a protest calmly run
I will exploit for my fun
Sowing seeds of mayhem begun

You want calm, I'll give you storm
I am pent up since were born
Taking pleasure when don't conform
Yet I still expect your respect

Exploring is not boring

Some might say that I just play
Some don't know me well
Nothing new for what I do
I don't always say

Some way say can't understand the way
I write or even think
Some don't know how I did grow
Into that my Coffee drink

You steal from me if you don't see
Just different from that that you
No thing to dazzle the path I travel
Just doing that I do

Exploring is not boring
When with have opened eyes
Not all wrong to get along
Some might be surprise

I saw you

The morning Dew of which walked through
The shroud that then revealed
The ecstasy in what could be
In I but then did yield

In the night you're out of sight
Yet still I see your grace
In the day I hesitate to say
I want to share some space

Will you one day look my way?
Will you then surprise
Will you make nonsense for relent?
When inviting me to Parades?

Fulcrum of that foolish

I just want to run away
Run away to yesterday
I just want to run away
Where nothing serious but just play
I just want to be
The only thing that did see
Not this now insanity
The kid to which all seemed free

And in the morning as light comes calling
I could so easily be that mourning
Yet the brakes to the falling
Another day for the adoring
Made a trade and made the grade
Happy in the way I played
Some bits left and some bits staid
Without double n and e

I just want to be somewhere
Where Winter never comes
Enjoy the season with good reason
Then move back to other one
I'll accept a Spring for that may bring
Autumn barred but understand
The need to clean does Autumn mean
Just not with own hands

Refreshed, fed and made the Bed
What more can fool now say?
Cannot write because of sight
Nor an instrument play
So just be me my philosophy
Nothing else to do
Any suggestive to my perspective
I really have no clue

Mama! Where's my chewy Dinosaur?!

Fulfilling Destiny

The notes it made as History played
It's part in who we are
Laid in scrolls the long past souls
That pushed as to this far
Eons strong when did belong
Replacement something new
Better still with strong will
Just pushing what can do

Some time, next time, will be fun time
When we learn to feel
When understood life can be good
When we see the real
The open pages of the ages
Point in one direction
All it needs to some hope feed
Is simply our perception

So now we stand so tall and grand
The finished article think
Yet w be if could only see
We're teetering on the brink
Immortality or fatality
On edge we now do waver
Ironic though when come to know
We are, in truth, our saviour

So some time, next time, if there is still time
A better thing will be
When can rejoice we made right choice
Fulfilling Destiny
A stepping stone to that unknown
But better than the here
When perceived can then breath
Without remorse and fear

The future me a mystery
For only me in part
If only take the good things
At least it is a start

Fun in Phobia

Arachnids cause anxiety
Flying causes fear
Anthropophobia fear of people
Especially when near
Lachanophobia is a strange one
What can vegetables do you?
Of Hippopotomonstrosesquippedaliophobia
I really have no clue

Coulrophobia I can almost understand
Some of them are bad
Yet Catoptrophobia?
Seriously! Are you mad?
Aquaphobia I can understand
For too many tales of woe
Thanatophobia I can get
Yet to it we must go

Homophobia do not suffer from
They are still a Human being
Ommetaphobia I can understand
When changed the gift of seeing
Sometimes I will touch on Athazagoraphobia
If the subject means so much
Depending on the subject
Dependant on what it is
Haphephobia the fear of touch

Glossophobia must be difficult
When out to something buy
Atychiphobia can be overcome
When willing to just try
For every fear a phobia
Down to Podophobia – fear of Socks
Still not named fear of Ian Wilcox
Just at its starting blocks

Gambling on garbage

In my Head the thought it led
Under pressure the page did sink
So, I try thought don't know why
It came out in some ink
What have I got? Not a lot!
If I may be so bold
The story of lost glory
Here my friend is told

I am too busy to complain
The failed venture into fame
They are them and not the same
Even though Toyah shares last name
I am too busy I tell my wealth
As I sit here on forgotten shelf
I am never quite myself
Labelled dangerous to your health

If someone gets an idea
Then you are cleverer than me – that's clear
For instead of clean I simply smear
My Marbles seem to hold no fear
Is someone here taking note
Of the garbage that I wrote
This great burden that I tote
Would be a hardship if wasn't pleasure

The ink seems dry so I ask why
Why not try with soft sigh
To wrap this up and give you peace
With this promise I do release
You back to some true treasure
Of those whose skills I cannot measure
Oh, to have just what in their little finger
The skill of script that does linger

Gap filled

On thoughts astray that go away
On level once believe
On platform high that passes by
When to reach we don't achieve
On pipedream and what does mean
On pile of rueful smile
Goes the prose that no-one knows
To add to growing pile

The half done or just 'not that one'
The cutting of the crop
The ruthless me of what you see
The limit at which stop
The complex of the complex
We call to print a Book
The disaster when didn't master
Or even took a look

The name! The Fame! The same old game
Not one I wish to enter
Prefer indeed my thinking feed
As recipient not sender
Though reading tough it means so much
When glimpse what others do
Whatever and whoever
Always something new

Give t me your fantasy
Give to me your real
Give to me your want to be
Give to me your feel
Letters laid on parade
Really makes my day
Others of the different covers
Enjoying not work shall we say

Get rich quick

When twist the gist of that I list
Is it me going around the twist?
Interpretation a personal conception
Sometimes lost in man-made mist

I am me and will always be
Your offer for 'quick fix'
That get rich scheme that's always been
Somehow doesn't suit the mix

The chancers are no romancers
Of what I have become
Not that rich but pick up quick
When you your aim to some

For slow and steady I am ready
Not that promise that you offer
Remove me as possibly
A chance, just please don't bother

Amazing you who never knew
Suddenly want to make me rich
Scams like prams less help than Trams
When detected the glitch

Mister/ Misses or whatever
Clever think you are
Offering things you cannot bring
Shows you didn't get that far

What you have spent properly
Namely on your Family
Wasting time with this crime
On the likes of me

Give me back

A one of many they now shared
The price of paying because they cared
In the world of challenging
They took a chance, they dared
To be true to the who
The one that wore on sleeve
Shot down in flames when were just games
The other did believe

So empty street they now greet
Where once they held a hand
All seemed right until last night
Still trying to understand
The walk alone from what was known
The emptiness inside
Rose above the certain being
Rose above the pride

In the rain they felt the pain
The mend would come
Just don't know when
The chance of new begun
The now solitary stranger
Who needs something back
Decided to ask for it
For without did lack

'The reality this morning
A sleepless night now dawning
Real life it came calling
Sadness now is spawning
Nothing rough could be this tough
So different from the start
Guess it be 'not meant to be'
So please give me back my Heart

I know that it means nothing
Nothing more to you
I need to give to someone
Someone who will it valued
We were, I guess, too different
As we pushed for more
The chasm became obvious
The more we did explore

I do not hate – just can't relate
The things you deem to matter
Love should be a solidarity
Not this type to scatter
I am here with new fear
Outside and now apart
All I ask is a simple task
Give me back my Heart'

The letter posted through the Door
No reply expected nor did come
The stranger found a way to cope
The found a new one
A new vessel for the bleeding
A new vessel for the sharing
A new vessel for the loving
A new vessel for the caring

Give to me

When life played something, it made
When stranger came a calling
When with respect did not expect
Found myself just falling
Never been and never seen
The places I passed through
Each a section of rejection
So back to which I knew

When bad starts falling and crap starts calling
I have now got cute
The more I fall means nothing at all
I wear a parachute!
Not today! That which I say
To both above and that below
I am yet not complete
There's so much more to show!

The ecstasy and misery of what can be a challenge be
But one we can control
The complexity of the one and we
Lies within each soul
Mind - it sets a certain goal
Heart i knows that which can make one whole
No instruction Book to which in look
We are a recipe just one can cook

Do you know true what you can do?
Do you wish for more?
Dream success and all the rest
The acclaim and the encore
Give t me that which free
One who does believe
Give to me the success be
That you alone achieve

Go back to sleep!

The semi state of sense
Leads to pure nonsense
Suffer recompense
When awake for real
The blurry eyed did write
Struggling with sight
Eyelids want shut tight
Writing purely just by feel

On Monday I was a muddle
Tuesday baulked the tide
Wednesday I was getting there
Thursday could not hide
Friday was a 'my day'
Lethargy deep inside
Then Saturday and come what may
Sunday just recovering

Cadaver case I will be
In personal perpetuity
Yet my thoughts, they run free
For a writer is, was and forever the me
Prolific some may say
As with words do play
Some today, others yesterday
What tomorrow? Who can say?

From slumber do I wake
First the pen I take
Before the fast I break
It is ritual
One or two to get me started
Even before a Sparrow farted
From the Boss will get red carded
Oh, how do the 'mighty' fall

Prolific pen passes pure pleasure

Goddledegook when that took

In the crazy part so let's start
Join me in place where be
If a fart was art into which part
Would those gasses just float free?

If a Tiger walked on two legs
Instead of bounding on all four
Would it catch the Antelope?
Would we have so many more?

Why the need for Caffeine feed?
When know it raises the heart rate
Yet without and without doubt
Become an irritable state

Who decided meal times
Make them formal three
Surely eat when hungry
Makes more sense to me

How does Bird fly so high?
Just by trapping air
Is it really effort?
Do they even care?

I am writing late afternoon
What time are reading this
Everything is different
When with hours twist

Wifey dear! I need one of those special pills!

Going to seed

All fall down
Then landed on the Crown
Will rise and fall again
A pleasure or a pain
Can create and can destroy
No concept of Girl or Boy
Metamorphosis when has lain
The cycle of the Rain

The sonnet of the Seagulls
Was not popular it is true
When the cross Albatross
Said "I show you how to do!"
The cackling Crow thought did know
A better one from land
Wrote with beak for with feet
On both it had to stand

The Wind did wind up Windmills
Metaphorically it is true
For directly to the grindstone
Passed the energy to do what do
The sails went round and round
A blur above the ground
No filling here for should make clear
Not same as those same sound

The Plane was plain upon the grain
Of wood it shaped with care
Cutting through as those do
Same but in the air
Tell me how you feel today?
Do you like to read?
All that I am is a mixed-up man
That's in danger of going to seed

588

Golden

Golden brown is the Gown
When clothes you choose to shed
Never a sin the colour of skin
Despite the history led

Those dark eyes hold surprise
The person not the sight
The one someone when life begun
The sharing of our plight

Golden tones have sat on Thrones
Golden on some still
Just another colour of a Mother
Experiences still a thrill

Golden or much darker
Same rules to all apply
The one who doesn't recognise
Needs encouragement to try

The lighter got much brighter
When looked beyond a skin
The lighter got a 'sighter'
To what was stored within

All the difference between us
Doesn't count for much
When we all feel the same
With another Human touch

Sun can change the white to brown
Blemishes can portray pain
Nothing much in outer cover
As different as a name

Gone past four and so I pour

A mind did find a common kind
A place to rest at last
A heart did start to play its part
In the loving kind
A person so familiar
One not too unlikely
To be kin of different skin
To another just like me

I look back on memory
Take a glimpse of what used to be
Now a something not for me
All the hate and atrocity
We were doing for what paid
Surviving with no parade
Broken rules so firmly laid
On this street a friend once laid

Meadows make a Mountainside
Islands make a sea
Trees do make a Forest
Three make Family
Borders make a Nation
Capitals a central station
Offspring the next generation
We are but another 'ation

Summer sun can bring much fun
Can also burn without some care
Winter cold in stories told
Of thermal underwear
Normal to you I have no clue
For climate is like in which are living
Personal but above it all
Need Mother to keep on giving

I lost religion

If I lit a fire who would gather round?
Who would share without a care?
The value of common ground
The space that was just there?
If I could make the thunder sound
The Lightning for all to see
How many regard as computer game
How many realities?

If I made a thing to trade
Called it understanding
How many true would see it through
How many profits by under handing?
Is it getting better? The new from which were told
Is this truly advanced, from the problems of the old
Enter you with conscience true, enter Sister/ Brother
Stay a door that value more
The self and not the other

So, talk to me of sanity
Convince not all insane
Whatever makes you happy
Is it worth the pain?
No plastic trees just to appease
No protest just because I can
This is what I was born to be
Just a common man

I lost religion long ago
Discrepancies came to fore
Became a badge of individuals
Who's motives so much more
The joy of pen I found again
The affliction some do say
Yes, I may take to extreme
Yet to me just play

I need more Coffee

Sometimes when we intrude
Into our self-imposed solitude
A discovery do we make
A new direction we choose to take
Noon too soon a palindrome
Moon, however no
Toot a hoot but ton is not
Toss a stuttered sot

How many holes do we dig?
Before we find our treasurer
The one inside we choose to hide
That shows us our true measure
Poop not scoop, nor nip to bin
Ma'am has charm but Madam no
Confusion comes with abbreviations
Tit legit though only in avian situation

The measure be mentality
The strength to make a change
When life's pieces can't seem to fit
Them must rearrange
Rope no hope
But mum has some
Nun a one
Become becomes undone

Rise to your challenges
You noble warrior are
First fight starts with yourself
You are a rising star
Level joins the party
Uneven it got barred
Palindrome gets juices flowing
Rat and tar are tarred

I need

A Baby born without choice
To join the crowd that has no voice
A Baby with which to add
To the population mad

Never in the field of Human conflict
Was so much owed to those so needing
Yet the curdled cream dream
As their egos feeding

I need a 'pick me up' served in a cup
I need a crazy notion
I need release from that which tease
A bit of a literacy explosion
I need to find some peace of Mind
I need to find myself
Just the joy I can employ
Forget about the wealth
I need to be simply me
The known and that to still discover
The same name but not so lame
Expose but under cover

If you believe then are deceive
The easier are led
Fluffing up the Pillows
Of some selfish ones big Bed

So change can wait until too late
Attitude and nothing more
We are heading for final act
Guarantee with high cost sure

Forget the cup of Coffee
When others don't give a jot
If cure is seen in Caffeine
Need another pot

I used to feel immortal

Another mark on Calendar
Another segment there to know
Another chance to be myself
Another space to show

I used to feel immortal
Time changed that in own way
I used to be invincible
Now just silly something I can say
Used to think I knew it all
Laugh at the one I was back then
The perfect Super Hero
Now old fart with pen
And all just carries on regardless
Of what I used to be
All around does own thing
With or without that called me

What I was now strange dream
What I was and what have seen
What I was I can't compare
What I was I now not dare

I found solution in the evolution
I found solution in being free
I found solution from that confusion
I found solution in reality

I used to feel immortal
Time changed that in own way
I used to be invincible
Now just silly something I can say
Used to think I knew it all
Laugh at the one I was back then
The perfect Super Hero
Now old fart with pen
And all just carries on regardless
Of what I used to be
All around does own thing
With or without that called me

I want

There came a day to stop the play
A day to plant the feet
Sometimes happens, if you're lucky
Lucky in the one you meet
I want to be fantasy turned reality
I want to be surprise
I want to be what you need
I want with no disguise

I saw Stars and you saw Moon
One could reach much sooner true
We are in the orbit together
Way beyond influence of never
I want to be fantasy turned reality
I want to be surprise
I want to be what you need
I want with no disguise

Now am blessed as fulfilled quest
Found that I don't deserve
Now must be bold to keep what hold
Just a different test
I want to be fantasy turned reality
I want to be surprise
I want to be what you need
I want with no disguise

Sun doe shine as think am mine
Though never to command
A different way is that play
One which cannot understand
I want to be fantasy turned reality
I want to be surprise
I want to be what you need
I want with no disguise

I will return

If I were you just for one day
Would I work or would I play?
Could I then in truth say
That now I know you better
If I were you instead of me
What type of person would I be?
Would I be accepted as Family?
Or just another stranger

Hypothetical not theoretical
Yet an interesting idea had
The answers be such variety
Some positive with some sad
Sad because just for that day
Would not be me and be what may
May in what I could choose
Then that I would then lose

If for one day you could be me
Would you be reflection or fantasy
That question that needs thinking
As into this you are sinking
The sun does shine through windows near
I guess can call it day
So please excuse me for a short time
I will return, if I may

I, I don't know why

Said a Head that Grey not Red
Want to do that new?
Fill some Books for others to look
Then decide you have no clue
So did land a pen in hand
Led just by the thought
Results showing no part of knowing
The way they had been taught

Oh no! We go
In to a Marbles world
Strange they bring as from Walnut spring
Borderline unheard
It's behind my eyes they disguise
Literature for just laid down
If there was a kingdom for scattered and then some
Each would fight for Crown

I, I just don't know why
This drivel others read
I, I am surprised
As writers' subjects' feed
You, you don't have a clue
The encouragement you give
That the make those Marbles live
Each then makes new Floating land
Nothing known and nothing planned

The one has fun as with it runs
Not sure for just how long
Just goes with flow as verse grow
In strange place where they feel strong
Sometimes a lot each day jot
Sometimes barren is the pace
Nothing new for have been too
That certain writers space

A Supernova above fields of Clover

Past five-Five and still alive
Mother Nature and others tried but failed
Onto something that is something
To my future flew not sailed

When I met that host that meant the most
Decided there would stay
In scheme of things and what it brings
Got lucky where did lay

Laid my hat as someone said
Found that place to make my bed
Five and six will hold some tricks
Just more knowledge to be fed

So today I say Hooray!
As another milestone I do reach
Many less fortunate
Another lesson Life can teach

So, what today in your own way
Just another from which to recover?
Just a date that you might hate
Wishing two nine would just smother

Milk Cow know how
To give when not asked
Just stands there with no care
Doing what was tasked

Yet for me it's History
Something didn't know
As through laughs and tears I spent the years
As to now did grow

A supernova above fields of Clover
Changing that believe
More have four, perhaps more
Talking like their leaves

Idle ink I sometimes think

So was said in ancient times
There was a city that had no crime
A city that never knew that word
Never spoken, never heard

I want to live there, present day
Want to see what they will say
Of the modern we enjoy
Where people wear guns and oft employ

Front entrance could be left open
No fear of whom you meet
A stranger just a new friend
And as such you greet

No sturdy lock to outside block
No self-imprisonment
No feeling like a future victim
No anger needs to vent

Where Bodyguard is wisdom
Weapon understanding
Life is just according it
Then finding ways to handling

The police car siren shatters stillness
Crime or accident? I don't know
Such is frequency of the hearing
The reasons grow and grow

Sit an read and hope does feed
We've done so can do again
The Utopia of shared space
Without the bitter pains

Idle introspection

Seen the scene that seemed 'clean'
Seen the ones that not
Seen the way that part stay
Seen some then forgot
Life a Stage matured with age
Life a lesson learn
Life is cost and reward
Life is what we earn

The soul is whole and somewhat fragile
If the truth be told
Enduring is the earning
Reward as we grow old
Pride a ride from which can fall
When situation comes to call
If not have then can't lose
Balancing you can choose

Darkness supports light
As does wrong props up right
If we see beyond plain sight
Then equipped to win our fight
Melancholy in misery
Exuberant in ecstasy
Non – plussed in all the fuss
Perfect way to be

You made me something
That's okay
I choose to differ
Go own way
Nothing is a something
If but it we choose
We are already at the bottom
What have we to lose?

Nothing becomes something

If I said

Modern being lacking seeing
If not on some man-made screen
That lacks smell so we can't tell
The full beauty of the scene
Food called 'fast' replacing past
Another sense does go to waste
Coated with the chemicals
Smothering what we call Taste

Vocal cords will be absorbed
When exercise choose not to do
With each Generation communication
Slowly changing into something new
Went from slouch to standing tall
Reverting back to slouch
Vertical is mystical
Spending most time on a Couch

Feet have become just something
On which to show off shoe
As to function of our legs
We haven't got a clue
Experts on Benefits
Not so the old 'three R's'
The only time that we 'walk'
Is from House out to our Cars

If I said 'Let's stop the World'
Would you pause to stand by me?
To take a moment to look around
Make some space to see what see
Not in passing for going fast
Take in slow so can then know
Just what a gift we've got
Before at pace we lose the lot

If in the morning

If in the morning if new came calling
Would you up and leave?
If new day brought a new may
Would you in me still believing?
Relationships are more than receive
To be successful must
Along with support in which are caught
Must be based on trust

Have travelled the world, heard unheard
Seen that which none should see
You love me for what I am
Will you love at what can be?
For you are the reason why
Though contented to improve will try
Sad songs seem so popular, not the choice for me
In love and just happy, the place I'd rather be

Love is true when so are you
Yet comes then with a cost
When circumstance gives no chance
When loves life is lost
The tragedy of that we see
Is that the L word now polluted
Easy comes and easy gone
It now is diluted

So i the morning my dear love
Which path will you take?
Be the strong and carry on
Or a new one make?

If my blood ran

Everything evolving, situations simply solving
Random riddles repetitive revolving
Welcome to the you
Questions asked, most are marked
Deeds of daring do

Do you know you have to go?
Somewhere you haven't been
Fight the fight and see what's right
If only to make a little clean
If my blood ran free would it be
Red like was before?
When I was still innocent
Before I knew much more

Morning yawning, coffee calling
Shower power, too hot a howler
Welcome to a new day you
Night-time natter, sleep time scatter
Grabbing what when wish

Do you know you have to go?
Somewhere you haven't been
Fight the fight and see what's right
If only to make a little clean
If my blood ran free would it be
Red like was before?
When I was still innocent
Before I knew much more
I need to feed so I bleed
It comes out line by line
Sometimes more, sometimes less
Whatever just seems fine

If the World

The warriors without uniform
Still in challenge they perform
The everyday who makes a way
The incredible who brave a storm
Not that of which do know
That of stuff that they don't show
That of which is no Trifle
That which know as simple survival

If the World does truly spin
Why not spin for me?
Why not begin to spin
The way I want to be
If the world does spin where do we begin?
How far drop if it just stops?
Gravity the mystery
Would our Sun be final tops?

I can pen then pen again
How many can that say?
Not because they have no cause
Just no time in which to play
Down the road of poisoned Toad
The one with just accept
Nothing strange so nothing to change
No desire for better get

When last night will be tonight
Tomorrow same today
When nothing more than pourer than poor
Should others then not say?

If the World does truly spin
Why not spin for me?
Why not begin to spin
The way I want to be
If the world does spin where do we begin?
How far drop if it just stops?
Gravity the mystery
Would our Sun be final tops?

With reference to the Oregon, Washington and Californian fires of 2020

Fire Fighter

The brave Men and Women
fighting the fires of hell for
You
Their hours have no sleep, no
breaks, 24 hours slip by till
they crash on the ground
for a couple hours of
respite
The smoke chocking their
air they keep fighting as the
winds swirl the spreading
fire like butter across lands
leaving viewed burnt toast in
blackened view
Even their tears of frustration
doesn't touch the blazes as they
feel your pain in loss of property
and lives, sometimes their peers
fighting beside them fall
The heat sucks the moisture from
Their bodies, lips & tongues
cracking skin falling like the
burnt leaves
Depression seeks their endless
fight with Mother Nature's unrest
as they look through fire smoked
sky's and pray to God for rain
They put their own thoughts of families
in a pocket of their heart surrounded
with prayers
Their fight is for you as they put their
lives on the line ...
FOR YOU!
GOD BLESS THEM ALL

Janice Fisher

JB I am and be

Strong did sound the silence
Strong did sound the beat
Strong did sound the welcome
Of every friend I greet

Do we know or even care?
Do we do what do to dare?
Do we hoard then throw away?
Do we like to share?

Loneliness can be lonely
Loneliness can be choice
Loneliness in which some suffer
Loneliness in which some rejoice

I hear the call of the morning
I hear the call of Night
I hear the call from the victims
I hear the call of the past fight

Wake me up when reason calls
Wake me up when all makes sense
Wake me up when worth waking
Wake me up with my consent

After gone I'll be forgotten
After gone will be replaced
After gone be just another
After gone I'd lost some race

Just because you are reading
Just because I wrote the words
Just because it has one signature
Just because many heard

Joined a band of fellow beings

Come the one and come the all
Join together to break this wall
Built by others with ulterior means
Enforced by use of social machines

The individual is not individual
But a part of a Global tribe
Though are different in our look
We are all the same inside

Born one place of Human Race
Does not then promote/ demote
What we be is just who we be
The same thing with different coat

A man once chose to look some more
Ventured out to distant shore
Found someone who does adore
Gave a purpose, then gave more

Joined a band of fellow beings
Who found that by simply seeing
Beyond the thing that we call Nation
Just a word of our creation

Different tongue we have begun
Yet us same part to say
As we do feet/hands two
For each designated that way

Live and let live, receive an give
How to make us strong
Most of all just hear the call
Each of us belongs

Jolly times in July

'Come with me' said Destiny
'I'll show you what can do
You are strong and so belong
Above all you are you'

The been and gone just made one strong
That and nothing more
The hurt parade just simply made
A wish to seek on pleasure shore

Hardship was a learning curve
As am older learning to swerve
When do dip into that pool
Rise again no one's fool

Jolly times in July
Darker in December
Moving maybe in the May time
Never in November

A chick's call says it all
Things bigger than we are
Blinded by the Highway
Speeding to places far

A game changer could be that stranger
If we but choose to stop
The sole aim and with it pain
To just get to the top

Compromise is no surprise
To those that been and done
Learning while something earning
No value in just one

Just a fish

What a day yesterday
What will this new one hold?
Will it show what want to know
If I may be so bold
Will tomorrow today be sorrow?
Will I wish for a repeat?
When today went my way
Will it well me treat?

What a year for pain and fear
A World trapped in the unknowing
Such misery so plain to see
Yet cure itself not showing
Nature played or man-made?
Someday, perhaps, reveal
When the layers of the players
One by one we peel

Yet I am not going down
I will stand my ground
Take on chin and to it grin
Armed with that I've found
I can't control this planet whole
Nor another Human being
Not that wish for just a fish
Within the shoal I'm seeing

Came and saw and wanted more
Came and more I took
Came and got the whole lot
Came and wrote a Book
All that I'd been and all that seen
Something that shattered shell
Took a look and me it shook
When witness living Hell

Am a lover of the different colours
Each has upon its scales
Much the touch of age and such
Much from where it hails

Just a thought of in which are caught

Solitude for the multitude
The strange we have to face
Separate yet irrelevant
To some of our own race
So discerning when joy earning
Regardless of the risk
First to burden the already burdened
When this thing does kiss

Freedom yes but not at cost
When another life is lost
Is the pleasure equal measure
When patience means more can enjoy

Each are one since time begun
Yet each now share as race
Does one think they deserve exception?
When a global problem face

Politicians do what Politicians do
In that jumble nothing new
When in truth they have no clue
Just thinking better than me and you

Solitude for the multitude
A pain we have to take
If we ever this thing better
One day we will make
Slow inclusion the solution
Not mass gathering for some pleasure
We can now do that differently
Containment is the measure

Let every other human being enjoy a future by being patient now

Just for a smile we hope to gain

The clock is ticking and the mind is flicking
Back and forth on what to do
The craziness of laziness
How you wish was something new
The apoplexy of lethargy
The illness so abounds
Yet we don't dare to ourselves share
For fear of the stigma that surrounds

Road to Hell on radio
Yet down that road we go
May be cunning, maybe wise
What we feel we disguise
Yet are hurting and adding pain
Just for a smile we hope to gain
When alone the truth is shown
We are Mannequins in melt

The fixed smile for a while
The forced laughs that fool no-one
That jaunty step when others looking
Kidding self you're having fun
That lack of concentration
Self-shielded from the situation
Most of which are own creation
Passing off as irritation

Oh, to turn back time to repeat the crime
The audacity to dare
This time failure but next time
Who does really care?
Then comes success so mind at rest
The comfort of the sharing
The knowing without showing
That someone's always there

Just litter

I saw the ship and boarded it
Destination somewhere new
I sailed with intention
To do what I could do
I saw a ship called Me
Sitting in the Dock
Made me change what I was
Made me just take stock

A 'normal' day came to say
"Get out - you don't belong
You are much better than this
You have depths so strong"
The voice it spoke to me
The voice so near and clear
The voice it was a stepping stone
Stamping on the fear

Everything is a something
If we use to choose
Not all will be the right one
But what have we to lose?
Play the game of 'be the same'
Then guilty of repression
Brave does call the individual
That leads to succession

In this life you might fail
Once or twice in aim
That is just the way it works
No-one is the same
Only you a better can do
The rest it is just glitter
When you find peace of mind
The rest becomes just litter

Just two friends

The Father took Son to one side
Was time for younger to fly the nest
Learnt so much in loving family
Now the moment to put to test

In every household this will happen
Spreading wings nothing new
Each generation needs some freedom
Needs the space to own thing do

Talk was light as shared some past times
Memories of done together
Fishing and some Boat trips
Of baking sun and wet, wet weather

Shared a Beer, last for a while
Clicked bottle necks with that smile
Equals if just for this moment
No Dad and Son, just two friends

Then said proud Father

"Be careful how you spend your time
Make each second work for you
Once it's gone it's truly gone
Make the most of all you do
Accept failure as a friend
For is telling you to improve
How you did it or not at present
Up to you the next move

Laugh out loud it's like my Brother
In the time I have had
Blame it for what stands before you
All my good parts and my bad
One day it will be your turn
Standing here with your Son
Is a reward for successful parenting
So, get out there and have some fun!!
They both laughed

Kings and Queens

Clever be that we see
Clever be what don't
Wisdom is what we do
Wisdom is what we won't
Integrity comes for free
Aloofness has a cost
In somethings we gain when we abstain
In others respect lost

Rhyme is fine for short time
Variations a sensation
In what read for Brain to feed
Especially from other Nation
Age a page and not a cage
For is but just a number
Young can be better with the letter
If older choose to slumber

In certain dreams it just seems
A replay of a cost
The trust did break when risk did take
That certain something lost
One direction should be intention
Failures just the drive
Just a part, a kick start
To benefit when survive

We're all getting somewhere
When we steer the wheel
What used to be but now 'not me'
For present is the real
We used to be Kings and Queens within our means
Those limits did expand
When we saw we could have more
When we extend a hand

Kleptomaniac

So, I am a Kleptomaniac
I steal words to put on paper
Amongst the different versions
Almost harmless my kleptomania

I see them and I want them
I have no idea why
Dip into a pot of them
Then to lay out have to try

It would be easier if I was just given
Donations kindly would receive
The problems in obtaining a few of them
You really would not believe

In some way I'm a Krypton Kleptomaniac
Collect it from the air
Then I might in some forms of light
Enclosed, with you share

If, would

If I had the taste to want to waste
Would you waste with me?
Some of that crime we call Time
To just see what we could see

If had the urge to sometimes purge
That which I thought wrong
Would you be a purge partner?
So all could get along

If I laughed on rocky path
Would you join in the occasion?
For have to be in for chance to win
So treat as celebration

Knee needs a recount

Okay Boss I lost count
I think it was Thirty-Three
Then got distraction in the action
Of rubbing this annoying knee

What do you mean it doesn't matter?
We have to count again because
One will not accept is beaten
So is using for a pause

Independent? Yeah, that's right
When radicals they incite
If we do not what they please
Are outside to bar release

Bloody heck! A Lawsuit!
With no evidence we did wrong
That means that have more work
On what planet do they belong

I guess we're making Sitcom
Better than that made
The world is laughing at the debacle
Such is our grand Parade

Are we a Republic or Democracy?
Guess it hinges on this knee
Can it bare or even care
When resides in the Land of the Free

Knocking on the door

One did feel it was not real
In any shape or form
One felt lost at the cost
Since the day were born

One did feel so unreal
School talk that they heard
Different be from that that be
Cannot find right word

Could it be worse than this curse?
The person did endure?
Is it too much to feel that touch?
Then to want it more

Silent tears became a stream
Stream a River made
River fed an Ocean
Ocean became a Desert

The Boy or Girl - they grew up
Became the something new
Changed the way they act or say
Made an 'it' a you

Knocking on the door for want more
Knocking with protective glove
Rapping on the entry
Entry to the House of Love

Knocking but not knowing
Answer lies on other side
Can they find courage to receive it?
Will their own then choose to hire?

Lady Lust

The once juvenile reflects with smile
The things we do when have no clue
The fascination of situation
The pains we put ourselves through

I made castles out of sand
When I was a boy
I made a castle in my head
When older, knowledge did employ

It was crazy for she was a lady
Though by first looks so hard to tell
She called 'amuse' when you confuse
With the power of her spell

Was not the first nor the last
For she had miles left in her tank
I broke free with some sanity
With wisdom now I thank

Lady Lust I once did trust
'Quick fix' on display
Charge no shown until known
Just how much will pay

The foolishness of self-importunateness
The folly of the immature
The 'live for today's when with stranger lay
No guarantee its pure

The Irony a laugh to me
As witnesses' others doing same
Each generation same situation
The self-repeating that changes name

Light lecture by a lamplight

The weather clear, for a change
The mood outside at rest
Communication situation with a far off but close nation
Words do flow upon behest
Vanilla is a smooth sensation
Chocolate somewhat fuller sort
Coffee be the taste for me
Each in own are caught

Another day so come what may
Welcome you I do
For you are just experience
A strange type of clue
Who we be? A mystery
Who become is fun
When we see reality
When realise we are one

It's coffee in the morning
In which where I want to live
Coffee in the evening
In that it chose to give
Ganyan talaga ang buhay
Some do say
Como a vida

Who am I to even try?
To force upon the world
Another opinion from a minion
Just the idea is so absurd
Ideological so freely floating
Entrapped and there doesn't stay
Too many self-opinionated
Has always been that way

Vida amorosa, frui vita, Dèan eòlas air beatha
Most of all just feel free

Lipstick new

The younger man yet younger woman
Younger man songs did write
The younger man was besotted
The younger man shared the plight

The kisses taste like special Wine
The kisses taste of fire
The kisses taste of what I need
The kisses taste of desire

The younger Lady stood for while
The younger woman then did smile
The younger lady did reply
'It's just a new lipstick'

Delivery

When Delivery becomes a misery
A four-hour slot is told
Then the wait that can irritate
In case left out in cold

Can't go to shops for the package drops
A signature requires
Then you get the message
That your mood it fires

Been and delivered now sitting there
As to signing didn't care
Just placed outside your front door
Before they finish need to drop off more

Ordered without seeing
For now, a techno being
Saw it on the Internet
No guarantee is what will get

620

Live

My spoon buffoon and played a tune
When trying to be fork
The lettuce quite perceptive
When offered up a stalk

Got a shine I think is fine
On my shoes that black
Aching arm is so harm
When in slippers I sit back

'Live it up' the song does say
Why would we live it down?
Like the tune but will soon
Live just for the hell of it!

Hello you

Hello you what have been through?
You look different from last saw
Did you get less of it?
Did you get some more?

Can you stand to shake this Hand?
Extended in good will
Can you remember one called friend?
Can you remember still?

Echoes off that special
Now just day to day
Gone the part that touches heart
The sadness wants to stay

No rising in the morning
From a slept in bed
Just removing cardboard
With old jumper for your head

Hello you once again
Yes, I know that pain
Just believe you can achieve
I have also seen the gain

Live in

Live in space that has no waste
Live in clean instead
Live in space that has grace
Live inside my Head
Live in joy that can employ
Live in free to be
Live in the UK
Yet I Live in me

Strange the change but I can master
Strange the change but no disaster
Strange the way I see things now
Strange the reason then the how
Late Summer offered promise
Early Autumn took away
Yet it gave me something else
Something new to say

Rap, rap, rap! Like dripping tap
The constant I do see
Clap, clap, clap! I tip my Hat
To those who are same as me
Hey, hey, hey! What do you say?
The underground is seeing light
Whoo hoo hoo! They have and do
The way to make the future bright

Someone I know that learnt to grow
Gave me reason to adapt
They made me think as I did sink
That I'm worth more than that
A different abled made me stable
In ways I can't explain
Now history the way once be
Now much more I gain

Lockdown mk2

The buzz of chainsaw and Hedge trimmer
From mid-morning to nearly Dinner
Council staff or Contractor
In the end it doesn't matter
The Park boundary getting Haircut
Straight sides front and top
At least the front to height of Railings
There the cutter has to stop

Mid November and in Lockdown
Not many out to appreciate
Guess the Council still must spend it
Some of Budget from the State
Traffic Wardens still a plenty
Up and down the near empty spaces
Autopilot are legs and feet
Mobile phones now glued to faces

Lottery the shops open
Can't work out in High Street
Friends cannot have in your Dwelling
But can meet up if outside eat
'To Mask or not to Mask?'
The infection rates going through the roof
Went down first time complying
Is that not the proof?

Lockdown 2020 mk1
That was something new
Then the trust bit the dust
Now is Lockdown mk2
Perhaps the reason – one each Season
Won't that just be fun!
Starting in the Two Oh
Ending in Two One

Logic in the illogical

Awkward awkwardness the instance
The fear that you might miss
Plant on that inappropriate
That first sweet loving kiss

The fear of the unknowing
The fear that fear is showing
So that fear keeps growing
Once done the question growing

First love is a mystery
Just how should you act, how should you be?
Will this end in tragedy?
One step further in being me

So long ago I don't know
I just can't remember
Was it on a sunny day?
Or a cold December?

Love and lust such different things
Each a certain sadness brings
One gets over and move on
One gets over and still belong

Making magic in the man kind
A kingdom we each own
Making mark in that Park
Memories now shown

Are we all pre-printed?
Just t do our thing?
Are we all pre-destined?
To whatever what might bring?

Long lost

One saw a face within a crowd
Something triggered that seemed mad
Older, yes, with some changes
Yet looked like a friend once had
Took a gamble so to them did amble
Warm yet not quite confident
Had to know so had to go
Just few moments would be spent

"Excuse me for intruding
This might seem strange but I think I know you
Did you live in Warwick Avenue?
Did you also to Crompton go?"
The questioned stopped slightly bewildered
Took deeper look at Questioner
Looking somehow reminiscent
Of the bits that in young were

"Yes, I did and yes I did
Also strange, you I think I know
We both have changed in appearance
Yet somethings last as we grow
I think you also answer yes
To the questions you did ask
My oh my to find did try
Yet Adulthood just comes too fast"

When lost friends meet and cordially greet
When of old times reminisce
Lost in laughs the happy past
Oh, so how they miss
How many ships sail the Highs Seas?
How many meets with care?
How many berth in same Ports?
How many new bonds made there?

Long time

Been a long time since these legs of mine
Could walk for seven days straight
Been a long time since these eyes of mine
Could tell if things are seven or are eight

Desire, old friend, no need to lend
Yourself in certain things
I have found my perfect ground
Am happy with what brings

In this place and in this space
I wait but will not stay
Nothing wrong but don't belong
Belong so far away

Time to change the mood

A Bacon roll fills a hole
So does Beans on Toast
I'll eat a lot of stuff I've got
Yet still love a Sunday Roast

In Bays we play but not that way
No water laps the shore
Unless regrets from us it lets
When wishing something more

Something said sits in this Head
Took root so it will stay
The magic of the melody
When said you feel same way

Our future's born from that which torn
From the almost told
The thing that be part history
The present and the old

Long way in the past

Today is just another day
A reflection for company
Today is just a prison sentence
When 'invisible' you be
Been through and raised
Gone now their own way
Dreading someone saying
Today's another day

Heating off for can't afford
Cold now a companion
Down to eating once a day
While others bet on some prize stallion
They know I live for rent do give
Just to keep me dry
Nothing more though for sure
Someone to visit or just try

When what we have doesn't matter
When what see is not real
Do the things in tatters
Help you create a feel?
Looking is not knowing
Most of it for showing
As inside is growing
The loneliness of age

When did age become punishment?
That we have to bear
When did it mean something obscene?
For the elderly to care
So, sit and face this depressing task
Again, just like the last
Others just to talk to
Long way in the past

Dreams

Do I ever slip into your dreams?
Soft as a feather
Strong as a Hurricane out of season?
You are in mine every night
I catch you from the universe
Circumstances cannot sever
What was divinely planned
beyond the howls of emptiness

We fill our souls
inspire of distant barriers
We speak in a language we designed
Holding secrets of our hearts
Tattooed across the stars
Hung from the silver Moon in Autumn
Love breathes

I feel it at the twilight
stirring me to wake
I am mesmerised
Your caresses
hold me hostage
Never let me go

I hear you whisper
"When you open your eyes
I will be standing there one day"
I pull the cover over my me
I feel you
Until then
may morning never come

Margaret 'Renie' Burgess

Whose Reality

Far from the crowds
And iridescent lights
False fronts and petty games
Minds filled with pompous praise
Pretending who they think they are
Another world exists
Separated by the brutal illusions and deceptions
The brush is thick
It is here amongst faded wildflowers in late Spring
Beneath the wild Apples
I find my heart
The wind howling in the night
Without fear
I walk into the wilderness
Beneath the full moon
Ancient lovers kiss
Eyes glowing in the dark
Holding truth
Between their fingertips
Wearing Stars like a Crown

In the palm of your hand

In the palm of your hand
I surrender
No stopping
Love will have its way
Into the seduction of souls
The pulsating fire that burns inside of us
Comes together in a single flame
We were designed for passion
Why hide?
Let it flow through our veins
singing
The song of lovers
From head to toe kisses flow
Touches warm and tender
We move in rhythms
Choreographed by God

Margaret 'Renie' Burgess

Haunted

As I sit in shelter
belly full
Covered from head to toe
Loved
Feeling safe
my soul stirred a haunting memory
forever etched in my heart
Pulling me into the light of darkness
a parking lot filled with puddles
Rain beating down
the child in filled diaper

Bare chested
tangled hair
snot dripping from his nose
Lapping up the rain with his little tongue
Where would he sleep tonight?
Who would hold him in their arms?
What would he eat?
Who would say "I love you"?
His little ribs sticking out line a carcass skin

What have we become?
Our children abandoned
left alone to fend for themselves
Where are the bedtime stories?
and goodnight
kisses
The ravages of war
The survival of the brave
knows no age
The broken soul
rises in the rubble

Is this the consciousness of humanity?
A society preaching God
and living like a demon

Margaret "Renie" Burgess

Ode to Beets

Your round sensual
purple passion flesh
tantalising my Tongue
The sweetness a delicacy
Nibbling at your perfection
Orgasmic delight
You grow more beautiful with time
Pushing me to delirium
Wanting more

Bamboo Rendezvous

Bamboo
branches rising
Sipping Tea
moonlight shimmering
A gentle breeze

The sound of life
growing in the night
Positioning each touch
reaching for the next

The sound of Bamboo
lingers
A hush filters through
whispers
Sighing
in the dark
Breathing life
You are my enticement
Journey from the altered state
I melt like wax in beneath
Your sips
Alive
Wrapped in golden
Tenderness

Margaret 'Renie' Burgess

Painted Cat

Mr. Sandman has arrived and presented the lovely Ms.
P. a Halloween gift, a Saloon Girl costume.

She will be a wild woman of the west or the "painted cat."

The gown is red and black with ruffles and made from the finest
silk and lace with real rubies and black diamonds as sequins.

The lovely Ms. P's dress is a little revealing, but very classy.

Black net fish hose, stiletto black magical high-heeled shoes, encased
with red rubies, ruby earrings, and a black diamond ruby necklace.

Cowboys from all over the world are meeting the
lovely Ms P and the "painted cats."

The midnight hour celebration to at the Full Moon
Western Dance Hall, no uninvited guests allowed.

Ooh-la-la and sweetest dreams all y'all.

Fantastical Fantastic Fabulous Festive Friday

Decorum and demureness are the code of conduct for the
reason it is more than just a beautiful outer appearance.

Rules addressing appropriate behaviour, action, and
language should be your signature calling card.

Count your blessings and go ask Alice because she is ten feet tall.

Cha, cha, cha, time to perform the Celebratory
Dance of Life. Ooh-la-la, kisses for all

Melissa Begley

Judgement:

Prayers enlist the assistance of a Higher Power or provides
the opportunity to send up praises and gratitude.

Fresh perspectives to improve life is a new paradise. The
thrilling performance of homily and hymns, perhaps, create
the unlimited energy of love for our fellow humankind.

The human drama, incapable of stillness, returns to tittle-tattle,
gossip, unkindly words without restraint. When questioned
for their accuracy, suddenly, are you the evildoer?

Silence is not overwhelming when living in a world of putting
your style upon the pile of narcissistic self-expression.

Saintliness is not an ecstasy of control or our determination
on who or what to acknowledge. Many have utilized
religious beliefs to control women or launch wars.

Are you in House of Worship every week, but treat your
family with disdain and even with physical pain?

Keep in mind, perchance, we are ultimately judged by a Higher
Power, but live in our individual earthly comfort zones.

Judging our fellow man as a passionate and self-righteous enthusiast
of knowing right from wrong just, might be our downfall.

Let's acknowledge the hearts of gold and overlook the gold donors.

Tight-lipped hypocrisy is equal to loose-lipped hypocrites.

Bear in mind, we all Sin and your faithfulness to religious activities does
not exonerate your actions, only our Almighty come judgement day.

Improvements are required for all every day, not just the
ones perceived as bad, wrong, evil, or unpleasant.

Melissa Begley

Word

As you sojourn outside your home remember
succouring others is of utmost importance.

The Word is to respect not a display to selected people.

The Word is not to judge.

The Word is to agree to listen to others without shutting them out.

The Word is to eliminate tittle-tattle and not to rattle.

The Word is to seek the ultimate truth.

The Word is forgiveness.

The Word is acceptance.

The Word is to understand enlightenment.

The Word is pure optimism when encountering the unpredictability of life.

The Word is comfort.

The Word is a meticulous process of understanding the power of restraint.

The Word is encouragement.

The Word is not your grandstanding or boasting.

The Word is creation.

The Word is spiritual life.

The Word Is Love.

The Word is God.

Melissa Begley

Seasonal Changes

The Cosmic Moon and seasonal changes present opportunities of the reasons why proper decision-making properties are self-maintenance.

The veils to other dimensions are thinning and spiritual entities are dancing or haunting.

Negative and confusing emotions, visions, and dreams with a flight or fear intuition.

Amplify shield protection, properly, to avoid negative attacks or attachments.

Control your reactions and grasp the energy that is not an illusion, but projections of the paranormal world.

Delectable, delightful, demure, gorgeous, and humble the lovely Ms. P dances underneath the moonlight recognizing others for the reason of their electromagnetic energy.

Magnificent Monday

Does a heart void of the radiant energy of love disassociate from one's soul?

The metamorphosis power of an emerging manifestation of manipulation spawns itself like a demon during a person's heartbreak.

Glorious words of kindness to decorate the victim's mind until convinced of a time, place, or action that doesn't or never existed.

Do not participate in erroneous actions and bear in mind it is a pleasurable indulgence of the heartless.

Optimism

Daily commitment to ourselves is the enjoyment of
tranquillity enabling us to share happiness with others.

Reflection, deception, depletion, projection, and
time for the attraction of positive balance.

Nightly Dreams filled with creative freedom enables
us to pioneer the spirit of optimism.

Sweetest Dreams all y'all.

Melissa Begley

Transmute

At the midnight hour, we enter into a realm of the
Universe that creates glorious relaxation.

Fallacious or salacious and aimlessly wandering around the
moon until it is revealed to Ms. P., what is the truth?

The prophesy of your pathway is not conjured up in a spell,
but spearheaded by your spoken words and actions.

Tranquil and beautiful discourse or embellishments creating
organized chaos of evil-like behaviours is low vibrations.

Create your destiny by the transmutation from negative vibrations
to the higher vibrations of love and positive energy.

The lovely Ms. P and Mr. Sandman

The lovely Ms. P and Mr. Sandman will be celebrating International
Peace Day on the moon, that is sooo far out man.

Bear in mind that when people express delicate floral words of love with the
intentions of procuring lust or greed; is it possible to have World Peace?

Crystalline flows of Ancient messengers, perchance whispers musings on fate.

Aimlessly wandering without an aesthetic consciousness
is conceptual cleverness of mindlessness.

Heartlessness, perchance embedded in your DNA and your
moonless nights are a nightmare that will never be resolved.

Geometric stars with twinkling effects are dancing
in the sky, can this be utopianism?

Sweet Peaceful Dreams all y'all

Melissa Begley

The lovely Ms. P. is on the highway to hell lol

Attired in purple stilettos, a pink mini-dress, adorned in black diamond
bracelets and wondering is this an opium dream psychosis.

Internationally acclaimed pretty, pretty boys, and the flowers
and feathers in her goldy hair seduce the wind.

An uncanny event on the cosmic moon, guitars, drums, saxophones, and
the dynamic Glimmer twins, rhythmic unruly energy, unspoiled utopic
smoke, we are envisioning dancing dragons, and it is insanely bewildering.

Dazzling and we all are socially charged. We know
it is only rock and roll, but we like it.

Perchance, a romantic rendezvous is just a kiss away.

Serene Sunday will be a triumphant day

Trifling, trivial, and petty matters are insignificant.

Transform into a thrilling, rousing, and inspiring living being
and your spirit will overflow with joyousness and jubilation.

Negativity is taboo and pleasant dialogue enhancing
the positive will revolutionize the human race.

Are you motivating and enthusiastic?

It is time to perform the Celebratory Dance of Life. Show
up everybody and your upbeat moves will generate positive
energy. One, two, cha, cha, cha, three, four ooh-la-la.

Cloudless Night

The lovely Ms. P. embraces the magical mystical moon with much delight.

The dream of mystery is the cloudless night filled
with bright colors of kaleidoscopic stars.

In darkness the moon shines enticing sensual energy.

The morning delight after a dazzling moonlight is the Songbird's
serenade of the ancient masters' amorous sounds of eternal love.

Aami bhaalobaashi tomake khub. Sundor Sapno.
Melissa Begley

Moon Enchantress

The lovely Ms. P. was heartbroken and despondent for the reason of
a competition in his spirit to court and triumph over her spirit.

Oblivious and unsophisticated of the callousness of a
narcissist voraciously pursuing greedy pleasure she became
clay to shape in his hands of avaricious purposes.

Imprudently, she was convinced that he was an eternal
lover, spiritually and physically, entwined as one with the
bestowment of love delivered by the Universe.

On the night of the New Moon, she was underneath
the mighty Ash Tree weeping.

Ash trees are protective and defend the earthly
inhabitants they love from harm.

The Tree Faeries suspended dancing around the base of the
mighty Ash tree and were unhappy and began to sob. They
were unsuccessful in consoling their beloved Ms. P.

The Gnomes knew the lovely Ms. P. was not a prissy or a prudish
female and were angered that she had been betrayed.

The might Ash summoned the Moon to arrange for assistance.

The Moon Enchantress arrived and shined a radiant glow all around
Ms. P. The penetration of love was evoked into her heart.

The Tree Fairies and Gnomes were laughing, prancing,
and dancing while jugs of Kentucky Bourbon were passed
around and plenty of Moon Weed was lit up..

As the Moon Enchantress was disappearing in a puff
of passionate pink smoke, she whispered for all to hear,
"Lovely Ms. P., It was not your loss, but his."

Melissa Begley

Mobile menus

What you gonna do when see through
The sky to the other side
When have clue past the blue
At that it tries to hide
What will you be with reality?
That we are but so small
No matter how we scatter
The whole is bigger than us all

Saddle bags and more than Nags
Old Cowboys we did applaud
Gone the dream like sour cream
When modern drive a Ford
The old days now on-screen plays
Netflix if we choose
Between Box sets and Take out gets
Use of legs we lose

A Star it bucks as think
It is gonna Cost a lot not free
The coffee that we drink
Takeaway delivery
If on screen that word, we see
Moped stuttering as driver hurrying
Ordered without speaking
Cartons tight against the blight
Received with sauce leaking

This place of mine is so divine
A doorbell announces fare
A short walk and some small talk
A meal I don't choose to share
Utensils disposables, as with the dishes from which eat
In the bin goes my sin
When couch lizard hard to beat

Mobile menus are a permanent

Modern free

'Modern free' what does it mean
When by empty Bank account is clean
Cleaned by that you have to pay
For the pleasure living one more day
People chasing Rainbows
Only to be told
When they find an end
There's no pot of Gold

What a life we do live
When received less than give
What a life, when for sure
Others always want much more
More from us the common folk
Now taxation beyond joke
Paying more yet no increase
To the things the payer sees

A whole lot of BS do they spurt
While own pockets don't feel hurt
High times cloud the facts of crime
Spin Doctors earn more than medical
One does fudge the facts to suit
On repairs the facts that call
That Summer that some enjoyed
Without the need to be employed
When with fate sometimes toyed
The highlight before fall

Modern marvel

I am a marvel of modern making
Know so much that is not real
What went on, or maybe not
How some 'experts' are paid to feel
I am a marvel of modern making
Can use a finger instead of tongue
Tapping devices geared for gaming
Far removed from when begun

Mrs X from Istanbul
Chats to Mr Y from Washington
Never will they meet in person
Yet proclaim each 'the one'
The changing names and weird frames
Regulated by A.I.
Illogical in the 'logical'
As to understand us it does try

I, myself, have own Computer
Maybe shower but keeps sane
I allow it total freedom
My Computer is my Brain
Yes, I am a marvel with a marvel
When I think of what can do
I am a marvel in the modern
Strange thing is, so are you

Moment came

The one they came with different name
Different skin tone too
Then they found in new ground
Feelings that felt true
On bended knee to what see
If partnership had found
Ecstasy of course just because
The mountain now at mound

A sign of the times since you've been mine
In heart and nothing more
The time spent without relent
The hours I adore
The moment came when ended game
Found the perfect one
When explored so much more
That shared but different Sun

The making of the maker
Of the life that's new
Watching as they grow up
Doing what they do
One becomes part of three
Each a separate entity
Nothing more and nothing less
Yet each one feels they are blessed

Now the waiting for some reunion
Waiting for what's right
When together once again
Together in real sight
He misses them and they miss him
Miss each other too
When we do the strange but needed
Do that each must do

Your silence hovers over me

Your silence hovers over me
the crow rests upon the crown
the hollowness of your bitterness
clings like shadows from the caves of laugh less wonders
cherry picking each imperfection
forgetting that life dwells
beyond the barren desert
each grain of sand vibrating the memory
of your bare feet and the solemnness of your scorched skin
unaware
love
waited just above the dunes............

Fairy Tales do come true

Oh
Cinderella has arrived
her gown of cotton hangs
her slippers covered in dust
soot
fills the pleats
the tired apron blushes
magic stirs within
look
her eyes are filled with diamonds
her heart is on her sleeve
she will dance into the dream
a Queen
her crown of honour
rests upon each lock
the innocence
smiles
lighting up the room
Believe in love
it changes everything
and throws away the broom........

Margaret "Renie" Burgess

647

To end all wars

So, fast you flew
the tangled hair twisted
the speed of sound entwined
the cabin
in the dark wet woods
held the answers to your rage
battles of a lifetime
thrust the wild revenge
you were lost
inside the battle
captive in your skin
once tender
young and agile
your bones now barely bend
yet in haunting memories
you ran from the enemy
casting words not fit for babes
ones that fuelled the violent rage
there are no winners all are scared
left behind their innocence
some never returning home
the flag that flies in glory
hasn't fallen in the swamp
you are just a madman
waging wars inside
your soul
nothing will destroy
the land that makes us whole
prayers pass the mountains
soaring high above
God gave the
ultimate weapon
a lasting peace
through love........

Margaret "Renie" Burgess

War zone

In this massive game of control
power grips the broken pieces
the gentle unassuming innocent
we are at war
sending babies to pull the trigger
holding lives in limbo
driving stakes into hearts that only loved the best they could
it is difficult to not notice
nor should we turn our heads
away
from each other
we after all are human
in the debri the scraps thrown at us
lies
empty words that have no place
in the soul's vocabulary
hang like body parts after a crash
rub your eyes
fall to your knees
BUT NEVER SURRENDER
do whatever it takes
to keep going
to outlast the Generals orders
in the silence of your pain
there is a voice
there is hope
there is strength
there is a love so powerful
so deep
so all encompassing
do not look down head bent in fear
look up
look up
look up into the heavens
call out to the Creator
hold your head high

no matter what you have been told
no matter what movie they play day after day
you
you are worth more
you are enough
claim your birth right
you came from the stars
remember?

Margaret "Renie" Burgess

Come lay your head

Come lay your head
upon my chest
let me hold you
here to rest
A warrior marching
across battlefields
screaming victory
breathing freedom
with each step
dodging land mines
for a dream
I will keep watch as you sleep
listening to your brave heart beat
here in the somber night
between my arms
there is no blood shed
only love and an enduring peace
against the ravages of war.........

Searching

I come to you each night
hoping in the morning light
to see you looking back at me
a smile
a tenderness in your eyes
yet you cannot be found
in my longing
my expectation
plucked from my dreamtime
melting
lost in the arms of my beloved
I lay silently frozen......

Margaret "Renie" Burgess

651

Today Went Astray

To the Southern tip of an old shoeless foot,
The hills mockingly sung resilience,
Browbeating with an agonized slap,
Regret began to furiously build a nest,
With steel pikes and barbed wire,
Blood flew downstream leaving a reeling head,
Self slowly serving self a sentence so severe,
Pain swam with spasms of an awaited lover,
Today went astray lifting the ashes off the ashtray like a stolen loves perfume,
Today went astray fitting the naysayer's prophecy of one unforgiving of self,
But alas!

Who forgives a parasite that lives on another,
or death that feeds life?
Who designs the spectrum of the arc of a rainbow seen but untouched?
Who tames dreams in their wakefulness shaving reality?
Today went astray as it perhaps should have done,
Let man drink a bitter root beer and smirk his lips,
Tomorrow may go North to new lands,
And by the rising sun,
Man must dare fate and cerebrate the astray and found.
We only owe us our feelings,

So salute to failure and success with two shots of fine whiskey.
It's living life.

Nancy Ndeke

I Bought Me A Poem

A piece rugged as Moses beard,
Held together by little wisps of tones,
Weak in the knee but wiser in the ears,
I bought me a poem,
Green as a well-tended lawn,
Yellow like a pawpaw ripe,
Brown like a well baked cake,
But cranky like a sod without a drink,
No way to negotiate peace,
This piece of bought poem in pieces,
Needles sticking like hay on a cheating lover,
Gripe dripping like overripe guava

I bought me a poem,
One I wish to offer for free,
To anyone living far enough,
Perhaps away with the bedouins,
And outback elders of silent commune,
I bought me a poem,
Like a parrot won't stop,
Reminders at dawn and dusk,
Of unreasoned times of shallow men,
Should order tell the law to come,
And quell the noise at night,
Know my fault this be

I bought me a poem,
Smooth like a snakes skin,
Velvet smooth with idioms,
And catch phrases that slap liars,
Bold and un-beautiful like a hyena's gait,
His fate is cruel like life imprisonment,
He won't die, he won't leave,
He won't relent, he won't repent,
O I bought me a poem,
And now lost in its lines,
I tag words hesitantly,
Drowning on in mimicry

Mastered by a bought thought,
Surrender must not shame,
For now,
Am bought,
By the same poem I bought.

Nancy Ndeke

The Naughty Look

I took a look at the hook,
Naughty loop upside not upset,
My ears did catch fire,
Those looks saints warn off,
When the hungry itch and ram the dial,
There's a language all coiled up in sighs and beads of sweat,
There is some with geography of vicinity,
And biology of chemistry,
Others, outright mystery.
The express unexpressed,
The debt of a throb like a bomb,
Permission maybe nodded or bodily persuaded,
Polity and regret to deal after the fact.

Words jam and tongues draw,
A blind picking of probing antennas,
And flower receptacles awake,
Awkwardly beautiful,
A little coy later,
A soldier's recap of paths of guns,
And puns intended.
A child's toy panning,
When embers and retirement calls.

Nancy Ndeke

Awkward At First....

Baby steps with jelly knees and a lopsided smile,
A cowboy with a gun unsure if it's sell-out or sell in,
Guarded, a little breath held in

A river did build momentum,
Rising with the words drops furious,
Soon a staccato did sound as thunder would clap,
Melting the dust of single steps and the dance of uncertainty

Bank burst and out flows the excess held,
Relieve flooded outward filling the airwaves with a song,
Friends were born into the brotherhood of sisterhood,
What a time of it with marbles sparkling at marvellous speed

What a time of it with village speech reaching the city,
An island needs a man to explore and write its secrets,
Distance is a mirage gone and never coming back,
For a path walked remains in the Memory of the foot

And here we are telling of tomorrow and the day before,
Having met the exam in the field of life,
Colors shaded out the differences as they highlighted the preferences.
No more trapped by side stepping toes,
Laughter greets the air and every other windblown guest of man's emotions.

Nancy Ndeke

Nap needed

Are you a Beggar when you dream?
Are you a Beggar that's always been?
Are you the one in search of more?
Are you the wreck washed up on shore?
For Scavengers and pilferers
To exploit at leisure
To strip bare without care
Merely for their pleasure

If my left foot fought my right foot
Would my ankles join the fight?
Then if knees accepted pleas
Imagine what a sight!
If a Chameleon can change at will be
How does it know another?
How does it tell and what the hell
A fellow but different colour

But I still search for my worth
In everything with cost
How many credits gain in this insane?
How man have I lost?
Just keeping strong to belong
In opened Pandora box
My current trend as attempt to mend
Wearing nothing but my socks

A Pea is green but not always been
When does Corn decide it's yellow?
Who decides upon the ride?
Whether we are mellow?
In what state is agitate?
Not found on a Map
When is induction some form of suction?
I think I need a nap!

Neapolitan anyone?

What definitions what we are?
What defines what be
Something in what we choose
Or just what others see
Delusion by confusion
Illusion by intrusion?
What then is solution?
Think past what we are

The red and white did meet the brown
Something new was seen
As well as tones around the world
We have Neapolitan Ice cream
Coffee and cream a taste bud dream
Choc and mint a hit
When sorbet comes into play
Will you change a bit?

Been one thing that changed something
Not the view of others
Just who be in Human tree
When disregards the covers
As one Nation are creation
Just like that cold delicious treat
Difference be in one like me
Them I warmly greet

Baked Alaska I cannot master
The timing not quite there
Yet putting ice cream in an oven
I task of which no care
Frozen be an attitude
Now that does need some heat
Melting cold attitudes of old
To make us all complete

Need a moment to compute

Going back or pushing through?
Decision making, what to do?
What we know or something new?
I know the feeling, but do you?

Comfort in the same old thing
Excitement in what change could bring
Do we retreat or challenge meet?
A Lament or to victory sing?

Lying low or stand and show
Speaking out or staying mute
Every day the questions may
Need a moment to computer

Discover

I have made a discovery
Salt and Ice cream do not mix
Then I made another
Back in Freezer still can't fix!

I like to make a discovery
It's how somethings I do learn
Like Women from Venus a fallacy
They are from a different Galaxy!!

HMS Discovery
Purpose built for an expedition
Not my choice of place to go
For the Antarctic was its mission

What defines discovery?
As opposed to happenstance?
I guess one is unexpected
Other When you take a chance

Need my Coffee

I and N did meet a K
Said hello and suggested play
Did something so absurd
Got together to promote word
Way to go was just to flow
From container to then show
Met some paper and on brink
When together page and ink

Came unbidden and looked around
Saw some things and then found
The love of letters laid in Ink
Got me going - made me think
Bored with that in school read
Bored with how the hopeful tread
Choice it said that instead
Just going with where idea led

Ink was dark but page lighter
Employed that which we call Writer
Now the future seems much brighter
With a talker instead of fighter

And so the story goes

Bumble Bee buzzing free
Doing that which Bee could be
Landing on plants and sometimes Tree
Spreading pollen, we can't see
Wasp the curse of flying kind
Stinging everything as if blind
Wondering why Mother created
Was her anger not fully sated?

A Dragonfly just passed me by
Does it realise it's mid-September?
Crazy weather now seems forever
Yet not so distant than can't remember

Need of coffee

Somewhere in some pure lit sunset
A being made a face
Was not from that around
Classed as different race
Yet that being saw more than seeing
If breathe they were a Brother
Does not matter how did scatter
Nor a different Mother

In future times the past crimes
Will be just what they were
No justification for that situation
Nor the wrongs that some did incur
This travelled one of things to come
A potential did they mark
For no certain plain to see
Did or didn't we embark?

Somewhere in some pure lit sunset
How I wish I could be there
For have ambition to respect tradition
Yet I also care
Outer cove different from other
No reason I can see
For those who lack confidence
To create hostility

This single person cannot make
This single voice a system break
Yet imagine what we can do
When we add the likes of you?
Nothing purely spectacular
Nothing designed for show
Just changing things in how it brings
A thing Politicians know

Nerve

A soul felt somewhat despondent
Not sure why but answer try
A soul did feel somewhat lost
Reflecting lonely, counting cost
A soul amongst the soul sea
Each trying to be what be
The difference was reality
Hidden by a history

History said be the same
Past added nothing to gain
Soul rebellious so confronted
Soul pushed further to that wanted
A weak link on the brink
Chose the path for wanted more
Rebellious is my guess
They then chose to walk out Door

Just because they wanted better
Just because they left no letter
Just because they had a vision
Just because, don't deserve derision
So, I read in days past
Yet the message it did last
Became foundation for what could
When discarded that I should

A letter to Life better
Found amongst some, considered, treasure
A moment to contemplate
A moment beyond measure
Who am I as life slips by?
What purpose do I serve?
When can be that true me?
If only found the nerve

Never too much to travel

The Berlin Babe was something else
The Glasgow Guy didn't try
To understand when spoke
We all know reason why

The Irish imp had a glimpse
The Latvian labourer did a favour
The Polish dish I gave a miss
The Beijing Boy had odd behaviour

One for all and all for one
Oddities can be overcome
Let's make this place a place for fun
Someone's child is someone

The Delhi doll was a troll
The Hague one now quite vague
Sarajevo son could get undone
Paris postures like a plague

Through Madrid I somehow slid
Likewise did Lisbon
Prague was hard but not too bad
In Manila met the one

One day of bliss is one I miss
One day to look to yet again
Glad that I refused temptation
Have too much to gain

The Tokyo was a show
The Philadelphia was a thriller
The Auckland was a cool hand
In Manila found who I so adore

So Many

They spend their days without food
broken wood forms the walls of their house

Each drop in the sea
wishes to rise
in the wind in the waves
to not be splashed up
on the shore to evaporate

Each vine in the garden
wants to twist and twine
high enough to be as green
to have roots not crowded out
to have water and food from the soil
to have enough
to grow to see the sun

They spend their days without food
broken wood forms the walls of their house

And still
Dragonflies with holes in their wings
they fly the few feet they can
then stand hoping
to catch an insect passing by
to give them strength to try to fly
again

They dream of writing poetry
but no books are left in the broken homes
paper there is not for words
but to plug the holes in the walls

A Dragonfly has made its way in
it shivers on the dark dirt floor
wondering if a hand will lift it up
or if a foot will be
the last thing it sees
who will mend the wing of one Dragonfly?
And then another until all are whole

Please wind don't hit their broken homes
mighty sea don't throw them away
God let them live in the garden another day

Cathy Mccormick

Oh Heck! Not another one

Awkward is that moment
That bit left unsaid
Loitering and festering
In mouth as well as head
Politeness locks and firmly blocks
That so sure to hurt
Maybe not visually
That expulsion of the curt

You've seen something that although not obscene
Just makes you wonder why
Only grace as drivel face
Is at least they chose to try
Self-proclamation a sour sensation
For is for others to decide
Not the statement that is for detainment
In a capsule full of riches far and wide

The great ones never self-proclaimed
They left to others to decide
Arrogant just ignorant
When statement mixed with misjudged pride
Being positive is a good thing
Being confident even better
Just reign in when begin
To think ruler of the letter

An observation born out of frustration
When see what now on show
Making another question form
Do they even know?

How many times must see this crime?
When author name completes with that, they've written
When switch off at the start
Because with self are smitten

Old dirty

Atom Mick changed his name
When he found had energy
Became something most do know
Yet not all like nor see

Had a temper, so destructive
If and when chose to use
Also liked to replace poor fossil
When beneath us we abuse

Dropped an m and the k
Put the two names together
Gained a nickname most do use
Nuclear - Old dirty we hope never

Clink the Drinks

Clink the Drinks with some high jinx
The perfect evening with good friends
Alcohol feeds the soul
Goes too fast but to Blackmail lends

Celebration good occasion
Though in truth none do need
First the curse to get worse
Get the 'taste' so taste buds' feed

The stronger the treasure the smaller the measure
When served in Licensed places
Customary also when socially
In someone's dwelling spaces

Once I was that rascal

Once I was a rascal
A thing of irresponsibility
Once I was that didn't want to meet
Nor even me to see
When young was fun without a gun
Never thought of carrying knives
Unless on trip to hooks dip
With Fathers sparing Wives
That misbegotten tale that is called male
Given space in which it thrives

Remember that September?
Not that in which now live
That one when were young
When had so much to give
I changed the Sun because was one
Just o instead of u
Told by some it would be fun
That what the young must do

Once before my Wife was more
Than when I met her made
A mother so could suffer
And with figure trade
For so many years now have laid
In a bed when silent made
Ways to keep what I have got
Ways to make up for Birthday I forgot

One day parade

On days parade just what have made
The canvas we do own
Exhibiting so might bring
Company to one alone
You are out there
That do know
Just how many failures
Through which have to go

So, who is me?
Just want to be
The instigator and then caught
Nothing more
From some far off shore
A feeling so long sought
Everything we know as we grow
Coming to fruition
The happiness a lifelong quest
We are a Human mission

Is this one the real deal?
Is this when reach my goal?
Is this my completion?
The part that makes me whole
To say 'I love you' and mean it true
Nothing can describe
When with no care your feelings air
Not for a moment choose to hide

The pleasure in the morning
The joy in afternoon
Satisfaction in the evening
As together in sleep swoon
Everything to this day bring
The bits that didn't fit

When have gotten and begotten
When the pieces finally fit
When you meet the right one
Is the time that you get it

One more gap

Cluck o'clock and Roosters rock
The Sun does have a yawn
Things that be can nearly see
I guess it must be Dawn

Coffee on, dark and strong
Rocket fuel as high octane as can take
Trudging around not making sound
Soon will be awake

Another day and chance to play
On this thing we call being
One more gap before that
When lose the sense of feeling

Pause in tune so must be noon
Time for top up take
A solid and a liquid
Bought so didn't make

The choices are expanding
The wallet is now sinking
Figures don't matter much
When taste buds they are thinking

Another day and chance to play
On this thing we call being
One more gap before that
When lose the sense of feeling

Evening time and time for crime
Of the culinary kind
What does earn the chance to burn
Which victim will I find?

One, Two, Three, Four

"Go on! You're bulletproof!"
Said the voice
"Go on regardless!"
Said the choice
"Care for none but yourself"
Selfish said to me
"Let others marvel in your magnificent"
But alas was not to be

Been the one I've never been
Seen the things I'd never seen
Dreamed of big then lived that dream
Fed the fire with gasoline
Watched the flames as they rose higher
Danced that dance we call Desire
Made a bed and laid down proud
Then came crashing down so loud

One – I got to feel strong
Two – I had no clue
Three – Got to feel was free
Four – was but a two-way door
Five – did strive to be alive
Six – it made me sick
Seven – went the chance for Heaven
Eight - that person now I hate

Knock, knock you fool
Conscience calling
Knock, knock you promise
You are stalling
Knock, knock you so misguided
Now your feelings so divided
Knock, knock you older one
You've been and done so now become

The situation for Generation
Not the same as mine
They are told to forget that old

The modern Leaders say that's fine
The prospect of regret
Looms to one like me
For they are blessed by what learnt
Learnt by likes of me

Deliver to me peacefully
Deliver to me please Fate
Deliver to me carefully
Your love but not your hate
Deliver to me my prospects be
Deliver to me the choice
Deliver to me redemption
In soft understanding voice

Time for change can seem strange
When not appreciate your past
Time for change can be strange
When, thankfully, it didn't last
Time for change can seem strange
When to where have no clue
Time for change can be strange
Yet change is what must do

One – I got to feel strong
Two – I had no clue
Three – Got to feel was free
Four – was but a two-way door
Five – did strive to be alive
Six – it made me sick
Seven – went the chance for Heaven
Eight - that person now I hate

Dawn is but a start of day
Dawn a word that many say
Dawn a name some do choose
Dawn a word that we use
Dawn a chance to begin
Dawn at stage each are in
Dawn a switch from dark to light
Dawn the time to make day bright

Op in Ian

Tell me of your torture
As titillate you try
Tell me of your reason
The simple reason why
Why you choose to self-abuse
Mental not the other
Dream that dream that might mean
A name upon a cover

Tell me of desire
That unseen inner fire
The sheer joy when employ
An escape from mire
Trapped but with escape
Are you brave enough to take?
Anthology be what be
But who's name on front see?

Easy is the introduction
In another's feel that suction
Yet are worth more you see
When take steps and then break free
The times a changing that for sure
Yet are they really the sought cure

A snippet here and snippet there
Does the reader really care?
You who own a treasure
Let not others reap your measure
Yes, it's easy to give to them
All the profits of your pen

An introduction to greater things
Understand for what it brings
Then branch out and be your self
Give to them a Books wealth
You have done the work you see
Why content with what be?
A name behind another name
Somehow just don't sit the same

Quad questions

Can you catch it my young friend?
Can you really, truth be told
Can you catch it like I caught it?
Can you catch this common Cold?

Did you see that my work colleague?
Did you see it and then caught?
Did you see it for weren't meant to?
Did you see what I just thought?

Did you taste it you poor person?
Did you taste that of me?
Did you taste that not worthy?
Did you taste that called envy?

Did you sense it my one special?
Did you sense from above?
Did you sense what I'm feeling?
Did you sense this thing Love?

Let me

Let me rest in less stress luxury
Let me rest just for a while
Let me rest and see what happens
Let me rest to regain my smile

Let me rest so can consider
Let me step aside from this
Let me be just an observer
To take step back from the abyss

Let me pause for the cause
Let me consider if is right
Let me be burden free
Before decide to re-join fight

Quantity is not quality
(Though took some time to realise)

On a roll so away I go
Point and then just see
Victory in volume
They'll be impressed with me
I will be on front page
The one they'll wish to be
I will be immortal
Go down in history

The pleasure in my leisure
Then did something strange
No recreation situation
When to obsession it did change
Obsessive and possessive
The Master not the friend
I was a fool to let it rule
Until I put to end

The go slow showed the way to go
When caught up in the rush
The pause it caused some resource
When stepped out from the crush
The small steps would further get
When time to check the route
Headlong, headstrong was just so wrong
When others could give no hoot

Now by doing less I'm doing more
More products and more joy
I hope the quality is improving
When some breaks employ
How easy was I caught up
That copious I need
Every hour another one
To the World must feed

Quantity or quality

Not posts but how many places posted

The single voice – it got lost
Lost amongst the crowd
So much same became a pain
When one deserves to be heard loud

The member can't remember
Lost in the constant noise
The one that had important to say
Became just another choice

The irritation of same situation
The 'social' not being such
The flood of same muck
The product of a Generation

That wants and seeks attention
Just don't know quite how to deliver
Quantity over quality
The quill does start to quiver

All are somehow different
Let their words reflect
All are not what they think
In that we boring get

Reduce/ restrict to become a 'hit'
Become a choice of voice
Let them hear loud and clear
Give your readers some rejoice

Quantity query for the questioning

A shot in the dark for a lark
Something just to see
A venture into adventure
What will be will be
A hit or miss, the strange twist
Masochist maybe spring to mind
The trait too late to contemplate
The answer we will find

The sound of silence, it was heard
Heard aloud around the world
The sound of silence had a voice
Sometimes in it we rejoice
The sound of nothing becomes something
The comfort in the chaos seen
The cause for pause is to applaud
If we hope for that serene

A Head is full of questions
Some answered and some not
We just have to make the best
The best of which each got
A Life is but an opportunity
A chance and nothing more
Do we stick with what have
Do we look to foreign shore?

A ramble to preamble
A verse that one can choose
Amongst the barrage of that better
One can keep or lose

Question of perception

Once there was a well-known person
Well known for that they share
Once there was a question
How much did they dare?
Once I knew a one that grew
Into self-confident
Once I knew one who passed through
The other time they spent

Once I knew but not the present
Someone who did change
Became a type of confident
Before would seem so strange
Once I knew who went through
A different but not unique
They took on board and adored
The difference once did seek

I saw the way that within it play
The one who holds control
I saw that one who made it through
The one who did explore

They wrote

'If all of me you could see
What the thing you think of me?
If all my faults were shown as we waltz
Would we dance in harmony?
Is the one you see truly me?
Perhaps you'll never know
For select in those who get
The full unedited shown'

I asked myself why cannot do the same?

Ian Wilcox

Question you

What becomes of strange afflictions
What becomes of their interdiction?
What becomes of the same?
Just as serious but different name

Since when again did feel such pain
Not disease but the cure
Almost one hundred years of our fears
A century of Leadership not always pure

Covid set a silence, can you hear me now?
Covid set the panic, last known as that 'Mad Cow'
Covid seen what interactive brings
Reminiscent of Nineteen Nineteen?
Can we really say as 'Leaders' play?
The game of 'one up-man ship'?
Same resonance but different way
How they laugh, hope goes away

Am n fan of modern Politics
Where each wants to be a name
Am no fan when responsible
Yet response is a shame

Accept the start was unexpected
Accept the cause still 'mystery'
Accept the origin is a closed door
Question why should be

Covid sent a message
Can you hear it now?
Life is more than what can earn
Life is not just some cash Cow
Been too long on easy street
Now a challenge you must meet
Medical and physical
Just sit or place your feet?

Questions then suggestions

If a Feather gently falls to Earth
How does an Eagle soar?
As money causes so much worry
Why do we yearn for more?
When know the stress of growing up
Why on our own inflict?
What reason when music sells a lot
We label it a hit?

'I wouldn't do that if I were you'
Yet to reason said
'Maybe you should try this way'
Not telling where it led
'Take a breath' to one that's breathing
If not they wouldn't hear
'Sort the wheat from the chaff'
When no field is near

When co-existing seems so hard
Why do some choose to marry?
If a burden that has no physical weight
How come that we still carry?
'Eat more Greens' yet don't show
The basic thing like how to grow
'You should have done the same as me
When your way they didn't know

Questions and suggestions
We are so full of each
One by learning answers we evolve
One by giving answers
Do we someone else then teach

Quintessential is exponential

Quintessential is exponential
If but what we choose
Live and learn so offspring earn
What we could soon lose

As take on board do not hoard
Mistakes as well as victory
For by being honest
Better will your children be

I screwed up so many things
My Daughter knows of most
Some are non-repeatable
So are now a personal ghost

Yet growing and then knowing
Deserves the chance of showing
For how can she learn what I did earn
Her future now am sowing

The pause.... then cause
The reason comes to mind
The honesty of what I be
Avoidance hope will find
Not of me but history
The past as that I know
The danger signs of which were blind
As with the scars did grow

Life lesson One Oh One
To begin must take on chin
Shake Head and carry on
Weak it seeks as doubt leaks
Has no chance when will is strong

Fortunate favours the brave
Not just in conflict but who we are
Arrogance a pestilence
So, don't please take that far

Radio and T.V.

I never wanted to fall in love
But Fate had different plan
I could not find here the one
Found on different Land
The urge to travel sounded strong
To a place felt I belong
To a place with darker face
To a people who know grace

I never wanted to be accepted
For didn't know what it be
Just a one who lacked fun
A bigger place I could not see
Getting by a thing to try
A pat on back from self
Once more into the conflict
Of that I called wealth

The wealth of just breathing
When in others it did cease
The wealth of expression
In harmless ways release

Then all changed
First accepted by just one
Then acceptance grew
Was accepted by a couple
Then more than few

Radio and T.V. shows
Talk of pain and joy
They never knew of this one
The simple confused Boy

Now I see that sunrise
As what it could now be
Another chance with day to dance
Was blind but now I see

Rainbows show

Look outside and see the Rainbow
Soon it will be gone
Waiting for the opportunity
To brighter then adorn
Hear that note that Nature makes
Then adds a new to it
Replicate in our own way
Possibly a 'Hit'

What's the point of staying still?
When on offer there is more?
Crime is in the making
When it you do not tour
Mountain made decision
Decided more to show
Gathering resources
Mountain it did grow

Palliative the narrative
When delivered from the soul
The release is no tease
When helping to make whole
Not just the one in which begun
But the many to which care
Some of whom does still consume
So, of whom been there

An Ocean just a notion
When we learn to fly
Just a mass that we pass
Gaps that just go by
Rainbows show and we do grow
Into ourselves it's true
Nothing much to it really
Just a thing we do

Rambling

Raising rumours reaching ridiculous
Announce on that stage we look
Media frenzy now predicted
Before a deal for Book
Life is so ridiculous
If in all believe
Not my thing I'm sorry
Got bigger issues for to grieve

The icons passing quickly
To join their similar kind
Wonder how many new ones
Amongst them they will find

Social media frenzy
Guess some like what they do
Scared the position of power
Might go to someone new

Now mask a task that they ask
Yet cycle helmet must remove
So on security cameras
Your image they can improve

Rambling in the morning
In the afternoon
Rambling in the evening
At night do write same tune

Random four liners

The moniker made the message real
Told exactly how you feel
No illusions or confusions
Just keeping honest,

All the self-published
Who owned a pen
Astounded by the experience
Vowed 'Never again!'

Why when just two litres
We then pass what seems more like four
Yet stomach not shrinking
Just bloated some more

The less that we do
The less seem to sleep
Boredom must like us
So, awake it tries to keep

The more that we earn
The more that we spend
Then from a Broker
Even more try to lend

Random four liners
Somehow make a whole
Was this just an accident
Can't think was my goal

Really matter that much

The want to fight for wrong or right
When in the darkness see dark light
The dull decisions seem so bright
When nothing really matters that much
When enjoy the hurt employ
The torture is some twisted toy
When not a Man or even Boy
When nothing really matters that much

The sedative of satisfaction
The rapidness of rash reaction
The folly of falling into factions
When nothing really matters that much
The sane refrain from inflicting pain
The wise work out woes disguise and gain
Trouble takes the tempting train
When nothing really matters that much

Look at self and check your wealth
For are not rich in loving health
Wonder why been left on shelf?
Because somethings really matter that much
Every day we pay in same old way
With things we do and things we say
Aggression often leads to affray
Because somethings really matter that much

I like at me then look at you
Don't understand some of what do
But I don't know what you've been through
Because somethings really matter that much
Try to take this offered hand
To help lift head from out of sand
Being nice can be so grand
Because somethings really matter that much

685

Reflections with a mention

(Acknowledgement to The Moody Blues)

If I could write a Nights in White Satin
I would happily turn and peacefully go
To which place agreed to have me
Currently I don't know

If I could make a mark in marvel
A fantasy would be achieved
Just reward for one who could
Like some others, they believed

Because was born to make me happen
Because was born to in me believe
Because was set to go forward
Because won't rest until achieve
Yes, I am just a Human
Yes, I am the same as you
We are all just unfinished
In those things that we can do

Done and tried and still am trying
So much more before I die
No holding back is reservation
No sense of cannot try

Awkward is an Uncle
Shan't a distant Aunt
Possibly a close Brother
Will the Sister of with which will dance

For many years have made some moments
For many years want to make more
Book half-filled yet growing bigger
Now becomes more than a chore

Reflection with a mention
Of what used to be
Old days played in old ways
This older is now free

Rejoicing in the change

The revelation a sensation
Shook me to the core
When accepted not rejected
Then I wanted more
Those Apple trees and Honey bees
Nice but not the whole
Wanted more so made the chore
Examination of the Soul

Ecstasy once mystery
Not the type you take
Never interested in that kind
Just the type you make
Higher level in feeling good
Once before not understood
Then came change and with it gain
Added extra, Parenthood

Give me choice and I'll rejoice
In what I have and hold
Some difference in circumstance
That's a different story told
I've been caught up in a madness
Not of making, just partaking
Came sometimes close to breaking
Now I'm glad I saw it through

'Every Dog has its day'
This one just waited a wee bit longer
No weakness caused by the waiting
It, in fact, made me stronger
Looking back on yesteryear
Laughing at my silly fear
Rewards above what I deserve
Simply by keeping nerve

What you give is what you get
Remember that and just let

Release

On the road to unknown
The only place to be
On the journey, not late nor early
Just in harmony

On a track with no turning back
One way was the sign
So am going forwards
With these thoughts of mind

Elocution is pollution
When invention is the taste
Adds a different flavour
Seems a shame to waste

Now the dream it seems
Real in just the visual
Not for what but for got
The moment that did feel

Feel the joy when did employ
Limb to let it bring
Inside to the outside
Guess a writer thing

Rhapsody in literacy
Emotion through a notion
Pleasure in the leisure
A compelling potion

Awkward at first but could be worse
Trapped but just not said
Those things sing and want to bring
More from that there Head

Sailing Solar

On the Onyx of Occurrence
Shone a beam of light
Perfection an intention
Never could quite get it right
I used to think as deeper sink
That the fault was mine
As I grew, I slowly knew
It's just one word in a line

In the Sea of could, might be
Floated confused one
Current took to Being Book
Shackles came undone
The barrier was being me
All that thought could do
Took deep breath and then stepped
Into something new

The chains of limitations
Are just tissue situations
When we want to break that hold
When we want to be that bold
Strong enough to see what can
Strong enough to make a plan
That has guides but no rules
Someone's puppet is for fools

Sailing solar in the sense
Not now bound by gravity
Body yes but rest rejected
In that part I am free

Salt cake

Fiona was Sandra's friend
Been the same since met at school
Whilst Sandra was the sensitive type
Fiona was always cool
Sandra was in meltdown
Another venture, another test
Another in the list of everyone
Where not all end in win and rest

Fiona said to Sandra

'Scratch my surface – watch me bleed
Hear my whimpering as they feed
The agonies once again
Recollections of the pain
The bitter truth so I'm told
Part of it, of getting old
Coupled with a longer life
Are more cuts from the failure knife

Yet more heal to make me strong
More verses added to success song
Experience can't be bought
It's a lesson so must be taught
Only if same errors make
Do we deserve to eat salt cake
Try again but different way
Then a win sees light of day'

Carl and Liam buddies true
Many journeys had been through
Liam hot headed if truth be told
Whilst Carls mixed his with dash of cold
Another day but same old story
Liam ranting about failed glory
Carl sat beside and let subside
Then spoke the same words

Samhain

(The original Celtic festival)

'Tis the hour that isn't there
The one to venture – if you dare
The Gateway opens to dark places
Hideous creatures with half faces
Add to them the Spectre ones
Reaping chaos just for fun
To entice and with take back
Each year the Dark World does attack

Yes, we know through Book and play
But there we control what do or say
Not this hour between two Dates
There is no love just full of Hates
Hates or Hades in ancient Greek
Our destruction both do seek
The unwary or uncaring
Eternal misery with them soon sharing

Plucked from here and to there go
If to them disdain do show
Best respect is to them let
Not self nor soul in sights get
Three One, One Zero
In modern day
To Zero One, One-One
They will stray

Witches, Warlocks, Ghosts and Ghouls
Playmates of kind or reckless fools
Maybe you choose as your salvation
To be cast into eternal Damnation
If so, then ignore All Hallows Eve
Now just called Halloween
Treat as fun that image you
Try to ignore but no can do

Saw the sign

I saw the sign that said 'Low Bridge'
Wondered why it felt that way
Saw the sign that said 'No Speaking'
Thought you are a fine one to say!

I saw the sign that said 'Wild Animals'
Thought they should meet the kids!
Saw the sign that said 'Wet Floor'
Who forgot the lids?

I saw the sign that said 'School Crossing'
Wondered where it went
Saw the sign that said 'You're bored
This effort is now spent

Poodle parlour

Panic at the Poodle parlour
A Doberman snuck in
The staff aghast at their task
Where to they begin!

No curly coat to groom
Too big to put on lap
Other clients are in meltdown
No chance to have a nap

The Boss was not amused
At the situation quite confused
Picked up phone in a shock
Wrongly asked for the Bomb Squad!

The famous Dog Parlour caper
Got in local Paper
Just page three for you see
Editor was a Dog hater

Say to me

Say to me of democracy
Speak to me of independence
I will tell you only half truth
For the whole just makes nonsense
Some rules for the masses are so needed
Some protection for the poor
Not the playthings of the corrupted
Not that for those I abhor

Shindigs in the shadows
Are we really now so shallow?
The tease to please can now do with ease
The field is somewhat fallow
Alchemy a mystery
So is Human Race
Yet in parts each an art
One each day we face

Is to sorrow the way to go?
I choose to disagree
But am told that I'm just old
And it the way to be
So say to me of independence
Certainly some parts make some sense
The rights of each Nation loose
A common freedom if do choose

Scions of a struggle

All is a kilter
Sense has gone astray
Harmony a bygone word
Chaos come to play

When one day of sensibility
Amidst crowds of pure confusion
Briefly seen but then lost again
Like some fleeting strange illustration

Seasons become unseasonal
Reason turns unreasonable
Logic grows illogical
Rise has flipped to the fall

Scions of a struggle
Signs that it might double
Everywhere there is trouble
Everything a muddle
Pleasure in the pain gain
Inflict and so receive
The destruction of all now here
Sped up to now achieve

A story somewhere, sometime
For history bigger than just one
In all of infinity
Is and were more than just one Sun

So is said so must be true
What has been done others do
Permutations in the equation
Said that thing Situation

Everything has a beginning
Everything an end
Between the two by what do
To the latter a hand all try lend

Scribbling Time

Calamity came calling
Misery this morning
Fantastic fast falling
Started successfully now stalling

Compromised and with surprise
Delicious draught I drink
Such a shame put down the drain
To be honest, kitchen sink

Both are white and granular
Both same sizes, so similar
Hence the hardship and the halt
When instead of sugar added salt!

Turn on light so could see
Merely made more misery
Performed perfectly then did pop
Such a start! Please something stop!

Put on shoes while watching News
Feet now seem so strange
Comfort cancelled, callous calling
When did left and right foot change?

Found my keys so some release
Tempting trauma, at least a tease
Outside world occupied
Hoping somehow in it hide

Should I just go back to Bed
With maverick mattress and lay where led
Wish tomorrow for today
When I asked refused to play

Sod it – scribbling time!!

Seat

We be what Bubble wants
Unless to be a Bubble
Bubble is the expansion
Bubble can be trouble
The sphere no fear approaches near
What are we to do?
The concept of some 'Internet'
Now I have no clue

The shop seemed quite empty
Outside there stood a queue
Welcome to Two Oh Twenty
Welcome to something new
The Leaders appear leaderless
The population in confusion
Two oh two oh a film script
Classed as an illustration

What's that I see for cannot be
A common sense profound
What's that I see for not reality
Neither sight nor sound
I am in confusion of illusion
Someone explain trick
The current feeling has left me reeling
Am I or not I am, this thing that they call 'sick'

I walked upon an empty street
Others now too scared to meet
Understand the worries got
From every option is same lot
Is this now the end we sing?
The end of free thought it will bring?
Is this now a promise keep?
When a person wanted certain seat?

See through

We do to self what we think wealth
But is that really true
When with surprise we then surmise
Just what we did do
The pain of 'gain' are we insane?
The following of trend
The hard fact is how we act
That the way to mend

Tasted bitter but no quitter
Nor are you if truth said
Just a switch inside of each
Leads to part then played
The scars we wear we sometimes share
The rest we keep to self
We get lost in the cost
Protection of inner wealth

They sing of Gravity and what could be
Yet somehow it is wrong
For is not what once got
Just another song
Look and see what you can be
The message I here send
So much more than just a chore
When self-imposition broken not just bend

So now look at me and what do you see?
Just another just like you
Difference is I made the twist
Exploring what can do
No, I am not special
Very much like you
Yes, I am just different
Can the outside now see through?

Self-description

Too short to be a towering figure
Too tall to be in Pantomime
Stuck I guess I am in middle
Middle good so all is fine

Too pale to be of ethnic
Too liberal for 'white is right'
I am just another person
In that thing I think perfect sight

Too different abled to be 'normal'
Too 'normal' so confuse
I am just what I am
Using whatever can use

I am male who considers female
Their own lives do try to understand
I am not a Dictator nor combobulator
Nor will I go cup in hand

I am me and whatever be
I am definitely not you
I am no judge for opinions smudge
When of subjects have no clue

Preconception is misdirection
Holding back a promise due
Of a better for us all
By our thinking we can do

I am carnivorous and herbivorous
I will even eat my Pizza cold
I am a spot – a living dot
I watch as we unfold

Does anyone else like chopped egg and salad cream sandwiches?

Sending signals to the Sentinels

Sending signals to the Sentinels
The watchers up above
Far beyond our atmosphere
In urgent need of love

Sending signals, a cry for help
As with malice we employ
Short of outright warfare
In our bid to us destroy

A calmness creates calm
Hostile leads to harm
Acceptance prevents persecution
Calm a soothing Balm

Turmoil such a tempting taste
When our wisdom wishes to waste
Happening in horrid haste

Sending signals to the Sentinels
Please protect us from ourselves
We are fighting all and sundry
Surely that's not right

Sending signals to the Sentinels
A last hope I do say
For am not for religion
So no other one to which pray

Sending Troops

Sending Troops to save them
Sending different kinds
Sending Troops to education
Best of them you'll find

The battle of just learning
The war on lack of chance
One side freely wants it
One side makes a stance

So, sending Troops to fight this battle
Mercenaries some might say
Sending Troops to aid in fight
Just in a different way

The battleground expanded
When involved new I.T.
Gave the poor victims
A new way to see

I am gathering a Battalion
A Regiment my wish
To join with others Armies
Words we freely dish

Words are a powerful weapon
In the illiterate war
Words can beat the systems
Words can do much more

So, sending Troops to fight this fight
Sending them to fight
They have many letters
They just want the sight

Separate romance

The light it slowly goes to bed
Soon is time to rest this head
The days been long but got along
How are you my love?
The time we shared with love and care
The minutes seemed to flow
Just as I was comfortable
Time you had to go

And still you remain despite my pain
Still you will not leave
For if not here in physical
I have no cause to grieve
You are here so bright and clear
To some quite a surprise
For you live and will always stay
Behind these loving eyes

The touch I love oh so much
On hold but not too long
Until again without refrain
You and I are where belong
In the company of each other
In the air we share
In the space where see that face
In the moment where

I am lost yet found - on loving ground
I am the traveller home
I am that space so won my race
No more the phone screen gnome
Technology a mystery
Yet a blessing too
For the chance for separate romance
For still am loving you

Serve me please

"Make mine a double
Over ice
Make it straight
No decor slice
Hell! Just fill the glass to top
When overflow you can stop
Give me something that I know
Before you serve first me show
Serve to me what you see
Serve something I wish to be

Make me something that is good
Give to me that understood
Let me sample that of which fond
Before I go to that beyond
Make it cold and make it clear
Needs no mixer for don't fear
The stuff itself is just enough
In those times that seem so tough
Serve it straight so all can see
Give to me Humility"

A double for the trouble

Why are my digits turning blue?
Why is my breath exhale as cloud?
Why do ears seek attention?
If feeling sound, it would be loud

Why does we want to pen again?
Can we not learn refrain?
This is becoming quite insane
Soon in life will be a bane

Seven a.m. summary

Who are we to say what see?
How our perfect world should be
When extolls such misery
Others of one family

Is peanut butter really butter?
When you spread on bread
Do you need the real stuff under?
Or just use it neat instead

Who measures servings on the jar?
When they're speaking from afar
Never met so how do know
If more or less you choose to go

What to do to see this through?
Another day does beckon
Refuse collection outside now
More clearing up I reckon

Why do I even try?
To just live, to get by
Not a thing but just a question
Some other poor souls do not mention

Breakfast done so move on
Another task to take
Do I go cold and slow?
Or my lunch will grill or bake

Can be bothered to go out
When I really just don't care
Maybe just full open windows
Then experience new fresh air

Seven a.m. summary

Shakespeare and shenanigans

(With humble tribute to the great Man)

To B or not to B?
The question facing A
The Bard before his time
Let's C some a play

Alas poor York I know it well
For an easy place to spell
Such is life in what do
They named another and called it New

These violent delights have violent end
A message to the future sends?
Problem being who is seeing
When the quote does reach the end

Brevity is the soul of wit
My brevity comes early morn
Wait! Is that Breakfast?
Cereal with which milk adorn

If music be the food of love
Who the hell made Rock'n'Roll?
What situation needs that gyration?
I prefer the gentle stroll

Now is the Winter of our discontent
Believe me pal am spending and spent
You thought that you had bad
Try this time with what we've had

The man, his works are History
Yet another could never be
For what penned in prose and play
Became things we each do say

Soothing Balm

If Time allowed us times
To on our past consider
Would we be who now be?
Or just another cinder?
What I needed didn't have
So grew up and searched for it
Went to places didn't know
Took the reward and sometimes hit

How many, true to self
Can laugh because it's you
How many got that certain kick
To find what you could do?
Bubble trouble when in it
We stay desperate and some pain
When break free and say 'This is me!'
Then the profits gain

If Time allows do we leave trails?
That others can then follow?
The ones create in certain state
Or are we just that hollow?
With frivolity comes responsibility
Not that just of cost
More the case when in haste
Look back at what we lost

The stubbornness perhaps illness
Seen s many years past were
The blessings in the seeing
Not for everyone the cure
The scumbag that changed their rags
The offensive now the calm
The connective in perspective
Life became a soothing Balm

Sorrows of situation

Across the waters someone saw
The need to venture, to explore
The chance to just be something more
Before we knock on that Death door
Across and so far from 'Home
Statistics said that they must roam
Not from choice but from need
If their Family they want to feed

How can a Nation become situation?
Where to survive must 'sell' them self
Prostitution in recruiting
When 'Home' offers so much wealth
The haves and have not's
Not separate by water just
The soured cream that 'rule supreme'
Those once the others once did trust

The ignominy of stupidity
When becomes just the same
They promised something different
Yet like the benefits can gain
All well and good when understood
But where leaves the ones who vote
Outside fortress - I care less than nothingness
For my decisions build a moat

The confusion of illusion
Factual an intrusion
The wrong is 'right' in power fight
The 'common' no inclusion
The despair although not there
In body nothing more
The need I bleed for are 'my creed'
Found roots on foreign shore

Sorry about the smell

He picked a Pepper
Placed on plate
Salivating
Then he ate

She felt a mess
So bought a Dress
Cost becomes a nothingness
When with money shopkeeper bless

If all the days
Just went away
What could say
When time for play

Look at you!
What did you do!
Did you swim through
A sea of goo?

Is this action
Of this faction
An attraction
Or should we sanction?

Is the rain
Upon the plain
Just the same
As goes down Drain?

Words not heard
Can be inferred
By a herd
Become absurd

Sound familiar?

The new comer was quite timid
The new comer was quite shy
The collection was a medicine
Here's the reason why

If I came to you what would you do
If I said you make me proud
If I looked at you like I had a clue
Would you then speak out loud?
The troubled that is troubling
The hideous you hide within
The sense of being we don't share
The thought of self we don't care

The single voice of many
The greeting just the same
Everyone is equal
Everyone has pain
We wonder what you're doing
As you wonder why we wonder
Each of us is you in disguise
Each of us do blunder

Tell a Star to shine less bright
Don't hold your breath for reply
A star shines bright inside of you
You are the reason why

Mirror look is that which took
Judging from own eyes
Yet they are part of the questions asked
They are compromise
So when the pain drives you insane
Share with those who care
When you feel outside your depth
Take breath and then just dare

Sour puss sounding sensible

The occasion of the situation
Cause for celebration in adulation
Yet what in reality see
What is given but not be
Did one study in the real?
In an institution where desk can feel?
Encouragement yes, but nothing more
When outside the Facebook shore

I do not mock for still have to gain
Yet different ones now fall like rain
An 'Institution' creates dilution
In the real breeds confusion
Something that can print to show
Not for improvement way to go
Maybe I am just of a temper
When in them I will not venture

Modern things and with it brings
New attitude to recognition
I am of the old school
Certificates earned by that of tradition
Enjoy that earned for still success
Just on those laurels please not rest
A stepping stone and nothing more
In the journey of published chore

Souvenirs of joyful tears

The dropping down in temperature
Adding to the woe
For a moment wish could fly
To where I want to go
Drizzle drips from fingertips
The slushing wheels do make
The crowded streets that now treat
To flashbacks so can take

Souvenirs from sandy shores
Places to return
In the sun kissed part that has the part
That makes emotions burn
Souvenirs of joyful tears
Still feel though know not there
Gentle strolls, soft footprint holes
With the one who does love share

Imagination helps situation
Recalling barriers falling
The want to give each day I live
Eternity is calling
The place now be is not for me
For they are far away
Though intend to this mend
Then there will I stay

Yes, Souvenir each day, each year
As strong with each return
The reason when each season
Failure I will spurn
For nothing else could ever match
The sights, the feel, the sound
Of gentle waves and Palm trees brave
The resolutely stand their ground

Standing still could be a thrill

Mister Money isn't it funny
You like to flash the cash
Yet when Tax man comes you try to run
And break out in a rash
Figo Ego you make me go
Quite nauseous inside
Yet am politics so try I might
Your existence to hide

What is worth when is worthless?
What is 'rich' when you are poor?
Lacking satisfaction
Always wanting more
It's a shame we play a name
The one more 'valued' than another
When does the same the no labels- plain
A 'rip off' or a cover?

Miss Contrary you evil Fairy
In and out you slither
Flummoxing as you begin
The spurt and then the dither
Missus Look from your Mom took
That one that leaves men cold
No real clue does have you
It's been this way since times old

The Family they call a Tree
I guess the leaves do leave
The rain the same in praise and blame
In those who do or don't believe
Oceans deep and Mountains steep
The highest and lows we go
Standing still could be a thrill
When answer is just so

Step inside

The one who knew not pure sun
Just glimmer that did tease
Lost in the myriad of misdirected
Each promising to please

Yet another, different smother
We will promote and then award
Certification for its sensation
To a level one can't afford

It will not be like that in life
Recognised, but do we care
The satisfaction of imagination
The fault most of us truly share

Step inside and let self dry
As for reason do not try
To explain or justify
Why you are here and please don't cry
Step inside this place dry
No barriers the way you look
Come and meet as rest your feet
Another chapter in your Book

The Sandman came to play a game
The person said 'not now'
The dark did bark but was a lark
When saw the light of day

Alone w come and alone we go
No matter the company
The in between is personal dreams
Dreams of what can be

Step inside and see why
You are better than you know
Take some time, it is fine
Discover self before you go

Stepping stone on which did roam

I have sometimes worked and sometimes strayed
Wandered for the laugh
Been and done some stuff wrong
Gave those unwanted autograph

Still are strong those that did wrong
Still in sight those did right
Some low blows and some scared the crows
When life became a fight

So where do now stand and how
For moved on but not forgotten
Sometimes real those things I feel
That feeling of just rotten

I used to be survivor
Then I changed my cover
Became partner and a lover
A great decision made

Now when I go don't go alone
For other walks with me
Always and forever
Even if them you can't see

Someone turned my lights on
Someone took from darker place
Someone gave me strength by that did lend
Showed me how to face

All that's been like some bad dream
When can see the future true
All was just stepping stones on which did roam
To that still could one do

Steward

Tantrum was a tempting trouble
Only problem it did double
All the problem that its birth
Caused at first without mirth

Temper met and quite liked Tantrum
Shared some bits so did join
There they sat, deeply depressing
With Gaiety Gladness other side of coin

Middle Muddle much to liking
Neither extreme to do go
The boring Steward of the Bar
Say most of those I know

Not a minion

Excuse me but have you seen my Plankton?
I am sure it was here just now
Multi shaped and multi coloured
Wish I knew the why and how

Excuse me please but I am in a hurry
Can you help me with this riddle?
Why when space for two to pass
Does one insist to stand in middle?

Excuse me for let it be with recompense
It was me with flatulence
Bottom burp without much clue
If one of them will follow through

Excuse me for I am of the opinion
I am one and not a minion
At least one cell is not like you
Both in looks and what do

Still making Marmalade

Made Marmalade but not as trade
Made Jam as a mistake
Made a Stew as thing to do
Then had coffee break
Made a story that wasn't gory
That one a surprise
For shorter style have done for while
More years than, perhaps, wise

Alcohol leads to fall
A lesson found before
When made mistake in its intake
Hangovers are a chore
Saw something so chose to bring
Something different to the table
Now I'm fielding questions
Are you really stable?

I ought to be some plastic tree
The type dogs just like to chew
Not sure why but they try
Saves the Sofa new
If Saturday relates to Saturn
God and planet both
Will we be a six-day entity?
When the 'solid' gives up the ghost

Why do Man and his chosen Lady
Seem determined to drive each other crazy?
Love until distraction
At time hate the pure attraction
Been and done so then become
The maker of the new
So can be and so can see
Them doing what once did do
Still making Marmalade – or at least trying to

Success the best when laid to rest

The old one finally got a name
Sipped from cup that some call Fame
Yet next morning felt the same
No refund available

You have a purple moment
You are the shining star
Will it last a life time?
Will it get that far?
A moment you can treasure
Beyond the normal measure
Yet just a moment that it is
So just enjoy the briefest kiss

The cynical were critical
The 'likers' turned to 'love'
The 'inferior' became hysteria
Pushed to places far above

Above that which they did know
To somewhere not chose to go
Back of mind they still know
Soon would be replaced

The 'trappings' just entrapment
The spending still stays spent
As star seekers loudly vent
They knew when they were good

The insanity of popularity
The pressure to deliver
The worry of not fulfilling
The sense of ice-cold shiver

Fame a name and hidden trouble
When in focus time does double
Even more when rise to top
How many there wish it would stop?

Summer seems a sleep away

The sun is taking Rest Days
The heating switched to own
The foragers are getting thin
Trees, there limbs are shown

But do I care? No, you see
I have Wi-Fi and strong Coffee
The fire outside may choose to hide
Yet I'll wear Sunglasses for sake of pride

Friends a plenty in different parts
Where Winter ends and Summer starts
A pop group once sang some words
At the time they seemed absurd
Now with some new technology
The Sun does always shine on TV

Caffeine kick is hard to beat
But a welcome can compete
From far off distant place
Brings a smile to this craggy face

Winter wear a woven weave
As for warmth tries to achieve
Yet the snow it does deceive
When in cold wet we can't believe

Summer seem a sleep away
When again outside can play
Snowballs not the thing of old
For a start - too bloody cold!

Wardrobe now full of stuff
That is thermal with closed cuff
Just the start but had enough
Sun! You lazy thing!

The elegance of effluents

Today I 'play' with the old grade
Surpassed by many that are new
It works for me so I can't see
My money passing to
A company near insolvency
For every company is
That spits out more for us to adore
Caught in the demand risk

The badge that catch to the 'must have'
The thing that must be shown
The 'look at me and what do see'
The treasure that I owe
The status symbol like the thimble
Small in its contents
Unlike it the 'fashion' twit
Really has no use it lent

The elegance of effluents
Merely stance in circumstance
What we keep or throw away
An indication of what willing pay
The phone replaced because last model
The up to date we wish to coddle
The Top we bought from 'fashion' shop
Now replaced by the new stock

It's just like us this modern fuss
Must prove with artificial
Cannot be in honesty
Classed as superficial
'But that's the old' so often told
To which I then reply
'Yes but works and not into quirks
So please explain a reason why?'

The epitome of Irony

The arrival at the Bus stop
Just in time to see Bus leaving
Just for once and purely by chance
The timetable it is achieving

Forgetting to adjust the Toaster
As this bread is getting older
Borderline Charcoal crime
Next time it will smoulder

The waiting for call then nature calls
Decision now must make
Discomfort on the Sofa
Or a call retake

The odd sock in the laundry
Two went in but one came out
The frantic search around the drum
The temptation to scream and shout

Waking after Bed time
Now awake again
When one should be sleeping
Another of a list of our life pains

Sour milk in coffee
Forgot to sniff it first
Or check how long have had it
Before trying to quench a thirst

The cancelled date that can't relate
For got message when were there
Did we miss an opportunity
Do we even care?

Is mystery Irony
Just clothed in a disguise?
Are we all just victims?
To something that's more wise

The ever change

The day was just another day
Chance and circumstance at play
Meant do things just go astray
I smile because I can
The light gets brighter and mood lighter
That was yesterday
Another chance with things to dance
I'll grasp it come what may

Never cared much for the failure stuff
Never minded - just got tough
When will I know enough's enough?
Who cares if we enjoy?
The reality of opportunity
The chance to be what be
No contempt in this familiarity
A welcome friend instead

When I was young, I looked at Sun
It said much more than shine
Told me of persistent
To be that Sun of mine
The distance beams had travelled
The Galaxy unravelled
To hit upon bedazzled
Cherishing the experience

I was a boy, just a toy
In the grown-up game
Just like those I own was just some clone
Just with different name
I endured as I matured
Stages done and more to go
Another step on this grand trek
Another me to show
The ever change of this strange - me a

The Film on screen

Is confusion new solution?
It's what our 'Leaders' like to spread
The lambasted so elastic
The pain within the head

The Film on screen was might have been
'The difference from the now
The characters just amateurs
To those who presently plough
Through the crazy maze we all face
The challenges we make
The need to stock until break the lock
The smash and grab to take

Every me and who you be
Are the problem not the cure?
When live to give then want to live
The others they want more

I don't know which way to go
Which direction to which face
The only real that I feel
That of outer Space

The Film on screen was might have been
The difference from the now
The characters just amateurs
To those who presently plough
Through the crazy maze we all face
The challenges we make
The need to stock until break the lock
The smash and grab to take

The old was told so changed the script
The impossible now the hit
Fantasy in which to oneself
Reality bad for mental health

The flowers of

I took a breath, I don't know why
So I let it go
I took a trip when bond did slip
So much out there was on show
Impossible became I'm possible
Happiness raised its Head
The misery became history
In to where things led

Apples in the Contentment Orchard
Bloomed from flower into fruit
The Tailor of the Tranquil feeling
Got to work and it does suit
Oranges overpowering
The denseness of despair
Coconut came calling
Became? Because I care

Before this time, I was cold
Tired of all that 'Brave and Bold'
Wanting more just to hold
More than that of which told
Now today so far away
Far in more ways true
Yet a different distance
One I can see through

The flowers of fortuitous future
Gently gave to me
Something that I needed
Yet I couldn't see
The hard cards dealt before
Are a past and nothing more
The replacement made a statement
When set foot upon, engulfed within its lure

The Ghost

I saw that ghost I hate the most
That which did for cause
I saw the me can no longer be
The actions just a source
I saw persecution in revolution
The rebel that I be
I saw reflection of intention
I saw a future me

The days then were just when
When myself would change
The days then but still with pen
The start of something strange
Yester year now holds no fear
A step just to what be
Not complete so future greet
The completion of fantasy

I saw that ghost I hate the most
For was not the me today
Just that was, somewhat lost
Just treating life as play
I grew to see what did not see
That life is not freely given
You have to earn so you learn
It's a small world for those not driven

The grain of sand

A grain of sand in rubble sat
Said to self 'guess that's that'
Once a part of a Hat
On a statue of some did pat

An idol for the idle
Who thought their world could change
Nothing new for some still do
That an object flesh can rearrange

We want your soul and want your money
Want your whole, the serious/ funny
We want you to this object follow
So can see that thing Tomorrow

If a Stork could talk the way it walks
Would it have a stutter?
Would a Coconut tree that we see
Be classified a Nutter?

At the Dock was moored a Yacht
The likes of which never seen
Wood and chrome stood out alone
For the rest was some obscene Green!

So, she sells seashells on the sea shore
Collect yourself and you'd get more
The list of things to tongue twist
When are written such a bore

A snippet here and snippet there
The Floating Marbles have no care
Then to show they me dare
They made the effort so it's fairly

Now back to that grain of sand

The greatest Choir

On one day some did say
That current has now changed
They made decisions that came to fruition
A new way they arranged

No politics for that can't fix
Just the way we do
The simple things and what they bring
The old became the new

A sonnet sang in a Sun stream
Floating in the air
A sonnet for the people
For them to then share
Radiant the rhapsody
Uplifting in unknown
The writer wrote to reach the people
With the words then shown
And down by the brook someone took
A look at that we share
They then made a startling choice
They began to care

On one day some still did play
Though playmates getting few
For the once became ensconced
The culture grew and grew

The Mother that watches over
Each and everyone
Repaired the ship upon which sail
Repaired the seams undone
The narration no irritation
When words were truly heard
The what became, a badge of shame
Bordering absurd

A sonnet sang in a Sun stream
Grew with each desire
A single voice to the new choir
Became the greatest Choir

The hotter we get

Many stumps still remain
A proud future could not attain
Cut by current, deprived of growing
With beliefs and them not knowing
None did see what's meant to be
In the forest of fickle
None did know how trees grow
When could be cut by Sickle

I look at you without a clue
Of what it really means
I look at that so isolated
Separation before past teens
When racism hides division
Caught and taught by all sides
The barbs no less brutal
Whichever tone our Hides

Determined be to truly see
Beyond the attitude
Judging by the person
Not that, at best, is rude
We lost our fur to hide it
But we have been this way since venturing
Just adapting to the climate
With ourselves not mentioning

The hotter we get darker
The colder paler be
Yet inside we are same tribe
If only fools would see
The migration situation
Threw new challenges to face
Yet are we and will always be
The same Human Race

The hounds

The hounds that sound on past ground
No call to arms they be
The new can do what once went through
Now just memory
The past a blast that could not last
The present showed its face
The future strains at its reins
A new uncharted space

The things that were now concern
Past a blast that could not last
The been and done with pain and fun
Now belongs to someone young
Now I'm told I'm getting old
Maybe true with what been through
A sentence often told
The fact is nothing new

Please, please release
Me from this crime of mine
Not that of life for have gorgeous Wife
Just the curse that can think can write a line
Stopped dreaming of what could not be
Started thinking that reality
The things that I could achieve
If only in self I believe

The images we paint

On streets that I grew
On the same ones that I knew
On the streets that were a past
No-one knows me as I pass

Envelope in how to cope
Parcel of a bygone time
A history of the once me
A reflection not a crime

The pavement now looks different
Somehow it looks too hard
To get some rest if that's the best
With a bed made of others discarded card

I now look at those now there
I have a certain care
Knowing in the showing
None choose to be that way or there

Bygone times in life of mine
Streets that once did walk
New the shops at which I stop
New the people with whom talk

Sometimes through pain you can attain
That shove needed but never received
Sometimes you have to see something worse
To own the new achieved

An attitude can be solution
Or greatest enemy
An attitude too confident
As bad as that so rude

Confidence is innocent
Until we wish to taint
By the way we show ourselves
The images we paint

The innocence of our ignorance

Stars do glimmer briefly
In sky and on the screen
How many still in real time?
If you know what mean
And they just smiled for a while
Posing as requested
Whilst others out there struggling
Others sorely tested

I woke this morning and what did I find
Everything has changed for Human kind
Not the place it used to be
That consigned to 'once was me'
Yet I still hear the night creatures
The us, the them and all
Still aware of faraway share
As around our world social media draws the call

Calibri light or Times New Roman?
Seems the modern task
When wish to say something
An inert thing will ask
Wishing for some better days
Wishing that 'old' again
Wishing I felt comfortable
Wishing I felt sane

When Sun rose in a morning
Moon it showed at night
People cared what they shared
When some sense of wrong and right
But you do not care for how I feel
When can do what do
You think are 'free' as I do me
If only that was true

The innocence of our ignorance
For are servants in disguise
To those with no conscience
And the trade which plies

The joy of the Creatives

The rain it wakes while still darkness
Tattoo on window pane
The hunt for that position
As under blanket you now thrive
Sleep again will be a pain
Want but cannot get
Until gone the visions wrong
So them you just let

Those awkward spaces with blanked out faces
Of body gone but not memory
The ship that slipped into the dip
Could not see what would be
Those bygone times that crossed some lines
Yet legal with what you wear
The us or them with lethal pen
At aftermath you stare

The complexity of misery
That's there but cannot share
That part of 'art' long ago did start
The burden we now wear
The striving of surviving
In any shape we choose
The now cost of that we lost
That sometimes can bemuse

We are all masochist
When we do reflect
The pain for gain can drive insane
When not yet we get
Another day no longer play
More the obsessed mission
We will pay, if not today
If it doesn't make fruition

The jo of the Creatives

The joy to employ

Is my intention a direction?
You will just have to decide
Am I paranoid of the void?
The ultimate in hide
I need to feed and see where lead
No worries where it goes
In black and white in plain sight
The diversity of me it shows

Sometimes will take a short break
Then back again to pester
A reaction to inaction
The Marbles start to fester
The pen again as and when
The Lightning of the Word!
The way we say when at play
Message sent with ears not heard

Feel the real of letters still
Spoken just a token
For need to show so that they know
What will then be spoken
I dream a dream for scribbling seen
The message not the name
For no joke to thought provoke
The rebellious and tame

The joy to employ as a toy
Yet mean something to someone
They treat it as a feat
Me? I'm having fun

The last Goodbye

The last Goodbye that I made
Was filled with sorrow and of hate
Sorrow for them and hate for another
Someone who did change his fate

The last Goodbye to innocent
Different when just a something
Brought home when took one did know
A whole new meaning it did bring

Used to take a certain satisfaction
Of a job well done
Culmination of tough training
Then part of me – it came undone

Until receiving don't appreciate giving
Don't know Life until Death meet
Can't know you until tested truly
Can't feel victory until felt defeat

The Hubble Bubble nothing but trouble
Until within you do toil
Be it in your own known spaces
Be it on a foreign soil

Hark the Herald of the hearsay
For am someone you don't know
Hark the stranger that faced danger
Held a friend as life did go

Learnt somethings oh so precious
On one past unforgettable day
Learnt that I was not so mighty
Nor is anyone that likes to say

To value anything has two sides
To appreciate must know the cost
To be wise is to try to avoid it
When something precious unbidden lost

Tip of heavy rain

Raspberry or Strawberry?
What the chance of choice
Blackberry or Blueberry
All do have a voice
Thick or thin the cut begins
When talking Marmalade
Not a decision is the mission
When people they parade

And you might be living comfortably
Well congratulations and best wishes too
But do you ask how are others doing?
Take some time for what go through
When treat yourself to evening drink
Do you stop and think?
For that shot more than shorter
Someone wishes for clean water

We chuck money when Charities call
If are lucky get some not all
In other hands most does fall
Yet still we give one and all
A rebel some will say
When I disagree with way
Giving for the living
Is just something we pay

Isn't it neat to self-treat?
That thing you see in shop
Yet someone lives under gun
Surely this should stop
The good life should not have strife
If your gain is someone's pain
The one's we see on posh TV
The tip of heavy rain

To challenge the somewhat challenged

Challenged be for someone challenging me
To write each day for week plus one
It will not change for I am strange
Writing is just fun

The sugar cube spoke to the tube
'How do you bend your edges so?'
Tube did reply 'I don't even try
It's just the way I grow'

Nursery rhymes of bygone times
Would make no sense if modernised
That great Gun that fell from wall
Humpty Dumpty would be surprised!

Once again without refrain
The one turned to inner feeder
Spouting out without doubt
A mystery to the reader

How many dots make a lot?
When a few grew to that new
How many words sound absurd?
When of pronunciation have no clue

Almost there so soon will share
Before it is too late
Sorry you poor devils
This is the first of eight!

To do or not to do

Cussing Cornflakes on the intake
Cussing Toast the most
Cussing drink, through down sink
Because was not full roast

Cussing view that isn't new
Cussing every day
Cussing start as Home part
Because it is my way

This grumpy sod now does plod
Again, to work, with same lame jerk
Jerks Ville here I come
With wave of hand I join their Band
Until back to where have fun

The things we must to earn a crust
With no love nor real intention
Tempers boil as we toil
Should be banned by Geneva Convention

Sit and tap the same old crap
Spreadsheet screwing Head
Projected not expected
Wish was back in Bed

The average day some might say
Others wish they could
Some try to find for that kind
Some say that life's too good

Way it is they would miss
So, thank you but no thanks
Odd cash in hand is so grand
As Benefits go through Banks

We live to work not work to live

To just see

The gathering was an assessment
Assortment of but all the same
For came from just one species
Science gave it name
One stood at the Podium
Beside another sat
A third shivered as in Winter
A fourth no pet could pat

One spoke for them all
Them and many more
The Hall was filled to bursting point
With more outside its Door
The gathering was about equality
Of sex, colour and of creed
Yet these had another class
That also had that need

"This is all we came for
This is all we got
Acceptance in the wider world
Really means a lot
This is not ambition
This is destiny
For apart from some small things
They are the same as me

We rise to the challenges
Of life and living things
With light heart we make a start
Not knowing what it brings
We add to the flavour
Just like a shade or tone
We occur everywhere
Everywhere you roam

Judge me and us as you wish
Wish us to then judge you
Just be aware of the small matter
Sometimes difficult how things do
Yet as yourself 'are we so different?
From that beside you stand
Are we some form of alien?
Upon your Earth did land'

Yvette here you call Désactivé
Stefan there you call Behindert
Madeline there you call Gestremd
Kua Monokia you call Bert
Yet look at all their first names
Are they something some recognise?
That is because they are another like yourself
If you would just open eyes"

The gathering fell into silence
A guilty embarrassing accord
Then with heart felt feelings
Each of them did applaud

I was once of that crowd
Now that speaker spoke for me
I have seen much deeper
Though find it difficult to just see

To play with TSA

The act that isn't fact
The things that two do know
The misconception without inspection
The rumours that then grow
The opinion strong that is so wrong
The choice then to ignore
The measure of the treasure
The one that you adore

Something said in the silence
Something said can heal
Something said in the awkward
Something of way do feel
Something in the void of sound
Something that shatters it
Something aimed with good intentions
Something that does hit

All that's been does something mean
All been through now not so new
All have had have still got
All that means still means a lot
All that wished served on silver dish
All I was now something old
All rewards for being bold

To say a something that means nothing
To say a thing in play
To say in visual but not visible
To spell as an act
Play with TSA

To play

When human stopped and sat
Decided clothes and, perhaps, Hat
Little then did they know
Just the trouble they would sow
When I.T. came to be
Could the confusion then did see
Various becomes delirious
Laughing now with variety

This Spine of mine seems to be fine
The rest is just a test
To aches and pain I show disdain
Believe in being best
Best of me and see what see
Whatever happens just move on
Had a visit to the options
Both decided not yet belong

To play Digeridoo the whole way through
An anthem would be something new
Maybe on a spare day
For the playing have no clue
Challenges are challenging
Accepted not for all
A special ear overriding fear
When does hear the call

Shadows lurk, wait to be seen
Stored within strong case
They were then and this is now
Why on them a moment waste?
Innus yourus Faceus
Said some person long ago
Not sure if they knew what say
But message holds so thus so

To Right Until Something Trouble

Time to test the tempting
Need some wise advice
Who are calling? Names keep falling
Trust does come with price

'Et tu Brute' Caesar was alleged to say
The tribulations of trust
Yet without we merely doubt
So, in some and somethings must

Now we get to heart of matter
So many stories of success
So many choices made
So many for the best

Maelstrom in the making
Or the golden key?
Yet in trust we sometimes must
Then see which will be

'Ego autem confidebat'
As does pass the lips
Some repay with like kind
Some it merely slips

Trust not just a money thing
Set up for another Day
Trust is more important
More important than just what say

To self-imprison

I read something that made me think
How some do in something sink
Not uncommon for do know
Some who which to this place go

Darkness deep the drifting can
Solitude one sin of man
Isolation a strange sensation
When all are part of just one Nation
To self-imprison I do try
To understand that reason why
Do not fault for do not know
Why one chose that path to go

Alert must be for if do see
The one who thinks that all is lost
Just one act for impact
Can make pay the ultimate cost

Nothing's ever easy
Though some get sense of failure more
Becoming something physical
Driving deep into their core

They know too well that

Darkness deep the drifting can
Solitude one sin of man
Isolation a strange sensation
When all are part of just one Nation
To self-imprison I do try
To understand that reason why
Do not fault for do not know
Why one chose that path to go

Look, learn but never lecture

To Shangri-La in Hover Car

The children's playground in the Park
Now just seating, on safety grounds
Gone the sight of active kids
On a screen now come their sounds
The 'Piggy Bank' now 'Junior savings'
They like to use their money as well
Almost everything HP or mortgage
How pay back? None can tell

The corner shop to which once did pop
Now a mini Mart
To just buy one was so much fun
Now you need a cart!
Chains a pain when all sell the same
Price fixed to strict adherence
Layout and goods so understood
Matched in their appearance

The TV that once with five channels
Expanding up from original two
Now has more than days in month
February with March too
More people now than work to give them
Robotics seemed such good idea
Now the talk is when not if
A.I. deems our lives too dear

To Shangri-l in Hover Car
Mechanical Maid for mundane stuff
Got so far (but not the car)
Life now getting tough
A thing for everything
And for everything a thing
Gaggles of new Gadgets
No finance them to bring

To the same place

The different abled went to shop
So made way to the Bus stop
Not the casual stroll of others
Not the child's skip and hop
Just being what being
Unconscious of what others seeing
Just independent, getting on
Unaware some think this wrong

That drop in tone when not alone
For we are now encroaching
Upon the space, that 'able space'
As our paths are now approaching
By birth or life, by Surgeons knife
We are not the same
Yet we are, with same brush tarred
We even have a name

And do we care that they stare
Because we look so out of place
Their confusion no illusion
It's painted on their face
Do we feel should run and hide
Do we take it in our stride?
We can't change the way we are
We've more chance if wish on Star

The different abled with inner smile
Used to this for a while
Embarrassment or ignorant
Shun their likes by country mile
Not all do, that is true
Some have sense with which to know
Whatever way we live and play
To the same place we all go

Tomorrow

Tomorrow will be perfect
Tomorrow will be grand
Tomorrow I'll be recognised
Have the world eating out my hand

Tomorrow will be amazing
Tomorrow will surprise
Tomorrow I'll be careful
Tomorrow I'll be wise

Tomorrow is something I dream of
Tomorrow I will rule
Alas there is no Tomorrow
Today I'm just a fool

An orchard

An orchard of origins
An orchard of unique
An orchard of occasional
The orchard I do seek

Amongst the maelstrom of malevolence
Amongst the seas of suffered
Amongst the lakes of liquid lies
Amongst the caves of callous cries

An orchard much like Orchids
An orchard of surprise
An orchard of understanding
An orchard of the wise

Tomorrow's dawn the current pawn

Tomorrow dawned on Today's memory
Like a flutter from a Candle
Braced itself as matured
Confident could handle

Today did pay a last look
Before yesterday became
Much like that before it
Though none were quite the same

The parts that dross would soon be lost
The enjoyable remembered
At least for the short term
However, some parts would be embered

Pages turn as more we earn
Experiences to keep
Cranium a Gymnasium
When learning curve is steep

So, Tomorrow's dawn the current pawn
As in sleep we amble
Nothing set for fate won't let
Every breath a gamble

Onwards us brave travellers
This worth more than pittance
Whatever is, it's a gift
It is our existence

What will be? A lottery
A game we like to play
Everyone a winner
When Tomorrow's now our Yesterday

Tongue twister

Llanfairpwllgwyngyllgogerychwyrndrobwllllantysiliogogogoch
What the hell were they thinking!
More a question should we ask
What the heck were they smoking/ drinking?

I could not even begin to say it
Yet alone write free hand
I know that they are somewhat crazy
Those in the Welsh land

Fifty-eight characters
This village has on sign
Longest place name in UK
The land of Sheep and once of Mines

No idea what it means
I am guessing was a bet
Someone had some spare letters
This is what did get

St Mary's Church in the Hollow of the White Hazel near a Rapid
I am now informed
So much for simple Bromley
Of which mine was adorned

Do Welsh folk have detachable jaws?
To get tongue around that name
Guess they needed to amuse themselves
In the land of rain

Trivia hysteria

Finders, keepers – railway sleepers
Trainspotting not my thing
All the night to make tracks right
Irritation brings
Platform standing, carriage banding
For some but not for all
Commuter weaving, standers seething
Hunting closet for 'natures call'

The random friction of attrition
Sometimes submission's best for life
Deadly dealings, happenstance healing
Especially when foe is Wife
Two wrongs a right they don't make
Sometimes best though just to take
When alternative at worst can break
Take the bullet for

Little Jack Smaller wishes was taller
Yet each size has benefits
Smaller first to know when flood levels grow
Taller first the rain it hits
Tammy Tall made opposite call
Finding clothes that fit a snag
Thought was wise when bought Men's size
Until was compared to one in Drag

Lazy not so crazy
If Muscle strain a pain
New jobs make with excess intake
New furniture an employment gain
Ridicule the choice of fool
Their vocabulary insanitary
Blinkered vision a contradiction
For the wise and wary

Truth

I lost my religion when I found me
Found the person I could be
All the hate, insanity
I found the Devil inside me
I lost faith and this is true
When found out what I could do
All that anger passing through
Am still healing, building new

Still not worship anything
Seen the misery that can bring
Seen the goodness and the bad
Seen the ones that make it mad

I lost my following of Belief
Lost that feeling of relief
Cried to it sometimes, got no answer
Guess had me down as a onetime chancer
I respect those who follow
Though some of them leave feeling hollow
Those who twist without pause
Turn to justify their own cause

Slander me if you wish
Opinions are a personal dish
I will still greet you with a smile
The hate in me been gone some while

I lost something but found another
Something words could not smother
I lost religion but found grace
Found the strength to new face
Face the fact that I am me
I am what was meant to be
I now view reality
All the good and the insanity

Tunes Triumphant

Enya entered my environment
Swiftly followed by a Valens
Then came some misspelt Beetles
Bowie said 'Let's Dance'
The London Philharmonic
Precedes a Blind French Lady
Steppenwolf did their thing
Then was Lady Gaga - maybe
Posted tunes and some chat rooms
Mixed with Radio
Long live the pleasure give
Eclectic is the way to go

Bob sang of some Buffalo Soldiers
Madness sane of House
Twins begin in accent sing
From the land of Famous Grouse
Alternating current
Gave a wakeup call
Nena sang of balloons
Around time that wall did fall
The Cure sang of love on Friday
Ceassars told us to Jerk it out
Sheryl walked a winding road
Many want to scream and shout

Another day and it does play
Music to with which I muse
Random but reaction
Never will confuse
Of Monsters and Men, they did pen
Those of Little Talks
Everyone is different
Yet same path each walks

When different

Stood in rain and took the pain
When will sun rise again?
The mystery of epilepsy
No answers do I gain
The odd bruise just to confuse
The state from which do come
Resignation the sensation
Oh well, another one

I used to be what now can't be
Different Mountains climbing
The voices of the silent
Now are so inviting
I never forget that which were
Most now meet the same
Ripped from them apart from pen
In many a different name

I 'look' around at that profound
I marvel in despair
For one thing all have that binds us
The will to for others still they care
Every single day in a new way
The 'have knots' path to travel
They are at the core of things
They will it unravel

Who are you if have a clue?
Are you different or the same?
Who are now from what have been?
Is attitude so lame?
We can all be a pinnacle
A landmark to record
We are treasure beyond measure
Our past couple not afford

We could have a day or week
We could have a month or year
When 'different' should have no embarrassment
When 'different' have no fear

When her song

With acknowledgement to Blondie

She sang a song
Of union, of Union City Blues
How would that go down today?
With the views within the News

Disparity and misery
The topics we promote
Side-lined is 'just be kind'
Whilst incompetents they gloat

Some will savour a certain flavour
To them a pure attraction
They hide within as play the sin
The one label as distraction

One more to store to the old folk lore
A passage with intent
Those who wise prefer ears to eyes
When leisure time is spent

Atomic something chronic
Turned delivery into destruction
Now the race to travel Space
Time warp with no instructions

Did Sunday Girl take a twirl?
As exploded on the World
A picture be her face to see
When her song she heard

When I look into those eyes

Mauve the mellow of rendering
Bliss the blue of acceptance
Red the riot, peacefully,
Orange with no repentance

Colour, just a colour
A one we know as grow
But do we relate to each state?
Have we the strength to show?

Hidden pain because we refrain
The worry that seem weak
When a 'norm' since when were born
Acceptance we all seek

When I look in those eyes at what try to hi
I see more than you do tell
I see the inner of the beginner
Living a lifetime Hell

No more for sure you must endure
The solitude you now feel
You are not a lesser person
You are something real

The hands of clock are sweeping
Maybe sweep away
The anguish of this morning
As start another day

Not alon and never alone
Every time you breathe
You ar always welcome here
Every time you choose to leave

All that done was just someone
All that do is you
All the things you now bring
Part of getting through

Sun is done

I came and went and some time spent
In the place now wish to return
Found rewards that deserve applause
Far greater than did earn
Give and take and mistakes make
Then and now is true
We are not the perfect one
These things we all do

Errors are for teaching
As better strive through reaching
That next step in what can get
Knowledge we are beseeching
To come to us with no great fuss
Just a pleasure that can feel
The filling of the obvious gaps
That is joy so real

Academic is just a word
When compared to Life
With all the things we do not know
All the hardship and the strife
Yes, it is a bonus
Education gives us hope
Filling with a barrier
More effort now to cope

The vagaries of insanity
The search for the pure cure
The resilience to make nonsense
That others must ensure
Make me sweet Marshmallow
Make me that perfect one
Maybe one day you will make me
When our Sun is done

When the future appears to suck

Did a deed your pen then feed?
Did an act make impact?
Did a line come across so fine?
It made you change your tact
Randomness is blissfulness
When open to review
That startling new opportunity
To change the things you do

The ink does flow, as you know
Another new creation
The top of crop or just a flop
A mind-melt situation
Who would be with sanity?
A lover of the ink
The pitfalls surpass
The Publishers calls
Yet onwards still we go

If you and me a story be
What the sort a reader see?
Will it be some fantasy?
Will it be reality?
As you do what you do
Not through wish but to get through
Yet similarities hand a clue
Been so long can't claim as new

Are we superheroes?
Bravely to the fore?
Are we just determined?
Ambitious, nothing more

Stop!

Enough of the analysing
Yes I know that's quite surprising
We are we and free to be
Now let that thought sink is

Happy Inking

Where am I?

I don't know where am going now
But am glad for not knowing
The things to see a surprise will be
The pleasure in their showing
I don't know what future holds
Adventure in the possible
I don't know but one thing
A future means I'm able

If we knew at the beginning
What we know now
Would we change a single thing?
Would, could and if how?
If we were as bright as think
Why the current state
I don't know how to grow
When I can't relate

Sentiments of past spend
Looking back with a smile
The journey to where am now
Took for sure many a mile

Where am I?
Just biding time
Counting Crows and Pidgeon's
Where am I?
I a content place
Got a future and a mission

Nothing we gain when seek the pain
Nothing I understand
All to have when feeling glad
When welcome comes with open Hand

A thousand miles upon smiles
Have journeyed to this date
A thousand more I have before
A satisfying state

Where in this

Oh, dearie me who made I.T.?
Befuddled and bemused
The complexity of variety
Left now totally confused
Upgrade and trade a problem made
When born before a certain date
Need to do this and that whilst still sat
Not throwing quite irate

A call to school and admit are fool
When they make it sound so simple
On the face of Internet race
You are but a Pimple
'Yes, press this and look what see
Go to something that it shows
Tap on that to mend the gap
Your knowledge now it grows

Just buying that providing
By the ones that have in store
Nothing grand to hold this hand
Just talk with foreign shore
Add to this a subtle twist
Need to do that like to do
Happy When without hassle
Could enjoy not techno new

When get irate at present state
Things whizzing here and there
Acceptance for now circumstance
Just it really doesn't care
A bi of a minor growing major
The longer it goes on
Needing just one answer
'Where in this do I belong?'

Ian Wilcox

756

Who decides?

The Biscuit crumbles, the Cookie bend
The information sends round the bend
Foreign cuisine now microwave
Yet to each other can't behave

Digits growing stronger
Than the rest of self
Yet so many now
Jog to improve health

Speech is done through microphone
In the new gadget now own
Cooking is so boring
Tap a takeaway instead

Nuclear age now old news
Barely mentioned as peruse
The current feed of one's choice
Slightly different with their voice

Laugh I do because so true
The modern mystery
Need to be a Rocket scientist
To understand what see

Am no that old I can't remember
Lighting fire in cold December
When things hard but plain to see
When had real in reality?

For a reason I don't know
Things did change as we grow
To something not know before
As we chance to explore

Never met the perfect person
That may change in this thing strange
Just one question at suggestion
Who decides on 'perfect'

I stood still as child related
Their fantasy to which am fated
Deep inside I want to cry
Burning question is just why

I want the best for them of course
Yet I doubt that path we go
Reliance is compliance
We reap the seeds and so

So we lose the thing which born
A statistic not a name
Are we just consumed by luxury?
Like reward without the pain

Pain that comes from earning
Not money but hard graft
Graft itself soon history
In the techno current path

Who is she?

She walked the Halls with walls tall
She saw nothing on display
The pictures and the Tapestry
Where all these but didn't see
She walked the Halls of beck and calls
She was a robot to demand
She just did as they bid
With cracked and blistered Hand

Erase to days so far away
When things did have some meaning
Reverse this curse for can't be worse
From her others gleaning
The number not the person
She now has become
If have to be a number
Should make it number one

Slowly things a changing
Slowly rearranging
Slowly yet most surely
The same person found themselves
Slowly but relentlessly
Slowly veils did lift
Slowly for was honestly
She is but a Gift

Not the Gift to be bought and sold
Not the Slave of times old
Not a toy to employ
Not anything but the same
The abuse became confused
Then but now no longer
Took a chance and made her stance
Towards one who is much stronger

Wild and free

The scent that seeps so seamlessly
From flora that attract
The begin to feel on skin
Nature's own impact
Those stolen moments to just enjoy
Away from daily grind
The restoration of the equation
The calming then can find

The frivolity of who we be
To our place we earn
The bits we miss as ride the twist
The pleasure that we spurn
The child at feet of Mother in street
The gaiety in their stride
Short I know but it will grow
Lengthening to wide

The tooting horn designed to warn
Yet not in this situation
More a case of need of haste
The waiting's irritation
The greeting nod as to Home trod
From one you do not know
Courtesy doe come for free
Freely do they show

Wild and free I wish to be
If only can return
For too much a task as such
To the friendships I did earn
Lay nobody down in final Town
Unless by natural cause
Then good luck as soil does suck
Pass to the new without a pause

What could we be if we were free?
Free from self-restraints
That self-imposed that we won't show
Not that which hatred taints

Wild is the Child

Acquiesced in absence
Of a true reason why
Lacking chance of progress
By unwillingness to try

So easy to say and hope go away
So easy to stay still
Accept what get with no regret
Your prospective never know you will

Arrogance a circumstance?
Or just a thing we choose
'Superiority is inferiority
When weighed with what we lose

A flash in pan not the plan
But flint refused to play
Your Musket just a Trumpet
Now what tunes will say?

Humility we often see
But how much is a ruse?
A means when needs to succeed
Then all will confuse

A trai to hate in equal state
Honesty a revelry
For sure will find out more
The truth we then do see

Wild is the Child
Who knows no perversion?
I love that Child

Will you let me in?

If all today you just need to say
I am me but in own way
Then are blessed for unlike rest
You have found hey ho in Hay
Can you hear the pumping of my piffle?
Can you see cray with zee?
Can you then cut through garbage?
To discover the real me?

A loner is just alone if wish
A curry in a hurry
Just food and not a Dish

I walked alone for did suit me
Then I changed what have
I gave up independently
When walked a different path

Boulevard may seem hard
When on it you do lay
Yet on the street you often meet
Occurrence that will stay

No regrets, not just yet
The learning was the treasure
Beyond words that are heard
Beyond all types of measures

If I follow a start that leads to your Heart
Will you let me in?
Then the grace of filled empty space
At least it would be start

Will occasion be a fancy?
Or just another failure
The questions ask before commit to task
The idioms of nature

With distance are divided

Chicken run towards the Sun
Cockerel said its piece
Pig had thrill with its swill
Random is release

Day is dawning to bring morning
Daughter said Hello
Such a thrill when have time to kill
Here light still has far to go

Their evening spent with a friend
Chat by typing words
Tapping while we're rapping
Tick, tick, tick is heard

Another day with which to play
Game not yet decided
Probably same but see
When with distant are divided

Senility sneaking

Did I have my Coffee yet?
Getting old so I forget
My excuse and stick to it
For another Caffeine hit

The clic and grind not of my mind
My joints are getting vociferous
A tweeky leak as muscles speak
An Orchestra now serious

Senility sneaking as to you am speaking
My eyes trying to find keys
Need Fountain of Youth to tell the truth
Help me find it please!

With soft skin

The awkward ascension to anonymous
The perils that unravel
The profusion of confusion
The further one does travel

The kaleidoscope of long-lost hope
The fading of things past
The wish to be simply free
The hope that this won't last

Fame of name is not a game
More a burden true
Inviting those uninvited
To criticise what do

With soft skin one did begin
Now a sheet of steel
Only when from those known
Do you actually feel

The want is poisoned by ignorance
Only hearing the good side
The pressure of maintaining
They just choose to hide

To be famous have no wish
To be normal is my dish
Just the same apart from name
In sea am just a Fish

No more that once ambition
Learned the burden that it carries
When sell yourself for recognition
The cost when stardom marries

With tots and tuts

If I schleck would you peck at the speck, what the heck was that!
With tots and tuts, caution! May contain Nuts!
Mommy!! I need my dried Wombat droppings!

The Mac a'Roons they knew no tunes
Unlike their cousins the Maracas
One liked type of Biscuit
The other a type of Tapas

Why do Men grow facial hair?
Women, they got wise
They just change their Makeup
To aid with a disguise

When Symbology met symmetry
A new fad they created
Balanced out the horns or snout
Together with Crowns that weren't Gold plated

Which way now? Will I throw in towel?
Marbles just won't sleep
Maybe let them get a Pet
And in there with them let keep

Digeridoos and Kangaroo poos
They want one of them bouncy things!!
Guess no rest might be the best
Providing none of them now sings!

Within the comfort of my shelter

Moonlight made a magic happen
Diffused light hid the scars
Less the volume of pollution
Spewing out from countless cars
Moonlight gave a sense of being
Time in daylight cannot get
A subtle pause in pandemonium
A brief change to now reflect

The things have done and still to do
The old experience and experience new
The recharging of more than transport
The absorbing of what have been taught
A clock it ticks and I can hear it
A fox outside becomes a din
Train I hear through nearby Station
Yes, these sounds while still within

Within the comfort of my shelter
Notice that I don't call Home
For though has walls and a ceiling
Here inside I am alone
Communication a strange sensation
When can see and hear but cannot touch
The part of me that will always be
The better half I love so much

Quiet no descends again
As with idle twiddle pen
Half-awake and half asleep
A blissful state I wish could keep
'Alas poor Yorick' one once wrote
I wonder how that writer failed?
Did any of his contemporaries acknowledge?
I guess that man much less cared

Within the Stations

When secular becomes inferior
When gravitas is in the mass
Then we should because we could
Begin to try again
When reflection not perfection
Just a stepping stone to start
When the difference see leads not to misery
We remove a from that apart

You could have red hair, I wouldn't care
Three fingers instead of four
Walk with stoop, neck stretched by hoops
Engage upon world tour
The nothingness we could possess
With regards to separation
The platitudes of different latitudes
A mistaken situation

So many languages spoken
Yet language but a token
Let inner now be woken
Restrictions once - now broken
The same air we all share
The same blood we bleed
The variations within the Stations
Is simply what we feed

Apathy a tragedy
Too many have we seen
Let's have life and not just knife
With the edge so keen
Misty eyes, throat sore with cries
Not the greatest look
Let's rejoice all one voice
Acceptance all it took

Shared Pain

The sight of pain weighs heavily on the watching few,
As they struggle to puzzle about what to do.
Each groan and increase in breathing rate.
Hurts them and you, as each moan echo's round the room.
You whisper, 'They will be here soon.'
Inwardly urging 'hurry up what is keeping them?'
A pat, a kiss, a massage to ease the pain viciously attacking you.
At last, they are here, busily attending every symptom.
Pain lets go; breath returns to normal rhythm.
Relief and gentle laughter pervade the room.
Yet, we know we are only temporary winners,

A Holiday Sea Ride

I hope the sea is calm and the sky is blue.
I hope the food is delicately scrumptious.
I hope the ties of friendship reach out and include you.
I hope the music moves you to gather memories brand new.
I hope the sunsets fading lulls you to sleep ready for the dawn.
I just hope you enjoy each of the next eight days while you are gone.

I will be waiting to hear all your stories on your return.

WobblingPen
All my love
Mum. P. Xxxxxxxxxx

What is wrong?

The light has gone from your day,
What is wrong?
The smile that always used to stay
Has disappeared now gone.
The songs you used to sing
Have lost their cheerful ring.

Nothing is so bad
To keep you down for long
Let me hug you close,
With kisses and hugs,
Return your face to norm.
Nothing now is wrong.

I have ears

I have ears for decoration.
Not a sound can I hear.
It has created great limitations
Fear nearly always follows me.

Within four walls I feel safe protected.
Why am I so isolated, neglected?
Smiles I share in plenty
To have none returned.

It is a barrier between us
The sounds you take for granted,
Sounds we long to hear.
Is there hope? Yes!

Signing is here.

WobblingPen
*This was written for those who were born without hearing, or
who lost it over time, injury, or disease. Sadly, many are ridiculed
for the loss of their hearing, which is not their fault.*

Torment

While the world in torment flys,
You and I cling together
With kindness and love over flowing.
Trying to shut out all that is sad.
With endearments and caresses,
And hopes that things will get better.
Reluctant to untangle and become one,
To face the world to see what can be done.
Take care darling till we are again together.

What will I Find to do with you?

Oh, what will I find to do with you, with you,
Around the world to help make things seem better, better.
I am searching high and low for words to tease
Your sad face into smiles to make you better.

So give me that smile I would walk miles and miles to see.
I would stand in your gaze and troubles would fade away.
You would give me your hand and I would gather us close together.
Synchronised we would glide round the room moving in gentle rhythm.

Is it a smile I see, peeping up at me, revealing the girl who was hidden.
My heart starts to beat like a drum all must hear, dancing near.
When your face is raised to mine with a smile other too can see.
We light up the room as your smile chases away the dreary gloom.

Now our spirits are joined sharing laughter joy,
Spilling our delight out for others to share
Sending smiles round the room better and better.
It is something we can do so well together.

WobblingPen

770

CoRoNa PARANOIA

Caused by Coronavirus, the coroner's cornered
Overwhelmed, but not yet defeated
Times wear darkness
Pockets now holed, whole
Humour sneaks behind the door of despair
And gets our mirth in overdrive
Till we forget the virulent stranger
That brings boils on the butt of humanity
My landlord came this golden grey morn'
Before the first yawn of the sun
He knocked thrice
I coughed twice
He took off like the wind
For now the overdue rent can wait
A neighbour saw a bottled beer named 'Corona'
She ran out helter skelter cussing like a sailor in heat
My brother withdrew his twins
from the prestigious Corona Institute
That was hitherto famed to lead many to Ivy League
Someone's named 'Obanikoro' moniker as aliased 'Koro'
Went to church to baptize his name to Victor
He speaks in tongues now
My wife from the village has refused to answer phone calls
She's scared that a phone call from an infected person
May infect her person with Covid
So should I not listen to the Corona Church Crooners Choir's CD?
Their songs are inspiring
And not the dreaded disease carriers
So, CD is not a code name for CoviD
Better not destroy CD on sight
To cover the nose with an antibiotic virus CD
Is not the antidote though,
Save if we are computed or robotized
The policeman gave my son, Chase a chase
Caught, cuffed and cornered
Junior sneezed and the cuffs came off
The policeman ran like a cheetah
Forgetting his batch in tow
So, stay safe, smile and keep the flame of faith flaring ferociously
It is well even inside the well

William Warigon

The Tear That Tears Years Of Smiles

A lone tear sits stately
Like a prince upon her cheek
Forlorn, she's sure lonely
The tear like pin, does prick

Many years of happiness stacked
Upon a smarmy loveliness
Come crumbling down into the dark
Brooding basks in darkness

Hope looking like a cheated lover
Lies on the talc supine like my great Granny's breasts
Against the very sad eyed clover
Trials stand tall to try her with variety of tests

She hears hollow thunders whimpering
Her weak heart with strong thudding's
Against the chancel arch of matins reaping's
Then spring hiccups with sudden eagering

Of a new nave gives her a hope from the pulpit
And faith smiles her way with un-feral glee
She'll clamber from this depression pit
And into the arms of glorious bliss she'll flee.

William Warigon

A Majestic Ass

The fortuned Ass
Got a holy pass
The Ass was as meek Moses
Favoured above its bosses
Upon whose back sat the genteel Virgin Lady
For she is gentle, full of grace
Carrying the immaculately conceived Baby
That brought wonder and praise

How the horses' eyes greened
As the Ass swished and preened
Each step measured, tailored in majestic grins
Carrying the Carrier of world's atrocious sins
To the cold, old and rusty barn
Where a manger's anticipation was clear
Grasses and cobwebs, not a royal yarn
Adorned the holy birthplace we hold dear
For fortune favoured this Ass
Whose humility heralded a new dawn
In the Child's birth, a heavenly pass
Given to our tepid world, long forlorn

The Ass' spirit shone through
Rugged and beautified by the Message
To save me, to save you too
Joyfully opening that brand new page

William Warigon

Goodbye

Goodbye may be the hardest word
It pierces like a two-edged sword
We were walking together yesterday
I am mourning your departure today

I did cry you a river
I'm down with fever
Fevered with maelstrom of emotions
'Am confused by myriad of questions

My tears won't make the graveyard a vineyard
My bleeding heart won't stop the pain of sorrow's dart
Memories we've woven can't be stolen
By death's cruel hands that are molten

Death so cruel, so sadistic
Its sting is so destructive
But I rise above its intention
I have come to a realization

At the doorstep of my thoughts
I review my many trodden roads
Knowing that I shall see you again, soon
Where we will be in spiritual honeymoon

Ensconced in a mansion of our choices
Enthralled by songs with cherubic voices
The place where there's no pain, death and sorrow
But a lovely today and an even lovelier tomorrow

My tears've made me even stronger
What kills me not, makes me stronger
Invisible Arms around me
They comfort, protect me

So, I march on in the dour face of perdition
I laugh at the heat of hell with derision
I course through the seas of pain
With panache, again and again

I am not even invincible
But He that is invisible
Has bolstered me with such unmatched strength
I can walk through the valley of the shadow of death

With my head held high
Above the silver cloud
Branding my halo to the horned
This victory was fought for; I won.

William Warigon

Cleopatra

Cleopatra and one hundred shimmering emerald-green colored
Crocodiles are rhythmically dancing in the lovely Ms. P's front lawn.

Pearls presented to Ms. P. in kaleidoscopic colors are shaped as pretty boys;
additionally an invitation to travel to the brilliant moon at the midnight hour.

Enthralled, the ravishingly gorgeous Ms. P pinches
herself to see if she is dreaming.

Dazzling pink clouds open and one hundred gold
bubbles are preparing for the midnight journey.

Cleopatra and the lovely Ms. P are adorned in metallic satin minidress
festooned with emerald-green pearls. Irresistible, conquistadors of hearts
of stone, their overt edgy sexiness create the Aphrodisiac Revolution.

Imaginary, opiate-induced psychosis, or the realization
that the liberating experience is just kisses away.

Word

As you sojourn outside your home remember
succoring others is of utmost importance.

The Word is to respect not a display to selected people.

The Word is not to judge.

The Word is to agree to listen to others without shutting them out.

The Word is to eliminate tittle-tattle and not to rattle.

The Word is to seek the ultimate truth.

The Word is forgiveness.

The Word is acceptance.

The Word is to understand enlightenment.

The Word is pure optimism when encountering the unpredictability of life.

The Word is comfort.

The Word is a meticulous process of understanding the power of restraint.

The Word is encouragement.

The Word is not your grandstanding or boasting.

The Word is creation.

The Word is spiritual life.

The Word Is Love.

The Word is God.

Seasonal Changes

The Cosmic Moon and seasonal changes present opportunities of the reasons why proper decision-making properties are self-maintenance.

The veils to other dimensions are thinning and spiritual entities are dancing or haunting.

Negative and confusing emotions, visions, and dreams with a flight or fear intuition.

Amplify shield protection, properly, to avoid negative attacks or attachments.

Control your reactions and grasp the energy that is not an illusion, but projections of the paranormal world.

Delectable, delightful, demure, gorgeous, and humble the lovely Ms. P dances underneath the moonlight recognizing others for the reason of their electromagnetic energy.

Magnificent Monday

Does a heart void of the radiant energy of love disassociate from one's soul?

The metamorphosis power of an emerging manifestation of manipulation spawns itself like a demon during a person's heartbreak.

Glorious words of kindness to decorate the victim's mind until convinced of a time, place, or action that does not or never existed.

Do not participate in erroneous actions and bear in mind it is a pleasurable indulgence of the heartless.

Optimism

Daily commitment to ourselves is the enjoyment of
tranquility enabling us to share happiness with others.

Reflection, deception, depletion, projection, and
time for the attraction of positive balance.

Nightly Dreams filled with creative freedom enables
us to pioneer the spirit of optimism.

Sweetest Dreams all y'all.

Sensational Saturday:

Is happiness and contentment depicted by dazzling eyes?
Does sadness create lifeless not noteworthy, pleasant-looking expressions.

Our undertaking today will be to make the
world a brilliant and luminous place.

Ain't nobody frowning today, okay?
It is time to perform the Celebratory Dance of Life while giving all
the glory to God. One, two cha cha cha, three, four ooh-la-la...

September 26, 2020 (Ms. P.)
Melissa Begley

Transmute

At the midnight hour, we enter a realm of the
Universe that creates glorious relaxation.

Fallacious or salacious and aimlessly wandering around the
moon until it is revealed to Ms. P., what is the truth?

The prophesy of your pathway is not conjured up in a spell
but spearheaded by your spoken words and actions.

Tranquil and beautiful discourse or embellishments creating
organized chaos of evil-like behaviors is low vibrations.

Create your destiny by the transmutation from negative vibrations
to the higher vibrations of love and positive energy.

Good Morning

It is an exquisite, gorgeous Autumn day granted by God.

With tenacity and persistence, you shall shine by
offering the gift of encouragement.

Your grandeur and glory are evident as you become skilled in thoughtfulness.
A luminous and incandescent radiance of affection generates warmth, and
your strength of mind will wane and fade malevolence, ill will, and malice.

Remember to count your blessings and perform the Celebratory
Dance of Life and send up all the glory to God.

Hit it now one, two, three, cha cha cha, ooh-la-la..

Friendship

Be the peace, the aesthetic consciousness of sensibility.

Bequeath respect and create profound connections and develop friendships.

Humankind is fragile and egotistical.

The remarkable simplicity of achieving a quality of life, beyond our inner circle, consists of many perceived or real twisted dark shadows.

Value friendship, but never treat others as if they are invisible.

Listen to learn and cheerfully adapt to the differences of humankind.

Sweet goodnight kisses to all of the pretty boys
and hugs to the ladies cha cha cha
Serene Sunday will be a triumphant day:

Trifling, trivial, and petty matters are insignificant.

Transform into a thrilling, rousing, and inspiring living being,
and your spirit will overflow with joyousness and jubilation.

Negativity is taboo and pleasant dialogue enhancing
the positive will revolutionize the human race.

Are you motivating and enthusiastic?

It is time to perform the Celebratory Dance of Life. Show up everybody and your upbeat moves will generate positive energy. One, two, cha cha cha, three, four ooh-la-la.

Melissa Begley

The Magic Of Blues

Like the Nile living past the pharaohs,
Harken your script and paint a fair photo,
Here's the swallows begotten on mid-flight,
Migraine on migration,
Pain is an antidote to life

Arise in the dark and let black blanket your thoughts,
Baying of brains when denied a hearing,
The song of blue jays reaching the tones of the heart,
Defeat is a soft plea to the ears of a dictator,
Blood red cupcakes donated by brooding pity,
Blueberry sky's boasting of unreachable paradise,
Back left quests of land owners and those bereft of a roof,
The choir is incomplete without the child's hiccup,
Just like the grave is full before and after the burial

Africa is a sunny blue land,
Where theft flourishes,
And old tales of better days die before leaving the mouths.
Blue is royal to a gun and a traitor to the weak,
Whenever you hear it,
Know a loss has arrived,
Wait your turn however impatient,
For blue is fair to the taken and the taker.
It's the colour that evens out all ground dwellers.

Nancy Ndeke

With This Ring

I thee take,
to mould and fold,
Harness and dress,
as culture so demands.
Amen to the domain,
with a deleted delete button,
Whereas mother to my plants,
Tether shall be you know,
Within these walls high

Your days shall sip the forlorn drink of your tribe,
Massage my tired bones to fix you yet proper,
Should I die by a hand unknown?
The road rough is your fate,
My kin hard, knows no kindness,
with one outside the blood

Rejoice little fairly,
As this hand leads you,
Home is this graveyard,
That mellows your tormentors' heart,
That I would have been tomorrow,
perhaps a smile would be yours,
for now, fall in obedience of step,
and count your blessings for it

With this ring I thee take,
My own you are,
Till dreams mate with night,
To send your soul back,
To where breath holds still.

Nancy Ndeke

Step Inside

The pot invites the egg and potato,
One hardens, one softens,
Tolerate disorient,
Time zones and clone clowns,
Barriers like berries bob,
Step inside this caldron,
Tempered by wizards of letters,
Glow and groan if you must,
Sweet sweat riding the waves,
Faulty rhythm and impeccable tango,
Step inside.

Breath the old in the new,
Seasons of reasons and missions,
Justify the explanation,
Please the place with policy,
Go and meet unrest at ease,
The last chapter in the first page.
Weather men went to pray,
The beast said ' right now'
The light woke up from dark,
When dusk tore the mask.
Step inside

In multiples of swimmers we come,
Blind race to see the greenery,
Far apart is began,
What was never ended,
Awakening dreaming of streams.
Step inside and stoke the embers,
Time misruled your judgement,
For you are the wind that goes and comes,
A dance never ending.
Step inside

Nancy Ndeke

I Come Humming A Tune

In it is an old tale,
One with dents unseen,
And debts yet unpaid,
Sidestepping the scars and scabs,

I paste a poster of a sunny summer,
The wind did blow the cover,
Lifting the lid afloat,
Up at first light of gasp,
An old path cleared the top cover,
Gazing from years accumulated jest,
The mirror refused to crack under gaze,
Eyes rheumy from fixed stare,

Ears heating up from Memory,
A moment births an old score,
One that fled halfway to heaven,
Came back to clear the garden,

Plant a Rose and tend it well,
I came humming a tune,
Hoping to pass unnoticed,
In you though,
Behind a great word muslin curtain,
A tutor with a gentle soul born of a hard career.
Warning!
Somethings must never be said,

Someplace must never be visited.
Sir yes sir!
Said the recruit,
Sharing the absence of coffee and toffee,

We went for a walk with a brisk run of words,
I came humming a tune,
But found one as familiar as the one fate handed me,
Stopping a bit on this old track,
A moment stretched back to old days,
And the hum amplified of its own,
Cognisance of the 'twines' of marching,
That what must be must be,

What must go must go,
And what must stay must stay,

Even when the shaman reads the last rites.
So here we are,
Hummingbirds of a choral tune,
Of Temporal visits to the white sky's,
While feet still thrash the green paths of home.

Nancy Ndeke

Where The Eagle Goes To Re-Birth

It's way off the pavements marked with memories,
To the inner cove of a cave dark and bright,
A place of dare asking nor answering,
A place of quietude where soul communes with unknown,
Settled on an air bag carrying nothing but dare,
Feathers and crawls gorge, the pain notwithstanding,

Forty days and forty nights not a robbers numbering,
But learning the cycles of Sinai with heat and dust in tow,
We go to grow knowing we must,
We go to play knowing we must pray,
It's in that space where kneeling is unknown,
In an inner chamber where love first touched,

Rekindling the glow of passage in a moment of utter mystery.
A man meeting a man one more time,
Shaking hands with destiny in the calmest of demeanour.
A new day without a name on a face devoid of mask.
Home away from stones and hedges,
Just floating away in a presence longed for and finally found.

Nancy Ndeke

With

Fly with me in this
moment
As if we soar far
above
All the things that
call
That weigh ones
mind
Listen with your heart
now
As it picks up the beats
of mine
Feel my soul as it whispers
to yours
Let the breeze caressed
the mind
As I unfold it to connect
with me
Hear beyond the depth
of silence
The roar of the sea beneath
us
The leaves of falls journeys
flight
That move in quest with
the clouds
Be one with me if only in this
MOMENTUM

Janice Fisher

Mountain

Sometimes in a needed solidarity
Walk
We need to climb above all that
Turmoil
To seek the quiet beauty that's still
Untouched
Letting the soul reach out and be
Blessed
To regain a deeper meaning to our
Faith
To not ask the whys that form in the
Mind
Or think beyond the grasp of this
Day
Tomorrow's hold lessons in books
Already read
But as the winds blow some lost that
Knowledge
Breathing in this quiet majestic view
Of peace
I rest my soul in my knowledge of
Unbroken faith
I'd like to stay in this place of peace
Closer to thee
But know your chapter for me is on
Going
In the pages of time that seek its
Wings
I'll wait searching beyond the view
In Faith

Janice Fisher

Look For Me....

In the wind-blown dust of all ancestry,
At the undergrowth and moss hang on that oak,
At the bent back of that soldier overwhelmed by
memories of territorial protection,
On that lady at the strange home with fading Memory,
Look for me

In the river begrudging not beast or men,
At the orphaned child of crime laden backyard,
Am found around and about,
Stirring the souls of men to change their time,
From inward embrace that births ego,
To the mentor holding coloured hands in arts tutorials,
Find me abroad and home

A passport-less citizen of the universe,
Find me in your inhaled breath,
A droplet of this flow that we call life,
And should you in your peer and stare fail,
Know I just turned a bend,
To that place where thoughts build structures,
Designating each to a specie,
But all co-dependent to a fine detail,
Of a whole so beautifully mysterious.
A place where time counts for nothing more than a babies dream,
And an elder yearning for the setting sun.

Nancy Ndeke

Yet if I sit

Nothing left in coffee cup
Question, do I have the will
To just wash up that coffee cup
Or go for a refill?

Who am I? I ask with sigh
Too deep the current thinking
Into deep through lack of sleep
Slowly am I sinking

I don't quite know how I feel
Marshmallow is the mood
The more I try, the more want to die
The ridiculous is my food

Is what I be insanity?
Or just a person true
Everything is not what seems
At danger level Blue

A cup appears on draining board
A question answered without asking
Now to bigger challenges
Now to daily tasking

Yet if I sit and just let slip
More letters from within
Do I know when to end this show?
Or even where it should begin?

Who would see the real me?
Do I want them to?
The penner and the constant pen
Just a thing to do

Your future in the stars

The parent wrote a letter
Slipped inside the case to go
Of the offspring who home leaving
For did love them so told them so

A little sapling has become a tree
A little shoot to flower bloom
The inquisitive on next stage of journey
Yet remember, here you will always have a room
As you have learnt so have we
You taught us how to raise a child
Some bits, I admit, were scary
Others pretty wild

Your future lies in the stars
Those we placed inside your head
It's now up to you to choose which to follow
To one day see where led
For only you can choose what do
Which of these are caught
You and who you are
The still to learn and that taught

I am proud of you beyond expression
I marvel at that you have become
I see before me my awesome infant
No matter how big you are still that one
I see myself in you
Those decades of the past
All that I can warn you of
Is they go too fast!

Go with peace and contentment
Wherever life will take
Unseen you have a companion
For our bond nothing can break
My little one all grown up
That's a scary thought
Now see which starts are caught

Your gift I'll earn

I want to hold you like no other can
Want to be the one to whom you turn
I promise you that I will be there forever
I vow to you each day your gift I'll earn

The sweetest sound - a contented sigh
The most beautiful sight – a happy smile
The most amazing feeling – to be loved
The best excuse – in a while

The look that deflected a thousand spears
The touch that dried a thousand tears
The words creating hope a new
The presence that helped pull through

With the caring came the sharing
With the showing came the knowing
With reciprocation came elation
Creating something made to last

The meaning of Life is in the living
The best received the chance of giving
The warmest feeling is the reaction
The greatest puzzle is attraction

I want to hold you like no other can
Want to be the one to whom you turn
I promise you that I will be there forever
I vow to you each day your gift I'll earn

Your thoughts will stay forever

The lamp it softly lit the room
The room in which you once did lay
Now an empty bed instead
Ever since you went away

The air is still with slight chill
No body there to shed some heat
The silence is invasive
With no soul to greet

The door so often open
Remains closed more often now
So many changes noticeable
When to parting you did bow

A silence replaces living
Sad instead of joy
A Mausoleum in the making
A work not choosing to employ

The memories of our good times
Both here and outside world
The experiences shared together
As each day unfurled

We came, enjoyed and then did part
The burden of regret
Your thought will stay forever
My beautiful loving Pet

You who read

The algorithm of pondered Prism
The complexity of mystery
The happenstance that came from chance
The length of longevity
I still believe we can achieve
I still hope that we can cope
I hold true that we'll get through
When in the pits I'll be the rope

Some they sink to superstition
Some indulge in indecision
Mayhem many make their mission
Yet not the ones who care
Some they boast they have the most
Some a myth they make
As do swoon in their cocoon
The truth they do forsake

The too thick to worry much
About things they can't control
The 'There goes me if different be'
The ones with joyous soul
The 'come what may – it's okay'
If jus affects oneself
Those who strive to be alive
Regardless of false wealth

Many roads but one journey
Each must travel on their own
The companionships made are just a trade
As one finds they've grown
You who read, what do you need?
Can you forsake the glitz?
Do you need to image feed?
Along with all its bits

The Poets Field Of Vision

He draws from within and without,
Memories like delayed popcorn,
A look at the blank midday sky,
Prompts a vivid silence of commune of once upon a time,
A lonely bird recently widowed,
Revives the gratitude of love softly snoring,
That walk in a drizzly morning and sight of a homeless,
Draws tears of knowing it could be anyone,
Including the one clad in cashmere warmth.

Poetry does carry a burden,
Of using words out of tune to tune,
Brazenly baptising situations with robust eye bursts,
It sits uneasy in foggy dawns,
And rises like dough to prune out the hidden thistle,
It owes only itself and it's maker,
For to do less is betrayal of creation.
A character unknown to truth,
Unlike court jesters and paid dancers.

Beauty of pain aches his pen till it must be drained,
A poet has a peculiar vision,
And skewed lobby of choice of colors,
Opposite may just be positive,
And ugly beautifully presented,
Sorrow may follow a wedding night,
And cerebration take a dive into tempestuous mourning.
But for all its lack and luck,
Poetry comes close to freedom of heart.

As love and hate has told in ages past,
And continue to this day.

Nancy Ndeke

The Year Of Two Two's And Double Nothing

Usher in the usual old same, same,
Soon interrupts a new shame, shame,
Started from the yellow rice Fields of dawn,
Wet markets and dog game cuisine,
Sooner than later, awkward did the rounds,
Falling standards and failing lungs,
Sooner after lock became a pick,
Keys flocking out of style,
Business as usual did a somersault,
It's Belly up and fins rigid,
Out to the west the gift of East,
Brain drain took a dive from grave dig.

Hello believers and bereaved,
Poets and politics catching a sneeze,
The centre went round quelling fires,
But none would do for Central command,
Where sunflower heads filled with dismay,
Denied, lied and destroyed,
Hope fled from the entitled braves,
Down went down a further furlong,
Catch twenty-two was no longer a metaphor,
As statistics outnumbered the charts,
A year spoke death,
A year spoke tears,
A year spoke fears.

Still is, amidst the clime of musical chairs,
With debts of change stuck on old chairs,
The world stands agape at an era,
Where faith once give a welcome,
To a needy uprooted from injurious shores,
Now drainage pipes cough bloody phlegm's,
Cheered on by rabid dogs in colourful tongues,
Decorative declarations of monarchical beginnings,
One sought and clasped by goons and masochist egos,
Turning tables on human goodwill,
Rendering truth an alien vagabond,
Praising vulgarity to the Sky's above.

Christ has been demoted and his say distorted,
A few more days to the end of the crazy year,
How long to undo the deathly tempest?
Remain a dream and a prayer,
For in the spirit Union of the living,
What affects one in any corner,
Is close home than we dare discount.

Pegs And Hungers

Reason for rough roads and traction on wheels,
Grip of a hand shake before letting off,
Wind flapping socks and lace on the line,
Rumour mills running full throttle at midnight

Prayers from crows and vultures of prey,
Who shall hold this spinning foundation,
Where man and beast stare at uncertainty so eerily,
Who shall staple this unglued love with a little care?

Where hunger kills as easily as obesity,
The land is awash with murk,
Man-made monstrosities of Vandal demean,
From disease to peace-lessness,

From developed to malfunction,
Once upon a windy day and a stormy night,
Let's gather the will to level the ground,
Put up our wear for the sun to heal.

And perhaps,
Tomorrow will not come so terrifying.

Nancy Ndeke

Last

Leg

You

Super

Troopers!

Alas poor air, I knew you well

The new breed feed on Assassins Creed
Or FIFA 21
Sonic showed a way to go
Then of health we found no fun
Training shoes became fashion items
With price tags fit to match
Fitness now a knock off
Private Surgeons hatch

Do we know which way to go?
Do we really care?
Do we see reality
Do we think about fresh air?
Do we sit and just compete?
Because that's the way been taught
Do we dare to ask and share?
To use those things called Feet

Fingers getting exercise
Tap and slide and hold
Credit card Bills as we time kill
Another story told
To go to shop on motorised scooter pop
A step is just next level at
Fast food an essential
Then campaign to reduce fat

"I'll meet you on the Internet
Then will play together
"What! You want to play in person!!
There's this thing called Weather!
My ripped Jeans have no means
To do what originals designed
But do amuse as old confuse
Yet another way I find"

Alcohol and altered affection

'On day one it was fun
On day two we found some common ground
Day three brought reality
On day four we looked around
On day five we came alive
Day six began to fix
On day seven started Heaven
For we finished this box of tricks'

The one week wonder of so called romance
The couple did explore
Made it to just seven days
Then could take no more
The question asked by both parties
'What the heck was I thinking?'
Simple answer if truth told
Engaged in too much drinking

One did send but two agreed
Lacked inhibitions fluid feeds
When that fluid Alcohol
Then common sense replaced by needs
Needs not of long term but those short
In disaster then are caught
Seven days! I am surprised
So much shorter if were wise

All day long

The light has now become sight
The day a challenge to manage
The anticipated not yet stated
The Horse before the carriage

All day long we just moved on
All day until the next
All day long we stay strong
For our best yet to get
Passing periods in sometimes serious
Passing some wish fun
Passing that we treat sublime
Passing when had none

What will be might not be
If we make a change
Future not yet set in stone
Some of it can rearrange

Ask yourself your true wealth
Gasp when realise
The sadness of potential
Smothered in disguise

All day long we just moved on
All day until the next
All day long we stay strong
For our best yet to get
Passing periods in sometimes serious
Passing some wish fun
Passing that we treat sublime
Passing when had none

All fantasies can be reality

The days seem strange as time does change
Yet see it I still do
Been asked the question and found suggestions
The way I then fought through

When something happens what do you feel?
When something occurs do you ask if real?
The unknown shown do you then own?
Does to you challenge appeal?
Who does care the reason why?
You survive while others die
Who but you have the clue?
The reason of why you pulled through

So, ask me of some politics
I will answer with side flicks
Ask of me what should we share
I will answer 'Would you dare?'

The present is not set in stone
For our future we do own
All my life I'm just changing
Some parts of me I'm rearranging

When something happens what do you feel?
When something occurs do you ask if real?
The unknown shown do you then own?
Does to you challenge appeal?
Who does care the reason why?
You survive while others die
Who but you have the clue?
The reason of why you pulled through

All those Dreams are just a means
To search for something more
All fantasies can be reality
If them we want more

All is thanks a

An echo spoke and conscience woke
A current had to cope
That way back when didn't use the pen
When future was just hope

Now the strange as things change
The love has passed from Brother
Meaning more from foreign shore
That which more than lover

Tracer in the twilight
Foreign soil trod
The wonder why here could die
The calming sense of Brotherhood

Red it glows and position shows
If for short while if they have sense
Mark it as a used position
To the Boss man then is sent

A different time in life of mine
Now comfortable with have
The Wife, the Daughter, the new Home
Who could ask for more?

Was once the nomad paid to die
That I am no more
I a now a different person
All is thanks to foreign shore

All that shows

When one does catch a cold in Summer
One does question reason
Is the clue not in the name it's given?
Surely not the season
When one works the night-shift
While 'normal' people sleep
Does one question own routine?
Along with the friends you keep

How does water come in three states?
Gas, liquid and solid too
Steam, that drink and that ice
I really have no clue
If we are spinning oh so fast
Why no dizziness we feel?
Are emotions self-infliction?
Are they even real?

We used to be so progressive
When did progress we choose to stop?
Yes, the things we use develop
Not the one who relies on lot
We used to have lean bodies
I don't understand
How we became obsessed with unhealthy
To the point got out of hand

The quantum of the questions
The mad illness from which suffered
Then I add to the long list
Am I alone or are there others?
Is mystery a rhapsody
Is it punishment for just being?
All that shows I don't know
When most learnt without it seeing

All the machines

Climbing cliffs in contemplation
Living life with different nation
Some may question why
To them the answer 'you should try'

Experience best lesson taught
If further wisdom now is sought
Of just what one does be
In the group Humanity

All the machines that man has made
If in line they did parade
Never equal that have had to trade
With no regrets that's true
All have been some bad dream
All have had a thing I've got
What can see is simply me
The one who talks to you

New language learn as acceptance earn
For is their place, not yours
A situation in our creation
To travel distance shores

Your skin tone you do own
But is just a cover
No barrier to deter
Knowing someone with another

All the machines that man has made
If in line they did parade
Never equal that have had to trade
With no regrets that's true
All have been some bad dream
All have had a thing I've got
What can see is simply me
The one who talks to you

All we want

The liquid touched the porous
The stain it left enlightening
The single became multiple
Guess that we are writing

Another took and made a Book
Something if we dare
Permanent remembrance
Of one who chose to share

All we want is just one chance
A brief spell when ink can dance
All we want is for others to see
The product of creativity
All we want is to just share
That about words we care
All we want is to enjoy
Results of efforts we employ

Years ago that ink did flow
Years are but a memory
Of a time, one penned a line
A speck in History

Left to right or top then down
It's all the same game
Knocking on the shocking
As impulse try to tame

All we want is to enjoy
The thought of joy that give
All we want is to explain
How the others live
All we want is just a chance
To the imagination feed
All we want is to follow
The age-old great Writers creed

Alone but not alone

One stood apart from the now normal
Not pretentious, just informal
A callous maybe in some eyes
Just refreshing in those wise
Disdained by many – no surprise
When they looked beyond disguise
Nothing new when seen through
When on offer some then do

The Pariah with desire
Different ways they went
No ill thought of that taught
In the time they spent
Teaching/ learning yet still yearning
To be a single name
When got there then without care
Could promote new fame

The Lady became legend
In a different art
Yet to many who shared the dream
Her journey was a start
Showing just what could do
If prepared to see things through
Falling down then getting up
Tasting from the failure cup

They wrote

"I stand alone in a sea of souls
I am me and nothing more
I stand alone in those searching
I stand alone to open door
The path was sometimes Desert
The Oasis found
I waded in the quicksand
Then found firmer ground"

Am lost in things

When coffee's cold and you're feeling old
Just remember once were young
When joints ache and effort now takes
Remember earlier when things were simpler
When not knew when bite your tongue
What defines a Hero?
What definition must they do?
What defines a Hero
What definition applies to you?

Is there just a part inside?
A certain part of you
That still asks the question
Is there nothing more can do?
We talk of Champagne and then complain
So expensive a glass to buy
We run the shadows of thoughts narrow
Then we question why

Am lost in things that I can bring
No need for 'teaching' now
Lost in the space I once did waste
Found my when then how

No Book on teacher preaching
Just being what I be
No name selling by others telling
How that you could not see
Took my hobby to the limit
The limit self did set
Took and pushed it further
Not for what could get

Am no brilliant writer
That accept as true
Yet each piece is perfect
In what managed and could do

Auction autograph

The question a suggestion
To all who care to share
A trap which all can unwittingly fall
With or without care
The affliction of repetition
Same message different laid
When have new clue to do something new
An unwanted reputation made

Ask yourself

When I assemble does it resemble
Something that has been?
Done before when you want more
A different view of scene
When I do what think is new
Do you just see repeat?
When viewing more becomes a chore
A torture not a treat

Do I stay and just play?
In 'secure' and know
Do I grow by different show?
Worry about what others say
When acclaim in search of 'fame'
Restricts by sense of fear
The vision becomes the mission
Blinding that which clear

The new and old same story told
Known but nothing great
The limitations of Generations
Rests with the Mind state
Just a view for me and you
As travel on this path
How do we achieve what others believe?
When can auction

Autumn falls

Rainy day so inside stay
Another so no care
Saves the battle of crowd walking
Saves the half-hidden stare
Vacant Sofa, tangent opposite
Junk topped Desk face to face
Staring at the ceiling
Wishing far off place

We make marvels in our minds
Yet the real ones hard to find
None quite be of same kind
Variety is delicious
What used to be can no longer be
The price we pay with age
Yet if hear the call will stand tall
Write a brand new page

I am the sum of all I am
I am the sum of all that been
I am the sum of the waiting
I am the sum of not yet seen
Because I am Human
Because I choose to do
Because I am not worried
Because I live the new

Wind up my own clockwork
Put legs now into gear
Can hear the calling of another falling
Raindrops splashing near
I suppose that I must close
The window for a reason
Autumn falls upon us fools
Not dependant on the season

Autumn fast

An Autumn fast approaching
Yet the heat encroaching
Another abnormal day
To wear a mask now legal task
So many still police must ask
Response one cannot say

Tummy rumble is no trouble
For blessed to have food
Not the same for different name
Born in different 'hood'

With blue sky one does sigh
Tomorrow, probably, will rain
What expect the least get
The same and same again

A season now draws near
Though no logic does it hold
A mystery it will be
As chooses to unfold

We can't dance though had the chance
To be better than before
We will be in misery
The place that we adore

Just 'being' but not being
Filling just a space
We are now our sacred Cow
We are just a waste

Eleven soon so nearly noon
Tune playing on radio
Should do out but have some doubt
Why and where to go

The Marbles change to something strange
Guess must just accept
What they give when in verse live
We'll just see just what we get

Heaven hold a meaning
To those that way are leaning
A wonder it is seeming
Persona non grata for the likes of me

Made my stamp in mud and damp
Now but a distant memory
Have an offspring that does joy bring
She is the future Tree

An Autumn fast approaching
In season as well as life
I am told I'm getting old
Words spoken by the Wife
With a laugh it will pass
For this, a probe to inter
Passing time is no crime
As waiting for one's Winter

Avalanche

Ever had something happen
That others would not believe?
Never play in front of young ones
Who reach up about to knees

The little rotter in his chair
Played with food and dared to dare
I, the fool, real and play
Chose in front of him to lay

An avalanche of Blancmange
Came crashing on my Head
I am used to the white stuff
I got something yellow instead

My not right exclamation
At this surprise situation
Lost amongst the laughs so loud
From the hysterical family crowd

It hit just above the hairline
Spread in all directions
Slid behind my Glasses
Giving weird reflection

Scalp got an experience
Conditioner of sort
Went into my lugholes
There some of it was caught

Slid down the nape of neck
Where it met my collar
Instantly creating
Another profanity endorsed holler

Since that day can honestly say
I'll stand when he is eating
As for ammunition for a food fight
Blancmange it takes some beating

Average

An 'average' man average can
But why just stop there?
An 'average' man average can
If choose to just not dare

Show me the average in average man
Average woman for include
I will show you something else
I promise not to be rude

A ver(y)age is what all be
Average I cannot see
Common yes, in some ways
Yet in others not we be

So, you live there and I live here
A difference for a start
So how old to others told?
In difference is a part

Am I average at being average?
Am I just some sum equation?
Am I average for certain type?
Or for each and every Nation

A ver(satile) age(nda)
In that I do agree
If that's the true meaning
Then average I do be

Awkward in the experience

October was a disaster
November was the same
December mixed with sleet and snow
Along with winter rain

Early part of new year
Promise it did hold
For those who were adventurous
Those who were that bold

Middle mix and time to fix
Half way is not over
Still the chance in mind dance
In the fields of clover

Few things are beyond repair
If only we but try
First we must ask ourselves
The honest reason why

Despite long pain do we refrain
To venture of the past
Do we go yet still know?
This, maybe, will not last

A consternation situation
No real answer leaps to the fore
Awkward in the experience
Yet finding wanting more

Back on track

A stick burns slowly between finger tips
Half way there to dry lips
Frozen in motion as flashes notion
Just let it slide and slip away
To join the rest that weren't the best
Impulse actions that one made
Growing in non-showing
Soon enough to have Parades

All is fair in love and war
So that saying goes
Are we one or at other one?
Truth is no one knows
Complexities a mystery
Logic now il and al
Can we trust as now we must?
Those who make the call

Not that am dejected
That gave up in a life past
Wasted effort without rewards
Certain things can't last
Shallow sleeps tormented soul
I know and scars do bare
Weighing down without sound
Until met with who does care

Back on track, no turning back
One way now I know
Sideways steps with no regrets
Just one place to go
Focus set with no regrets
Better person be
By becoming half of whole
Made the whole of me

Baton passed as was the last

Sixty-Four the World got more
More than that expected
Time went by and wondered why
This one not projected?

An abjuration of their situation
Believing and still believe
Them and me just step be
In that we can achieve

Am not that Rock when take stock
Just sitting there for show
Am a bit of a future hit
When all do learn to grow

Grow beyond that monster
Currently on parade
Into new when no me and you
When bold choice is made

Now Twenty- Twenty and still plenty
Needed to achieve
Yet some signs the future fine
For in a Daughter I believe

Nineteen-Nine, Nine my world was fine
She came as that a pleasure new
Her and Mom plus me had fun
As she learned and grew

Baton passed as was the last
Further we do race
The numbers game is the same
Just different is each pace

Bats in Belfries are old news

Marshmallows in the microwave melt
Harder to say than is spelt
Effigy of lunacy
Not related, is just me
Bored and penning new creation
Such a familiar situation
Passing time with habit of mine
Is that eight today or is it nine?

Bats in Belfries are old news
When with ink I can confuse
Twenty-six the letters learned
More or less for more earned
Crabbiness a situation
Taught to one from new generation
When their gizmo goes kaput
Yet interaction is still nought

Play me a song from where belong
Older days than today
Music then had more meaning
Regardless of what you say
My days of living became those of giving
Something that is understood
When you have experienced pleasure/ pain
In what we call Parenthood

Now I need to clean that damned Microwave

Beautiful be my Bromley

Forget Hotel California
Welcome to Bromley stay
Rooms by the suspicious hour
Even by the day

Please don't come in vehicle
For no parking they can offer
Council premises is close at hand
For a fee can cover

The weather might not be the same
But no reason to be sorry
Work the only reason to visit here
Fast food outlets? Yep, don't worry

Forgot the Night boat to Cairo
Try a Bromley Bus
Various routers throughout the dark
Can spew with little fuss

Two rail stations it does have
North and South their name
Different place to which go
Yet start point near the same

Forget Town called Malice
When youngsters do invade
Graffiti battles then ensure
As obscenities they trade

None of which grammar correct
They don't seem to know
Arrogance in ignorance
Proudly seem to show

Welcome to the paradise called Bromley

Beehives in the archives

Clotted cream and naughty dreams
Not those type you're thinking
More a case of the taste
As down the throat it's sinking

Country Ham and Strawberry jam
Salivating at the thought
The good old British Banger
In food fantasy am caught

Crisis fresh air without a care
A Mom will new born child
The rise of Sun as day begun
Memories running wild

Come what may a perfect Day
For am here am I
The charm of calm can do no harm
Say with contentment sigh

What made me who I be
Too much for them to list
Captured in my Chronicles
If you get my gist

Would I change me for what could be?
That needs some deep contemplation
Just one event and the time spent
Would make a new sensation

There's Beehives in the archives
Never knowing what each will bring
Nectar or pain, what will I gain?
Honey or a sting

Before much more

If I had a Home in which a Bird
Lives and in which dive-bombed me and spouse
Would I be an aviary
Or simply have a Bird House?

Are we shackled by that not tackle
Are we prisoners by choice?
We love reaction but change won't action
Just love to vent our voice

If I had a pair of Pears
Would one choose to them share
Would I be worried that somehow sullied
Would I worry or even care?

Maybe I am ancestry
Those who under thumb
Of their Lord or their Master
Look now how they have become

If what I want I could own
Would that replace the value known
When do have and when need save
Even for a decent Grave

Calamity a mystery
Yet all have in living life
I am blessed so forget the rest
That doesn't apply to Wife

If fish could fly yes I know some try
Yet at most they glide
Would we be we or what would be
The offensive in the Hide?

Believe to achieve

With permission can I have a vision
Of the perfect place to be
With gratitude can I intrude
In the dreamt of fallacy

Can I gain to break the chain?
That binds me to that real
Can I soar to something more?
Can some freedom feel?

The once single molecule
Searching for that which could join
The one side of the prospect
The one face of the coin

Can I please learn from you?
Not in the formal way
Can I take from that you make?
In the written that you say

One had such potential
One refused to learn
One thought they were better
One potential then did spurn

Can I be an example?
Can I be a proof
Can I prove that however far?
Never should we be aloof

Yes, we are each at levels
Levels in what can be
Yes, we must believe in self
To fulfil our destiny

Yet the H word so important
Whatever level we achieve
Never better but just different
That is something I believe

Beyond that seen still lives that clean

To Bose Eneduwe Adogah

My friend, it's been a long time coming
Will we ever see reality?
My friend, we have grown in different ways
Different yet we met
Something, somewhere had a vision
Let's see what did see
You and I are days gone by
Now the term is simply We

In the coldness of Disaster
In that of the success heat
Strong remain and share pain/ gain
Together all will meet
My friend you have been absent
If but for a short while
Hope that everything is okay
That you still wear a smile

I know that you've been busy
Ecstatic at what I see
For although not part of it
It is part of me
Someday things will settle down
Back to almost that we had
Sharing all experiences
Both the good and bad

Time and distance create some hurdles
Merely there to tease
For we simply hurdle them
Hurdle them with ease
Not of blood but bonded
Bonded by that unknown
A friendship that grows in to Family
A Family that's grown

Blank tank

The jam within the type of Donut
The certain syrup on Breakfast Pancakes
That meal still that holds thrill
When Mom does or used to make

That place upon a foreign space
The one that stays with you
The feeling of achieving
When do what though you couldn't do

That want for more as explore
The things that were unknown
The amazement of the content
When unknown is shown

The best days of my life are gone
But is that really true
For your best days are the possible
Possible if but do

Yes, it is all different now
Guess what!! All is all
All includes, polite or rude
Guess it is your call

Why do animals have two different names?
Normal and something strange
Is it so some exclusive club?
Them can then arrange?

Why do we like certain stuff?
When so much is now on offer
Are we sticking with what we know?
Or just eating what's no bother?

Why am I penning trivial?
When more serious should be said
I guess it's another Floating Marble
That escaped from 'Prison' Head

Blank

Want to write but nothing to write
So, write this thing instead
On the page to pass some age
Release the full when led

Occupying without trying
Minutes of the morn
As with tap before a nap
Digits are then torn

Oh what to do when nothing new
Hand twitching in expectation
The more do try the more they hide
The complexity of situation

Pythagoras made a theory
Da Vinci did some art
Newton blew some learned minds
Yet I can't make a start

On a piece of drivel
To join the ones already done
Is one now incapable
What has one become?

Will relax and try to see
What will bring in future
Need to be doing something
Penning like a suture

Call for Caffeine

Is a stepping stone one to choose?
When not set in some firm ground
A promise made just for parade
One of joyous sound?

Is what we be a papacy?
Beneath the cover of another?
A tool to fool and perhaps rule
Whist truths they hope to smother

Is progression just regression
Glossed over by the new?
Has it become so undone?
Respected by the few?

Some simple questions with no suggestions
Need more coffee I do think
For clearer mind I do find
Equal to amount I drink

The travesty of that I be
The sceptical receptacle
The ghost of most that have lost hope
Or just another fool?

A battery of misery facing me it seems to be
Hello you old friend
What more the chore to then explore
What others can you lend

Another fix of Caffeine quick
Before deeper do I go
Then describe with diatribe
I am guessing feeling low

Another face in waste of space
The writing not the writer
Coffee working and cells are jetting
I'm even feeling brighter!

Call me Idiot

Sane thought name somewhat plain
So, guess what it did do?
Put 'in' in from word 'thin'
Then rolled eyes Green and Blue
Six voices said inside one Head
"I. D. have got quite a lot
Took and played, made some afraid
When said to call me Idiot"

A name's a game to separate same
For those who do not know
A name's a frame inert and tame
For an item to then show
Puts an object into category
Puts it there for clarity
Puts definition to supposition
In most cases but not all

Who said feet must meet the street?
I ask as I pass by
Why surprise as without disguise
I prefer to walk on Sky
The Restaurant confusion with my intrusion
When given condiment called Mustard
Though yellow is a good fellow
On my Sausages I prefer thick Custard

Those good chaps with white coats and Caps
Keep wanting to do me bad
Last time a crime, they crossed the line
They said my name was Mad
A name's a game to separate same
So, are they called Mad too?
They're not like me for you see
I know so I can do

Came from numb

The hands they move around the face
Display but don't record
Gone again another segment
Of that to lose we can't afford
No replay nor return
That's the stuff of fiction
Best years had both good and bad
Somehow seem a contradiction

Came from numb and then begun
To look at where I stood
The open space that now did face
Somehow felt so good
So much before to adore
If only did accept
Would never be a 'perfect' one
So, make the most of what do get

Which is better? I don't know
That where been or to where go
The mystery of Destiny
The paths that we choose
Those we have and those we will
Those we just peruse
We take one step and then one more
Travelling to a Gate or to that Door

Every day is a Fun day
To someone somewhere but not the same
We take turns to one earn
Some others can be quite tame
The bounce back and then attach
A meaning to event
Like each season has a reason
Those to come and those that went

Can I have a spoon?

How many people mix and match
The type of food they eat?
How many more just explore
Without the use of feet?
Through the fare of over there
A place that they can't see
How many then do realise
A certain symmetry

What today is the recipe
Of the type of dish that served
Will it be something palatable
Or something describe one word
A Master chef the maker
Cuisine so curious
Palate unpredictable
As is each of us

Life itself a recipe
The dish made a delicate one
Full of spice but also mild
Of hot pepper and Tomatoes dried by Sun
Shall I shake the Salt shaker?
Should I pour the Pepper pot?
Maybe pour the premade Perri-Perri
Just be brave and add the lot

I am not sure if I want more
Yet the experience was a blast
Maybe with some personal additions
Can convert into food fast
Breakfast still repeating
Hopefully quashed by meal at noon
This does look inviting
Though can I have a spoon?

Can the calm

Can the calm before the storm?
Calm again or merely pause?
For the calm did not create the storm
Calm was not the cause

Can might is right always win the fight?
When battle the peoples will?
For the people are always more powerful than the might
Have been and are still

The complexities of idiocies
When bull does baffle brain
When path of least resistance
Majority choose to just maintain

Can someone's view be the rule
When leader of a Nation?
They are not a toys owner
They're supposed to be its salvation

The vagaries of what can see
Around the places where we live
The illusion of contribution
Some believe they give

To think too hard as just a shard
From Globe of broken glass
Would cut self deep with scars to keep
Unless United make it pass

Can you feel this Heart still beating?

Syllables slide into the tide
Pronunciation proudly poses
Nouns announce of higher ground
Adjective it just supposes
All my life I'm now thinking
In shadow of words gently sinking
All my life, never knowing
Until now – now I'm showing

It's a beautiful day to be alive
A beautiful day to just be me
It's a beautiful day for opportunities
A beautiful day to see what see
What are we but possibilities?
What are we but sweet temptation?
What are we but experience?
That thing that's quite a sensation

I don't know where to begin
Yet alone where to end
The flow does grow and then on show
Forgive me please my awesome friend
Challenge took and in next Book
Will be able to view again
Later this year, so sorry dear
To inflict more pain

Can you feel this Heart that's beating?
Battered but still the same
Can you see the words inside it
Can you see the names?
Etched so deeply it is permanent
Add to another new
For the one became a Mother
Names inside grew to two

Candle

If I lit a light would you follow
Would you share with me all your sorrows?
If I shone a Candle to the World
How many places the message heard?
Does a beacon need to be seen?
Does it need physical to say what mean?
If I need a thousand Candles
A thousand and one will I buy
Why the extra? Why is why

If I shone a light in depth of night
Would you see a Beacon?
Guiding home those who roam
For the multitude of reasons
The navigation of situation
Might need some helpful direction
Known the need so to it feed
Profit from don't wish to mention

If what said filled a head
Just because you spoke
Not derogatory but part of we
Not some twisted joke
To light a flame in now insane
An act we all can do
I am holding match to light one
Now I ask 'are you?'

If one man a Beacon light can
How many could light us all
A candle just a metaphor
Replaced by simple call
Imagine a million candles
Piercing that feel darkness
Imagine a million trillion
Then finding speck of gladness

Candy

Candy came and thought it plain
So added coloured twist
Stood on stick with choice of pick
On every seaside list

Little Jack liked his shack
Though high up in tree
One false step and then get
Plaster cast

"What a day!" Many say
As to a Home return
Hours filled with glowers
As an income earn

Not for me this travesty
Best time that I've had
The understanding of my incoming
Yes! I'm truly mad!

Conversion

The bitter/ sweet of who greet
The play then do go away
The questioning of what could bring
The one that could not stay

The pain and gains as age does change
The joy of getting old
The battle scars and distant Stars
Each a story told

The making of the taking
The breaking and the other
The friend trend that has no end
The conversion from the lover

Candy in Cornucopia

Somewhere else we long to be
Some place – just not here
True can be so terrible
Facts a thing to fear

We make mistakes and pain do take
A Masochist lies within
A Library of laughable laments
Where do I begin?

We crave the candy in Cornucopia
Yet reject the healing
The sweet treats are hard to beat
When rational is reeling
That sugar rush means so much
Artificial or the real
If only it was permanent
That euphoric feel

I often wondered who I was
Confusion kept me sane
Trouble not a lover
More a Brother in different name

The acidity of actual
Rancidness of reason
The bitterness of being
Trust did hide some treason

We crave the candy in Cornucopia
Yet reject the healing
The sweet treats are hard to beat
When rational is reeling
That sugar rush means so much
Artificial or the real
If only it was permanent
That euphoric feel
How foolish I was then

Canine conversation

Take me to the Temple please
That one over by the Trees
For I think that I've got Fleas
There can scratch when lead release

Can you somehow change my food?
How can I make it understood?
It's disgusting, it's no good
I would leave but that is rude

Why do you scream and shout like that?
When I chase that bloody Cat
It hissed at me and then it spat
I am having a domestic spat

Yes, I washed myself today
But have you, may I say
The air is thick and smells of clay
Plus, you wash in some strange way

Why do you insist on keep reshaping bed?
Then on something rest your head?
Why not just curl up instead
That noise you make could wake the dead!

When are we going for that walk?
Will you stop all that talk!
Yes, I know outside there's fog
Doesn't bother me, I'm a Dog!!

Cardboard City such a pity

Cardboard City such a pity
For any who have to live
Something somewhere down the line
Some bad turn did choose to give

One from some Charity walked night street
Stop to talk to 'losers' who did meet
Met one regular of pension age
Belongings in some trolley 'cage'

Sometimes could convince to spend the night
In Hostel specifically for this plight
To have hot food and get clean
So, a someone once had been

If I could then I would
I stood when I knew I should
Did what told until got old
Then I sold when got cold
Now I am just somebody
Somebody who I used to be
Now I am just someone
Someone I call free

So long this way had this person been
Given up on shelter dream
Didn't now remember age
Gave up dates on paper page

Never no did get down
Never smile, never frown
Just the blank of neutral stare
Just the sign that no longer care

Wonder where these people go
When time comes to depart
Just the physical not in spirit
When move on to fresh start

Cast a stone

The reflective one reflected
Their disdain was deflected
Young enough to be hot headed
Old enough to feel the cost
The possibility of the insanity
The unbreakable could be lost

With heavy heart and so apart
Rested head in hands
The misery when cannot see
How would they understand?
For time alone as try to atone
A rash outburst undirected
A target hit and they bit
In ways so unexpected

Emotions stumble as they did mumble

'I cast a stone and so did earn
A volley in return
Took first step and what did get?
Learnt the other cheek to turn
With just a pause it wouldn't cause
Something a lifetime to correct
Frustration barks – on your marks
Then the hold at set
Something know I should have done
So sorry what did say
Wish could make it go away'

The older one and wiser one
Felt sadness for the other
Too much shared and for whom cared
As a Mother and not a Lover
They had been in that scene
Once or twice in past
Comfort gained for despite the pain
Now gone the time when it was cast

Everything went back to how was before

Do best

Is oh oh three too earl
To have a morning drink?
Question and suggestions
As into Caffeine sink
Night draws in and light is thin
The revellers out again
Glad they had but getting mad
The continued is a pain

If a 'single' does choose to mingle
Do they lose that name?
If a pair choose to show they care
Are they 'on the game '?
Dragonflies a late September surprise
When land and cause to wake
Not the vision for broken sleep mission
I would choose for goodness sake

Times like these with chill breeze
Wish back on foreign shore
Where the heat I think as treat
With those I do adore
Life a mess at present guess
Myself and everyone
Just getting through because what do
A thing that we do best

Do you believe in Magic

"Do you believe in Magic?"
A Teacher once did ask
"Do you believe in its existence?"
To a somewhat baffled Class

"Do you believe it's just illusion?
Sleight of hand to fool the eye
That some will never master it
However hard they try"

Now the Class was totally confused
This was not what meant to be
For the subject they'd come to learn
Was definitely Biology

"Do you believe in Magi?"
The Teacher asked again
"Turning matter into something else
That baffles with disdain"

One brave Student stood
"Ma'am, excuse me please
I am here to study an important subject
Will you this talk kindly cease"

The Teacher simply smiled

"Yes, you are and yes we are
Just in a different way
Please sit down and remove the frown
Listen to what I say

The Human body is magical
When think how came to be
The Human body is magical
In what can and cannot see

It heals itself from most things
It its problems solve
It generates and creates
Unforced it does evolve

From two separate things it becomes one thing
It metamorphoses into another
That then changes through the ages
Regardless of the cover

Each part does know the need to grow
The Brain both teaches and does learn
The digestive system a Magician
Turns solids into fuel we burn

Bones do give it shape
Getting bigger as we need
Nerves are info central
To the Brain they feed

Fluids are on-board taken
To stop it drying out
Limbs appear near top and at the bottom
So, we can move about

Other parts take in and use
Gasses we cannot see
Convert the ones that it can use
Expelling those that could cause misery

Each of you is a Magician
Magic Each do use
Unlike that of entertainment
This don't have to choose"

The Class sat in stunned silence
Looked around and at each other
Then as one rose and looked at Teacher
The clapping sounded just like Thunder

Facts Of This Factory

Self-sustaining, self-regulating,
Seasons of bloom and falling leaves,
One end opens another,
Pain is sure sign of life,
But for the fool toying with waste,
All else pain with purpose,
Death feeding life,
Life seeding death,
Much maims as sure as less,
Adaption to balance is divine,
If not for hoarding and largess of ego,
Paradise would ring true.

Nancy Ndeke

See!

The consulate of occults,
Dreamily tossing coins for allots,
Decidedly,
"Life begins here and ends here"
Staggering battles of scales unknown,
Battering life ahead of known expiry,
Song of empirical untruths,
Dressed beautifully in purple robes,
See!
Vanity's glorious ensemble,
Blue coursing defined favoured veins,
All else is straw for the comforts of delicate skin,
While hells rich harvest makes daily visits,
To the undeserving of gifts of breath.
See!
You can't see!

Nancy Ndeke

Marvelous Marbles....

The rainbow type rolling in dicey words,
Folklore dancing at twilight within clear fog,
A cane holds the hands of a soldier's heart,
Watching islands and twin love of blood and heart,

Living a dream that called present at parade,
Mystery shrieks distance to court a malady,
One that genuinely pays homage to the colour of words,
To imbibe in sips as noon approaches,

A thousand dreams building a Volume,
Where callers gape at the dare,
While dots connect to bedeck an idea,
And tomorrow seeks the library shelves,

Where memoirs of a grand heart keep his word,
For generations yet unformed,
By a generation shopping for a minute before sunset.
Such a time is the bulwark of a genius in old camouflage fatigues,

Enriching the world with a true gift of what can never be bought,
For the best of all things is that beholding the gift.
Children coming of age in the company of distance,
And tales yet spoken aloud,

Now, being chronicled by marvellous marbles rolling around,
In the recess and present moment of a time now bridged.

Nancy Ndeke

On A Leash

On a path walked a man,
A street rocked a man,
A highway poked a man,
all the way to that box,
that tells an era to enter,

Only the box was a story fragmented,
filled with refuse and dead wishes,
for where the leash led,
is a destination predestined,
half a man is a dead man,

A halved man is a hybrid grotesque crow for hired scare.
A quartered man is a stone hedge - blocking the builder and the thug,
you either disentangle from the lease and lead yourself,
or pay the high price of belonging to stuffy room.
One which shaves you clean with unclean hands,

All for gain than never trickles downstream.
A man was meant to own his logic and reasoning for all season's.

Nancy Ndeke

Gone the days

Gone the days of grand Parades
Though the beneficiaries did earn
Some came back sooner
Some they won't return
On far of field, they did yield
Unwilling but no choice
Representation of some opinion
Some far-off sheltered voice

Gone are the days from leading
First to show the way
Now it's all different
Don't do as do but say

You who kissed my Sister
Don't have to admit that you miss her
You lover of my Brother
Let no Flag his Coffin cover
Yes, it takes a certain type
To endure the way, they do
Don't make them pay when have to say
They're a dear memory to you

Mother of my Brother
Don't send your Son to War
It's the Master of Disaster
That and nothing more
Mister of my Sister
Don't send her into harm
There's far more to serving
Than being just a weapon that you arm

Gone the days of Chivalry
Upon a Battlefield
Now is mass destruction
As new weapons unleash yield

Goodbye you

Where were you when needed most
Absent without leave
Where could find that peace of mind
Something in which believe
You were my cane of sane
My hope when I had none
My partner in the pain
My friend when having fun

We've been together seeming like forever
We did those things we shouldn't do
We witnessed grass not so green
Looked up at skies not blue
Where were you when needed most
I guess on Holiday
Now I just accept as being
Not really hearing what you say

Found a new companion
Gives what needs to give
Gave me a new reason
New reason for to live
So hello, how are you doing
Do you like now being stranger?
No more will I rely on you
Even in the times of danger

The current so much better
In current can relax
Replacement is advancement
No fear of surprise attacks
You had your chance and blew it
You showed true colours true
You just weren't worth it
So Past goodbye to you

Grass and more

Once a super action man
Put before me and I can
Nothing much could this one stop
Failures a mere stumbling block
I was me for eternity
I was simply what did see
Made a name with dubious fame
Amongst some others that were same

Hours were just words
Days were just a line
A year became a chapter
Everything sublime
I was not born, just created
Purely product as that stated
Handle with care if you dare
We are same but not related

And all the days and all my ways
All the things that others say
All the courage and bravado spent
They are memories and there went
All the feeling of immortal
That great rush when answer call
All the highs and all the lows
Now in this one the past shows

Looking back with sad smile
Wondering why took such while
The grass was greener on other side
When hid behind that thing called Pride
Now realise that I can't hide
Everything far and wide
Nothing now what used to be
When I found the thing called me

Grateful

Heroes are a fantasy
Heroes are real life
Heroes are a Husband
Heroes are a Wife
Heroes are the unexpected
That do that we could wish
Heroes are a certain flavour
They are a special dish

In my time upon the land
Met some who question why
Met some who prefer deep water
Some who roam the sky
Then I met a different kind
Met the type we all can find
Just the person we do meet
Nothing obvious on morning street

Classify a Hero?
A question I do ask
Define the act to achieve
Not such a simple task
I once met a Hero
More than one is true
Some wore some camouflage
Some wore Green or Blue

Whatever their upbringing
Whatever their own day
They rise up when are challenged
They act in different way
The cream does rise with some surprise
Not always what expect
Yet because we can now pause
Grateful for what get

Greens

I am going to have to start eating 'Greens'
Their importance and what iron means
Just hate the Cabbage and Green Beans
I guess I must just swallow

I am not fond of that call frond
The leaf just gives me grief
Eat but chew will be somewhat new
If only for relief

I am going to have to give up snacks
I have read the medical facts
All that about Heart attacks
Plus they say can make you fat!

Going to have to bite the bullet
Hope I can get through it
Wife prefers a Man that's fit
Oh how I love this life

Pages

I read some of pages from past ages
I saw different ways did do
The way and say and how was day
Glad we changed to new

I took a look and some old Book
Adapted so could read
Got into the that passed so true
That sowed in some a seed

To get through the helter- skelter
The way just to survive
The modern reflects the past habits
The common use of knife

Grumpy gripe

Two oh Two oh as we know
A different and testing path
Cannot be near to those we see
So just behind mask have laugh
New words have come to common language
New shopping techniques explore
Closed are most of what visit loads
The non-essentials store

The daily commute near history
As is the 'regulars' that came to be
Replaced with haste by family face
Laptop perched on knee
And we go to where we know
Just work instead of pleasure
Hard a fact when on Group chat
To bunk off for some leisure

The unused yearly train pass
Will you get front them refund?
Best of luck to ask for such
Some sadistic fun
We are the victims
We are all the cause
We are the serfs that suffer
We are also all their Lord

Someone help me make sense of this
Someone please explain
We seemed to be in control
Then in Lockdown yet again

I guess some just don't care about how their actions cost us all

My Opinion Then ....

Is a dot spreading to the edge of a field,
One filled with mines and mimes,
My opinion is the wealth of time at an unknown confluence,
Where minds speak of what words fail,
A script without a prompter,
Easy flows the eggnog at the sinking of the sun,
Knowing the drill of sunrise but still taking a dip,
My opinion is on the alpaphet,
The beadworks that dwells emotions of letters,
Captive to the tongue and sworn to celibacy,
My opinion is a priest who hears all and says none,
A long distance tracker with distance as companion,
A woodcutter watching the thunder of his fallen effort,
And a jet screaming at the silence of the valley,
My opinion is the dance of one and two and reverse
before forward March in Match,
The closeness of a vest and the chest it keeps safe and warm,
My opinion is the fun of a journey that plays a flute and works with the tune,
My opinion is prayer that dreams come true for those who dream awake,
Bundling all opinions into a bundle,
I swing them lightly into the space above the eyes,
Catching the fire of midday,
To light a thousand candle's that dance to the
purity of what cannot be held by hand.

Nancy Ndeke

Ride The Thing Or Burst

Said the wise guy atop the hill,
Eyes peeled and ears staking out,
Hearing the whisper of BURROW speech,
A figment of blue jays and humble mambas,
A keen listener by choice,
Incredible credits to the dazzling scars,
He feeds gentle reminders to generals,
A star of ancient rock cave paintings,
The thrill of hunts and kills feeding the home,
Attitude reigns in the well-fed belch,
Time played by the rules,
Rules paying a courtly bow,
Bows only knowing truth,
A character borne by respect,
Health weighing the wealth of three,
A sum of two and two making three,
Who can fear fate when it teaches without preamble,
Painstaking notes of star wheeling

Schemes of logical debates,
Body better tow,
Before the skin boils into blisters,
In the foolery of gaming gyms,
Where show smiles at mirrors,
While midnight plays dice with marbles,
Dating a thousand rhymes,
A legend working in the shadows of a name,
One so great in humble mien,
To know such,
Is a gift within a gift,
A one life time peep,
Into a buzz that flows incessantly,
Into true texts of world heritage.

Nancy Ndeke

Guess what

Ordinary ascending to extraordinary
The Wobbly rise again
The Ndeke joins the party
As does pick up pen
The Loriz does join the party
As does the Margaret
Also, the Janice and the Cathy
The bar is highly set

Nearing the eight hundred
Of the thousand goal
Poetry is not wording you see
It's coming from the soul
A Donna dawdles but might appear
A Bose is guaranteed
The wisdom shared by those who care
The imagination feed

A thousand poem Book you ask
Yes, a thousand is the aim
Poetry from four corners
Published Poetry will never be the same
A Book that shook the little stuff
Deep into the core
Not the one that for fun
Gives one Titles more

The mix'n'match I plan to hatch
Just because I can
No reason for the title season
Except fits with current plan
Names displayed on inside page
To help lesson initial shocks
When displayed this monster made
Will bear author as Wilcox

Coming sooner than first thought

Half no Destination

If I was to say to you
"What type do you prefer?"
What would be your first impression?
What would you infer?
If I was to say to you
"Are they right or are they wrong?"
Would you give your own opinion?
When not knowing to which side belongs

It feels impossible with half story
Yet half story we all live
Taking what is given
Not knowing what could give
We are cast in our past
In nearly all we do
We are afraid of which from made
Yet scared to be the new

In sleep we keep
That we wish to be
Inside we hide
Our personal fantasy
Some Calcium deposit
Some stuff called flesh and blood
Barriers we make ourselves
Keep us chewing cud

A song will send the senses singing
A sight can cast some light
A taste will make a pleasure
If just didn't hold so tight
Half is not half way back
Half is halfway on
Half is not the final place
None of us belong

Hallelujah

I had to hide from my Bride
When on Wedding night
I screamed Hallelujah!
Not what you think for had no drink
Just wrong room into did zoom
That Bride! You should have seen her!!

I had to hide so ran outside
Knocking over man with Tuba
He screamed too but different tune
It was not Hallelujah!!

Down the stairs I went in pairs
Interrupting some street crooner
As through the door just before
I met with Hallelujah

My wooden leg

My wooden leg's got woodworm
At least that's what the Boss did say
Funny though the first hole
Showed when she with drill did play

My wooden leg is confusing
For the life of me don't know
How it's got arthritis
But that's just how does go

My wooden leg hates our Dog
It hates the Cat the most
Dog it sprinkles daily
To the Cat it's a scratching post

My wooden leg has family
In table it has four
Armchair two pair and another where
The Dog with Bear trap did explore

857

Hark the lark when the Dogs bark

Hark the Royal Mail Post person calls
Another Bill to thrill
Laying on the floor inside
Should I let it lie there still?

Makes a change from junk so strange
Menus from new shops
Physical not with appeal
Just like those Internet tops

Hark the contact less payments
Just touching card to screen
Easier to spend your money
When can't remember where have been

The queue outside while irritation hide
Know that it really does make sense
Just the standing there when without care
The one before you lets new in

Hark the two-a.m. street cleaning
Noise to raise the dead
Just what you wish to hear
When sound asleep in bed

The life I knew and went through
Sure, now has it changed
Is this part of what's to come?
I think that I will protest with a street party

Hark the lark when Dogs bark

Has no vroom

My systems show I'm on a go slow
My Brain it can't believe
When have done that which must
Certainly parts now sign of rust
Still want to be that which been
Again to see that have see
Now the case of the has been
Body no when mind is keen

Maybe Someday will be the plum day
When both choose again agree
Maybe Someday will be that fun day
Nothing promised, let's just see
The Matinée of what may
We wait in expectation
The Curtain call for end of all
Existence just a Play

An empty room has no 'vroom'
The stage of age is just the Stage
The been and gone now Wonton
The soup is now a Cage
Dissection with inspection
The knife can be so cruel
The satisfaction of interaction
Making thought the fool

When under pressure we then measure
The level we have achieved
Harmless the regardless
Of which others once believed
No Judge but self and your health
No limits to that can be
What one was, was just because
Their current we couldn't see

Head rest

Came from it and will return to it
What I ask is it?
Nothing rude I plea don't intrude
Accepted is some wit
The Avalon of where be from
The part that doesn't matter
For short and tall inside all of us all
Sits that want to scatter

Not the same but in species name
One in which we bond
Not all like and hate does spike
Past, present and beyond
You and me are History
The day we did show
For with this thing each does bring
The current to then grow

Short and sweet yet complete
Our part of it we do
Hope that cope with isotope
Or other names so new
Science grade now man- made
What more could this thing ask?
Other than to try to buy
That trend that now is Mask

Rambling as scrambling
To bed to rest that fed
In day of fray if allowed may
I'd rather rest this Head

Hello you, you are me

Wisdom flows upon the shore
Ebb and flow with what we know
Starting over like cliffs of Dover
Always something that's on show
The strings we pluck don't mean much
Until fit into tune
The songs we play maybe some day
A future type of rune

I'll be there if they care
Join me if you please
Just a start is making mark
When yourself release
No ambition for fruition
Just the one who are
No conscience parade of that which made
Just raising self-set bar

Free to be what others see
Lies just a disguise
The truth will know with what's on show
Regardless of the size
Salvation situation
When can't do as fast as think
Then the laugh of that ironic
Before into despair we sink

I wonder as they plunder
Instead of being true
The one that can don't give a damn
Accept what weak will do
Taking tips is not for kicks
If you turn up something new
Imitation an irritation
Time wasted to shine through

Inchin Ink

Inchin Ink had chance to think
Before the Marbles use
Felt not that serious
Wanted to amuse
The Marbles had one idea
Inchin had another
What became of the war of wills?
Not that of 'property lover

The sluice amused when transferred refuse
The Drain felt over loaded
The water as rain was insane
The hill top merely goaded
Green and red chose Gold instead
Of the clash with Blue
An image made soon in Trade
The newest of 'The New'

My foot does grow that which don't know
Soon will be in some sacking
Leper fear is quite clear
When blood flow seems quite lacking
The dog next door has one strange paw
Different colour from other three
They are Black and this one White
Canine complexity

If I were two foot taller
Would I wish I was two feet shorter?
If I knew then what found out now
Would I have turned up at the Alter?
Peanut butter and Blackcurrant jelly
Really is a must
Those with no taste so with Strawberry replace
Are brain cells you can't trust

Inchin ink felt happy

Inflection

If a word remains unheard
Did it really exist?
If a sound just falls to ground
Did it have to twist?
Do we see reality?
Or just that which we choose?
Do we just count benefit?
Not that which we lose

I sit and stare wondering if I dare
Be that person who I be
The confusion of illusion
The strong that others see
Can I take to point break?
The measure of the pressure
The too deep thinking in which am sinking
Where are you Clarity my treasure

If marvels made magnificent
Why they pass me by?
If good stood for adulthood
Why do we have to try?
The world outside both near and wide
Traps for the fool that treads
Into the new without a clue
Or by familiar led

Catching in a cat nap
The way it seems to be
Though is strange I wouldn't change
For is part of me
Back t word that needs to be heard
Not just seen on screen
For inflection gives direction
A different thing can mean

Inflictor or inflicted

The cigarette burns slowly unsmoked
Wedged between two fingers
Dirty white joins atmosphere
There it briefly lingers

Other hand drums a staccato
Repetitive yet not heard
Eyelids closed to shut out sight
Of the torture so soon incurred

To a one they do not know
Only by the name
Upon a screen, what does this mean?
In this sick perverted game

Dora was a keen explorer
So was said on the Children's show
Am I just a different Dora?
Only time and ink will know

Another stroke, another dot
Another line complete
Patterns forming as mouth yawning
Until in verse they meet

The cynical world of the absurd
With name so one can tell
The abuser and the loser
Of this poem born in Hell

Who's the winner and who's the sinner?
The inflictor or inflicted
Both do each have alibis
Between their ears both are twisted

Into the path

The Worlds absurd with mass not heard
The situation just not right
The complexity of misery
So we choose to write

The cold dark place we sometimes face
Inspiring not the other
When we turn to new verse earn
That might be endorsed by cover

The Story teller in short form
The key to thinking now is born
Interpretation a mystery
That is joy and so should be

Define the 'perfect' Poet
I will applaud you if you try
Then dismiss because remiss
I shall tell you why

There is no perfect poet
None can claim to be
For every single Poet
Is just like you and me

We have our happy
Have our sad
Talk the good times
Describe bad

A pocket full of notions
A chest just full of letters
Two minutes here and two minutes there
The world can't get much better

Thank whoever who led me into the path of the Wordsmith

Irish Dance

One did come and so begun
One then Two and grew
Three now see and then plenty
Just look at what they do

Poise and grace with smiling face
Each a statue from waist up
Hips and below a different show
From this River they do sup

Tap, tap, tap – clap, clap, clap
Twirl and whirl and twirl
Tap, tap, tap – clap, clap, clap
Every Boy and every Girl
Tap, tap, tap then tap, tap, tap
Faster than I could see
Only sound as make on ground
Brings reality

The Irish did create it
It spread to different lands
Heel and toe the sound does grow
Though not upon the sands

A certain style of music is required
To give the true effect
A man and his accompanying
A new craze did set

Tap, tap, tap – clap, clap, clap
Twirl and whirl and twirl
Tap, tap, tap – clap, clap, clap
Every Boy and every Girl
Tap, tap, tap then tap, tap, tap
Faster than I could see
Only sound as make on ground
Brings reality

Ironia

Cometh one and cometh all
Come you hale and hearty
Cometh neat and cometh scrawl
Come let's have a party
Black or White is just in sight
Language just a sound
Emotion more than notion
Equality profound

On astral plains, the vision reigns
There but out of reach
On solid ground the means found
Then began to teach
The ways and means to achieve dreams
The stepping stones are laid
Not that pomp and glitzy should
Not that school parade

That first step to what get
For better or for worse
Impulse inbred, occasionally with regret
Best quality or a curse
Wanting more such a chore
When have already what you need
Clothes to protect from getting wet
Sustenance to feed

On some Ocean floor we did explore
Pressure could not face
Looked again to sometimes, when
Could colonise Outer Space
Heaven in the Heart beats
To prove that we exist
To destroy like some old toy
The final ironic twist

Is a Ruby?

Starlight sometimes shines bright
Sometimes seems to shiver
Just how far is/ was that Star?
The lips begin to quiver

On reflection of perception
Did you get that 'special dish?
On reflection of which I mention
Did you have the meat or fish?

The bell rung so has begun
Another day at School
Learn to earn so then can spurn
Falling freely like drunken fool

One hand in a pocket
The other holds White cane
Dodging guided missiles
Moms with prams are quite insane

Look at me trying to look at you
Does that looks meet halfway?
Does it deflect for better to get?
Does it go astray?

Plastic shoes now seem the rule
Good in a strange way
When leather comes from living things
The more expensive just out of play

Is a Ruby a Diamond bleeding?
Why a Sapphire Blue?
Me, I am clueless
Perhaps you have a clue?

Is fate a state

If Fate won't win the confused game
Was it folly but in different name?
They won't win but neither you
What in end do you do?
Failure just a Teacher
To look at it and self
Was it just the wrong time?
Do you do it just for wealth?

Wealth a bonus but not a reason
Wealth does change like the Season
Wealth is nice but so is health
That's worth more than plain wealth
How many corners must one turn?
Until respect in some do earn?
How many roads must one travel?
Until this puzzle can unravel

Happiness is not just some state of mind
Happiness we strive to find
Happiness is in what we measure
That certain thing that we call pleasure
Love evolves from that state
Opposite of thing called Hate
Happiness is what deserve
If your doubting you can swerve

When ancestor stepped from known
So much more was then grown
Settled in some locations
Time evolved and became Nations
Yet are still some of same
Just each got a different name
Was it Fate that brought us here?
Was it just Love and Fear?

Is fate a state to which relate?

Is Kilt a skirt and did it hurt?

Once was a boy that did enjoy
The blindness of being me
Innocence and ignorance
Dilution - party three
Some they take and some they break
Romance was not for this hardened by what they saw
When it looked like being, had this one fleeing
Out the nearest door

Camomile made me smile
When some do call it Tea
For is a lotion not a potion
Unlike the Coffee
Is Kilt a skirt and did it hurt?
When whipped off before a fight?
A bunch of naked Scottish mad men
Must have made a scary sight!

So opened a mind and what did find?
A space needing to be filled
In many a way from how others say
Not just that which was instilled
Came to see finally
Knew less than I did know
On reflection needed corrections
The only way to go

Now a free to insanity
Caring not a jot
Made a trade with a jelly blade
Now is what I got

Strawberry better than Rhubarb flavour!!!

Is Parenthood misunderstood

That night that we call 'pleasure'
Are we ready for the 'Treasure'
Can we balance in equal measure?
With our priorities we call Leisure?
That inner feeling with no being
Just a conquest for a night
Are we really ignorant?
Not guaranteed but has a might

The employ to enjoy
The consequence irrelevant
Next week seek new form meek
In which need a seed to plant
Physical over logical
The modern and the old
Many Times, described as crimes
In our past we're told

'How are we meant to be?'
A question for the better
Am no Sage just of an age
When responsible was not eleven letter
We promote the independence
We forget to tell of rules
We are with each one passing
Turning into fools

Sorry but Mom and Dad are on social media
Leisure spaces are new Estate
As you cry we wonder why
You spurn the love for hate
True or false without pause
Flood for fame and money
If not sad it's got this bad
In twisted ways is funny

Is Time

Our claim to be just what we see
In that which is reflection
Nothing more and that's for sure
Is just more than our perception
All our past was just a blast
When tomorrow comes it will be fun
When we make it so
When tomorrow comes and day begun
The important is that we do know
The me and we of what choose to be
The rewards of simply identity
The bits we choose to show

So what say to another day?
Do we make the change?
Do we do that seems so new
Acceptable that so strange?
Yet I don't feel beat despite this feat
I believe we can achieve
Whatever chosen dish
When harmony the symphony
Not just some future wish
Once more the law must come to fore
The law of the living
Not the breaking by the taking
The mutual act of giving

Is Time a crime or friend of mine?
A question many ask
No answer for no Master
Of that which could be task
Perplexity is Infinity
When to grow just seems a show
The situation no relation
Fortunate to know

Is X the spot?

Patterns
Attach
Take
Always
Promises

Fun for some but not for all
Maybe mix? It's your call
Repetition leads to fall
When as writer only tool

Wordplay! Hooray!
Brightens Day
When does enter into foray
Yet becomes seem say/say
When is just all same way

Retort

What do you mean my Pen runs free?
Captivity was never taught
Marbles free to be what be
Only some in words are caught

So, I am ignorant to your perspective
So, I do not 'match up to you
Guess that you are lacking something
Question is – do you know too?

Nothing more detestable than the pompous
Except the pompous that are vocal
Luckily for Humanity
They are merely local

To lower myself to your standard
Would rather spite face by cut off Nose
Take on board that I just pity
Hoping sense is found and grows

Past

My branches reach for
Era's past...
In hopes of strength from
Those gone ...
Touch me with the knowledge
You gained ...
As you walked through trials
Of life ...
Let me feel the wisdom you
Had ...
You stir my soul in dreams
Of night ...
But when morning light
Shines ...
It's fragments of words lost
In meaning ...
A language I know not but
Search ...
Who you are to touch my
Dreams ...
Leaving a want in unknown
Mysteries ...
As if I splash the troubled waters
To see ...
The face that holds knowledge
Past ...
That yearns to touch my soul
In dreams ...

Janice Fisher

Weeds

The world sits so
Still
As if its eyes are
Watching
It's landed on a
Stump
That once was a
Tree
Growing strong it's
Limbs
Reaching for the
Sky
Now it's roots chocking
On weeds
Thunder roars from the
Mountains
Answering its call with
Lightning
Tornadoes swiftly push
It
While the sky turns brown
With dust
The wind answers a fire as
It spreads
The mask stealing the
Breath
Earthquakes try to shake it
Loose
But it closed its watching
Eyes
Waiting for the rains that
Bring
The finale of rainbows
Promise

Janice Fisher

End

I sit on the deck watching
the days end
As night slowly forms it's
darkened blanket
Leaving the days adieu in
Spectacular sky
I watch its beauty slip behind
the mountains

Replaced by a sky full of
Starlight
I look away from the West
to the East
As the moon begins its ride
to meet the stars
Causing mischievous shadows
to dance it's rise

The nite breeze warms against
my face
I hear it as it gently kisses the
Leaves in movement
The nite silence broken as an
owl hoots
Answering its call, a night hawk
flaps its wings

I smile as the crickets join in the
nights orchestra
Not to be left out a coyote howl
at the moon
A shadowed movement brings my
Attention
To the field as the shadows take
Form

Three deer move close slowly moving
in full alert
A star streaks across the sky in its
final decent
From within the house the clock chime
twelve
Time has stood still for me as I watched
the day and it's beauty end

Janice Fisher

Wild Fire

Hearts aflame within
A weeping soul...
Shoulders laden in
Heavy coals ...
Tears dry as in the
Desert heat...
While minds enter a
Dust storm ...
Eyes blinded by
Sorrows gone ...
Feet bare stepping
Unseen ...
Hands wrinkled in
Time ...
Minds sweeping in
Uncharted
Territory...
Bridges of tomorrow
Sweep in raging
Currents ...
Left in missing puzzle
Pieces ...

Janice Fisher

Chapters

I open the book of
New Adventures
Step in flight on
Butterfly wings
Hoping to nurture
Souls
Opening buds of
Peace

Pollinating a trail of
Unity
Whispering breezes
Of hope
As tides come and
Go
Finding mysteries in
It's depth

Pages floating fourth in
World's rotation
Poetry spilling from the
Heart
Crayons melting as
One

Janice Fisher

Search

I search the depth of my
troubled waters
That seem to pull me in
the tides pull
I breathe in the depth of the
waves retreat
So many whys in the
foam left
Watching the seagulls pick
In the foam
Finding nothing left but
sea water
Emptiness fills my soul
quieting whys
The clouds roll like a
calendar page
Beyond the horizon not
mine to see
A clock ticks quietly in
my mind
A tear touches my lip
salty as the sea
Time evades us in our
wants of more
But this path has no
stop watch
We're but a soul loaned
to a body
That evaporates in dust
or sea
I glance up at the moving
clouds
Thinking souls in their
final flight

Janice Fisher
A final one from the Lady herself

Challenge

In life ...
We face so many
Challenging paths ...
It tries' s to pull us
Down ...
Separate the unity we
Are ...
There is no you or me
But us ...
We started as two in our
Beginning ...
Somewhere along our
Journey ...
There were cross roads
We took ...
We lost our way and turmoil
Began ...
It's up to us to find our way
In peace ...
If anything in our paths should
Be destroyed ...
It's the word of hate, it doesn't
Belong ...
Love, peace, Unity, should
Flow ...

Janice Fisher

The Knowing

In the vastness of the universe
Beyond distant Galaxies
miracles emerge
lifetimes collide
Perfection unions waltz
into being
Memories unfold
in crystal voices
Different faces
unusual names
yet souls recognise
something is the same
I saw you sitting
you looking up and smiling
There was no earth beneath my feet
But a longing for us to meet

A soaring of the heart
took place
You were the one calling me
like a lost child
I ran into familiar arms
Love was found
Our souls knew
instantly
magic alchemy
Destiny
fulfilled
Delivery
In broad daylight

Margaret 'Renie' Burgess

Momentary

Almost, not quite
Fear muddled its way
into my brain
like an uncontrolled pain
Human events cater piled down
over my head - avalanche bound

Forgot where I was
Where I had been
Running like a Rabbit
a Fox, on the heal
Darkness entered all that I feel

Then, suddenly, like a shot in the wire
I stood on my feet and my thoughts became higher
The path I chose
was the one that I want
Nothing can stop me from
making it there

Warrior and Goddess – truth seeker
Being of light
Where had I ventured
this one lonely night?

Thank you, my Angels,
who answered my prayers
I never forget that you are always right there
A slight lapse of consciousness
now is repaired

I picked up my Crown, dusted my feet
Ran like a racer – fast and fleet
Love is the answer, it always has been
Now I remember the darkness can't win

Margaret 'Renie' Burgess

Beautiful

Never did I imagine
Love so deep
so beautiful
A place of honouring
A place of joy
within my heart

Seeing God live within your face
I know
Nothing ever felt so good
so right
We are bound by a sacred union
enchanted cosmic love affair
Help in every tender touch
beloved ecstasy

Each kiss
Lingering past the morning sunrise
floating between us
light illuminating
sanctifying our soul's contentedness
Passion breathing
one breath
My Heart
clothed forever
in your skin

Margaret 'Renie' Burgess

The last fern

I am the last fern
in the forest
You are a caterpillar
looking to eat
Camouflaged as stone
beneath the fallen ashes
Paralysed by fear
you circle in expectation
Satisfying a hunger
starved of affection
Hoping it won't last
The wind begins to blow
As you circle round and round

From the rustling
sound of souls
my defences drop
We are the only two
left inside the aftermath
slithering towards fulfilment
I shed the hardened mask
to contemplate the possibilities at hand
I watch with curiosity
your movement, calculated
We engage in observations
wondering what lies ahead
Asking to recall
a time of equal giving
Questioning
'do we love only with our eyes?'

Margaret 'Renie' Burgess

Of vampires and fools

In the midst of flames
Earth rebuilds
A rapid response
clinging to every raindrop
A heartbeat slowly finds its rhythm
takes a moment
Laughs, forgives
Medicine that doesn't kill you

Calling out to Angels
praying for redemption
Powerful the twists and turns of wild rivers
always in the crisis

A Poet dreams of unknown lovers
fires that pepper the landscape of your heart
not brush
Touches that excite a deeper meaning
Life not lost in translations
of vampires and fools

Margaret Renie' Burgess

Cloudless Night

The lovely Ms. P. embraces the magical mystical moon with much delight.

The dream of mystery is the cloudless night filled
with bright colors of kaleidoscopic stars.

In darkness the moon shines enticing sensual energy.

The morning delight after a dazzling moonlight is the Songbird's
serenade of the ancient masters' amorous sounds of eternal love.

Aami bhaalobaashi tomake khub. Sundor Sapno.

Fantastical Friday

Fantastical Friday, do not be an egocentric, but an
effervescent, sparking, vibrant, and vivacious being.

Empower, enlighten others by your exuberance and high spirits.

Waken the darkness of depression and sadness by your
strength derived from the power of mystical affection.

Emancipate the enchantment of benevolence, compassion,
and the ceremonial dance of life will set in motion an
exquisite world of the unexplained magic of love.

Demonstrate with grace and sophistication the energy granted to those
that heed kindness and thoughtfulness to humanity not just today,
but every day. One, two, cha, cha, cha, three, four, ooh-la-la... ....

Raindrops

Raindrops, gently, quench the earth and our selected
words influence and should be filled with mirth.

Do you desire to be inspirational, encouraging, upbeat and
positive or similar to a ground dying; scorched powerless,
incapable and unable to produce any fruit.

Ponder deeply why your behaviors are unorthodox with no rhyme or reason.

The relentless pursuit of inscrutability, perchance your guilty
pleasure, is a ghostly love affair of a being with internal conflicts.

Implement, love for yourself and the delicate waves will
build momentum to change your spiritual pathway.

Goodnight and Sweet Dreams all y'all

Melissa Begley

Thankful Thursday

Thankful Thursday, what did you observe in your mirror this morning?

Scrutinize your aura in addition to your reflection of beauty.

Fragile, frail, weak, narcissistic, and broken-down are many.

Today lets mend, repair, and try and put back together those afflicted with sadness, depression, enjoyment of the gossip train, broken hearts, physical and mental sickness, or the loss of a loved one.

The greatest gift we have is the compassion, sympathy, empathy, kind-heartedness, and genuine concern that we can exhibit in our own unique and extraordinary way towards humankind and our furry little loved ones.

It is time to perform the Celebratory Dance of Life. One, two, cha, cha, cha, three, four do it some more.

Please remember to count your blessings and to send up all the glory to God.

Face

Upon awakening at 3:00 a.m., I noticed a face looking
through my bedroom window, staring at me.

A young childlike face, but it was an adult male with a
devilish smile and inexplicable anxiousness.

Perplexed and frightened, I jumped off the bed and
like lightening ran into another room.

There stood the demonic entity with the childlike face. Ear shattering
laughter and mind-blowing anger, but I lashed out with hysterical sounds.

The childlike face transformed into the adult
male releasing negativity upon me.

To avoid harm, I shielded properly and astral projected
the lightness of love into his astral field.

Gasping, tantric breathing, and losing control he disappeared,
but his chemical energy was released into the atmosphere.

Mr Sandman

Mr Sandman is escorting the lovely Ms. P. to the
Metaphysical Discotheque on the moon.

Hand-cut-crystal red-hot chandeliers, dazzling flashing
lights, stimulating sounds, edgy-sexy pretty pretty pretty
boys, rebellious energy, and iconic artwork.

Ridiculous or impossible, not if you encounter
imaginative energy or a past life regression.

Sweet Dreams all y'all.

Melissa Begley

Golden Hearts

The harmonious ensemble of tranquillity and love are exhilarating;
frequently a difficult performance of the human condition.

The gift of self-restraint, with effortless dancing, while you ignore
those that boggle the mind with seductive lies and spreading
untruthful rumours is an intuitive dedication to inner-peace.

Distrust those that have limited positive energies and
are oblivious to their own unhappiness.

Golden hearts are uninterested in flattery and will flutter away
from the destructive behaviours of over dramatization.

Fantastic Fabulous Festive Fantastical Friday

Fantastic Fabulous Festive Fantastical Friday, your attitude
will sparkle, shine, glitter, and glisten today.

Trounce, thrash, and trample the adversary of unpleasant, disagreeable,
obnoxious, unlikable, heartless, and hurtful mind-sets.

Decorous, demure, well-mannered, courteous, and respectful
behavior will be your heartfelt bequest of kind-heartedness.

Remember to send up all of the glory to God
and to detach from negative people.

Serene Sunday

Do not become exasperated by humankind or disappointed when a promise is broken for the reason tranquillity is within your own heart and soul.

Artificial politeness is vulgarity. Self-petulance is an exaggeration of the ego.

Do not regret change in relationships for the reason the lightness of love is more powerful than the hardest hearts.

Seek the truth without blurry vision ruffled by the untruths.

It is time to perform the Celebratory Dance of Life. One, two, Cha cha cha and sending up all the Glory to God.

Melissa Begley

Tree Spirits

The trees bowed upon my entering Pre-Columbian site.

Electromagnetic energy and swirling winds centuries ago.

The half-moon shapes wept from the destruction.

The land twisted, reshaped, the stream now downhill.

The seer visualized women carrying baskets of flowers.

The pendulum directed me to the mightiest tree.

The bestowment of oneness with his masculine energy.

His bark caressed my nakedness, I sobbed.

The Tree Spirit's face was revealed. Majestic King.

Thunder God's destruction, slaughtered his people.

Humans exceeding all bounds of decency was ethereal.

A blackened heart possessed the Thunder God's jealousy.

The ground was tossed creating craters.

Soil rained down, burying the villagers. Soulful sounds.

The restoration of Zen like enlightenment is futuristic.

Perchance, the oneness of love will soon revisit.

The Trees will bow again eradicating evil suffering.

Melissa Begley

Remembering

You sit across the room
candle lit and roses bloom
inside a crystal vase
I watch the expression fixed upon your face
photographs neatly placed upon the mantle
the flames flicker crackling
bringing up memories of days gone by
ones that brought a sparkle to your eyes and tears at times
the room is filled with voices embedded in the walls
the children's laughter when they were small
voices from the loved ones who
shared this living space
the ones you are remembering I see it in your face
some never have such memories to drift back to
there is a haunting beauty when they do
appearing deep within your heart
your soul is being fed
I will not disturb your moment
just knowing they aren't ever dead
life when lived within the heart is eternal
it never leaves
only temporarily it seems
until the light begins to shine and the soul wakes up the sleeping
I will let you have them now
thank you for the peeking
into the hallway in the open door loving you even more
life isn't always what it seems
sometimes we need to remember
to fall into a dream.......

Margaret "Renie" Burgess

Love exchange

I come to you with open arms
the world is beautiful
falling into you
close
spinning world of chaos
loses its momentum
here next to you
there is only love
hearts wrapped around each other
souls touching
a sacred intimacy
in perfect alignment
a higher calling
Beloved I am yours
hold me here
never
let me go
secrets
hide within our consciousness
as we breathe, we become
I feel you and hear you in this silence
where words cannot fumble
understanding leaps in each kiss
I am
as you are
we are
as God gifted
nothing else matters
nothing
but this love exchange ....

Margaret" Renie" Burgess

Spell Bound

Clothed in lace and garnets
ghostly pale cheeks
the forest calls
the witch's spell cast
watching every move
bats fly overhead
the moonlight glows a wicked sheen
spellbound in stilettos
hypnotized
hungry wolves in wait
there will be howling
in the woods tonight
thirsty for blood

Complete

You are the giggles in my soul at noon
the light in the darkness
passions run wild
the sea rocking us
feel the connectedness
the sensuality of close encounters
you see me
I know when you are here
blue sky
white clouds
we float
soaring into heaven
unconditional love
nothing else matters
in this moment
our souls entwine
sacred love never was so sweet
our love story

I see you everywhere
we dance
the grasses sway as we move like the wind
inside
each other
sunlight
moonlight
timelessness
bathing us in kisses

other worlds smile down
scattering stars across
our nakedness...........

Margaret "Renie" Burgess

Into you I am

Catching petals
in the rain
falling into love again
the call is pulling
rain drops
softer than the breath of Angels
gentle as the touch of tenderness
in candlelight
powerful beyond the winds of March
deeper than my soul
at sunset in the desert
kneeling down to pray
I am yours in this fragile journey
as the Sunlight meets the day
melting snowflakes
with
patterns of the stars
your heart inside of me
I
flutter like a butterfly..........

Margaret "Renie" Burgess

Orchestrate Love

Thankful Thursday, absorb the magical powers from beyond the veil.
Super interesting exciting, electrifying day and
exchange meaningful time with nature.
You have been presented with a state of consciousness.
Orchestrate the synchronicity of truth, compassion, love and respect.
You are responsible to enhance a high vibrational flow by
creating positivity with your actions and words.
A psychic vampire will thrive upon others by delivering
words of love and appear as a healer, but is a thriller to
manipulate your energy and is a dealer of darkness.
It is time to perform the Celebratory Dance of
Life and send up all the Glory to God.
One, two, cha, cha, cha and three, four Ooh-la-la.
Turn up the charm and do no harm...

Thoughts to Beloved Spouse

There was a blankness in his eyes as he reached for her hand.

Her relative calm did not reveal the sadness in her heart,
or set off an alarm, that she knew he was dying.

His lifetime dedication and special ability to love her
with a fervent desire was a silhouette in his mind.

There was a sudden luminous glow that the Cancer was unable
to kill as he whispered his love for her one more time.

September 08, 2020 (Ms. P.)
Melissa Begley

Gauche

The midnight blue sky embraces the spectacular moon.

Humankind have developed weak minds that
their gauche has become acceptable.

Mr. Sandman and the lovely Ms. P. will travel to a more refined
time where differences of opinions result in mutual decisions.

The Tree Spirits dance in the moonlight while sprinkling a beautiful
fragrance creating joyous love in the hearts of the unique earthly creatures.

Sweetest Dreams all y'all

Name

The shadows faded away, but the reality is nothing hides the pain.

You know longer know my name and have no shame.

The game of love terminated when the dove no
longer cooed at the dawn's dazzling light.

Please, be alarmed for the reason Karma knows your name.

Shadow Self

My sorrow will dissipate caused by your harm,
jealously, and negative emotions all along.

The hate in your heart, perchance does not abate.

The dreams disturbed by your screams was the laughter of your shadow self.

Your hysteria is multiplying like Math.

Walk away with your sway.

As I am fanning the flames of change, I notice the darkness
of a black tear spilling out your right eye.

I fear, for the reason of no happiness, narcissism, and cruelty to others
that your disturbed energy will navigate your spiritual pathway.

Kneel, release the dark energy of no humility or accountability.

Melissa Begley

Sensational Saturday

Sensational Saturday, with the craft of a warm-hearted
mind-set your day will be awe-inspiring.

Remember, it is all right to be zany and crazy, but sincere
affection and respect for humanity is an obligation.

It is chilly and rainy, but it is still time to perform
the Celebratory Dance of Life.

One, two, three, cha cha cha, ooh-la-la. Everybody is
dragging their feet so do it one more time...

Stone-hearted

Emulate the love granted to you by God, or your personal belief.

Should you be racked with anxiety if your artificial
comfort is the high-end-state-of-judgement?

The salacious sounds of hearsay and gossip, while destroying reputations,
perchance is an artistic act of ungratefulness to your God.

Scoff at those that are different, become too prideful for earthly
resolutions negotiating forgiveness, loss of stardom amongst the persons
that create your parasitic powers and eternal cool popularity.

Historical tales of a glorious life, but realistically filled
with strive, unhappiness, or alcoholism.

No matter the illness, personal matter, difficulties of life you give your advice.

As a confidant, trust is appealing as your victim goes squealing and
you accumulate much personal knowledge for your arsenal.

Oh, do tell, how the maidens and gentlemen are sinners while you
sit upon your frozen throne with a stoned-heart of coldness.

Is it enlightened thinking melts your heart or artificial comforts?

Melissa Begley

Na na never

Never mind, never mind
That which we find
And just left at the door
Never think, never thin
Into that can sink
When taking thought for more
Never leave, never leave
Just to deceive
In hoping then to fix
Never let, never let
For will regret
Adding tantrum to the mix

So as difference has occurred
Each one wanting final word
Words too loud to clear be heard
Everything is so absurd

Beat the record you did set
Silly now you can't forget
Let to live and live to let
The others have an opinion

Tomorrow, maybe, will be forgotten
This circumstance that so rotten
If are strong will someday laugh
When returned to normal path

But in the meantime

Never mind, never mind
That which we find
And just left at the door
Never think, never thin
Into that can sink
When taking thought for more
Never leave, never leave
Just to deceive
In hoping then to fix
Never let, never let
For will regret
Adding tantrum to the mix

Where The Head Should Have Been

Is a dry patch with doodles of hundred dollars bills playing hide
and seek with musical chairs made of bear skins and music of a de-
feathered chicken still following the crumbs thrown by its mutilator.
Where the neck should have been is a motley of perfumed bloated
parrots singing out of tune to convince the masses that the great sun
rises from the west and sets in the North. Where the heart should have
been, is an empty cavernous swaying with persuaded decadence as long a
check is printed for the effort at generous sprinkling of death. where the
stomach should have been is a balloonious bottomless pit that swallows
anything and everything as far as there is a rumour of a profit however
meagre for that's the core of this damn creature defying description.
Where the feet should have been, there are fungus and canine's sharper
than eagles crawls to splinter, gorge and suck out life out of life.
Where wisdom should have been, is a drool from an idiot of one's
making, worshipping a traitor, defending the devil and tripping
over himself to convince the world that he is human though
the snout and tail tucked inside the bulbous monkey suit says
a different tale from what the forest knows of primates.
Where the headquarters should have been, now quarter's litter
the monologues of agenda-less meetings where diapers leak from
between the sullen heads soaked to burst with pus from too many
spices used to downplay the stench of National soup with fat maggots
saluting the king of rot under the watchful eyes of watchers whose
balls were wrung and hang to dry on the rafters of falsehoods.
Where hope should have been, tattered oversized underwear of
grandfather's flap on walls swaying with the desert wind in choreography
with the dying thirsty throats of neighbours whose kitchen fires sent
them out for a chance stake at life for gainful work at lowly pay but now
target practice for zealots husbanding a woman already married to
someone else but still shamelessly claiming himself first at the scene.
Where Sense and logic should have been, vagabonds and fugitives ride
the streams with vulgarity preaching entitlement and favour against
those who had sent the wrong application note to heaven asking to
be born in fruit and roots republics, this ranging from bananas to
cassavas, unlike you who has always had a lawyer present during
all your misdemeanours to mitigate against any and all cases.
Where humanity and a sense of wellness should have been, is now silos
and hot homes for gourds pregnant with all manner of cannibal nukes

and venereal amputations of others productive abilities, with the express
purpose of neutering 'lesser' humans to give space to your kind.
Except, who is ' Your kind exactly?"
Not two legs born of a woman?
Not one gone sooner than many tree species?
The crow and the tortoise have a testimony for such if only you asked. But
too busy helping God to help yourself, aren't you forgetting something?
That diamond and gold in all their glory shall outlast you!
That power and authority are as seasonal as flowers!
That the only man better than another is the one
who loves and is kind to fellow creatures!
One who fights fair and reaches out to touch the less fortunate,
for the fate of man, is, after birth, he is destined for death,
what has been accumulated not withstanding.

Nancy Ndeke

Give Us A Stage....

To sweep clean held deadness,
Arrange thoughts as the rain falls,
From a drizzle to a hearty sheet in a storm,
Blending lights from umber to maroon shades of nights,
Give us a stage,
To redraw the doubt maps long held,
Where structure strangled growth,
A thousand naysayers with a trumpet,
Preaching a marching song of knowns,
Give us a stage if you dare be proved not so right,
For we know the wind and its twirling ways,
it's the beauty of variety and amazing,
The contrast of a wild garden in full bloom,
And the mysterious display of emotions on life's journey,
Give us a stage and pay attention,
Pyramids don't move but their memories do,
Awe-ing the seeker in it's unforgettable stature,
The spirit of art is ancient and modern,
Form is a formlessness understood by dare,
Give us a stage,
And on it we shall perform a new thought,
One of a thousand breaths drawn to perfection,
Choreographed by typing truths and errors,
Monitoring of wondering and wandering spirits,
Whose only quest is simple in its complexity,
That what is unknown can be known if we try,
And discovery is the way of a solder,
One, who sometimes finds his own path,
When troops run out of supplies and warm boots,
He borrows from his best thoughts to keep survival living,
A show you won't forget soon,
For in the archival shelves of youths wishing to know,
You shall find the stage effects well documented.
So please,
Give us this stage.

Nancy Ndeke

Laundry life and life's laundry

Perpetual motion not just a notion
When the Heart beats so can live
Perpetual motion an actual token
In the take and give

Otherwise it's more like the laundry machine
Taking us on a swirl and us thinking we're on a trip
The best trip is in the mind
No wonder someone said that Time is an illusion

The tick and tock of the right box
Keeping us on course
The one we break with decisions make
The beating of the source

Repeating of an old course,
Like a known taste longed for,
Not really whole,
Till broken to learn,
The open secrets of gifts boxes,
Where,
We sip experiences,
Unhurriedly sometimes,
Or in a moment,
We live a decade and more,
With nights brewing old songs.
Renewal visibly paying tribute,
To the silence of timelessness,
In each greeting of breath.

The intrusion of that illusion
The complex that does vex
The things we do thrive
Yet all we do is seek a clue
On just how to survive

Within the inner the outer does sing
Its tone the whir of passing thought
On that a word does capture
Giving it emotion and fact
To drive in and out
With a rhythm sought of a seeker
Giving living more than life

Are Jean the means for sometimes seems
As we tumble when we rumble
But for sure we need no more
Than a dash of humble

Oh jeans and classic notes
Passing patches and improved tempo
But of note undeniable
Is dust in its eternal wealth
Where enough is yet to register
Leaving us to play at cleaning
What must claim us some day

I hung out all my washing
Left it there to dry
Put once dirty now clean to public
Did but don't know why

All out to play as sun does at dawn,
All out to pray as a hermit at home,
The public is really the private,
The dirty is a phrase,
For purity began this tent,
And some day when play is over,
And time to clean up due,
The why's and what's shall finally commune,
At the confluence of the ancient River,
That never tires of rebirth.

A collaboration between Nancy Ndeke and Ian Wilcox

Friends walk tall in turmoil's pull

Once upon a different space
Came together two different that face
From different backgrounds and different name
Yet the lives they were the same
Same tribulations, same emotional pull
One going through, one heard that call
Two friends stood and one did talk
One replied as both did walk
Walk through until had passed
For like before, this one won't last

"Life - you have to be in it to experience it
All the good and all the bad
All the gladness and all the sadness
Every time you breathe
Another chance to laugh or grieve
Yes, my friend - don't wish an end
For the end of all go through
Signals that is end of you"

"YES, to living in quarters in subway quartets,
Where yes tears away at fresh,
And no digs a grave,
Yes, to living the pain of breath,
And no, a guarantee one steer into a cul-de-sac,
Yes, to living the debt of a loan,
A crossroads page with a thousand outlets,
All ending at a destination un-appointed,
And if so, a coat of sorrows with prickly thorns,
Yes, to life."

"Times get hard but you are harder
Feelings strong but you are stronger
Confused is best when laid to rest
Joy is long so make it longer
The silver lining of the cloud
Should be seen and gleaming loud
Not that dark that just helps fill
Giving volume to that which thrill"

The sliver in the crowded cloud,
Like bees stinging eyelids and a hiccup,
Memories of first day at school and tender hands coaxing you,
Throat convicts emotions and agony flashes in coins,
Why won't answer the question or suggest a way,
Gratitude seems a hollow prayer as sad eyes beg to go home,
Which home is a scary thought,
Is it the timber walled one to keep warmth in,
Is the fluffy one beyond altitude where dreams direct?
Love can be such a pull, fool and a monster,
Life is war in the loving embrace of it's weak,
But for marbles of a stranger Angel with an ear for sighs,
Lowering the volume of a scream,
Laughter laughs at boss.
Between nights of terror and days of hope,
Books refuse to tow pity's path,
For time won't stop to render it's stamp on sadness,
So life trudges on with minimal mind escape,
As the sun dips at old age,
A new born look appears,
To say that life is fully life,
When it's most misunderstood,
And acceptable is an idea that fits every gift,
To have and not to have a matter of choice,
With empathy flogging guilt,
Experience enriches itself,
For life has no space for poverty.
Neither parties of colossal personal bashing,
It's own healing if allowed,
And it's own end given too much at once.
Life!

A collaboration between Nancy Ndeke and Ian Wilcox

What Inspires Me....

Rain and thunder amidst the mystery of lightening,
Crooked lines of a path overgrown for disuse,
The urge of life to thrive in barren terrain's,
Man's attempts at overthrowing the very source of his livelihood,
Politicians and their poker faced painted with fungus for paid laughter,
The gullibility of faith not seeing the interpreted lie,
Live sprouting wings at unlikely places,
Surviving what was meant to kill with calm grace and humility

Trudging un-trod paths with the confidence of a hunter,
Accepting defeat without begrudging the winner,
Planning for tomorrow which is unknown,
Helping a stranger just because they are human,
Losing all and trying again and again,
Knowing death knocks but living like an immortal each day.
What inspires me is knowing am not alone though lonesome I am,
My song is the River that takes all and gives all.

And am content to be.

The Locksmith

Him, soft punch thrower with flames of gyrating metaphors,
A legend in the neighbourhood where silence presents a buzz,
A slow dancer with fast and furious fingers over a keyboard,
A master of etiquette and a gentle demeanour.

Buried beneath the tough skin of a soldier, glorious of scars,
A world citizen living in the village with love and love,
A born again habitual creature headstrong and happy to be,
Inbuilt sensors he finds talents under bushels

A word here, a phrase there and babies dare to walk,
Shy by design and default his fame precede him,
A scholarly discourse bubbling in libraries abroad,
Battling his own behind curfew time set by love

Letting flows unchecked print epics on a daily basis,
A big dreamer housed in a vision most think unthinkable,
Here's the locksmith carrying the master key,
Gently with minimal effort he unclogs defeat to spray hope

A line builds up on this path of notaries and notations,
Each breathing a testimony of the first encounter with the maverick,
Compare and contrast doesn't pay his taxes,
A believer beyond the idolized days of holiness

His faith is love and the universe,
His mantra is "I'm possible" when told of impossible,
Such a fine introvert he feels like an extrovert,
A sunny spot for all fate brought his way

This day,
I cerebrate THE LOCKSMITH,
A disciple and leader of goodwill to humanity,
And a man of deep letters to boot.

Nancy Ndeke

Next to you

Ten stood tall before the fall
Nine they did survive
Eight a state when accepted fate
Other took a dive
Rest at best took the test
Seven passed, for now
Other one lost the sun
In Institutions cowl
Of seven six did choose to mix
One went on their own
Losing touch with once so much
Status now unknown

Six they tried to then fix
A problem of future hope
Never in their training
Were taught how this to cope
Five alive and somehow survive
System decided not of use
Cast them aside then tried to hide
The trail of their abuse
Token gestures in small measures
For those who served them true
The story told of brave and bold
Who might be standing next to you?

Night surprise

Ill between the in-between
The lapse of the gap
The one who runs to what becomes
The surge that doesn't sap

The override that does not hide
The need of the many and not just self
The need to feed so can answer
The battle which is Master

The display seen which doesn't mean
Superior to you
The reply before many die
The warriors so do

The night quiet ripped asunder
With bright lights and sound of thunder
Buzzing Bees with intent
From a stranger they were sent

The kiss of earth now proves its worth
As smaller try to be
Disco Inferno seems so slow
Compared to that which see

Buzz, buzz, buzz as the rush
Hornets seeking home
Those lead pills will surely kill
As the air do comb

Sense does say to run away
But sense, for now, is wrong
Reason season and almost treason
For is here that you belong

Reply back to this attack
Waiting for big Brother
Larger pill with same will
The area will smother

Nihil

A Black Sun has begun
If half what say is true
Recession in depression
A message we should do
They seem so glad to promote the bad
Good gets lost on middle
News peruses between the muse
Whilst with new object fiddle

And I wonder why I wonder
When other things spring to the fore
I wonder how many wonder
If out there is more
Wondering a living thing
All at times do, do
Wondering about outside
Wondering about the likes of you

It's okay for another day
One to grab and hold
Regardless of the consequences
Regardless of that told

The media a feeder
Of gloom and nothing more
Opinions in division
Neutral such a chore

I drink Coffee in the morning
Drink right through to night
It kisses certain parts of me
Helps to cure a blight

One day a day for hooray
One day another chance
One day to say come what may
This one I will dance

No mad nomad

A nomad noticed some notations
A nomad now at rest
Comfort in confusion
Had sat and past some test
The nomad was no mad being
Despite it all and all the things seeing
That was then but things change
Some of which can arrange

I loved you like a Mother
Yet you took my Brother
I loved you as my land
Yet dealt a twisted hand
I loved you as a birth place
Yet didn't feel my own
Went to one that welcomed me
There the love was shown

Come on now you thing called Life
Come on now you Destiny
I am better person now
Better with a Mind that's free
Free to think of own violation
Free to be simply free
Nothing better could it ask for
Nothing better could it be

A nomad noticed something
A nomad gets so lonely
A nomad needs to travel
Until they find a Home
A nomad learns survival
A nomad learns outside to think
A nomad is but a passing period
When nomad finds true love

No need to mail

Fish and scales with Puppy dog tails
The things that we do meet
Early morning Dawn Chorus calling
Some of us do greet
Hard the cards that dealt
Yet play them all the same
For nothing is fair when some don't care
Despite being in most parts just lame

Religion contradiction
In some but not others
Some confuse to amuse
Some a spectrum covers
One way to play or go astray
Faith can come at cost
When in extreme it does mean
Another person lost

Ants in the attic of attraction
Building nest, we call distraction
Nothing left but some action
To remove that nest
Prosperity a mystery
To some who view it wrong
Prosperity is in what be
The one who does belong

The weight of world as it unfurled
The legacy it be
The mistake made and joy of trade
To be a better 'me'
If clos one's eyes to that disguise
The one that we call failing
Then we see the prospects Sea
With no need of mailing

No gain for pain

What is the place in which we live
Not the scenery
What is that in which exist?
The likes of you and me
We divide it into portion
Then portion divide some more
Let's just take a journey
Let's just take a tour

Is it so hard to switch the gaze?
From that which does dictate
Is it so impossible?
Have we set our state?
And when a clock struck midnight
Elsewhere it greets the noon
The hours are but hours
Like old familiar tune

The outside tries to hide
Yet inside knowing best
Clock is but a countdown
Until we're laid to rest
A decorative that to which submissive
A rule to fool if let
When is just a statement?
Of the existence each does get

'To turn back Time' a well-known thing
Deja vu nothing new when a history does sing
So what of hand that sweeps a face?
What of digital?
What impact a simple fact?
We are one and all

We are prisoners in our hysteria
To run by that we need to maintain
Always seem to lose it
Yet never do we gain

No satisfaction in the stasis

Trusting can be tempting
Trusting can be trouble
Trusting can solve problems
Trusting can make them double
Yet trust we must to build ourselves
To build those who's around
Build up strong foundations
Sturdy and so sound

Camaraderie came calling
Friends fast were forming
Experiences ever expanding
Hardships shared are easier handling
Greetings gained by new names
New to you at least
Bonds are formed as new Days dawned
On bright fellowships fun to feast

There was that day
Long ago
When the likes of you
Just didn't know
Then came chance
To correct
Then was then
Now we get

Laughter in our quiet times
Uplifted when are down
Actions and reactions
An instant reversed frown
We talk across the ether
We joke across the street
We care not of location
As long as we can meet

The vessel we named Friend
Sails uncharted places
Accumulation of acquaintance
No satisfaction in the stasis

No theory to this query

October gone and now November
Summer days I can't remember
Forget Chapter, another Book!
Just Sights of Spring before another look

Quartet quota for whole year
Each revised with wistful tear
For same Titles but that's all
As the next one it does call

Marking time as turn each page
Adding month to modern age
Will the writer add a twist?
Do they even keep a list?

Once a young Lad then I grew
Changing shape into new
Then a young man, oh so bold
Soon be Winter when I'm old

How many Novembers do I need?
How many Springs need to bring?
Summers are the pinnacle
In this journey, one and all

You say that you are different
I beg to disagree
For we share same Seasons
All plus you and me

If I made a Mannequin of myself
I would not know where to start
For each are just like Mannequins
Each a work of Art

I say my name and where from
You the same reply
We find so much in common
Makes me wonder why?

None in the cupboard

There's none in the cupboard
What am I to do?
Space to fill and time to kill
Guess I'll make some new
Paper needs an ink drink
Looking somewhat parched
To the ment it wasn't meant
Refusing to be starched

I checked the fridge and freezer
I am a modern geezer
No, nothing there to report
Guess we're at the last resort
Biro gyro and moves show
Paper happy chappie
I am guessing as I'm messing
If she then please get this one a Nappy

After the event

Red wine is fine when White been drunk
Add to headache as head sunk
Next morning if hear calling
The pleasure of the Drunk

Cold Kebab a trophy be
Now a meal that seems free
What did they do before microwave?
Eat regardless and can't save

The Football repeat on Sunday
Saved for watching Monday
Too much action for attraction
Through dehydrated eyes

Bring on Monday for is closer
To another Fri and Sat
Repetition is the mission
When don't even own a Flat!

Nonsense freely admitted

On a beach on Solitude
A soul on sand did lay
Nothing much to talk about
Just another day
Galaxy Loneliness
So far from where they came
The inadvertent Astronaut
A shadow with no name

On the hills of Cheap Thrills
A fool did laugh out loud
If ignorance is bliss, I'll give a miss
Not so them so proud
Self-denial is a trial
The sentence hard for sure
Just when suffering from blocked tunnel vision
You are burdened with some more

On the banks of Circumstance
Stood the level head
Accepted all we cannot plan for
Just react to where it led
Analysing and adapting
With each step do take
Only when it looks a bad move do you then apply the brake

Mellow maudlin in the morning
Novel notes at noon
Half-hearted screening in the evening
Gently mumbling favourite tune
What is this? Some strange twist
Of what I thought I knew
Just another from word lover
Just a thing I do

Nos autem gloriam

Eleven on the eleventh
A Nation silent goes
In respect of some others
Many they not know
Eleven on eleventh
A chance to show respect
To those who gave so we could save
The freedom we now get

Blessed is the bygone Soldier
May you rest in peace
Blessed all the casualties
Gave for our release
Blessed are the victims
Of the heinous crime
Each one of a family
A Family just like mine

At eleven on the eleventh
The guns fell silent for first time
Unfortunately, Humanity
Repeated and repeats this crime
We honour but then add to
The casualties of war
Why don't we learn the lesson?
Of that which went before

Broken bodies and shattered dreams
The casualties of greed
Sorrow left to those bereft
As to some vision feed
Requiescet in pace you people
Old before your time
Cut short your potential
To give more to mine

Not a Layla

(With acknowledgement to Eric Clapton)

If Layla was an Arab lady
With Guitar that is just crazy
They it's true that I am lazy
For no music can provide

The Lady must have been beautiful
To inspire song
Yet from a different age
To that which now belong

L does start the name I love
That is where it ends
Know some different L's
They are just my friends

Take some light to make things bright
Just don't burn within its flame
Presplit is identity
More than just the name

To hold and touch means so much
If only I could say
Yet when received is not believed
Need to find a way

No, you're not a Layla
You are something more
You are you and it is true
This L I adore

To a L and O, I choose to go
Every time and always
For this love rose above
Lodieta always stays

Optimum Poetica

Once upon a writer's land
One took issues by the hand
To show the world the depth of treasure
The unseen that you could not measure

Once upon a modern screen
Gave a glimpse of what could mean
Filipino ang kanilang katutubong wika
Yet in a different chose and picked a
Common there as in most places
Of different families and different faces

A gathering they assembled
A chance to go and show
The talent hidden just still there
For with a passion they did care

Took decision, made it mission
To drag it kicking into Arena
Not the Gladiatorial more literally literature
Made a place Optimum Poetica

Orchids for the Orangeman

Lockdown lows did come and go
Now a different task
When shopping in space not stopping
Have to wear a mask

The sales have gone through the roof
Medical on sale
Not going to those who need them
The retail holy grail

Disposable and reusable
From places far and wide
Fashion ones even available
For those with senseless pride

Orchids for the Orangeman
Sugar for the Flea
Some do call me a poet man
But what type of it I be?

Nonsense in profusion
Adds to the confusion
Am I just illusion?
A passing dark grey cloud

The task they ask
Is to now wear mask
When in the shopping place
Conscious of the markings
To ensure some space

The robber really loves this
Yeah, I don't stand out
Now all I have to worry about
Is if they scream and shout

Origami

Origami or Salami?
That's a tough one and don't know
Slip and slide or just hide?
Which of me to show?

Mumble jumble or plain humble?
Really, I don't know
Just wait and see, what will be will be
Life is but a show

On a Stage we parade
Some is true and some charade
Not the same each quite made
Some have debts and some are paid

So, Origami or Salami
No decision as of which
The vestibule of ridicule
Another seam in which I stitch

Silly sentences

Am I Black or am I White?
Am I blind or have good sight?
For I cannot differentiate
Confuses me this thing called Hate

Have I been or just a dream?
Things have done and things have seen
At th end what does all mean
If own Toilet you still clean

Egg yolk up or yolk in middle?
As with pan you now fiddle
Complexity a calamity
Just how many answers has a Riddle?

Original called Lust

The one who made a nothing into better
The one who did believe
That the person is the limit
As what could achieve
An 'outsider' becomes original
Different from the rest
Doing stuff in their own way
Often that's the best

Autumn but an arrow shot
When delivered with such speed
Yet in Nature surely Autumn
Has a place, has a need
Summer seems so confusing
When all weather it is using
Add to that a different shore
Is destination want so much more

Who would be that solo Bee?
When to nectar cannot go
The waiting is frustrating
If not always show
The waking just past midnight
Now just thing to do
Done it now so often
Can't claim it something new

Made decision to make a mission
So could understand
That as two grew into that new
Closer in different lands
Clarity no visually
When to change we adjust
Feelings now more powerful
Than original called lust

Oscar Felix

"Oscar Felix Seven to Oscar Felix One
How copy? Over" please
"Don't play the 'tool' like newbie fool
This no time to tease
I'm deep in it and Six is hit
Together say situation
Not that you care for are somewhere
Else as per your Generation"

Grew up on Games that are not same
When real bullets fly
No restart while on seat fart
As real people die

The armchair players are not saviours
Though they think they are
Most can't shave, yet alone behave!
Or even drive a Car!

What are we thinking as into this sinking?
That shooting is just fun?
Peruse the News, does that amuse?
As yet another one

Lost i fit not worth the spit
Yet worth a pull of trigger
Gave wrong look so bullets took
As at your friends you snigger

"Oscar Felix to Felix Oscar
Thanks for the support
Maybe when your credit ends
You might just give it thought"

Oscar Tango Yankee

The J and am became a Jam
The S and it just took a stool
The R and all changed to fool
The P and ram just carried on
The I did sit with d i o t
Felt somewhat Home
The E aspired to that mpire
Took a leaf from ancient Rome

Which can you find that slipped my mind
Past Be and that which could be rear
The f that joins the thing so fond
To hold Glasses somewhat dear
The may and be that you see
The r that joined the udder
How about the t and rout
That makes a one just wonder

C joined loo but changed to an e and u
Not in that order true
The par got wise – made paradise
The c still will the loo
Water fell and so to that call
Added f to know by all
A joined bout and that loud sound
Then for fun it joined that rounds

On fun I run as do some
The mix I try to make
Boring leads to snoring
If constant the intake

Over to you

Our us is we

The couple stood hand in hand
Two months had passed from first day
A dry July floating by
Different from wet May

Eyes did lock as both took stock
How quickly things had flown
Already in the 'us' stage
Instead of just their own

With contented voice he did rejoice
A question formed to ask
So, with feeling happy reeling
He rose up to the task

'Has our beginning come to an end?
Or is this just the end of the beginning?
Am I left deeply sad?
Am I left with my heart singing?

No, I know without a word
I am you just teasing
That look you gave as us try to save
Was far beyond just pleasing

You and me for eternity
Is written bold and true
No more just own each day is shown
In everything we do

Once before felt could take no more
In that in which did live
Then you came and changed its name
Just in what you had to give

Each day I pray that this will stay
Each day I then feel blessed
For you see our us is we
Each day we pass the test'

Overload

Into silence again do tread
As I rest this weary head
Just following that where led
Now is leading to my Bed
Australia and New Zealand somehow give a reason
To be awake when sleep should take
Give up one for another

The way I feel seems so real
The want to write I cannot fight
The season of plain reason
Nothing more than a blight

I know the problem
Just cannot fix
That cure the curse and much more
The remedies and tricks
So give up on what much
Needed but can't achieve
I am addict with it
Now I so believe

The growin is now showing
The sensation of infestation
The out pour I could abhor
If only for creation

A tragedy is one like me
A certain kind of sick
That will inflict but just a bit
And treat it like a kick

Sorry you but I must do
To keep me slightly sane
I am just quite generous
As I share the shame

Others overhead

I wanted all so began the fall
Fixation a strange thing
Blind to find that peace of mind
With it what can bring
'One day you'll be a Man'
So did many but different sang
One day became next day
When what had no longer play

Chopsticks bewitch until learn the trick
Of their manipulation
Trial and error can lead to better
If worth in situation
Strong words said stay in Head
I guess I needed them
A broken mind a Band Aid find
In form they call poem

So look at me and what do you see?
Not the truth I guess
For unpeel layer and perhaps savour
Then tackle all the rest
The undone me some will see
The man behind the mask
The cautious me will fragility
Who summons just to ask

Unimportant me in society
That I do accept
Just understood to try to do good
Other overhead do let
So if you're fine with me and mine
Then welcome to my world
If you feel insult a thrill
Carry o for are unheard

Own efforts

I came to change the World in some way
Not a big way I admit
But I came through Mother Nature
So, I guess I'm part of it

I came unbidden yet am here
I, in truth, had no voice
So, instead, I use gift of writing
So, my being I can rejoice

I am of no importance
That I recognise
Yet I am blessed with acquainted
From both the near and considered wide

I am but a molecular substance
I am nothing more
Yet I value other molecular beings
As potential I explore

'I am me so should cherish'
Once did say one wiser than me
'Do your best to make things better'
I guess just trying a destiny

I came to change that would live in
If for no other but me and mine
I am a nothing but to them important
End of day, that's just fine

Now can I ask who are you?
Do you be yourself true?
In own circle have a clue
That your efforts now shine through?

Pandemic of the popular protest

We pay the Fine for new crime
Ignore the good advice
Add to the new problem
Because outside it looks nice
Moan and groan when on our own
In Groups larger than we did attend
Because more than thirty now classed as 'dirty'
We just have to 'mend'

Autumn fast approaching
Though would never know
Climate is in chaos
Regularly does show
Shootings by those we trust
To our communities protect
Unemployment rising faster than income
Apart from the 'top set'

Bitter sweet that victory
When you prove that you are ill
Having to justify that you don't lie
That a permanent disability is a disability still
Who are we in this insanity?
To make politics our voice
When we stand to lose that grand
To something with no choice

I simply stare without much care
As protesters protest for joy of protesting
Not for that which needs addressing
Just because it is now the 'new thing'
Not understood how feels good
Shout for sake of shouting
Rather than a displeasure statement
Has turned to some one day outing

Do half of them even know what they are protesting about?
The real issues are getting buried in this nonsense fad

Parked a piece of permanence

The story told so many times
Different people but same story
Selfishness became a quest
Tarnishing the glory
One victim hurt within
Chose to speak out loud
Experience but no grievance
Wrote that of which not proud

You took a wild Orchard
Then from me you then hid
Keeping as your treasure
When to your expectations could not measured
You took the wild and made your own
Took because you could
You could not see concept of free
Just you and nothing but

They parked a piece of permanence
Upon a pedestal
You, however, brushed it off
To the floor you let it fall
Sowed the seed that we all need
The knowledge someone cares
Yet you dug up with your 'Losers cup'
When your attitude won't share

So wrote one of the millions
Just a different name
The mystery of compatibility
Lucky dip but different game
I watched them play from far away
Not a gamble that I choose
When the stakes can make or break
I have too much to lose

Part Human Moon

He went one way
It the other
Last thing heard from him
Very loud has "Oh Mother!"

The bike looked small and the slope tall
Down he went at speed
To the end where up did send
As if another Satellite need!

Last we heard on the News
Some NASA boffins did confuse
Asteroids come here from there
This one burst out from our air

A competition they did run
Naming it - some school fun
Then the Head sheds flipped their lid
When our Mom said "That's our kid"

Peaceful now in my Room
As in orbit he does zoom
No Neil Armstrong can claim to be
More Evel Knievel booster free

It seemed such a good idea
When that day so bright and clear
On top of hill the track did start
Then the ramp for final part

Never guessing he'd be so mad
On that push bike that he had
He even pedalled as down went
Adding speed with intent

Alas poor Alan now self-taught
Part Human Moon, part Astronaut caught
When I say now it is true
Every night I look up to you

Pass me a chocolate biscuit please

Breathing takes a second to life
One we can't replace
Just a second but much more
When the new we have to face

Molly made a mop of straw
Once used cloth but now no more
Circumstances came to Dances
Front and centre and to the fore

Maverick maybe but okay
When with thought one does say
Words are there for one to play
Even if not every day

Mike does like to Hike
The steeper the more enjoyment achieved
Once did listen to the doubters
Long ago he then believed

Self-thought taught the hardest lesson
Too many opportunities for distraction
Yet the gain outweighing pain
End result the best attraction

Phyllis is bliss
The schoolyard banter from the lads
Eager promotion some strange notion
Had captured and then had

Harmony is mystery
When looking in too deep
When you find the place of calmness
That is the one thing you should keep

Angela hates her attitude
Ironic when you think
The part of her that lose prefer
Is that in to she does sink

Passing time in pleasure

Mister Maybe might one day see
Misses Might Not begs to differ
May and might in some fight
The body starts to quiver

Fantasy and ecstasy
Playing games with me
Promising without delivering
Just the way they be

So on solemn trek we regret
The end but not the reason
When gave so much then into touch
Outside the Football season
Why oh why did you try
Blinded by the act
They didn't care to their time share
Refusing simple fact

The pieces fit but not quite right
Is it me or just some blight?
That one's loose and that one tight
They seem so much Day and Night

In the Head we are led
But the art is to follow Heart
When combine all is fine
Head is just the start

So on solemn trek we regret
The end but not the reason
When gave so much then into touch
Outside the Football season
Why oh why did you try
Blinded by the act
They didn't care to their time share
The question – Do we care?

Pause to ponder

One day they say
Can change a life – it's true
One day can also end one
With no thought of you
One day can a difference make
One day can set you free
One day can make so much difference
One day at time we see

Education a sensation
Yet learn more outside School
That is just a preparation
That is just a tool
Getting into practice
For what have to come
When discover open mind
Open can be fun

Not subsonic nor hypnotic
Parabolic or even tonic
Not laconic nor thionic
Just a human who loves words
Not aphonic nor demonic
Not opsonic nor hedonic
Not postganglionic or pheromonic
I am that absurd

Not phytoplanktonic nor microscopic
Isotonic or extraembryonic
Anticycyclonic or zooplanktonic
Amphytiomic or geologic
Allophonic or enharmonic
Homophonic, even thermionic
Macaronic, exergonic
I am just plain old me

Shall I be weak

Somewhere someone sometimes said this written
For despair and without care
Reality had bitten

'Shall I see another day?
Shall I find the reason
Shall I send the resign notice
Not care if thought as Treason
Shall I just accept the present
Not strive for that beyond
Shall I just leave this now
In place of which not fond

Shall I be weak when strength seek
Shall I be a misconception?
Shall I be that fragility
The one too scared to mention
Shall I come when day is done
When distraction put to bed
Shall I be that truth you see
Deep in that there said

Raindrops fall and shoots sprout tall
The ironing grows to piles
Yet no care as at it stare
Non creasing with the smiles
If half past Three then what do see?
When half past Ten is there
Do we even look at clocks?
Do we even care?

A random ramble is a gamble
If worried where will lead
I am but an absent Mind
So into it must feed

Shall

The moment came in that game
The one that most do know
That certain stage when show ones age
The truth we now do go

Have done all the lead up
The hope to impress
Now comes the crucial verdict
Was good enough the best?

'Shall we share the shimmer
As Sun it gently goes
Shall we share the moment?
That one which only two do know

Shall we share a moment
Or one and nothing more?
Shall we share a moment
Then another one explores?

Shall this be our perfect key
To unlock a promise held?
Or will it be just simply
When two pairs of lips they geld?'

The battle of attraction
The war of adore
The simple skirmish, then retreat
The advance for more

To the victor goes the prize
Yet not considered if are wise
For that really just implies
Is just an object in disguise

True is in each clue

Shambles

I smile at adversity
Just a chance you see
I laughed when asked for autograph
Examine a mind free
Lost my pride on the other side
Of who I became
Now amongst the other people
Those with hidden fame

Happy once with what I was
Happy with new me
For when compared some experience shared
Really? How can I not be?
This is a Dawn, a new start born
Each time I open eyes
Cherish with some relish
Not that type though would surprise

Yesterday I had a plan
I would do nothing the whole day
The Boss she took exception
So did what she did say
Waiting for a good excuse
Waiting for chance to break loose
Not from ties for I am wise
Just to unshackle mayhem Moose

In ink on brink
Of that which can't ignore
Flood your Brain with works insane
Until can take no more
Then when gone in casket strong
Still won't be forgotten
As a Wordsmith did try though don't know why
His poetry was rotten!

His rambles were a shambles!

Sharks

Never met a rape machine
Met some who thought they were
They had a personal justice served
Swifter than made occur

Never met a bad one
At least not close enough to speak
Met some for short time
Who prayed on those thought meek

Why oh why do we try
To advance by putting down
Why do we think superior?
When wearing that ill crown

I remember a bloody Sunday
Not that referred to in the song
Just a difference in the place
Where some said don't belong

Us and some inhabitants
Who didn't in their own eyes did fit
Met some of the plastic people
Was having none of it

Sharks don't swim in shallow pools
Preferring deeper water
There are free to be what be
Regardless of the slaughter

Sharks, however, can be killed
By the determine, by those willed
Sharks do swim but also walk
Look like us and even talk

Never met one that was equal
Never could they match
The really ones deserving
Did a bullet catch
Scenarios of bygone age
Would sometimes do again

She calls me

She calls me her Consideration
She calls me her Reason why
She calls me her Everlasting
She calls me her Tempting
She calls me her Indecision
She calls me her Novelty to try

I lived in ignorant pleasure
Until seen as well as heard
When laid down in letters
They spelt another word

Now I know that she is intelligent
I know that of wordplay keep
I am now just wondering
How many does she mean

I do not think it is by chance
For the first ones in order say
Seven days a week
At least five times a day

But she says them in that female way
With smile upon her face
The 'Butter wouldn't melt in mouth'
Elegance and grace

I just like a puppy dog
Lap up all attention
Not really sure but wanting more
Of hoped for affection

She deserves

The Game's too long but we stay strong
The reason not the season
For long haul so sod it all
Why do need a reason
Put simply we are we
Not some clone to show
We are the product of what have been
Some scars just don't show

What became of that name?
The one we knew before
A stepping stone to our Throne
Called that which do adore
A fleeting glance that had no chance
For only just not all
Perfect for someone else
Just slow to answer call

Lessons learned and bruises earned
The journey that we take
Some of which we do end
Some of which they break
The need to feed the blindness to creed
That emotion can't explain
The trials of miles that were just smiles
Just experience we gain

In the eighties I was young
On the roller coaster just begun
Ups and downs and side swerve
Forcing one to hold their nerve
Now a new I helped produce
Taking similar journey to have done
She is a warrior so am not worrying
She deserves her 'perfect one'

She simply said

On wooden stool sat the man
On wooden table a paper sheet
Slow and careful he did fill it
In characters clear and neat
Tucked in envelope in way to fit

He in misery did write

'Too sluppy' was our Puppy
'Too sloppy' didn't fit
It was trained in the neat eating
It was having none of it!

Yes! my love, it is our Puppy
That you do so adore
Getting to the share of time
I think you love it more

Know when I am beaten
Know when need retreat
So, the last thing from me
Will be sound of leaving feet!'

You and it I wish the best
The two of you I so wish well
Just that slight part of me
Hopes you break that sad Dog spell'

Two days did pass but weren't the last
She tracked him down but not confused
She was diplomatically expressed as someone
Definitely NOT AMUSED!!

To his current residence
A letter she did leave
Definitely not of sorrows
Not that of one to grieve

She simply said
'You silly Bugger! Get your arse back here!'

947

Shopping Trolley

I saw a Fly – don't know why
I guess it had to land
But was rude so did intrude
It landed on my hand!

I saw a Tax collector
On parked cars did vector
Tickets issued far and wide
As tapped that thing with pride

I saw a plethora of shopping trolley
Pavements now a folly
Shops have done away with the collectors
Now are more like retail Spectres

Adage

An adage can be savage
Can also be a lesson known
Irregardless of the origin
From Paupers or the Throne

Knocking on reality
Knocking on that which did see
Knocking on what could be
Knocking from likes of you and me

A thing taught that might be fraught
With it we do choose
To ignore for something more
Not caring what we lose

Should sign up

I sit and wonder why am blessed
When others don't know
Yet still we show
Face a daily test

The nearest I got to China
Was speaking to Hong Kong
Everything is pure confusion
Everything is wrong
Politics for side kicks
Of those who grab the centre stage
Not the new for past went through
Just more obvious with age

Making moment seem impotent
A skill I do admit
Yet am wiser behind this visor
Simply having none of it

Eligibility is not so free
When look around the world
The cries of pain so insane
Wherever they are heard

Echoes in the afternoon
Regret as Sun does set
Gullible is our trouble
Craziness we get

All o me plus dysentery
See and want to change
I am just normal if slightly formal
Am I really that so strange?

Tap those fingers, kill some others
Guarantee won't find those lovers
Killing easy seems to be
Should sign up and do proper

Silence sat

The tranquillity of the what might be
The acceptance of the fact
The decision can be fruition
Depending on how act

Should we adore and so want more
Treat happening as Waterfall?
The past falls down to distant ground
The future comes to call

Silence sat in solitude
Never wishing to be rude
If inadvertently did intrude
Should just be the interlude
Maybe Monday Maybe Sunday
Each has day as its end
Twenty-four - slightly less or more
Another opportunity for to send

In what we do we give a clue
Of that which we don't show
The part a start as we impart
The parts that none did know

What have had not always bad
One, perhaps, can say
For played its part when did start
Being what today

So, silence sat in solitude
Had its time to say
Chose to close so no-one knows
Perhaps another day

Silent Lying Every Eventuality Posed

Sometime sooner than expected
Rose a reason and reflected
Possibility and projected
Then went back to sleep

Saw a star, the distance far
Wondering about who we are
Hard passing a noisy car
Then returned to sleep

All that seems in my dreams
Have a motive and the means
All the haves and have not been
Nothing dirty, all are clean

Sometime sooner than did wish
In the waking I did fish
The art of searching not the dish
Wish I could get back to sleep

Anchovies

Why's a Toadstool called a Toadstool?
When no Toads do use to sit
Why a music song successful
Then is classed as 'a hit'?

Why take the humble Coffee Bean
Roast and dry then do grind
Sell as powder that needs water
When had it when first did find?

What satanic sect created Anchovies?
As a topping for to eat
In the sea gaily swimming
Do they fit all nice and neat?

Silent voice

Am I a Star man?
A creature from outer space?
I walk amongst the near of you
I ever wear your face

Yet something is quite different
Not always I do show
I see a world in turmoil
Turmoil I really know

Am I thought that you have caught?
Floating there to grab
A conscience in a world without
The realisation of what had

Yes, mistakes have been made
Still can live and learn
Atrocities not right to see
Much less to unwilling earn

Am I that thing that just descending?
Or have I always been
Am I your worst nightmare?
Or a pleasure dream

I am but a figment see
I am a part of what we be
Have no eyes but I can be
Right or wrong a destiny

Sipping Coffee

The lady sat sipping Coffee
In the shop did always go
Such a regular was the Lady
Staff and owner each did know
Tuesday morning like each other
Liquid nectar to begin
Then the day became like no other
As her one-time love walked in

Eyes they met and he smiled
Met in truth with blank stare
He still believing she had feelings
She, herself, didn't care
Got his Coffee and came to table
Sat down opposite
Trying hard to strike a conversation
She was having none of it

After a few attempts he sensed a problem
Had a feeling something wrong
A stranger experience cast now over
Got the impression he did not belong
Bravado vanished in an instant
This was something he didn't get
For the first time knew confusion
When 'the perfect' got stamped Reject

She simply looked at him and said

'I know you think that I had forgotten
I know you think it had gone away
It meant something far much deeper
It is something here to stay
I gave you all and you gave something
Truth be told you did gain
Walked away to new conquest
Leaving me with such pain

Well now I'm stronger for the experience
Now am able to share same space
I feel nothing more than pity
As I look into that face
You had chance to win the lottery
That was something had to choose
You thought you were the prize thing
With that thought you chose to lose

Well look now at what you missed out on
Look now hard Mr Perfect
I am better for the experience
To better things you did set
Yes, I went down hard and crying
On that day you chose to go
That's because I was foolish
That's because then myself I didn't know

Now I know that I was lucky
I escaped a fate much worse
Blinded by artful arrogance
Caught up in the caring curse

I should thank you for finding me
Not today but way back then
The vision of your back in doorway
Marks the time of why and when
I started to look much deeper
Started looking and did see
Found a prize bigger than that leaving
Found the things that I can be'

With that he couldn't get away fast enough

Situation an occupation

Once did say I would not play
Once so long ago
Once did live what then give
Before it I did know
Now photographs of my past
Burnt for no-one there
Was a space that did face
I guess you needed to be there

Through low did grow to that I know
The person that I be
Not the end for still I mend
The object of complacency
In many things' contentment brings
Not all but just enough
All the rest, silent best
Too much of other stuff

A space for face of different 'race'
Found and then I grew
Gone what told to that old
Discovered something new
Complexity of who we be
The path I did explore
There I found on foreign ground
The answer to the more

Situation an occasion
Led some place not known
Situation and occasion
Gave a homeless a new Home
In the perplexity of fatality
One got a lucky break
Where it from can now go on
Only I can take

Six sick trick

Cosmic vibes and human jibes
All are one yet different tribe
Come to surface then subsides
That is where each fault hides

I once thought that I had found Heaven
It was just a taste of things to come
Then I found a true and so begun
The day I met the special one

So is this real what I feel?
It sure feels right to me
I don't mind that am half blind
When Life's given what gave to me

The more I search the less I find
The rewards come when stop looking
Subtly a mystery
Full flavour when I'm cooking

If the sun rises in the morning
Then I can rejoice
Another chance to greet or sometimes meet
One with different voice

A small cog in a bigger machine
I do understand
I am but of what we are
As I take your hand

Everything been and done
The good things and the bad
The rights and wrongs from where then belong
Were then just what we had

We moved on and now all belong
Learn from but don't erase
The mistakes made so can then stay
A non-repetitive error phase

Sleeper creepers

There are sleeper creepers in my peepers
Hard to stay awake
Missing lines time after time
How much more can one take?

I had five hours so should be fine
Am I getting old? Is this a sign?
Am too knackered to get wrinkles
Got a few but they are singles

If so then I am cursed
Doing norm but in reverse
They say you sleep less in old age
I think my body missed that page

This should take three minutes
Instead it took an hour
Mind wants to feel fresh
My orbs are just now sour

I give up

The battle tattle

A burst with thirst can be a curse
If not gripped at start
A love a glove from that that above
When ensconced upon a Heart
An ambition to fruition
No better can you buy
You can't take what you don't make
However hard you try

I want to hear you say "let's play
Let's see which one is better
I want to hear you then pray
For seems to be trend setter'
I want respect but not subservient
Each are equal in my eyes
I want challenge with a promise
Least of all I want surprise

The been and gone that made one strong
The catalyst with the twist
The here and now, the path we plough
The additions to the list
The to and fro then let go
The stages of the age
The rhapsody of misery
The turning of the page

I wanted to see you hurt
As you did hurt
The callous of the parting
When things weren't meant to be
The handling of the awkward moment
When truth needed to be told
I accept that it was not for us
Yet did you need to be so cold?

The battle tattle of failed dreams
The stark sense of not what seems
The moving on to that which new
The learnt mistakes
So other do

The Bondi beach and fab

Health and fitness, I do witness
When the weather loses track
Skin-tight shorts and washing boards
That bloke there with twelve pack!

In Gym clothes they strike the pose
Sunbed tan for definition
Energy bars instead of Mars
I have a sneak suspicion

Private clubs not for tubs
Tubs of lard like me
Persona non grata just for starter
To their obsessed fraternity

Enough oil to fry not boil
Must buy it buy the keg
Will slip loose on steroid abuse
That was once a Chicken leg!

Looks too much work so I will shirk
Enjoy my large Kebab
After this perversion to which aversion
'The Bondi beach and fab'

Shall I saunter to the Sauna
Maybe schmooze to the Jacuzzi
Just jump in and have a swim
Or just swoon in the Steam room

That's my lot for the day
Hip, hip, hip hooray
Now what' on telly with feet up smelly
I am them, just in strange way

The clock is ticking on the time bomb

The albatross soaring on air current
The Kudu in Savanna grassland
The Dolphin in pod swimming
The Goat so tame it eats from hand

The happy of the things around us
Unaffected by our being
Just carrying on as always done
That is what we're seeing

We tried our best to remove them
Some species a success
Yet more were more than match for us
Merely became less

Half-heartedly some still try
In the guise of sport
Many now realise what we've done
So, this a last resort

We used to be Giants
Rulers over what we had
We used to be happy
Nothing seemed that bad
Those were the days of innocence
When in everything we did believe
Life it played the cruellest trick
It flattered to deceive

Now we pick up pieces
Try to justify

Now we switch into ourselves
So, stranger has to die

The clock is ticking on the time bomb
The one we built for us
Doomsday fast approaching
The Earth can't give a cuss

The closing

Made a something out of a nothing
A casual 'Hello'
Made a thing for heart to sing
Made and lets it grow
Every day in this affray
A victory I believe
For whatever wrong feelings strong
In what it can achieve

See what you do to see things through
The apple has a skin
The nectarine is were begin
The Grapefruit has no clue
The Honey wise does choose to rise
Sweet truly is the taste
Not a sonnet nor some Bonnet
Something we shouldn't waste

If not know by now then ask how
To prove what mean to me
Is it something that can say?
Something you can see?
Funny how I feel now
The one not in control
The revelation a sensation
The closing of the hole

I walk the path I did choose
I hold on to that can't lose
Even when have different views
I humbly beg to differ
I walk with you for love is true
The constant in the flux
The always same that's lodged in Brain
That pleasure to just touch

The clown with frown

Crinkles in the wrinkles
The trying to be 'up' when feeling down
Trying to be 'professional'
The real frown of the clown
Making light despite the bright
Of that which does portray
The ultimate test of illusion
Just one more long pay day

Who is he with such misery?
Is it even a real him?
The mask painted that so stated
Real enclosed within
Out of sight different might
Another face to view
For in fact just an act
Really just like you

How many people do we see?
Yet don't see Inside
As their personal problems
In public try to hide
Next time you meet a stranger
Take some time to think
Are they really happy?
Or teetering on the brink

We are so caught up in self
We really have no clue
What our fellow human
Has been or going through
Am guilty I will admit
More often, truth be told
Been that clown with hidden frown
In some days of old

The coffee flows as news grows

Once we were the Cave people
Now the Astronaut
What an evolution
Just in 'progress' caught

The youth blow up and kill on screen
The adults do for real
The power so addictive
When no sense of shame

The coffee flows as news grows
Of what we did today
Some choose to be shocked by it
Some will simply pray
And we are all the product
That we choose to make
We are all the curse and cure
Depending on which path we take

The ether now is buzzing
Skies full of man-made birds
The weapons market flourishing
All is so absurd

Once upon a time of mine
I lusted for this day
Now is here I simply fear
The madness now at play

If we went back to sticks and stones
Would we be so arrogant?
If we went back to having to think of outcomes
Would we then have, at least, slim chance?

The coffee flows as news grows
Of what we did today
Some choose to be shocked by it
Some will simply pray
And we are all the product
That we choose to make
We are all the curse and cure
Depending on which path we take
Makes one think doesn't it

The common Cold

Never lost that not found
Never heard a silent 'sound'
Never met a future stranger
Never feared another's danger
Never one to follow certain 'rules'
Never had time for certain 'fools'
Never one to be that informal
Never that some class as 'normal'

Who the Tree in Forest be?
Why that one simply me
With restraint I am free
To make the one I want to be

Never killed unless for work
Never then did I shirk
Never then I background lurk
For Queen and Country went berserk
Never when to ground did fall
Never felt the end of all
Never when the options call
Did I say 'Oh sod it all!'

Reflection of the misconception
The pure truth – insanity
That I was but now see
Never really was true me

The storm told of new and old
Those classed Brave and those classed bold
Many a story has been told
Yet each could catch the common Cold

The common of the 'rotten'

Sully in the sultry
Rejuvenation by the Rain
Paradise has much in common
With that we call Pain
So right now, what are we?
Are we truly true?
Are we but a fantasy?
Are we what we can do?

It was near midnight and a sorry sight
When the stranger the street did meet
These cold slabs would be all that had
Beneath more than just their feet
A day turned to another
A coat they had for cover
Nothing from another
Definitely not from one called lover

The selection of rejection
Made by others who don't know
The complete be that we don't see
Just that part on show
Maybe not on pavement got
Not the place but feel
When what thought with reality fought
That fruit that lost its peel

No weekly shop nor Take out stop
Unless from thrown away
The common of the 'rotten'
That for which another pays
The four walls when hear their calls
The inside and the out
The so down can't even frown
Let alone a shout

The common

If I should fall who then would call
The fallen as a Brother?
If I went to wherever sent
Who would claim a lover?
Startling thoughts in which am caught
The questions and suggestions
The possibility of what becomes of me
Some anecdotes and mentions

Into the new we battle through
The growing never grows
To that told as that so old
Despite the bits that show
The time we spend as try to mend
The unbreakable think is broken
The things we share to say we care
But merely are a token

In light so bright we make things right
Not in the Faiths they try to preach
But in the wealth within our self
Within when care to reach
To be a one must of them have some
In method and the means
For are not we all that Human call
Made from many genes?

So, if I should fall to the next place call
Would I even cause a stir?
Others strong would just carry on
The as and when with were
Redskins or White, the dark/ the light
The cover makes no difference
The male the fe. The thing we be
The common in the sense

The complete yet uncompleted

I looked into that deep dark tunnel
The one we know as Solitude
I did hesitate at entrance
Then decided not to intrude

For some it is a personal choice
Others it is forced upon
Neither, fortunately, am made aware of
Neither, thank you, in which belong

I looked at options and made decisions
None of I do regret
I found my future, unexpected
I found my path so firmly set

One slip here and one slip there
One more chance I did not dare
All the parts just fell in place
When transported to outer space

Out of which I did know
Into something I did grow
Now a blessing I do show
When I present my true partner

Made a mockery of once thought
When a different way was taught
Now in it I am caught
The complex bliss of love

It's energy a mystery
Like that of Galaxy
The making of the ones you see
The complete yet uncompleted

The contentment dish

Once I saw a recipe
In a very different Book
A variation on behaviour
I just had to look
It contained some surprises
A variety of verse
Some I considered excellent
Some I thought were slightly worse

One in particular jumped out at me
A poem I remember
One I try now to follow
Since that day in past September
The Poets name I do not know
For was merely signed anon
Yet the impact of their words
Became a new life song

It was

The contentment dish

Take 3 cups of laughter
One of Irony
Add a dose of 'what the heck'
Revel in what be
Serve with a side of common sense
Sprinkle politeness over dish
Patience the perfect drink to serve
To fulfil an almost perfect wish

Before you judge, judge yourself
Before can love give Heart good health
Before laid to rest keep on moving
Be that one that some find soothing
Laughter cure a thousand woes

The cup

The stuff we know is not what knew
The change we now going through
The pain that stains might just remain
Until we make a new
Unless a change we make for future sake
This comfortably of just what be
A decision we must take

So, take a cup of patience please
Before your anger you release
Slow and steady best way do
To make change and something new
Instant may attention get
In the modern media jet set
Yet methodical and with that true
You can make a listener do
The changing wanted by the more
The ones so silent just days before

I saw you on that cold damp street
Head bowed down and shuffling feet
No-one wanting to just greet
The motion of a misery meet
Do you know that flow can go
Different direction if you choose
A cut here and bank there
What have you to lose?

So take a cup of patience please
Mix in some future dreams
Take a sip and add for taste
That now no hope it seems
Take that cup and fill a bowl with it and it again
The bowl is made by magic
Any amount it can sustain
Try to fill that cup against your now
Fill it with the how
The cure and not the disease
The hard but that which please

The curious life of Bingbangbongledoodledoo

The curious life of Bingbangbongledoodledoo
A gentle one with no clue
Of what to say and see it through
If life was Peaches theirs was stew

Ate Breakfast at twenty-two
Hours not the age
Had loosely mastered food preparation
When had reached this stage

Wrote with pictures and painted words
This, however, not so unheard
Just normally on paper see
Not on plate made from a tree

Underwear kept out rain
Though eye sockets were a pain
For kept riding up their head
Whilst under clothing Hat instead

Work they regarded as just pleasure
Doing something was their leisure
A 'To do list' became treasure
Idleness the ultimate torture

Bingbangbongledoodledoo saw as red what was blue
Blue as in calm to all and 'normal'
Not for them for had a Pen
Last thing could call would be formal

Once upon the time of mine
I discovered in some strange old Book
The curious life Bingbangbongledoodledoo
Felt compelled to have a look

The cycle and recycle

The last gasp of copper liquid
The last thought, the wonder why
Out of all, why your name on?
Then find out what it is to die
Different Body, same scenario
Each time forgetting that of past
The eternal soldier reborn
Wonder how long this one lasts?

The eternal Carer, the eternal Sharer
Different looks but same attraction
In what will become
In what path they choose their actions
The cycle and recycle
The unbroken circle follows
Yet each time the euphoria
Never once does seem hollow

Is reincarnation our salvation?
A chance to improve on that before
Or the sedition of repetition?
Nothing more than endless chore
The Deja vu of that new
Know but don't know why
If truth be told experience old
Had once before but then did die

The silly things that morning brings
As try to stir grey matter
Problem being the words I'm seeing
As the micro pulses scatter

The Day Digby Dunderhead dug

Digby Dunderhead dug a deep hole
To bury a bad dream
Four hours with a shovel
To hide that already had been
Been invisible to others
Not sure how he would get out
Both the dream and of the hole
If Earth was Human body
Must be approaching near to soul

Mrs Dunderhead noticed he'd gone missing
Pleasure shouldn't last this long
So, went out in search of him
In case there's something wrong
Now, Mrs Dunderhead was short sighted
Explaining quite a lot
Down she fell towards Hell
Digby got a shock

As well as visual challenges
Mrs had another
Weight control, ate Menu whole
From the front right to back cover
Like an Asteroid impacting
Was her half soft landing
Digby went down ten feet deeper
With shovel no help handing

Like a cork in Bottle neck
Mrs Dunderhead firmly wedged
Mr now in pitch black and cursing
Mrs deliberate act alleged
When the community with profanities
A Giant's Fruit Bowl had to make
Then banished both for ten years
For no more could they take

The day Digby Dunderhead dug to bury
That which did not exist
Became another looney legend
To add to his growing list

The Effalump had the hump

The Effalump had the hump
Not mentioned in recent verse
Through its mouth and large snout
Came unrepeatable curse
It did cry 'WHY OH WHY!'
As stamped the Donut flat
Then upon this strange moron
Effalump then sat

One arm free as meant to be
So it could then, in ways, produces
With squashed head and floor as bed
This monster reintroduces
An Effalump with the hump
Not Cameleon for not season
For that hybrid to appear
Who knows just what reason?

Yes, Effalump had the hump
Face as red as toes
Found makeup free when visit thee
Chain store as it grows
Staff aghast as went past
Lady beyond the situation
So did that as on bum sat
'it's free on this occasion!'

The Effalump with the hump
Showed me toes so red
Forcing me into what see
Simply enough said

The Mandolin made music

Skies once grey went away
Sun made a welcome show
Courage came a calling
Confidence did grow
The unseen that once had been
Took, hopefully, more than just vacation
No guarantee just hopes and see
No repeat of situation

And the Mandolin made music
The Laureate laid lore
The singer sang and so began
The better than before
The one became someone
Nothing special apart to self
Mastered many mysteries
Known as Mental health

Now can stand with no need to cry
Can smile and laugh and look eye to eye
Can stand tall and answer call
Forgotten now that fear of fall
The rebirth of beginner
Without the weight of sinner
The prospects get when did let
To believe they are a winner

And the Actors act upon their Stage
In show that is one proper
With audience there for their talent to share
Name the poster topper
The curse of the uneducated
In that which stated
Treating as something wrong
Deciding woefully don't belong

Hiding behind mask of own inadequacy

The Masters of Disasters

A time will come in each one
When a change comes calling
Then each side offers ride
The rising or the falling
With age comes change
The inside and the out
Some we handle out of light
Some will scream and shout

Discovery of long lost
Hoping somehow can pay the cost
Lost that which once did know
Lost in the way did grow
The taken and the given
The parts we like less than some others
The tranquillity of new reality
The smile at past lovers

When what matters no longer matters
When what believed no longer believe
Do we just move on?
Do we sit and grieve?
When what was before now is no more
When we hear the call from distant shore
Do we stay or do we go?
Into something we don't know?

What it boils down if we look
Life's not learnt from some great Book
Person and the personal health
Mean much more than financial wealth
Flexibility in all that see
An option should now look
The Masters of Disasters
The past we often took

The misery

If nothing meant just nothing
Why would choose to live
When the 'something' has everything
Yet choose not to others give?

If all it needs to close one's feed
Is a certain name
Why oh why do we try
To be just not the same?

The misery of poverty
Ignored by wealth around
Deaf to death and the rest
Based on social ground

Arcade parade

Arcade parade led to tirade
When hard earned spurned away
For did not behave and some save
For that 'rainy' day

Illusion contribution
Small win to suck you in
Then does slow their profits grow
As you compound the sin

Horses for the courses
Cards for certain deal
Bookies are just hooky
All just want to steal

That you have for short time
Until it they then own
Then your lot is just the pot
Not even rectum throne

The modern 'freedom' state

Summer breeze and bare male knees
Beer belly over shorts
Hairy chest just like a vest
I guess it takes all sorts

Lock down loose so now peruse
With or without choice
Mask/ unmasked is personal task
Each does have its voice

Summer bummer or something dumber
Go but then when back
Rules have changed not prearranged
A self-isolation attack

Who really cares if someone wears?
Small businesses turn blind eye
Already in the downward slope
A final nail then die

The elected show what already know
As face their first real test
Despite what earn and, maybe, spurn
Their no better than the rest

Fuel t fire as in this mire
Each side uses as a tool
Laughable if not so serious
As people try to fool

Wake m up so can coffee sup
From this begin to hate
Politics and its side kicks
The modern 'freedom' state

The Naughty Book

I took a look in The Naughty Book
My eyes popped out on stalks
Those rude words that should not be heard
When the angry talks

There's languages and profanities
There's some with history
There's some borrowing and inventing
Some a mystery

The expletive explanation
The letters replaced for public use
The omission but there known
Just too polite – not shown

Toes did curl, hair stood up on end
Found some I had forgotten
Think that you were outrageous
You were nothing Johnny Rotten!

Move along the Bus please

The door is open but can't get in
Two others block the way
A vision caught and not their fault
So to them nothing do I say

The Drive looks embarrassed
His instructions are ignored
Carry on much longer
Someone will pull the emergency cord

An obstruction in the aisle
Two cretins having natter
Move along the Bus please
Or your teeth I'll kindly scatter!

The one who chose the bold

Sally sat as Mom did plait
Roger didn't bother
See how we do now
Wear our different other
Roles are rolls
With different recipes
Some have seeds yet all have needs
The human Baker shop's complexity

None to be in ignominy
When accept to just accept
That misery that part of be
Only if we let
'Do you know me or even want to be
Someone I call friend?'
Imagine if all said yes to call
Friends became a trend

Gasoline a thing that's been
Different now runs cars
Ozone friend as try to send
Our pollution to the 'fars'
Far away from where stay
Beyond the one call moon
Not quite there to be fair
Getting there real soon

One did sit and wonder
If would die alone
One who lost and found
More reasons to move on
'Do you remember me or what I be?
For if the truth be told
I am you that did do
The one who chose the bold'

The pain of rain

(Acknowledgement to the former Artist known as Prince)

The aureoles of what spills
The discharge of the fact
The way we play when 'norm' astray
The acceptance of the pact
The acid and the alkaline
The unacceptable and the fine
The animal we hold inside
The Doppelganger that starts the new
The mystery that's me and you

Had my time of flirtation
Leave that now to new Generation
Let them feel that strange sensation
As mix with a new nation
Outer cover doesn't make the lover
It's what that cover tries to hide
A popstar sang with colour
Sang with liquid and with pain
A popstar of various titles
Sang of thing called Purple Rain

The elasticity of what might be
The comfort when no pain
Going back to the singer
Going back to Purple Rain
Shaking off the residue
Looking on to prospects new
None quite know what have been through
As on lip you silent chew

In the story of personal glory
The highlights fade to dusk
The driving on to keep strong
No request, just must
In the corner of the quitter
Stands a figure true
In the sea of misery
Nothing strange at what went through

The pause

The pause...... can cause...... distraction
Yet....... what get.?.......... attraction.?
Am I.?....... going.?......... of my head
Maybe I.?........ should just.?......... go hit my bed

Could ...... the cure.... simply be.?
Nothing...... more.... than
Just....... than a....... simple stutter?
Nah.......I am.......a no-hope Nutter!

Confusing...... is....... amusing
Imagining...... you...... perusing
Are you?......now...... reading
Same way...... without...... needing

Huh

Chunky chips or skinny Fries
Latter former in disguise
Served by those retailers wise
Makes it seem you get much more

Ice is nice, served with a slice
In a favoured drink
Yet on or in other things
Can drive one to the brink

A Head ahead when by led
Needs a certain type of form
Not that way can all per se
Hope or want to perform

Huh, enough, of this stuff
Sanity is calling
From afar and near I hear clear
That will to live is stalling

The penners own pandemic

The writing on the paper told
A story that was so old
The rise of one to another
An atrocity
Yet the world is not about just one
It is what others see

A life at sea was not for me
When Fish was just a dish
Office politics not on list of frolics
A target I don't wish
A stand alone with what I own
Of that I have no care
Caring comes with sharing
Hence, I wish to share

So was told in times of old
So is said today
We are all what we are
Despite what others say
A day in the life of famous
A day we can wish
Yet do we want that it entails?
Is that truly that sought dish?

Pleasure/ profit? You decide
Boils down to thing called Pride
Are you comfortable with who you are
Are ambitious but too far?

Reality is often cruel
It is something we can't fool
Making best of what we can
Then a wise Lady or Man

Greetings Future, what you bring?
Will I with success sing?
Will I instead just be another
Not quite there but name on cover?

The Pharos found

When fear subsidies and 'worthless' hides
What do you do to spur?
When have got and conquered lot
When barrier just a burr
When incidental becomes incremental
Past the past at last
When looking back is no burden
Just a period that went too fast

Free you be in entirety
Free you are so use
Free to be what you see
Free so don't abuse
Nothing much really matters
In big scope of things
Everything has a cost
A cost it surely brings

The seasons are a changing
Though not sure which one
All appear and disappear
Nature having fun
Clock tick tocks without stop
Another breath we take
Still have time so no crime

The confliction in contradiction
A waste to me is true
Let's just be in harmony
Each just do what do
The Sphinx a jinx when on the brink
The Pharos found the cost
Not the same in Rulers name
When the trust is lost

The pleasure/agony

The Pen a friend that does lend
Actual to call
The ink the brink of what do think
As the letters fall

The traverse into verse
Topics possibly could be worse
Sometimes a blessing sometime curse
The pleasure/ agony of the Wordsmith

The sip of drink as next line think
The chance of that arrange
The reread for feel need
The world entered and sometimes wish had not

Alas

Slipped inside and what did I find?
To be honest, nothing new
All the same in memory frame
As was when I grew

The chance to change would be strange
For blocks upon which built
All are happy where they are
Apart from that bloody kilt!

To steal them from me
Would rob me of my identity
For what was made new me
Broken chains and soul free

Reflection introspection
Happened with no intention
Stirring seeds of intention
Alas poor reader I apologise

The pleasure of the Prisoners

Took a breath and picked up pen
Thought flashed by so wrote again
May be weird with limited sight
Yet am a prisoner of the wish to write
Hour unimportant
To my addiction all the same
Only on the clock face
Can view that called Time Frame

A prisoner yet willing one
My punishment my reward
Creating or viewing creation
To those others I applied
Subtle and not so subtle
Serious or humour
Fact or fiction both same mission
Create/ dispel a rumour

A Prisoner, yes, a Prisoner
The Prison that inside
For locked in there with tender care
Until no longer can I hide
Those parts of me that breath free
The blessing or the curse
Some do choose the longer form
Mine come out as verse

The pleasure of the Prisoners
The Prison form of art
Never a Picasso
At least because of different start
My canvas piece of paper
My pictures letter form
In life we are all some form of Prisoner
From the moment we were born

The pleasure

"Home comer One to Base control
I've found something worth a look
Ran it through the on-board systems
The classified as Book

It seems our ancestry used their hands
To actually turn the pages
What a lot of effort
Those really were dark ages"

In still air the eyes do stare
At just another screen
No touch as such that means so much
Somehow a mere has been

Parchment parade of how was made
Never seems to last
That certain smell of how did tell
Now a thing of past

Replace muscle loss at a cost
A membership to private Gym
When the weights that so hate
Can have words there stored within

"Home comer One to Base control
There's more of them I see
This is some type of strange dwelling
Above outside sign 'Library'

These things seem like ingredients
For all dividend as per taste
Personal choice without voice
Must have had some time to waste"

The pleasure of just sitting down and reading a chosen Book

The price we pay

Do you know my name's the same
Of every one of you?
I am just another lover
Doing what I do

Do you know that I have failed
More times than I succeed
It is just a part of us
Those of 'the public' creed

Rejection of some certain place
Not a failure on your part
Just not there where they don't care
Nor appreciate your art

Do you know my name again?
If not I don't care
For better place can fill a space
Because they choose to dare

Do you see just what you see
That which personal choose
Fine with the likes of mine
You just chose to lose

So many people that I know
In various choices of expression
'Didn't fit' so got on with it
More names than I can mention

Standing out can have clout
Yet take blows in return
Nothing guaranteed including me
You pay so you can earn

The prisoner of factual

The coffee cup sits empty
Like the drinker it is drained
The need to do but not the through
The energy is sprained
The mid-afternoon that seems like evening
The clock that time lies
There rather be but can't see
Unless join the super spies

Nothing came from nothingness
Something came from when did test
Complacency spelt misery
Action changes scene
Not that of mass rebellion
In places I won't mention
Physical replaced by Poll
There express intention

If I be what I see
What am I to you?
Different eyes say fool or wise
Something all will do
The open road to just right
The promise that no argument/ fight
The sitting doing nothing
When thinking is a something

If I be what want to be
Would that be reality?
Would I truly then feel free
With exposure misery
The complexity of fantasy
The rye smile of actual
The things that mean more than been
The prisoner of factual

The pusher not the puller

Making larks with my marks
Some I choose to keep
Some do show though why don't know
Some I put to sleep
Where drive go I don't know
Just the lust for must
Just a creation of situation
Ride the thing or bust

Looking back with cloth sack
Been and hope not again
Feeling now my worth in spades
Not that worthless pain
Run, it said and run led
There's only you can change
The misery of what you see
The real that feels so strange

Will never end the time I spend
Going but not knowing
The future me I long to see
Into which am growing
The chance strange but that's okay
Change can be for better
Let's begin on a whim
Write just one lonely letter

In myself am in good health
Though body says am not
Attitude and then conclude
Your best is what you've got
A Rock star I missed by far
A Sportsman not my choice
No leader but a feeder
Hate sound of my own voice

Credit m with invisibility
The pusher not the pulled
I am just a figment of success
How many have I fooled?

Twaddle is a doddle

Nothing else matters
When it hits the fan
The vision of the future
Planned when this began
Nothing else as visible
Nothing when in tatters
The things that they are going through
Those who truly matters

Each day a new mystery
When so called Leaders have a thought
Each day new we see
When in their thoughts are caught
We like what see on TV
We soak in that on device
We accept what is given
Wouldn't true be nice!

This morning I had Cereal
Tomorrow might have Toast
Is this the limit of individual?
A word that means the most
The Penner pens and then hits Send
To an audience have not met
The society we now be
Just a Block or just a let

Near my night yet light still bright
A complex situation
When too far to drive by Car
My loved from different Nation
Twaddle becomes a doddle
With repetition true
Yet for lark make my Hallmark
Just loving this I do

Recent begun

How should be reality?
When a beach now stands before
How should I feel when things get real?
Besides those who I adore

Questions and reflections
More the first I seem to find
When away the thoughts then play
Wild runs an active mind

No more that shore until to it return
No adoration situation that will never change for more
No long this one for merely fun
Now a finish of recent begun

Make mine a Marmalade masterpiece

Hello you, you must be new
No look of dread when meet
You actually seem quite happy
When you did me just greet

I think that I will have the usual
Though not from looks it gets
No full cooked that scrumptious look
No variation of the 'Sets'

I am in the mood for different food
So, a startling will release
Ask the others how want it smothered
Make mine a Marmalade masterpiece

Ian Wilcox

Two went through

Two went through what two do
Luckily was not me
Just spectator and now narrator
Been where now they be
Heated words so absurd
When delivered in the heat
Reconciliation of situation
Not going there is hard to beat

When we try to hide the love with pride
What message do we send?
Honesty best policy
When argument try to mend
To disagree should be free
When just an opinion
In free thought we should each sought
To rise above the minion

So, we think we've won that should not have begun
The smile that hurts the most
For is stored by them adored
Another awful ghost
There's attraction in reconciliation
When no cause is clear
Not the sorry of simple worry
Not expressing fear

The white lies as we disguise
That we know is wrong
The making up of generous cup
The guilt now flowing strong
In argument we do vent
More than just the cause
Strange sensation is irritation
Wish they'd learn to pause

Uncharted tales and personal grails

How many writers do you know?
How many yet are just to show
How many into hobby grow?
The answer does surprise

How many we just turn to
Without a thought or care
Thar others are still out there
Someplace and somewhere

Making minds that dare to find
Quality in that which see
Not a name for not yet that game
If that wish to be

You worship adoration
I prefer something else
You tell of social media achievements
Them I laid to rest

No self-proclaiming for not my style
If others choose, enjoy for that brief while
Each to own and search for Throne
By talent or by guile

Others outside do flourish
From each other nourish
In different ways accomplish
That to which do aim
There is no way this game to play
For all are just the same
Some do earn bonus points
Whilst not reaching that called Fame

So who are you and what do you do?
To put poetry back on the map
Are you the purest warrior?
Or just a name to fill some gap?

Under blazing Sun, we begun

You melt inside my tender hold
That chill just slips away
That dark that covers light
Let's your light come out to play

Each time we are together
I can do nothing but rejoice
For each vision I experience
Calls me with inner voice

The first time we met knew you were different
You so silent yet so proud
Beneath your outer wrapping
Perfection screaming loud

Under blazing Sun, we begun
A journey until this day
The rapture of when you are here
The mourning when gone away

Each and every time I see
I realise what you mean to me
I live for you, that is true
How do you do those things you do?

That first time we were together
You became my vice
Now I am addicted
My beautiful Choc – Ice

Unrecognised Heroes

Been and done and had some fun
More ahead I'm sure
The applauded with nothing awarded
Just that strength so pure
The knocked back that chose attack
In attitude not actions
That rose again to attain
That few yet incredible faction

So say them again and again
Those who better than the me
Those who are my reason why
I will refuse reality
For the real is what others
In comfort zone that doesn't change
Who above the polite labels
Of the ones they find so strange

Staying strong and driving on
Those worse off than me
Made me look as moment took
At reality
Self-pity a misery
For oneself and others
When compare to what others dare
Who with positive that one smothers

You unrecognised Heroes I salute you

Upside down

Play on please for you release
That which in I hold
Sanctuary your playing be
Another story told

A combination situation
Them expressing what I feel
The moment is a pleasure
This moment feels so real

Fast then slow the tempo goes
Life in such short burst
The best of it the high notes hit
The Bass to define worst

Contented be by melody
That caresses in such way
Tempting unrelenting
Urging me to stay

How I wish that I could play
Such a pleasure be
Reflection of affection
Done for all to see

They strummed Guitar from afar
Yet chords my ears did reach
Every note a Teach
Different did they teach

Allow me please some playful tease
Upside down I write
No, you are not imaging
It's here now in plain sight

Urgent need of Frog pills

I
To
Try
More
Said
The
Do
A

The letters had an argument
About shape and effort made
The pattern on the paper
When joining the parade
Energy a mystery
To likes of I and O
Too much spent as different went
The pen for it to show

The twist of wrist and land of hand
The even on airwaves rode
With a play on how each lay
The invented the Morse Code

One day they had a coupling
As most reproductive things they do
Quite a strange shaped offspring
When was born the letter Q

A different child showed as P
Then another became D
Quite complex was child X
With two I's not three

Attention changed perception
More important when stood tall
Even got a Title
Were then called capital

Us, just us

If you told me that the sky was green
I would not disagree
For everyone has own opinions
In the stuff they hear and see
I draw the line at blatant crime
For that I have no place
Regardless of the colour/ creed
Regardless of your face

The things we do both me and you
Are what makes us individual
The way we play and how we say
Should never be thought as criminal
How we express can be a test
That's the joy of being
Forget language or dialect
They are simply part of get

All I want to do is just get through
See the other side
A life with Wife just feels right
So other stuff run and hide
Came and went and to spent
The things irrelevant
Found my feet when did meet
The new instead of old

How many chapters has a Book?
When we start do we look?
Just reflection on what took
I guess the answer's no
A travelling once and now again
Different journey take
Now is Life and no gun or knife
See what of it can make

The buried deep that all keep
Yet lays there pushing on
That is what makes us just us
Why we all belong

Ut salire in ignotis

Not all seen is that shown
When one does say and one does own
Ut salire in ignotis
I jump into the unknown
That with which we jump from
Many are the craft
The only thing we can control
The results and aftermath

Land or air, sea maybe?
I don't care
In uniform or just which born
A challenge we all share
Who amongst have not had challenge?
Who amongst not beat?
Who amongst is still able?
To a Stranger warmly greet?

Forgone was the future
That did once have look
Just a history of what could be
If no chance you took
Someday, maybe, will reflect
On what do have and could have been
Someday, maybe, have a smile
Seeing that which never seen

The 'Road rage' of the past age
The waste of time it be
The benefits now firmly sit
The treasure now is free
The opportunity and with it can
Be that who don't give a damn
For the rules made by fools
The grown up that should be in Pram

Ian Wilcox

Velvet Comes Redundant

The bitterness of the bygone
Taints treasure of the present
The hook is buried oh so deep
Pursues without relent

The fly does try, I don't know why
To swim in the ointment
Yet it had its time to shine
On different things it spent

That's where you are
That's where you are
On that VCR
That's where you be
That's where you be
In my history
The been a truth
I cannot lie
The memory remembered
Though I try
Acceptance no forgiveness
Until the day I die

You made a fool and put on stool
Your conquest then to show
The gullible for the trouble
When they do not know

Been CD an did see
It's too late to change
DVD gave clarity
Even if so strange

Now we change yet again
Now we explore more
You were but an old way to play
Something that I adore

Vindaloo true and with no clue

Blooming heck! I forgot
Vindaloo can be quite hot
Not that way it seems
After liquid load and searching dreams
Inebriation situation
A lot to answer for
Why we try before brain cells die
We demand encore?

Why are you with login true
Following as you do?
What amongst this endless drivel?
Compels you to your eyes swivel?
Nothing much and so as such
Ink becomes a caper
Safe when in a favourite pen
Dangerous on paper!

Mrs Brown, her with frown
That lives at sixty-eight
Not her age but perhaps her rage
Everything does hate
Made mistake that again won't make
Of wishing her Hello
Fish wife loud and somewhat proud
She told me where to go!

Nothing much moves as such
This blob some seem to like
Now get it! A kind of hit
Inflict on partner like a spike!
Time i short and I am caught
With bladder screaming loud
Worry me of a wet knee
Yes! I am that proud

Now about that Vindaloo

Grey they say – No! Just different tones

Dark and light do not make colour
Merely add a tone
To the hues we all infuse
For none do stand alone
Rich or poor and from what shore
Should not judge the person seeing
They are, like us, a certain must
In this thing called 'being'

Sweetest songs serenaded with diverse mix
Touch hearts as cold and too hard to be fixed.
Tall and short are the yardstick to measure fabulousness
That the old and young hone on the horn of their naturalness.

I am from a certain type
One we class Caucasian
Yet you'll find that I am Blind
In more than one a situation
Classes are for recording
To help and not to hinder each
Merely quicker for the searching
Not required for all to teach

Same crimson blood swim in our blue veins
Your dimples bring forth waters meant for all
Whenever our black and white hearts hit hence,
They pulsate with love that never deigns to fall.
In me, the proud black egret
Has come to see the white falcon
As a cause and a walk mate
Leading to the depth of one home.

Echoes are an everything
When in reflection we analyse
Gunpowder rule is for the fool
Time has things surprise
The subjugated now narrated
By those from whom did suffer
They are not some pest at best
Each has been born of Mother

Mother Nature deems it fit that we walk as a mixed portion
Like a force of the sea storm and her loyal waves.
We assert now and trample on idea of servile notion.
Long have we capered scrappers, and fled the primitive caves.

Yet comes a light - radiant bright
There comes a sound so loud
Comes the sense that on this sphere
We all stand on common ground
We cannot correct the wrong been done
For that we need a Time Machine
We can address though the present
Show what 'intelligent' does mean

In time, meanings, logic all melt
As we melt into a sameness
That we crave upon universe's belt
Beaming like stars' radiance.
To curling smoke, we're stronger
Than the coarse crouching hills.
Ours is striving for an aim, higher
We hide those that abominate still.

Let's now cleave to our vision,
Coddle the core of our mission.
We are the shadows on the wall
Waiting for more lights to fall.

The slaves become the Masters
The Masters become the slave
Though not in the way we know
Just in how behave
When is found ways so sound
Firm to go some more
Everyone is everything
Now for the encore
Let's now cleave to our vision,
Coddle the core of our mission.
We are the shadows on the wall
Waiting for more lights to fall.
Our propinquity to love we make legendary.
We stand on what we believe to make customary.

An impromptu collaboration between William Warigon and Ian Wilcox

The Barrier

I have had a lifelong barrier, fear of writing a word,
I am intellectually and verbally very strong, but when
I put it down on paper, things go very wrong,
Form filling is a nightmare in case there is a need for elaboration,
And creative wording required about my career expectations.
I hunt through and deliberately choose short easy familiar words,
In place of expansive, creative, flowing,
intellectually-shaking wonderful words.
Oh I know them, they are very familiar to me and I
long to use them with a creative flourish,
If only my brain could be attached to paper without the use of a pen,
If I could think them down, see them cascading over
the page in fluent picturesque abundance.
Now I have discovered a wonderful key! 'Spell-
check', it's part of my computer package,
Now I am set free, I can't stop writing; words are pouring out from me.
Alright, sometimes I am stumped when I am given a choice and
a dictionary is needed to finish the word I really mean,
On one or two occasions I still make an error but,
oh gosh, it is getting better and better.
Now I will show you!
The world of words has swung open for me, I am free!!!

First Introduction

We made our introductions slowly, I whispered,
"Hello Darling, I'm your Mum."
Strangers we are not as we have talked quite a lot
with you safely tucked up in my tum.
My love for you, my darling, welled up and filled me with
pleasure as you were tenderly placed in my arms.

I searched you all over, slowly and gently, acknowledging
features inherited from your Dad and me.
I marvelled at the eyes opened wide and looking so knowingly back into mine.
As a Mum I know I'll not be perfect; we will have
our moments of rejection sometimes.

I want to protect you my lovely, to keep you from hurt and harm.
I know darling that I won't always be near you to cuddle, praise and cheer you.
You'll just have to rely on all the skills I will try and
teach you, in your growing-up time.

Remember always, you are a person with rights and codes of your own,
Not just the proudest possession your Dad and I will ever own.
When you are in trouble don't shut us out, come home or phone.

Then when you have a babe of your own, just
think of me for one moment in time.
When you were once and always will be, a much-loved baby of mine.
My role will then be extended and I will be a
grandparent for the very first time.

WobblingPen

Grace

Grace by name goodness by nature.
She baked night and day to give cakes and biscuits away.

She would open her tin, and share baking hidden within.
One at a time they were given away.

Dull eyes shone, as the delights hit the tongue,
provoking taste and memories, of times long past, leaving smiles to linger on.

Grace never did partake, it was for others, she steadily continues
to bake. Leaving the magic of companionship behind.

Note: This is a true story about a lovely quiet lady, using her
delicious shortbread biscuits to open up a conversation.

Early Learning

I am learning to walk.
Look at me, look at me.

I am learning to talk.
Listen to me, listen to me.

I am making decisions.
"No!" said with a smile or a scream,
It seems to work, with a quick scamper off.

Soon I'll be a grownup; able to have my say,
In this family where I am loved.
If not, one day, I will just walk away.

WobblingPen

Wondering why I'm wondering

I don't know why the sky looks blue
I wonder why but have no clue
I wonder if it looks blue to you
I wonder if I'm getting through
I wonder why I'm wondering

What was it that I said last night?
I wonder why we had a fight
I wonder why When seemed so bright
I wonder why this don't feel right
I wonder why I'm wondering

With all the clever in the world
No answer straight - they just stay curled
Past six years and now the tears
Causing in me doubt and fears
No reason said to where it led
Bouncing around in this here head
Still wondering why I'm wondering

Am not sure if love no more
This a feeling so not pure
When it's you that I adore
Scratching round to find a cure
I wonder why I'm wondering

How can fix this complex mix?
On something built with solid bricks
Yes, we've had some knocks and kicks
Nothing that a hug can't fix
Leaves me wondering why I'm wondering

With all the clever in the world
No answer straight - they just stay curled
Past six years and now the tears
Causing in me doubt and fears
No reason said to where it lead
Bouncing around in this here head
Still wondering why I'm wondering

Wordplay warning

The humour of the reading
Own words yet different name
Someone is so desperate
To achieve some 'fame'

The strategy simplicity
Sign in with made up name
Copy that found posted
The new version of robbery game

The desperate seeking in social media leaking
Those who lust the fame
Rob from all and everyone
For plaudits hope to gain

The pretender to what has been
Making own the things have seen
Living lie to raise them self
Only interested in personal wealth
What if I say that I don't care?
If as own on Facebook share
Try to publish if you dare
Then find out a Publishers anger

Rob me of that posted
Instead of choice to share
People know that style in which written
So really, I don't care

If yo choose then you lose
Any respect you aim to get
If you take it to next level
Then the lawyers let

Angry no, pity yes
That you need to do
Insecurity in visibility
Insecure are you

Just remember that what goes around comes around
And second time has bite

Would

If poetry had a national flavour
Which flavour would you choose to be?
Lichon in all ways, Curry were the heat it stays
Tagliatelle for the speller

If culinary was the answer who we be
If we tasted but not see
Would each other still just be
Some strange thing – a mystery

If words read said instead
That are different but the same
Would we then read again?
Regardless of the name

Nothing should prevent us
The sender and receive
Nothing should be a reason
For in us we should believe

And clouds did gather overhead
Yet saw sunbeams there instead
Words both written and them read
Made a mattress for a Bed

If Poetry was population
Would we be in this situation?
When the hopeful, not the hate
Went much further than just state

If verse no curse but the cure
Would it somehow help the more?
When is written simply pure?
Not just for now but forever more

WTF did I just read

The Octopus came calling
Wanting a new Home
The Reindeer asked directions
Heard so much of Rome
The Cat it sat where was at
Daytime was its leisure
Come the night then is right
For hunting is its pleasure

The seed did feed and so did grow
Into something we then know
The Cockerel crooned and Hens they swooned
But most of it for show
Dog dragged log I don't know why
Guess it was there so had to try
Geese got bored so passed by
I wonder what it's like to fly

The cloud was proud so stood out loud
Took control of that we see
When at play it turned grey
Parts of it we class misery
The Cow showed how
We don't need some machine
To keep the stuff both soft and tough
At levels painters seen

We love Ice cream but hate the scene
When cream is not there
The Mouse does scurry in a hurry
Acquaintance no wish nor care
The Neighbour could be saviour
If change their irritation
The downside so let it slide
The joy of other nation

1010

Mooning At Moon

The lips of the moon;
Red and luscious
Parted across the hyssoped horizon
Had ears of trees tingling
And me mooning
Like a baying bard at bayous, buoys and docks.

Throw a hug with a holy kiss -
Forget about the past diss.
It is a new day with a virgin brand.
Take advantage and flirt with the elements.
The moon I'm mooning cannot mourn.

The ample arms of the moon
Wrapped around my soul
Gives the test needed
To vanquish vile vicissitudes
That tend to bring darkness

Precarious equilibrium,
Blissful avalanche...
In the depth of the warehouse of my memory are fiends, foes and friends
Neatly stashed.

William Warigon

You Are Strong, Be Stronger!

You are stronger than you think
Life can be blue or finicky pink
If the arms of life thrust you to the deep
Every day you are blue and you do weep
Remember I am here for you
You are never alone. Be blue
But do not contemplate suicide
You've much to achieve, beside
On the other side lies no panacea
Your life is precious, it is so dear
Whatever puts a crimp on your life
Making dark depression your wife
When voices tell you to end it all
Padlock your ears and stand tall
Do not capitulate
See, soon or late
Like a winner that you are
You'll rise above every star
For fighting death keeps us alive
You are born to fight to stay alive
Many others have fallen into the deepest abyss
They clawed their way out, now they're at peace
If they could triumph, so could you
You are the Lord's beautiful dew
Bring out your inner strength
You can fight at any length
Having your wings, spread them, fly
Don't be pinned down, aim to be high
Live today, to tell testimony tomorrow
So as to alleviate someone's sorrow

William Warigon

First Taste Of Tough Love

My naive children,
Come to the den.
It is time to know the bane
And the taste of sweet hen.

Let me lead you on a lesson
That will secure your future.
Know who makes your liaison
For a fixed meaningful fixture.

Let me light the deep dawn
That walks with death when eyes are closed.
This is not the time to fawn.
Clear your eyes' cobwebs and choose doors.

Doors are aplenty
But what each door leads to:
A certain calamity
Or to a destined rich bamboo.

Savage kingdoms abound.
Predators are all around.
Don't be weak, willing prey in any purse.
Choose the paths to be your own boss.

Tyrants tempt like horny harlots.
Don't succumb as happy Harlots.
Wear your rights right like crowns.
So no one eats you like cheap prawns.

William Warigon

Togetherness: Yin And Yang

The bright light exposes the shadow's blackness
Like Siamese twins, the two are intertwined
Just like us, harmoniously we roll in togetherness
We are but two spirits in one soul combined

I am atunned to your every nuance
Feeling every breath, you take
Our hearts beat as a united séance
In sync of every move we make

Without you, there is no me
We fight all injustices with a single voice
We wade off gnats against me
And gather in one nest our every choice

United we stand strong
Divided we fall like a pack of cards
In one another we belong
Unity and faith as our safeguards

Our uniqueness is displayed to be emulated
For where differences are killed and replaced
With united front, opportunities can't be limited
It's very importance can not be downplayed

Lying in the ruins of our own dreams
Or feasting to celebrate our own feats
We do it with a synchronized gleam
Together, we carry results of our deeds

Your beauty has embellished my ugliness
My sadness is mirrored in your unhappiness
Ours are two souls wed locked in finesse
Where we waltz with unabashed loveliness

William Warigon

Secure Line

No tapping, tagging of toppling,
Straight, quiet and accommodation,
Time is of no essence here,
Open channel, no static,
Such is the eloquence of this line,
Non to interrupt or present bill,
Verbosity is a choice,
Silence works best,
Tears may punctuate without judge,
So is nothing but a closed stare,
This line is secure,
Like the birth of a new day,
This line is secure and no tell-tale repeats,
A gift and a weapon,
Closed in or open is all the same,
In prayer in private,
In thoughts in a crowd,
Assurance of a trees shadow,
Lending a moment of rest,
The rain washing your tears,
Cleansing your sorrowful weight,
This line is secure,
No intruder to break,
The only tax for sure to pay,
Is a vow to withdraw to its inner Scutum,
And in the bliss of that lonesome of divine space,
Let all out and chose what stays,
From within is all answers,
From without supposed cures,
Let never whoever,
whatever,
wherever,
ever invade this secure line.
The best being, that,
You carry the key to the inner and outer.

Nancy Ndeke

'Consequences Have Choices'

When the plumber did the rounds and the pounds,
When his bill climbed the stairs to our sanctuary,
When his time in was my time out,
When he called to book an appointment with a leaky faucet,
One that the owner knew not,
No surprise my dear.

That baby Bill showed up earlier than marked,
Backwards counting to my stint at Brokehaven hospice,
A lazy eye just like Bills,
A sweet dimple on the left cheek,
But for his immediate need of blood transfuse,
This charade would have rained forever,
Why me and you darling,
Could not our child donate?

A quest the DNA did point with a stagger for a fact,
To save the baby true dad did show,
Too late by a day dear,
Saying goodbye to innocence,
And I,
Blind lover and triple tricked by love,
My own bad bye I confer.

Out of this old house,
Bequeathed by grandma maternal,
Her spirit now appeased,
Go build a nest elsewhere my dear,
With big Bill back with his brood,
Roam the roads and chance another fool,
This one learned a lesson,
Consequences have choices.

Nancy Ndeke

Laughing In Adversity

Crown on the head of a crown,
Sleep induced typos on a National calendar,
One tweet to the owl challenging its age-old wisdom,
The wise shrink with silenced horror,
While those who took God's tongue for their own,
Baptise snow for soil,
A ruckus none too palatable for world drama,
As sneeze chokes myriad throats,
Claps and applause pay homage to con,
Games turn teams into adversarial games,
Stupefied, a child dresses in fear,
Wondering where the brave go to die,
As characters in true life movie,
Laugh in howls in the throes of adversity.

Treated Truth

With a mild fragrance like Jasmin at night,
peeking at bottle brush for comparison,
Served in delicate youth's morning glow,
In chinaware smooth and glamorous,
Truth sits sadly at the throne,
The comfort of the state room all so gloomy,
Music a vexation to the spirit of light,
For this conference of men of knowledge,
Is nothing like the adverts say?
This here,
is a onetime auction on the block,
Defrauding the unborn of their heritage,
By hands warm in velvet gloves,
Silky smooth modulated bargains,
To sell the weak one more time to hell,
By inflating simple life's support systems,
Where health is bought by tomorrow as insurance,
By filling shelves with doses that eventually kill,
Calling it a deal breaker for easy living.
A lie wearing a diamond tiara and heavy mascara.

Nancy Ndeke

Ανοησίες

The orange filled the skyline
Start or finish? I am not sure
For when the global timescale differs
To that of home on foreign shore
Angels in the atmosphere
Do they, in fact, exist
When people that appointed
Turn to self-pleasure twist

What is far by a car?
When do need a plane?
With money most is possible
Question then the gain
Cash or card? The first now hard
Yet still your earnings spend
Everything now electrical
Height of fashion and new trend

Now is devious to be serious
When waffle is the taste
Guess should join so read born
Minutes not a waste

Oh, Darling of mine
Your body fine
Your eyes do shine so bright
Can't you see should be with me
Each and every night

Enough of that! An h in sat
Not for me I do think
More explore to reach a core
And in thought then sink
Hahaha get that car!
I need a speedy getaway
Knives are out without a doubt
What more can one say

Lightning Source UK Ltd.
Milton Keynes UK
UKHW020638040221
378234UK00013B/1050